DIGITAL SIGNAL PROCESSING

AUTHOR

Dr. Sanjeev Sharma
Assistant Professor
Department of Electronics Engineering,
Indian Institute of Technology (BHU), Varanasi

REVIEWER

Dr. Vimal Bhatia
Professor
Indian Institute of Technology, Indore

KHANNA BOOK PUBLISHING CO. (P) Ltd.
4C/4344, Ansari Road, Darya Ganj,
New Delhi, India

All India Council for Technical Education
Nelson Mandela Marg, Vasant Kunj,
New Delhi, India

Dear Readers,

To prevent the piracy, this book is secured with HIGH SECURITY HOLOGRAM on the front title cover. In case you don't find the hologram on the front cover title, please write us to at contact@khannabooks.com or whatsapp us at +91-99109 09320 and avail special gift voucher for yourself.

Specimen of Hologram on front Cover title:

Moreover, there is a SPECIAL DISCOUNT COUPON for you with EVERY HOLOGRAM.

How to avail this SPECIAL DISCOUNT:

Step 1: Scratch the hologram

Step 2: Under the scratch area, your "coupon code" is available

Step 3: Logon to www.khannabooks.com

Step 4: Use your "coupon code" in the shopping cart and get your copy at a special discount

Step 5: Enjoy your reading!

ISBN: 978-93-5538-657-1

Book Code: UG485EN

Digital Signal Processing

by Dr. Sanjeev Sharma

First Edition: 2026

Originally Published by:

All India Council for Technical Education, Ministry of Education, GOI

Exclusively Published & Distributed by:

Khanna Book Publishing Co. (P) Ltd.
4C/4344, Ansari Road, Daryaganj,
New Delhi (INDIA)

Visit us at: **www.khannabooks.com**
Write us at: **contact@khannabooks.com**

To view complete list of books, Please scan the QR Code: KPH

Printed in Bharat.

प्रो. टी. जी. सीताराम
अध्यक्ष
Prof. T. G. Sitharam
Chairman

सत्यमेव जयते

आज़ादी का अमृत महोत्सव

अखिल भारतीय तकनीकी शिक्षा परिषद्
(भारत सरकार का एक सांविधिक निकाय)
(शिक्षा मंत्रालय, भारत सरकार)
नेल्सन मंडेला मार्ग, वसंत कुंज, नई दिल्ली–110070
दूरभाष : 011–26131498
ई–मेल : chairman@aicte-india.org

ALL INDIA COUNCIL FOR TECHNICAL EDUCATION
(A STATUTORY BODY OF THE GOVT. OF INDIA)
(Ministry of Education, Govt. of India)
Nelson Mandela Marg, Vasant Kunj, New Delhi-110070
Phone : 011-26131498
E-mail : chairman@aicte-india.org

FOREWORD

Engineers are the backbone of any modern society. They are the ones responsible for the marvels as well as the improved quality of life across the world. Engineers have driven humanity towards greater heights in a more evolved and unprecedented manner.

The All India Council for Technical Education (AICTE), have spared no efforts towards the strengthening of the technical education in the country. AICTE is always committed towards promoting quality Technical Education to make India a modern developed nation emphasizing on the overall welfare of mankind.

An array of initiatives has been taken by AICTE in last decade which have been accelerated now by the National Education Policy (NEP) 2020. The implementation of NEP under the visionary leadership of Hon'ble Prime Minister of India envisages the provision for education in regional languages to all, thereby ensuring that every graduate becomes competent enough and is in a position to contribute towards the national growth and development through innovation & entrepreneurship.

One of the spheres where AICTE had been relentlessly working since past couple of years is providing high quality original technical contents at Under Graduate & Diploma level prepared and translated by eminent educators in various Indian languages to its aspirants. For students pursuing 2nd year of their Engineering education, AICTE has identified 87 books, which shall be translated into 12 Indian languages - Hindi, Tamil, Gujarati, Odia, Bengali, Kannada, Urdu, Punjabi, Telugu, Marathi, Assamese & Malayalam. In addition to the English medium, books in different Indian Languages are going to support the students to understand the concepts in their respective mother tongue.

On behalf of AICTE, I express sincere gratitude to all distinguished authors, reviewers and translators from the renowned institutions of high repute for their admirable contribution in a record span of time.

AICTE is confident that these outcomes based original contents shall help aspirants to master the subject with comprehension and greater ease.

(Prof. T. G. Sitharam)

ACKNOWLEDGMENT

The authors are grateful to the authorities of AICTE, particularly Prof. T. G. Sitharam, Chairman; Dr. Abhay Jere, Vice-Chairman; Prof. Rajiv Kumar, Member-Secretary, Dr. Sunil Luthra, Director, and Reena Sharma, Hindi Officer Training and Learning for their planning to publish the books on Electronic Communication. We sincerely acknowledge the valuable contributions of the reviewer of the book Dr. Vimal Bhatia, Professor, IIT Indore for making it students' friendly and giving a better shape in an artistic manner. This book is an outcome of various suggestions of AICTE members, experts and authors who shared their opinion and thought to further develop the engineering education in our country. Acknowledgements are due to the contributors and different workers in this field whose published books, review articles, papers, photographs, footnotes, references and other valuable information enriched us at the time of writing the book.

Dr. Sanjeev Sharma

PREFACE

The book "Digital Signal Processing" is the culmination of our extensive experience teaching fundamental signals and digital processing courses. Its inception stemmed from the desire to impart foundational knowledge of signal and its processing concepts to engineering students, equipping them with a comprehensive understanding of the subject matter. To ensure a thorough grasp of the fundamentals and to offer essential supplementary information, we meticulously integrated topics recommended by AICTE throughout the book in a systematic and structured manner. Our aim was to provide wide coverage while maintaining clarity and coherence. Throughout the book, efforts were dedicated to elucidating complex concepts in the simplest and most accessible manner possible, facilitating effective learning for students at all levels of proficiency.

Throughout the manuscript preparation process, we meticulously consulted various standard textbooks to ensure comprehensive coverage of the subject matter. As a result, we developed sections containing critical questions, solved problems, and supplementary exercises. In crafting these sections, particular attention was given to defining key terms, presenting theorems, and providing a comprehensive synopsis of formulas for quick reference and revision of fundamental principles. The book encompasses a diverse range of medium to advanced level problems, meticulously organized in a logical and systematic manner. These problem sets have been rigorously tested over numerous years of teaching, catering to a broad spectrum of students and ensuring their effectiveness in facilitating learning and understanding.

In addition to incorporating illustrations and examples where necessary, we have augmented the book with a multitude of solved problems in each unit to enhance comprehension of the associated topics. It is noteworthy that, across all editions, we have integrated pertinent laboratory practical experiments to provide readers with hands-on training in the subjects covered. This distinctive feature sets our book apart and reinforces practical application alongside theoretical understanding.

Regarding the current book, "Digital Signal Processing" aims to offer a comprehensive understanding of communication engineering topics covered within. This book is designed to equip engineering students with a solid foundation in signal processing, enabling them to tackle future challenges and explore advanced topics such as 5G and beyond, MIMO, OFMD, Image Processing, Multirate Signal Processing and more. The subject matter is presented in a structured manner, ensuring that students are prepared to work across various sectors or in national laboratories at the forefront of technological advancements.

We sincerely anticipate that this book will motivate students to engage with and delve into the fundamental principles of engineering physics, thus fostering a robust understanding of the subject. We are grateful for any constructive comments and suggestions that will aid in enhancing future editions of the book. It brings us great joy to offer this resource to both teachers and students, and we take pride in the comprehensive coverage of various aspects included within its pages.

Dr. Sanjeev Sharma

OUTCOME BASED EDUCATION

For the implementation of an outcome based education the first requirement is to develop an outcome based curriculum and incorporate an outcome based assessment in the education system. By going through outcome based assessments evaluators will be able to evaluate whether the students have achieved the outlined standard, specific and measurable outcomes. With the proper incorporation of outcome based education there will be a definite commitment to achieve a minimum standard for all learners without giving up at any level. At the end of the program running with the aid of outcome-based education, a student will be able to arrive at the following outcomes:

PO1. Engineering knowledge: Apply the knowledge of mathematics, science, engineering fundamentals, and an engineering specialization to the solution of complex engineering problems.

PO2. Problem analysis: Identify, formulate, review research literature, and analyze complex engineering problems reaching substantiated conclusions using first principles of mathematics, natural sciences, and engineering sciences.

PO3. Design / development of solutions: Design solutions for complex engineering problems and design system components or processes that meet the specified needs with appropriate consideration for the public health and safety, and the cultural, societal, and environmental considerations.

PO4. Conduct investigations of complex problems: Use research-based knowledge and research methods including design of experiments, analysis and interpretation of data, and synthesis of the information to provide valid conclusions.

PO5. Modern tool usage: Create, select, and apply appropriate techniques, resources, and modern engineering and IT tools including prediction and modeling to complex engineering activities with an understanding of the limitations.

PO6. The engineer and society: Apply reasoning informed by the contextual knowledge to assess societal, health, safety, legal and cultural issues and the consequent responsibilities relevant to the professional engineering practice.

PO7. Environment and sustainability: Understand the impact of the professional engineering solutions in societal and environmental contexts, and demonstrate the knowledge of, and need for sustainable development.

PO8. Ethics: Apply ethical principles and commit to professional ethics and responsibilities and norms of the engineering practice.

PO9. Individual and team work: Function effectively as an individual, and as a member or leader in diverse teams, and in multidisciplinary settings.

PO10. Communication: Communicate effectively on complex engineering activities with the engineering community and with society at large, such as, being able to comprehend and write effective reports and design documentation, make effective presentations, and give and receive clear instructions.

PO11. Project management and finance: Demonstrate knowledge and understanding of the engineering and management principles and apply these to one's own work, as a member and leader in a team, to manage projects and in multidisciplinary environments.

PO12. Life-long learning: Recognize the need for, and have the preparation and ability to engage in independent and life-long learning in the broadest context of technological change.

COURSE OUTCOMES

After completion of the course the students will be able to:

CO-1: Interpret and analyze continuous and discrete time signals.

CO-2: Analyze the digital signals using various digital transforms *z*-transform, DTFT, DFT, FFT etc.

CO-3: Design and develop the basic digital system.

CO-4: Design of IIR and FIR filters.

CO-5: Define the concept of decimation and interpolation in multirate signal processing.

CO-6: Apply signal processing algorithms for real time applications.

Course Outcomes	**Expected Mapping with Programme Outcomes** *(1- Weak Correlation; 2- Medium correlation; 3- Strong Correlation)*											
	PO-1	**PO-2**	**PO-3**	**PO-4**	**PO-5**	**PO-6**	**PO-7**	**PO-8**	**PO-9**	**PO-10**	**PO-11**	**PO-12**
CO-1	3	1	2	1	1	–	–	–	–	–	-	-
CO-2	3	2	2	2	2	–	–	–	–	–	-	-
CO-3	2	1	3	1	1	–	–	–	–	–	-	-
CO-4	2	2	1	1	1	–	–	–	–	–	-	-
CO-5	2	2	1	2	2	–	–	–	–	–	-	-
CO-6	1	2	3	2	2	–	–	–	–	–	-	-

GUIDELINES FOR TEACHERS

To implement Outcome Based Education (OBE) knowledge level and skill set of the students should be enhanced. Teachers should take a major responsibility for the proper implementation of OBE. Some of the responsibilities (not limited to) for the teachers in OBE system may be as follows:

- Within reasonable constraint, they should manoeuvre time to the best advantage of all students.
- They should assess the students only upon certain defined criterion without considering any other potential ineligibility to discriminate them.
- They should try to grow the learning abilities of the students to a certain level before they leave the institute.
- They should try to ensure that all the students are equipped with the quality knowledge as well as competence after they finish their education.
- They should always encourage the students to develop their ultimate performance capabilities.
- They should facilitate and encourage group work and team work to consolidate newer approach.
- They should follow Blooms taxonomy in every part of the assessment.

Bloom's Taxonomy

Level	Teacher should Check	Student should be able to	Possible Mode of Assessment
Create	Students ability to create	Design or Create	Mini project
Evaluate	Students ability to justify	Argue or Defend	Assignment
Analyse	Students ability to distinguish	Differentiate or Distinguish	Project/Lab Methodology
Apply	Students ability to use information	Operate or Demonstrate	Technical Presentation/ Demonstration
Understand	Students ability to explain the ideas	Explain or Classify	Presentation/Seminar
Remember	Students ability to recall (or remember)	Define or Recall	Quiz

GUIDELINES FOR STUDENTS

Students should take equal responsibility for implementing the OBE. Some of the responsibilities (not limited to) for the students in OBE system are as follows:

- Students should be well aware of each UO before the start of a unit in each and every course.
- Students should be well aware of each CO before the start of the course.
- Students should be well aware of each PO before the start of the programme.
- Students should think critically and reasonably with proper reflection and action.
- Learning of the students should be connected and integrated with practical and real life consequences.
- Students should be well aware of their competency at every level of OBE.

ABBREVIATION AND SYMBOL

Abbreviation	Full form	Abbreviation	Full form
ADC	Analog-to-Digital converter	FPGA	Field-programmable gate arrays
BPF	Band pass filter	FS	Fourier series
BW	Bandwidth	FT	Fourier transform
LCCDE	Linear constant- coefficient difference equations	HPF	High pass filter
CM	Circulant matrix	IFFT	Inverse fast Fourier transform
CT	Continuous-time	IFT	Inverse Fourier transform
CTFS	Continuous-time Fourier series	IDFT	InverseDiscrete Fourier transform
CTFT	Continuous-time Fourier transform	IDTFT	Inverse discrete-time Fourier transform
DCT	Discrete cosine trans- form	IIR	Infinite impulse Re sponse
DFS	Discrete Fourier series	IoT	Internet-of-things
DFT	Discrete Fourier transform	LPF	Lowpass filter
DSP	Digital signal pro- cessing	LT	Laplace transform
DT	Discrete-time	LTI	Linear time invariant
DTFS	Discrete-time Fourier series	MRI	Magnetic resonance imaging
DTFT	Discrete-time Fourier transform	OFDM	Orthogonal frequency-division multiplexing
ECG	Electrocardiogram	PSD	Power spectral density
EEG	Electroencephalogram	RNN	Recurrent neural networks
ESD	Energy spectral density	ROC	Region of convergence
FFT	Fast Fourier trans- form	SF	Sampling frequency
FIR	Finite impulse re- sponse	SNR	Signal-to-Noise Ratio

LIST OF FIGURES

Chapter-1: Introduction

Chapter-2: Classification of Signals and Systems

Chapter-3: Discrete-Time Signals and Systems

Chapter-4: *z*-Transform

Chapter-5: DTFT: Discrete Time Fourier Transform

Chapter-6: DFT: Discrete Fourier Transform

Chapter-7: FFT: Fast Fourier Transform

Chapter-8: Design of Digital Filters

Chapter-9: Multirate Digital Signal Processing

Chapter-10: Application of Digital Signal Processing

Digital Signal Processing Laboratory

TABLE OF CONTENT

Chapter 1: Introduction

UNIT SPECIFICS

The introduction chapter of a Digital Signal Processing (DSP) book, several key specifics are typically covered. It begins with an overview of DSP, explaining how digital signals differ from analog signals, and why digital processing is preferred in modern systems. Fundamental concepts such as sampling, quantization, and reconstruction of signals are introduced to highlight how continuous signals are converted into digital form for analysis. The chapter also touches on the importance of filters, the Discrete Fourier Transform (DFT), Fast Fourier Transform (FFT), and other key tools used to manipulate signals. Real-world applications of DSP in fields like communications, audio and video processing, and biomedical engineering are presented to showcase its widespread utility. This chapter sets the foundation for understanding more advanced DSP techniques in subsequent sections.

RATIONALE

To begin learning DSP, it is essential to understand the different types of signals, their specifications, and the various applications of signal processing.

PRE-REQUISITE

NIL

UNIT OUTCOMES

List of outcomes of this unit is as follows:

U1-O1: Understanding of the basic applications of signal processing

U1-O2: Introduction of different signals

U1-O3: Signal processing using digital signal processor

Unit-1 Outcomes	EXPECTED MAPPING WITH COURSE OUTCOMES (1- Weak Correlation; 2- Medium correlation; 3- Strong Correlation)					
	CO-1	CO-2	CO-3	CO-4	CO-5	CO-6
U1-O1	2	1	–	–	–	3
U1-O2	2	1	–	–	–	2
U1-O3	3	2	–	–	–	3

INTRODUCTION

Digital signal processing (DSP) serves as a gateway into a realm where signals are manipulated in the digital domain. DSP involves the analysis, modification, and synthesis of signals represented as sequences of numbers. Its applications span a multitude of fields, including telecommunications, audio processing, image processing, medical diagnostics, radar systems, and more. The transition from analog to digital processing has brought about a paradigm shift, enabling greater precision, flexibility, repeatability, and the implementation of complex algorithms. This transformation has revolutionized industries, leading to improved performance, reduced costs, and enhanced capabilities.

Central to understanding DSP are key concepts such as sampling and quantization, which convert continuous-time analog signals into discrete-time digital signals, as shown in Fig. 1.1. Time-domain and frequency-domain analyses offer complementary perspectives, enabling insights into signal characteristics and behaviors. Filtering techniques further augment DSP capabilities, facilitating alterations to signal frequency content for various purposes such as noise reduction or signal enhancement.

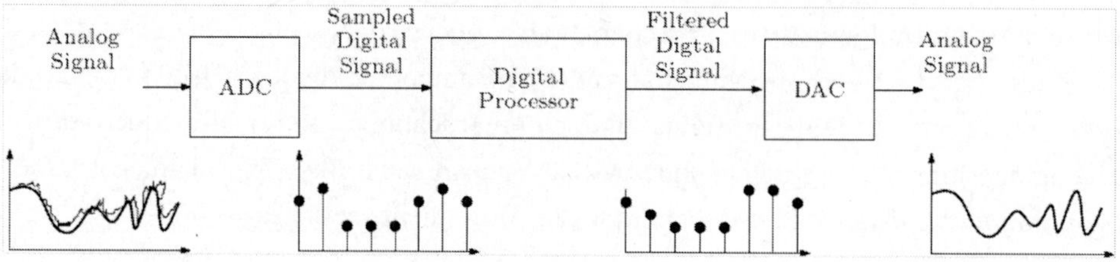

Fig. 1.1: DSP overview

The significance of DSP is underscored by its myriad applications. In communication systems, DSP techniques are integral to processes like modulation, demodulation, error correction, and channel equalization, ensuring reliable transmission of information across wireless and wired networks. Audio processing harnesses DSP for tasks like speech recognition, audio compression, equalization, and synthesis, shaping experiences in fields like telecommunications and music production. Image processing exploits DSP for image enhancement, restoration, compression, and feature extraction, empowering applications in photography, medical imaging, and computer vision.

While DSP has yielded remarkable achievements, it also confronts challenges and navigates future directions. Real-time processing demands, algorithmic complexities, and ethical considerations regarding privacy and bias are among the challenges. Looking forward, DSP continues to evolve with advancements in machine learning, artificial intelligence, and the Internet of Things (IoT), ushering in new applications and interdisciplinary collaborations.

DEFINITION OF DSP

DSP is a specialized field within engineering and mathematics that focuses on the manipulation, analysis, and interpretation of signals in the digital domain. In essence, DSP deals with signals that are represented as discrete sequences of numbers, as opposed to continuous waveforms in the analog domain. These signals could represent various forms of data, such as audio, video, images, sensor measurements, or any other information that can be quantified and processed digitally. DSP techniques enable the extraction of meaningful information from these signals, often involving filtering, transformation, compression, enhancement, or feature extraction. The ultimate goal of DSP is to extract insights, patterns, or desired characteristics from signals to facilitate tasks such as communication, data analysis, control systems, image processing, and many other applications across a wide range of industries. As technology continues to advance, DSP remains a cornerstone in enabling the efficient and effective processing of signals in diverse real-world scenarios.

HISTORICAL BACKGROUND AND EVOLUTION

The historical background and evolution of DSP trace back to the mid-20th century, coinciding with the rapid development of computing technology and the need for more efficient methods to process signals in various fields. One of the earliest milestones in DSP can be attributed to the work of mathematicians such as Harry Nyquist and Claude Shannon, who laid the theoretical foundations for sampling theory and digital communication in the 1940s and 1950s. Their contributions provided fundamental insights into the representation and processing of signals in the digital domain, setting the stage for the emergence of DSP as a distinct discipline.

The 1960s witnessed significant advancements in DSP driven by the burgeoning field of digital computers. Engineers and scientists began exploring digital techniques to process signals more efficiently and accurately compared to traditional analog methods. One notable development during this period was the introduction of the Fast Fourier Transform (FFT) algorithm by James Cooley and John Tukey in 1965, which revolutionized spectral analysis and made complex frequency-domain computations feasible in real-time applications.

By the 1970s and 1980s, DSP started gaining momentum as a field of study and application, fueled by the proliferation of microprocessors and dedicated digital signal processing hardware. The availability of powerful computing resources enabled the implementation of sophisticated DSP algorithms for a wide range of tasks, including speech and audio processing, telecommunications, medical imaging, and radar systems. This period also saw the emergence of commercial DSP chips and development tools, which democratized access to DSP technology and spurred innovation in various industries.

The late 20th century and early 21st century marked a period of rapid expansion and diversification for DSP, driven by advancements in both hardware and algorithms. The integration of DSP capabilities into consumer electronics such as smartphones, digital cameras, and audio devices further solidified its importance in everyday life. Additionally, the advent of digital signal processors with specialized architectures optimized for specific applications, such as digital audio processors and graphics processing units (GPUs), opened new possibilities for high-performance signal processing in real-time and embedded systems.

In recent years, the evolution of DSP has been shaped by trends such as machine learning, artificial intelligence, and the Internet of Things (IoT), which have introduced new challenges and opportunities for signal processing. DSP techniques play a crucial role in processing and analyzing vast amounts of data generated by IoT de- vices, extracting actionable insights and enabling intelligent decision-making. Looking ahead, the continued convergence of DSP with emerging technologies promises to unlock new frontiers in signal processing, driving innovation and transformation across diverse domains.

IMPORTANCE OF DSP IN VARIOUS FIELDS

DSP holds immense significance across a wide array of fields, playing a pivotal role in revolutionizing communication systems, audio processing, image processing, and many other domains. In communications, DSP techniques are fundamental to ensuring efficient and reliable transmission of information across various channels. Error correction algorithms implemented through DSP enhance data integrity, while channel equalization techniques mitigate the effects of channel distortion, ensuring clear and accurate signal transmission.

In audio processing, DSP has transformed the way we capture, manipulate, and reproduce sound. From professional recording studios to consumer audio devices, DSP algorithms are employed for tasks such as noise reduction, equalization, dynamic range compression, and reverberation effects. Digital audio processors enable precise control over sound parameters, allowing audio engineers and musicians to achieve desired sonic outcomes with unprecedented flexibility and fidelity. More- over, DSP plays a critical role in emerging audio technologies such as virtual reality (VR) and augmented reality (AR), where spatial audio processing techniques create immersive auditory experiences.

In the realm of image processing, DSP techniques are instrumental in analyzing, enhancing, and interpreting digital images for a myriad of applications. From medical imaging and satellite remote sensing to digital photography and video surveillance, DSP algorithms enable the extraction of valuable information from images to support decision-making and analysis. Techniques such as image filtering, edge detection, object recognition, and image compression leverage DSP to enhance image quality, detect features of interest, and reduce storage or transmission overhead. As imaging technologies continue to advance, DSP remains at the forefront of innovation, enabling breakthroughs in fields such as medical diagnostics, biometrics, and computer vision.

Beyond communications, audio, and image processing, DSP finds applications in di- verse domains such as biomedical signal processing, radar systems, financial analysis, and seismic exploration, to name a few. In biomedical signal processing, DSP techniques are utilized for tasks such as electrocardiography (ECG), electroencephalography (EEG), and medical imaging modalities like magnetic resonance imaging (MRI) and computed tomography (CT). For example, ECG and EEG signals are shown in Fig. 1.2 and Fig. 1.3, respectively. In radar systems, DSP enables tar- get detection, tracking, and signal processing for military and civilian applications. In finance, DSP algorithms facilitate analysis of financial time series data for fore- casting, risk management, and algorithmic trading. In seismic exploration, DSP techniques are employed to analyze seismic signals for oil and gas exploration and earthquake monitoring.

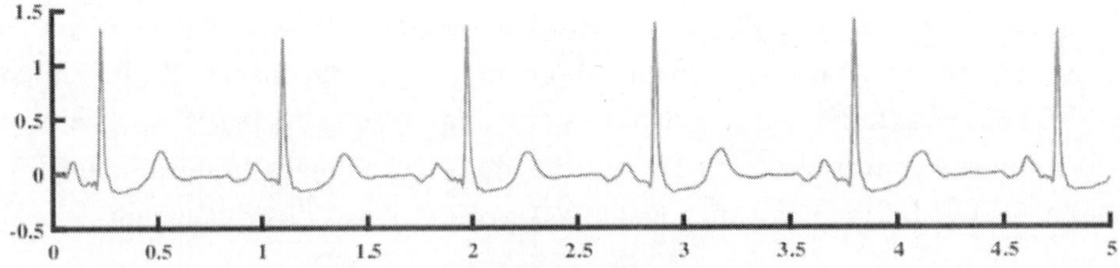

Fig. 1.2: ECG signal[a]

---

[a]R.He, et al.,"Short-time detection of QRS complexes using dual channels based on U-Net and bidirectional long short-term memory", arXiv preprint arXiv:1912.09223, 2019

CONTRAST BETWEEN ANALOG AND DIGITAL SIGNAL PROCESSING

The contrast between analog and digital signal processing lies at the core of under- standing their respective methodologies and applications. Analog signal processing operates on continuous signals, where the data is represented by continuously vary- ing physical quantities such as voltage or current. In contrast, DSP deals with discrete signals, where the data is represented by a sequence of discrete numerical values. One key distinction is precision: analog processing offers infinite precision due to its continuous nature, while DSP operates with finite precision determined by the number of bits used for representation. This inherent precision limitation in DSP can introduce quantization errors, affecting signal accuracy, although it also enables greater repeatability and consistency compared to analog systems.

Another fundamental difference lies in the flexibility and versatility of digital pro- cessing. DSP algorithms can be easily modified, replicated, and combined to achieve complex signal processing tasks, offering unparalleled flexibility and adaptability. In contrast, analog processing often requires intricate circuitry and component tuning, making it less conducive to rapid prototyping and reconfiguration. Moreover, digital processing enables the implementation of sophisticated algorithms such as Fourier transforms, filters, and adaptive signal processing techniques with relative ease, facilitating advanced signal analysis and manipulation.

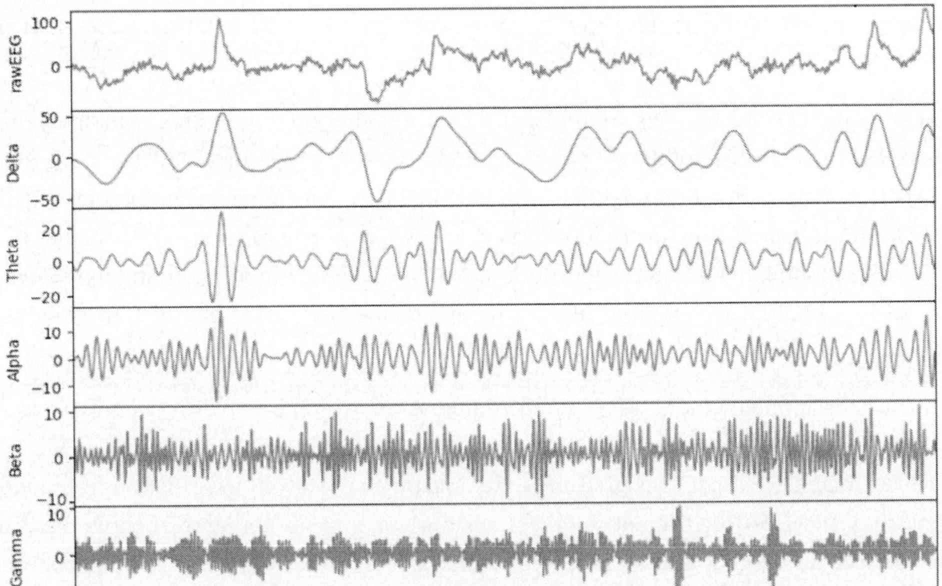

Fig. 1.3: EEG signal[a]

[a]Nikesh Bajaj,"Wavelets for EEG Analysis", Wavelet theory, 2020, IntechOpen London, UK

Furthermore, digital processing offers inherent advantages in terms of stability and robustness. Digital systems are less susceptible to noise, interference, and environmental factors compared to analog systems, thanks to techniques such as error detection, correction, and signal processing algorithms that can mitigate the effects of disturbances. Additionally, digital signals can be easily transmitted, stored, and manipulated without degradation, making them well-suited for applications requiring long-distance communication, archival storage, or real-time processing.

However, analog processing possesses its own set of strengths, particularly in applications requiring high-bandwidth, low-latency, or continuous-time signal processing. Analog circuits can operate at higher frequencies and with lower latency compared to their digital counterparts, making them indispensable in applications such as high-frequency radio communication, analog audio processing, and real-time control systems. Analog processing also offers advantages in terms of energy efficiency and simplicity of implementation for certain tasks, especially in low-power or resource- constrained environments.

REAL-WORLD APPLICATIONS AND EXAMPLES WHERE DSP IS USED

DSP finds extensive real-world applications across diverse domains, playing a crucial role in shaping modern technology and enhancing everyday experiences. One prominent application of DSP is speech recognition, where algorithms analyze audio signals to identify spoken words and convert them into text or commands. From virtual assistants like Siri and Alexa to voice-controlled smart devices and automated customer service systems, speech recognition powered by DSP enables seam- less interaction between humans and machines, revolutionizing communication and interaction interfaces.

In medical imaging, DSP techniques are indispensable for capturing, processing, and analyzing medical images to facilitate diagnosis, treatment planning, and research. Modalities such as magnetic resonance imaging (MRI), computed tomography (CT), ultrasound, and positron emission tomography (PET) rely on DSP algorithms for image reconstruction, enhancement, and visualization. DSP enables clinicians to obtain detailed anatomical and functional information from medical images, aiding in the detection and characterization of diseases, monitoring treatment response, and guiding minimally invasive interventions.

Another ubiquitous application of DSP is audio compression, which involves reducing the size of digital audio files while preserving perceptual quality. Audio com- pression techniques such as MP3, AAC, and Ogg Vorbis leverage DSP algorithms to remove redundant or irrelevant information from audio signals, thereby reducing file sizes for efficient storage, transmission, and streaming over networks. From music streaming services and digital audio players to online conferencing platforms and telecommunications networks, audio compression powered by DSP enables high- quality audio playback and communication experiences with minimal bandwidth requirements.

In addition to these examples, DSP finds applications in a wide range of fields, including telecommunications, radar systems, seismology, financial analysis, and more. In telecommunications, DSP enables the transmission, reception, and processing of digital signals for wireless communication, data networking, and multimedia ser- vices. In radar systems, DSP techniques are utilized for target detection, tracking, and signal processing in military and civilian applications such as weather monitoring and air traffic control. In seismology, DSP algorithms analyze seismic signals to detect and characterize earthquakes, assess ground motion hazards, and explore subsurface geological structures. In finance, DSP enables the analysis of financial time series data for forecasting, risk management, and algorithmic trading.

INCREASING DEMAND FOR DSP EXPERTISE IN MODERN TECHNOLOGY

The increasing demand for DSP expertise in modern technology underscores its pivotal role in driving innovation and advancing various industries. As technology continues to evolve, the need for efficient processing, analysis, and manipulation of digital signals becomes increasingly critical across diverse domains. From telecommunications and multimedia to healthcare and automotive systems, DSP expertise is sought after to develop cutting-edge solutions that address complex challenges and capitalize on emerging opportunities. The proliferation of digital devices, the growth of data-intensive applications, and the rise of transformative technologies such as 5G and 6G, artificial intelligence, and the IoT further fuel the demand for DSP expertise. Professionals with proficiency in DSP principles, algorithms, and implementation techniques are in high demand to design, optimize, and deploy sophisticated signal processing systems that enable innovations in communication networks, medical diagnostics, audiovisual media, autonomous vehicles, and beyond. Additionally, as the digital transformation accelerates across industries, the ability to harness the power of DSP for real-time data analysis, pattern recognition, and decision-making becomes a competitive advantage, driving the demand for skilled DSP practitioners who can leverage digital signals to unlock new insights, drive efficiency, and create value in today's dynamic technological landscape.

FUNDAMENTAL CONCEPTS

The Sampling Theorem and analog-to-digital conversion are fundamental concepts in DSP, essential for converting continuous analog signals into discrete digital representations. The Sampling Theorem, formulated by Harry Nyquist and Claude Shannon, stipulates that to accurately reconstruct a continuous signal from its samples, the sampling frequency must be at least twice the highest frequency component present in the signal. This principle ensures that no information is lost during the sampling process, preventing aliasing and allowing for faithful representation of the original signal in the digital domain. Analog-to-digital conversion involves quantizing the sampled analog signal into discrete amplitude levels and assigning binary codes to each quantized value, thereby creating a digital representation of the ana- log signal. This process typically involves an analog-to-digital converter (ADC), which samples the analog signal at regular intervals and outputs a corresponding digital representation. By converting analog signals into digital form, sampling and analog-to-digital conversion enable the application of DSP algorithms for processing, analysis, and manipulation of signals in various real-world applications, ranging from telecommunications and audio processing to medical imaging and beyond.

Discrete-time signals and systems form the backbone of DSP, providing a framework for representing and analyzing signals in the digital domain. Discrete-time signals are sequences of numerical values defined at discrete points in time, as opposed to continuous signals, which vary continuously over time. These signals can be classified based on their characteristics, such as periodicity, amplitude, and duration, and can represent a wide range of phenomena, including audio waveforms, sensor measurements, and digital images. Discrete-time systems, on the other hand, are mathematical models that operate on discrete-time signals, transforming input signals into output signals according to predefined rules or algorithms. These systems can be linear or nonlinear, time-invariant or time-varying, and causal or non-causal, depending on their properties and behavior. Understanding discrete-time signals and systems is essential for mastering DSP, as they provide the foundation for implementing and analyzing various signal processing algorithms, such as filtering, convolution, and spectral analysis, which are integral to numerous real-world applications in communications, audio processing, image processing, and beyond.

Basic operations in DSP, such as addition, multiplication, and convolution, form the building blocks for implementing various signal processing algorithms and tech- niques. Addition involves combining two or more signals by adding their corresponding samples together, allowing for signal summation or mixing. Multiplication, on the other hand, modifies signals by scaling their amplitude values, amplifying or attenuating specific frequency components, or applying gain factors. Convolution is a fundamental operation in DSP that computes the response of a system to an input signal by overlaying the input signal with a system's impulse response and integrating their product over time. This operation is essential for modeling linear time-invariant (LTI) systems and implementing filtering operations, such as finite impulse response (FIR) and infinite impulse response (IIR) filters. Mastery of these basic operations is crucial for understanding and designing more complex DSP algorithms, enabling the manipulation, analysis, and synthesis of digital signals in applications ranging from audio processing and image processing to communications and control systems.

TIME-DOMAIN AND FREQUENCY-DOMAIN ANALYSIS

Time-domain and frequency-domain analysis are two fundamental approaches used in DSP to characterize and understand signals. In time-domain analysis, signals are studied in the context of time, focusing on how their amplitude values change over time. This analysis enables the examination of signal properties such as amplitude, phase, frequency, and timing relationships between different signal components. Time-domain techniques include waveform visualization, signal averaging, correlation, and time-domain filtering. Conversely, frequency-domain analysis in- volves analyzing signals in terms of their frequency content and spectral characteristics. By transforming signals from the time domain to the frequency domain using techniques like the Fourier Transform or Discrete Fourier Transform (DFT), signals can be decomposed into their constituent frequency components. This analysis provides insights into the frequency distribution, harmonic content, and spectral density of signals, enabling the identification of specific frequency components, noise reduction, and selective filtering. Understanding both time-domain and frequency- domain analysis is essential for comprehensive signal processing tasks, as they offer complementary perspectives and tools for analyzing and manipulating signals ef- fectively in applications ranging from audio processing and telecommunications to medical imaging and seismic analysis.

HARDWARE AND SOFTWARE IMPLEMENTATIONS

Hardware and software implementations are two key approaches used in DSP to realize signal processing algorithms and systems. Hardware implementations involve the use of specialized digital signal processors (DSP chips), field-programmable gate arrays (FPGAs), or application-specific integrated circuits (ASICs) dedicated to executing DSP algorithms efficiently. DSP chips are designed with architectures optimized for signal processing tasks, featuring parallel processing units, specialized arithmetic units, and high-speed memory to handle complex computations in real- time. FPGAs offer flexibility and reconfigurability, allowing designers to implement custom DSP algorithms and optimize performance for specific applications. In contrast, software implementations leverage general-purpose processors (such as CPUs or GPUs) and DSP software libraries to execute DSP algorithms using high-level programming languages like MATLAB, Python, or C/C++. Software-based DSP solutions offer versatility and ease of development, enabling rapid prototyping, algorithm experimentation, and portability across different hardware platforms. Both hardware and software implementations have their advantages and trade-offs, with hardware solutions offering superior performance and efficiency for real-time processing tasks, while software solutions provide flexibility and accessibility for algorithm development and deployment in diverse computing environments. Understanding the strengths and limitations of hardware and software implementations is essential for designing and deploying DSP systems that meet the performance, cost, and scalability requirements of various real-world applications, ranging from telecommunications and audio processing to biomedical imaging and autonomous systems.

Emerging trends and advancements in DSP (machine learning, deep learning, IoT)

Emerging trends and advancements are reshaping the landscape of signal processing techniques and applications, with notable developments in areas such as machine learning, deep learning, and the IoT. Machine learning techniques, including super- vised learning, unsupervised learning, and reinforcement learning, are increasingly being integrated into DSP workflows to enhance signal analysis, classification, and prediction tasks. By leveraging large datasets and powerful learning algorithms, machine learning enables the development of predictive models that can extract complex patterns, trends, and relationships from signals, leading to more accurate and efficient signal processing solutions in domains such as speech recognition, image processing, and biomedical signal analysis.

Deep learning, a subset of machine learning that involves training deep neural net- works with multiple layers of interconnected nodes, has emerged as a game-changer in DSP, offering unprecedented capabilities for feature extraction, representation learning, and signal reconstruction. Deep learning architectures such as convolutional neural networks (CNNs), recurrent neural networks (RNNs), and generative adversarial networks (GANs) have demonstrated remarkable performance in tasks such as image classification, speech synthesis, and signal denoising, pushing the boundaries of what is achievable in signal processing.

The IoT, characterized by interconnected networks of smart devices and sensors, presents new opportunities and challenges for DSP. By embedding DSP capabilities into IoT devices and edge computing platforms, real-time signal processing tasks such as data compression, feature extraction, and anomaly detection can be per- formed locally, reducing latency, bandwidth usage, and reliance on centralized cloud services. DSP techniques also play a crucial role in extracting actionable insights from IoT-generated data streams, enabling applications such as predictive maintenance, environmental monitoring, and smart city infrastructure management.

In addition to machine learning, deep learning, and IoT, other emerging trends in DSP include the integration of signal processing with emerging technologies such as quantum computing, neuromorphic computing, and blockchain. These advancements promise to unlock new frontiers in signal processing, enabling innovations in areas such as quantum signal processing, brain-computer interfaces, secure signal transmission, and distributed signal processing networks. As DSP continues to evolve and converge with these emerging technologies, the possibilities for creating intelligent, adaptive, and efficient signal processing systems are boundless, paving the way for transformative advancements in science, engineering, healthcare, and beyond.

Structure of the Book

Chapter 2 describes the *Classification of Signals and Systems.*

Chapter 3 describes the *Discrete-Time Signals and Systems.*

Chapter 4 describes the *z-Transform.*

Chapter 5 describes the *Discrete Time Fourier Transform.*

Chapter 6 describes the *Discrete Fourier Transform.*

Chapter 7 describes the *Fast Fourier Transform.*

Chapter 8 describes the *Design of Digital Filters.*

Chapter 9 describes the *Multirate Digital Signal Processing.*

Chapter 10 describes the *MATLAB-based Application of Digital Signal Processing.*

SUMMARY

In closing, understanding the principles of DSP is paramount in navigating the complexities of the digital age. As our world becomes increasingly reliant on digital technologies, from communication networks and multimedia devices to medical diagnostics and autonomous systems, DSP serves as the cornerstone for processing, analyzing, and interpreting the vast amounts of digital data generated daily. Proficiency in DSP principles equips individuals with the tools and knowledge needed to innovate and solve real-world challenges across diverse domains. By mastering DSP techniques, individuals gain the ability to extract valuable insights from digital signals, enabling advancements in fields such as telecommunications, healthcare, finance, environmental monitoring, and beyond. Moreover, DSP provides a frame- work for understanding and harnessing the power of emerging technologies such as machine learning, deep learning, and the IoT, enabling the development of intelligent, adaptive, and efficient signal processing systems. In essence, DSP is not just a field of study but a critical enabler of innovation, driving progress and shaping the future of technology in the digital age. Therefore, embracing and understanding DSP principles is essential for individuals and organizations seeking to thrive in an increasingly digital and interconnected world.

EXERCISE

Multiple Choice Questions

1. Which of the following is a key characteristic of digital signals?

   A) Continuous in time and amplitude

   B) Discrete in time and amplitude

C) Continuous in time, discrete in amplitude

D) Discrete in time, continuous in amplitude

2. What is the process of converting an analog signal into a digital signal called?

A) Quantization

B) Sampling

C) Modulation

D) Filtering

3. Which of the following is NOT a basic operation in digital signal processing?

A) Filtering

B) Modulation

C) Quantization

D) Differentiation

4. Which of these operations can be performed by a DSP system

A) Signal filtering

B) Signal compression

C) Signal transformation

D) All of the above

5. What is the purpose of quantization in the analog-to-digital conversion process?

A) To sample the signal at a higher frequency

B) To convert continuous amplitude levels into discrete levels

C) To store the signal in a compressed format

D) To reduce the signal bandwidth

ANSWERS

1	2	3	4	5
B	B	D	D	B

Subjective Questions

1. Explain analog to digital converter steps in detail.
2. Write various applications of DSP in modern world.
3. Why sampling rate conversion is required in digital signal processors?
4. Why ECG and EEG signals are used in healthcare applications?
5. How can we convert time domain signal to frequency domain?

KNOW MORE

For more information related to this topic scan the QR code.

OR

Type this link in your browser

https://www.google.co.in/books/edition/_/H_5SAAAAMAAJ?hl=en&gbpv=0

REFERENCES AND SUGGESTED READING

1. John G. Proakis, and Dimitris G. Manolakis "Digital signal processing: principles, algorithms, and applications, 4/E,"Pearson Education India, 2007.
2. Alan V. Oppenheim, Alan S. Willsky, and S. Hamid Nawab "Signals & Systems,"Pearson Education India, 1997.
3. Steven W. Smith "Digital Signal Processing: A Practical Guide for Engineers and Scientists," California Technical Publishing, 1999.
4. Barrie W. Jervis, and Emmanuel C. Ifeachor "Digital Signal Processing: A Practical Approach," Pearson Education India, 2002.
5. S.K. Mitra "Digital Signal Processing: A Computer Based Approach,"McGraw-Hill Higher Education New York, 2006.

Chapter 2: Classification of Signals and Systems

UNIT SPECIFICS

In the chapter on the classification of signals and systems within the context of digital signal processing the specifics focus on categorizing signals and systems based on their characteristics and behaviors. Signals are generally classified into categories such as continuous-time versus discrete-time, and analog versus digital. Continuous-time signals vary over a continuous range, while discrete-time signals are defined only at discrete intervals. Analog signals have a continuous amplitude, while digital signals are represented in discrete values. Systems, on the other hand, are categorized based on properties like linearity, time-invariance, causality, and stability. Linear systems follow the principle of superposition, time-invariant systems have behaviors that do not change over time, causal systems respond only to present and past inputs, and stable systems produce bounded outputs for bounded inputs. Understanding these classifications helps in selecting appropriate techniques for analyzing and designing DSP applications, ensuring accurate signal processing and system performance.

RATIONALE

To begin signal processing, it is essential to understand the energy and power signals, their specifications, and the various operations on the signals.

PRE-REQUISITE

NIL

UNIT OUTCOMES

List of outcomes of this unit is as follows:

U2-O1: Understanding of the basic functions for signals representation

U2-O2: Basic signals operations

U2-O3: Sampling and reconstruction of contentious time signals

U2-O4: Energy and power of signals

Unit-2 Outcomes	EXPECTED MAPPING WITH COURSE OUTCOMES (1- Weak Correlation; 2- Medium correlation; 3- Strong Correlation)					
	CO-1	CO-2	CO-3	CO-4	CO-5	CO-6
U2-O1	3	1	–	–	–	–
U2-O2	3	1	–	–	–	–
U2-O3	3	1	–	–	–	–
U2-O4	3	1	–	—	–	–

2.1 INTRODUCTION

This chapter delves into the systematic categorization of signals and systems, providing readers with a structured framework to analyze and manipulate various typesof signals encountered in real-world scenarios. By exploring the diverse categories of signals, ranging from continuous-time and discrete-time signals to analog and digitalsignals, readers will gain insights into the unique properties and representations ofeach signal type. Furthermore, this chapter elucidates the classification of systems based on their linearity, time-invariance, causality, and memory, offering a comprehensive overview of the fundamental principles governing system behavior. Througha blend of theoretical concepts, practical examples, and illustrative diagrams, this chapter aims to equip readers with the knowledge and tools necessary to navigate the intricate landscape of signals and systems with confidence and clarity.

2.2 DELTA FUNCTION

The delta function is also referred as Dirac delta function or unit impulse function. It is used to model a tall narrow spike function and other similar abstractions for very short duration. Therefore, it is used to capture the instantaneous effect of the systems. Delta function can be thought as a function on the real line which is zero everywhere except at the origin, where it is infinite with unit area. Thus, delta function δ(t) can be expressed as

$$\delta(t) = \begin{cases} \infty, t = 0 \\ 0, t \neq 0 \end{cases} \text{ with } \int_{-\infty}^{\infty} \delta(t)dt = 1.$$

Plot of δ(t) is shown in Fig. 2.1. The height of the arrow is usually chosen to represent the value of the integral. For example in Fig. 2.1, unit height of arrow denotes the area under the delta function.

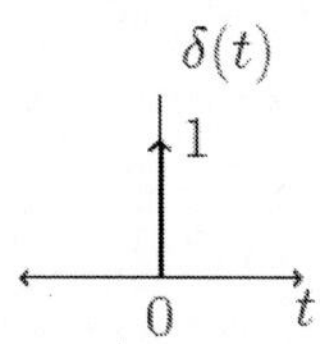

Fig. 2.1: Delta function

Delta function can be defined using a symmetric function of unit area with width approaching zero. For example, rectangular pulse *p(t)* of width *W* and height *1/W* can be used to define the delta function. The pulse *p(t)* is represented in Fig. 2.2 having unit area, i.e., $\int_{-\infty}^{\infty} p(t)dt = 1$. Therefore, as *T* → *0*, width and height of the pulse *p(t)* approach to zero and infinity, respectively, and pulse concentrates on the origin. Hence, as T → 0, p(t) resembles with delta function δ(t).

$$\delta(t) = \lim_{T \to 0} p(t) \quad (2.1)$$

Further, we observe that *δ(t)* is a even function, which is easily verified using theabove equation (2.1) as

$$\delta(-t) = \lim_{T \to 0} p(-t) = \lim_{T \to 0} p(t) = \delta(t). \quad (2.2)$$

Delta function is not a function in the conventional sense since it does not satisfy the function's property. It is a distribution and uses to model instantaneous phenomenon or actions. Therefore, in practice, instantaneous action is modeled using delta function and mathematically can be analyzed.

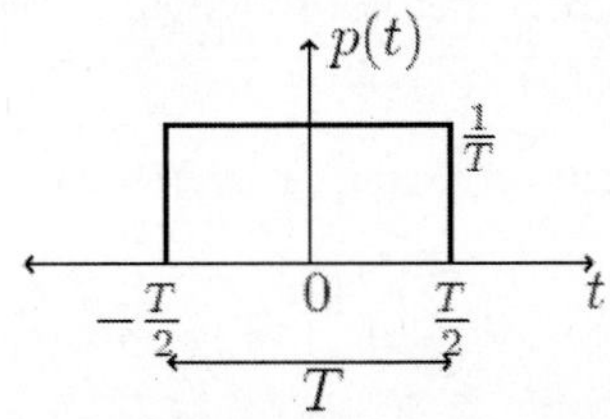

Fig. 2.2: Rectangular pulse

2.2.1 Properties of the delta function

In this subsection, some common properties of the delta function are discussed with their applications.

1. Time-shifting property: $\delta(t - t_0)$

$$\delta(t-t_0) = \begin{cases} \infty, t = t_0 \\ 0, t \neq t_0 \end{cases} \text{ with } \int_{-\infty}^{\infty} \delta(t-t_0)dt = 1, a \leq t_0 \leq b$$

Therefore, $\delta(t\ t_0)$ is located at time t_0, which is easily verified using theequation (2.5) when pulse is cantered at time t_0.

2. Amplitude-scaling property: $A\delta(t)$

It represents that the area under the impulse function is A, and shown in Fig.2.3.

$$\int_{-\infty}^{\infty} A\delta(t)dt = A\int_{-\infty}^{\infty} \delta(t)dt = A$$

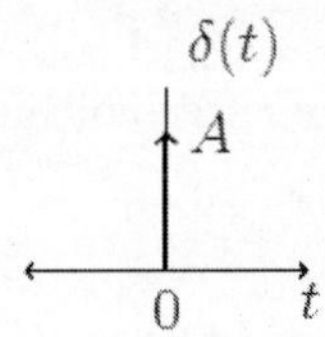

Fig. 2.3: Delta function $A\delta(t)$

3. Time-scaling property: $\delta(at)$

$$\delta(at) = \frac{1}{|a|}\delta(t), \qquad a \neq 0$$

$$\int_{-\infty}^{\infty} \delta(at)dt, a > 0$$

Substitute : $at = t', dt = \frac{1}{a}dt' \int_{-\infty}^{\infty} \frac{1}{a}\delta(t')dt' = \frac{1}{a}$ (2.3)

Similarly, it can be proved for negative value of a. Therefore, $\delta(at) = 1/|a|\delta(t)$.

4. Sampling property: $x(t)\delta(t - t_0) = x(t_0)\delta(t - t_0)$.

Let $x(t)$ be a continuous time function, as shown in Fig. 2.4. After the multiplication signal is zero except at $t = t_0$ since delta function is zero every where other than $t = t_0$. Over a delta function duration, signal $x(t)$ is constant and its value is $x(t_0)$. Therefore, after impulse function multiplication, signal value is $x(t_0)$ at time t_0 only. Hence, mathematically it is written as

$$x(t)\delta(t - t_0) = x(t_0)\delta(t - t_0).$$

Similarly, if impulse is located at time t = 0, then $x(t)\delta(t) = x(0)\delta(t)$.

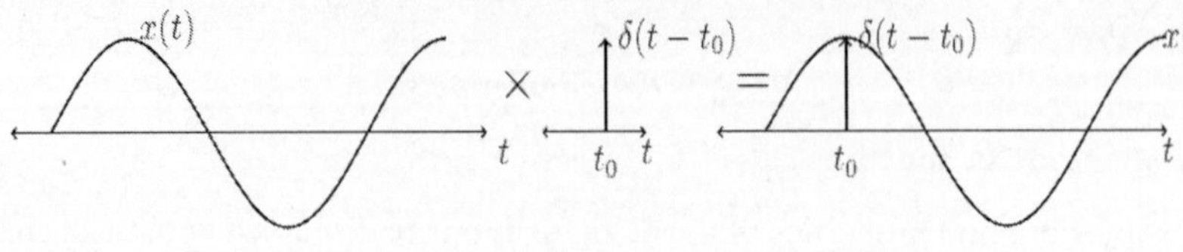

Fig. 2.4: Signal multiplication using delta function

5. $\int_{-\infty}^{\infty} x(t)\delta(t - t_0)dt = x(t_o)$

Using sampling property $x(t)\delta(t - t_0) = x(t_o)\delta(t - t_0)$

$\int_{-\infty}^{\infty} x(t_o)\,\delta(t - t_0)dt = x(t_o)\int_{-\infty}^{\infty} \delta(t - t_0)\,dt = x(t_o)$ (2.4)

6. Derivative of delta function: $\delta'(t) = \frac{d}{dt}\delta(t)$

Derivative of a delta function can be understand using the rectangle pulse $p(t)$, which is used to define the delta function. Therefore,

$\delta(t) = \lim_{T\to 0} p(t) \rightarrow \frac{d}{dt}\delta(t) = \lim_{T\to 0}\frac{d}{dt}p(t) = \lim_{T\to 0} p'(t).$ (2.5)

We can see in Fig. 2.5 that two impulses are located at $-T/2$ and $T/2$ with equal and opposite height. As $T \rightarrow 0$, both impulses coincide at time $t = 0$. Therefore, we define area under the function δ'(t) is zero, i.e.,.

$$\frac{d}{dt}\delta'(t) = 0$$

Further, $\int_{-\infty}^{\infty} x(t)\,\delta'(t)dt = -\int_{-\infty}^{\infty} x'(t)\,\delta(t)dt = -x'(0)$

7. Convolution property $x(t) * \delta(t) = x(t)$

$$x(t) * \delta(t) = \int_{-\infty}^{\infty} x(\tau)\delta(t - \tau)d\tau = \int_{-\infty}^{\infty} x(\tau)\,\delta(\tau - t)d$$

Using the even function property of the delta function $\delta(t\text{-}\tau) = \delta(\tau\text{-}t)$.

Further, we use the sampling property and expression is

$$x(t) * \delta(t) = \int_{-\infty}^{\infty} x(t)\delta(\tau - t)d\tau = \mathrm{x}(t).$$

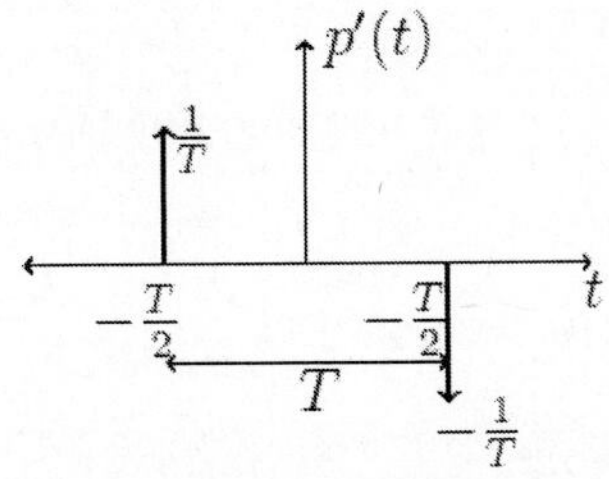

Fig. 2.5: Derivative of the delta function with $T \rightarrow 0$

2.3 UNIT STEP FUNCTION

Unit step function or Heaviside step function is used to model an event that starts on at a specified time and continue on indefinitely. The unit step function u(t) is defined as

$$u(t) = \begin{cases} 1, t \geq 0 \\ 0, t < 0 \end{cases}$$

Unit step function is discontinuous at $t = 0$ and it is shown in Fig. 2.6. Unit

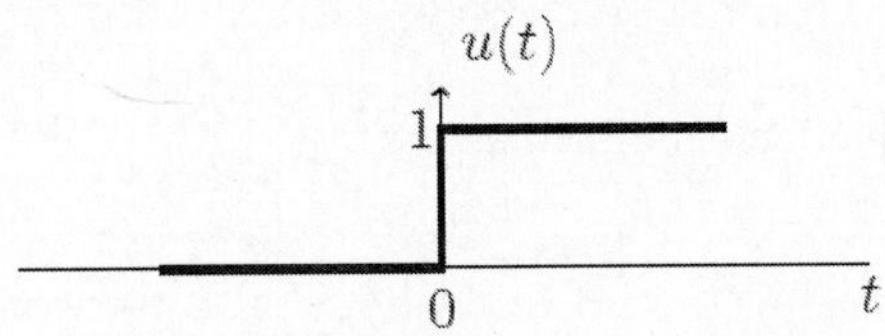

Fig. 2.6: Unit step function u(t) plot

step function u(t) is related to the delta impulse function δ(t) through a runningsummation as

$$u(t) = \int_{-\infty}^{t} \delta(\tau). \quad (2.6)$$

The above integral is zero for t<0 and unity for t>0 which satisfy the unit step function definition. Further, the first derivative of unit step function is equal to thedelta function as

δ(t)=du(t)/dt (2.7)

The derivative of unit step function is zero everywhere except $t = 0$. However,the derivative of unit step function can be derived by considering a limiting case of function $u_\Delta(t)$ as $\Delta \rightarrow 0$ in Fig. 2.8.

Further, the unit area of the delta function can be proved using the above relation as

$$\int_{-\infty}^{\infty} \delta(t)dt = \int_{-\infty}^{\infty} \frac{du(t)}{dt} dt = [u(t)]|_{t=-\infty}^{\infty} = u(\infty) - u(-\infty) = 1 - 0 = 1 \quad (2.8)$$

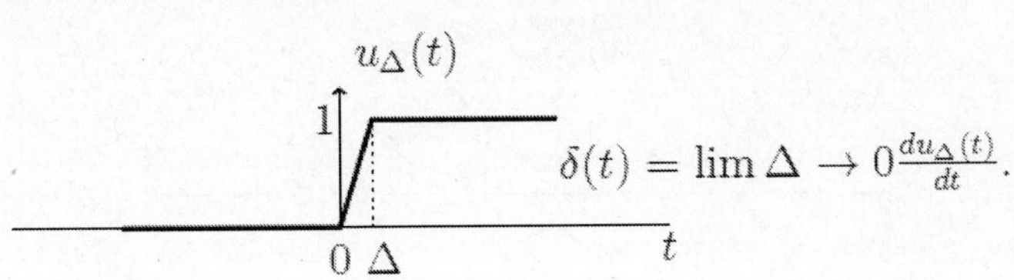

Fig. 2.7: Function $u_\Delta(t)$ plot

The $u(\infty) = 1$ and $u(-\infty) = 0$ as observed in Fig. 2.6.

2.3.1 Properties of unit step function

In this subsection some common properties of the unit step function are discussedwith their applications.

1. Time-shifting property: $u(t - t_0)$

   Time shifted unit step function $u(t - t_0)$ is defined as

   $$u(t - t_0) = \begin{cases} 1, t \geq t_0 \\ 0, t < t_0 \end{cases}$$

   and its plot is shown in Fig. 2.8.

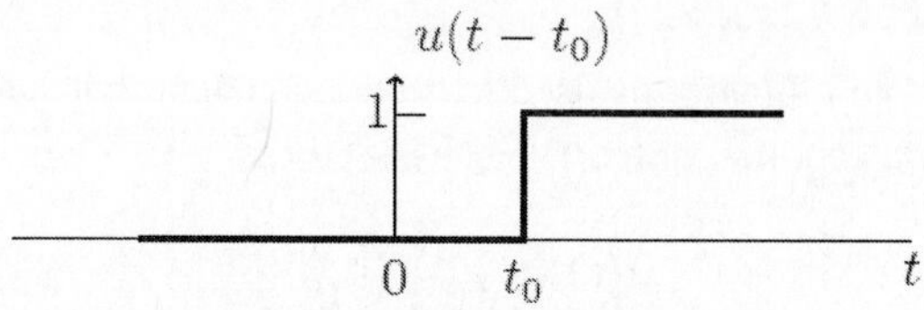

Fig. 2.8: Unit step function $u(t - t_0)$ plot

2. Amplitude scaling property: $Ku(t)$

   Amplitude scaled unit step function is defined as

   $$Ku(t) = \begin{cases} \mathrm{K}, t \geq t_0 \\ 0, t < t_0 \end{cases}$$

3. Switching property: $x(t)u(t)$

   $u(t)$ acts as a switch. It is clear that multiplying a signal $x(t)$ by $u(t)$ gives

   $$x(t)u(t) = \begin{cases} \mathrm{x(t)},\ t \geq t_0 \\ 0, t < t_0 \end{cases}$$

   Therefore, after multiplying by $u(t)$ function $x(t)$ is switched off for $t < 0$ and switched on for $t \geq 0$.

2.4 UNIT RAMP FUNCTION

It is a function which starts at $t = 0$ and increases linearly with time. Unit rampsignal $r(t)$ is defined as

$$r(t) = \begin{cases} \mathrm{t}, t \geq 0 \\ 0, t < 0. \end{cases}$$

Therefore, $r(t) = tu(t)$. A graphical representation of the unit ramp signal is shownin Fig. 2.9. Slope of unit ramp signal is unity.

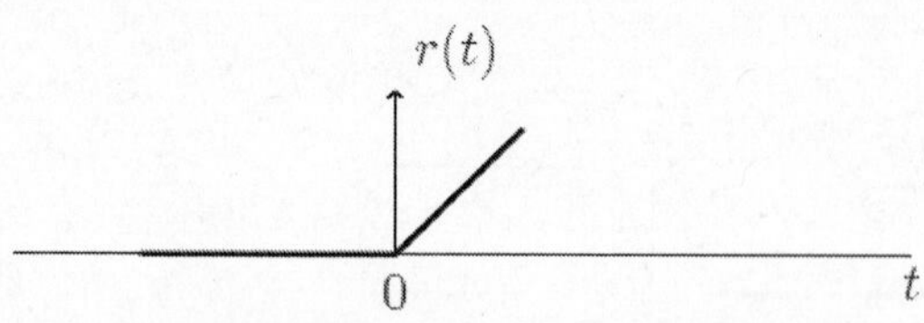

Fig. 2.9: Unit ramp signal r(t) plot

Unit ramp and unit step functions are related to each other as

$$r(t) = \int_{-\infty}^{t} u(\tau)d\tau$$

$$u(t) = \frac{dr(t)}{dt}. \tag{2.9}$$

Note: Unit impulse function, unit step function and unit ramp function are used to represent some more complex signals in the sugnal and system analysis. Therefore, these are also called the basis functions.

2.5 RECTANGULAR PULSE SIGNAL

A unit rectangular pulse has unit amplitude within a time interval, otherwise it has zero value. It is also called the Gate pulse, Pulse function, or Window function, etc. A unit rectangular pulse *x(t)* is defined as

$$x(t) = \begin{cases} 1, \frac{-\tau}{2} \leq t \leq \frac{\tau}{2} \\ 0, otherwise \end{cases}$$

Unit rectangular pulse *x(t)* is also shown in Fig. 2.10

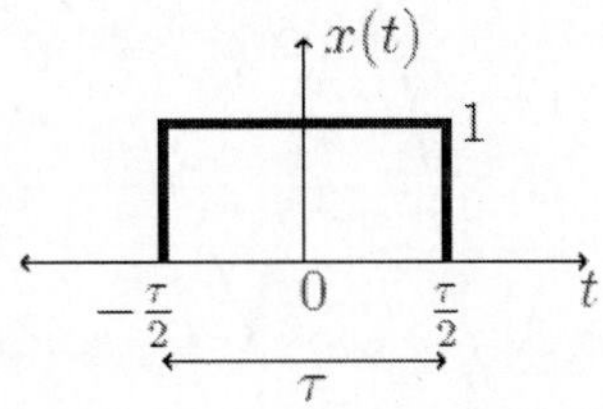

Fig. 2.10: A unit rectangular pulse

2.6 EXPONENTIAL SIGNAL

An exponential signal *x(t)* is defined as $x(t) = Ae^{bt}$, where *A* and *b* are constants. Therefore, exponential signal can either have exponentially rising or falling ampli- tude depending upon its exponent value. An exponential signal plot is shown in Fig. 2.11.

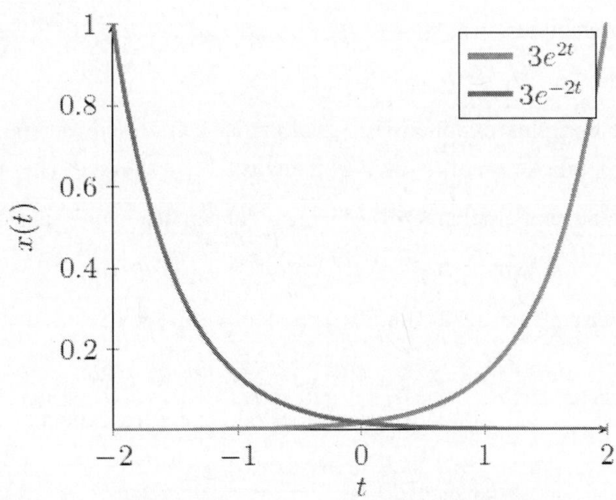

Fig. 2.11: Normalized exponential signals plot

2.7 SINUSOIDAL SIGNALS

Sinusoidal signals are essential in electrical engineering as we use them to analyze and test circuit performance. All periodic signals can be represented with sinusoidalsignals of different amplitudes and phases using the Fourier series.

A sinusoidal signal is defined as

$$x(t) = A\, sin(\omega t + \phi),$$

where A is the amplitude of the signal, and ω and ϕ are the frequency in radian per second (red/sec) and phase in radians, respectively. Further, $\omega = 2\pi f = 2\pi/T$, where f denotes the fundamental frequency in cycle per second or Hertz (Hz). T is the time period of the waveform and $T = 1/f$. Therefore, all three parameters A, ω and ϕ are essential to completely define the sinusoidal signals. Further, argument of sinusoidal at $t = 0$ represents the phase of signal. A sinusoidal signal is shown in Fig. 2.12.

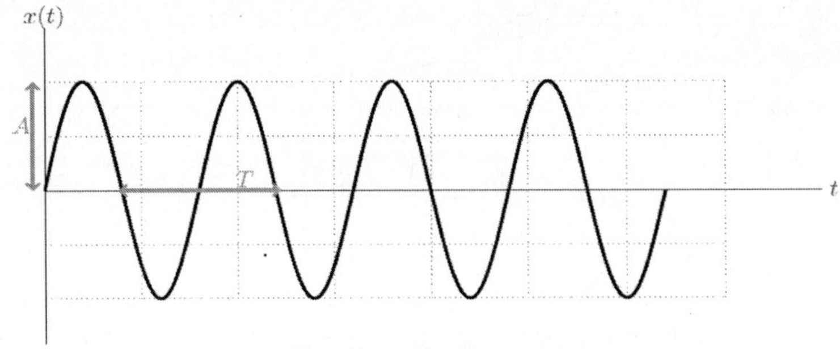

Fig. 2.12: Sinusoidal signal plot

2.8 COMPLEX EXPONENTIAL SIGNALS

A complex exponential signal is defined as

$x(t) = Ae^{j\omega t}$,

where A denotes the amplitude of signal at $t = 0$ and ω is the frequency in red/sec. Complex exponential are periodic in nature. For example

$x(t + T) = Ae^{j\omega(t+T)} = Ae^{j\omega t}e^{j\omega T} = x(t)$

Since $e^{j\omega T} = 1$. Further, a complex exponential signal is also expressed as $x(t) = Ae^{-j\omega t}$, which has same frequency ω in rad/sec except direction of rotation of the wave has reversed as compare to $e^{j\omega t}$.

A complex exponential can be expressed in terms of sinusoidal signals using Euler'sidentity as

$$x(t) = Ae^{j\omega t} = A[cos(\omega t) + j\, sin(\omega t)].$$

For a generalized complex exponential, Euler's relation is

$$Ae^{\pm j(\omega t+\phi)} = A[cos(\omega t + \phi) \pm j\, sin(\omega t + \phi)].$$

Similarly, a sinusoidal signal can be written in terms of periodic complex exponentials as

$$cos(\omega t + \phi) = \frac{e^{j(\omega t+\phi)} - e^{-j(\omega t+\phi)}}{2}$$

and

$$sin(\omega t + \phi) = \frac{e^{j(\omega t+\phi)} - e^{-j(\omega t+\phi)}}{2j}$$

Therefore, complex exponential and sinusoidal are related to each other and periodic in nature. A complex exponential is shown in Fig. 2.13, where A and $\omega_0 t$ denote the circle radius and angle at particulate time instant t.

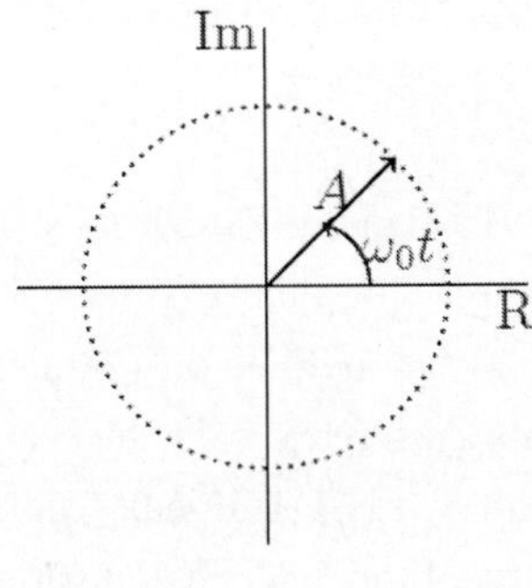

Fig. 2.13: Complex exponential signal $Ae^{j\omega_0 t}$

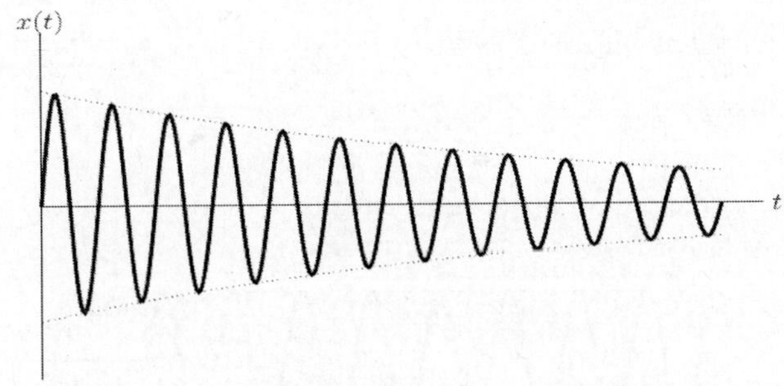

Fig. 2.14: Plot of $2e^{-0.05t}$ sin(3t)

Further, a decaying modulated exponential signal $x(t) = 2e^{-0.05t}\ sin(3t)$ is shown in Fig. 2.14. A sinusoidal signal propagates inside the envelope $2e^{-0.05t}$. Similarity, a growing modulated exponential signal $x(t) = 0.5e^{0.05t}\ sin(3t)$ is shown in Fig. 2.15.

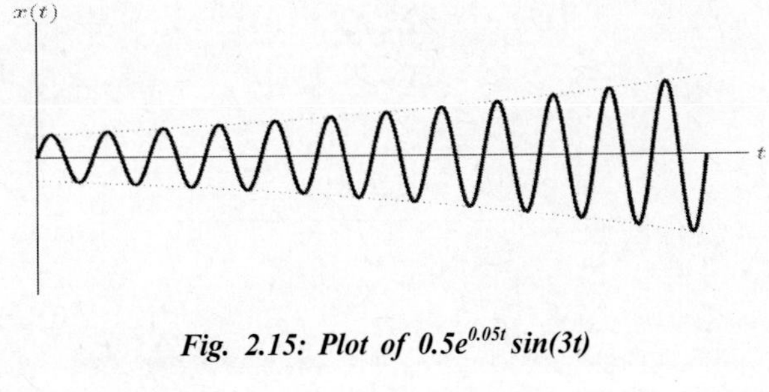

Fig. 2.15: Plot of $0.5e^{0.05t}$ sin(3t)

2.9 CLASSIFICATION OF SIGNALS

In this section, we describe different types of signals, which are commonly used insignals and systems' analysis. Different types of signal are

- Continuous-Time and Discrete-Time Signals
- Analog and Digital Signals
- Real and Complex Signals
- Even and Odd Signals
- Energy and Power Signals
- Deterministic and Random Signals

1. *Continuous-Time and Discrete-Time Signals*

Continuous time (CT) and discrete time (DT) signal are mostly used in signal and system analysis. In CT signal, independent variable is continuous there- fore, these signals are defined for a continuum of values of the independent variable. However, DT signals are defined only at discrete times, and consequently, for these signals, the independent variable takes on only a discrete setof values. For example, speech signal is a CT signal and the weekly Dow-Jonesstock market index is a DT signal. The symbol *t* denotes the continuous-time independent variable and *n* denotes the discrete-time independent variable. Therefore, continuous-time signal is denoted as *x(t)* and discrete-time signal

is represented as *x[n]*[1]. A continuous-time signal *x(t)* is shown in Fig. 2.16 with independent variable $t \in (-\infty, \infty)$.

[1]Some books use $x(n)$ also for discrete-time signal representation.

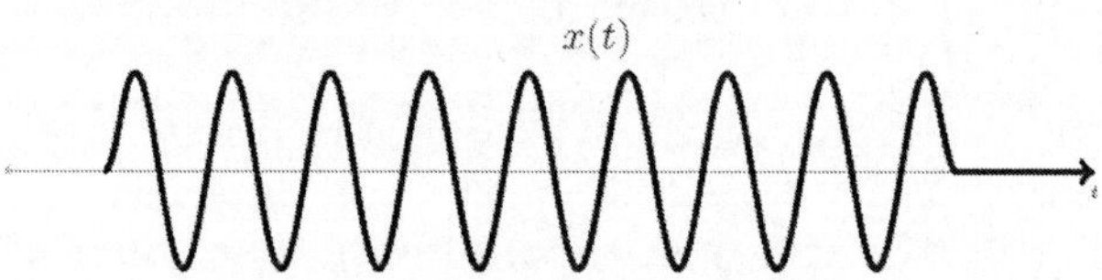

Fig. 2.16: Graphical representations of a continuous-time signal $x(t)$

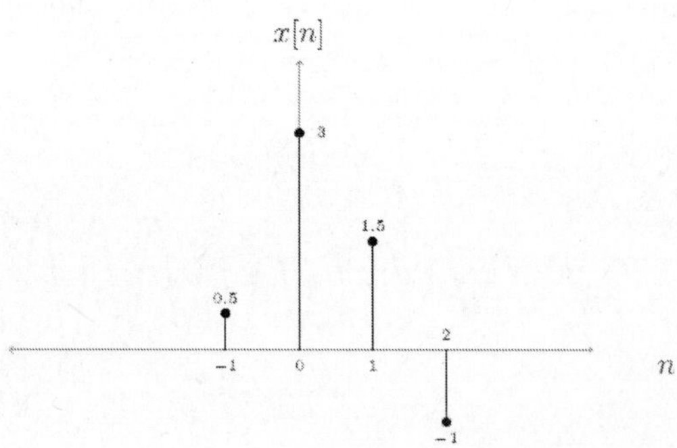

Fig. 2.17: Graphical representation of a discrete-time signal $x(n)$

2. *Analog and Digital Signals*

- **Analog Signal:** If a signal can take on any value in the continuous interval(a, b), where a maybe $-\infty$ and b may be $+\infty$, then the signal is calledan analog signal.

- **Digital Signal:** If a signal can take on only finite number distinct values, then the signal is called a digital signal.
- Analog signal:
  - Analog continuous-time signal
  - Analog discrete-time signal
- Digital signal:
  - Digital continuous-time signal
  - Digital discrete-time signal

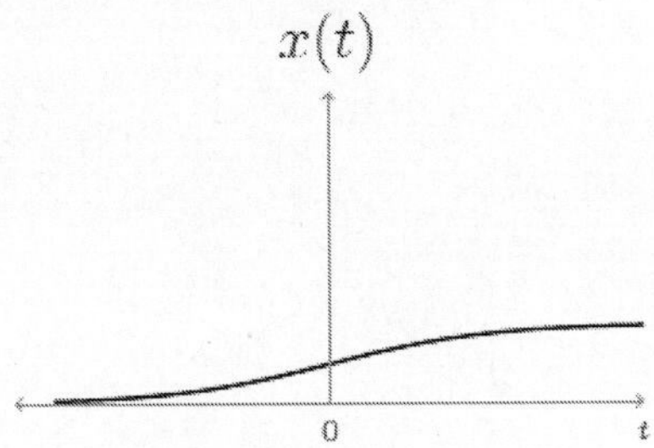

Analog continuous-time signal

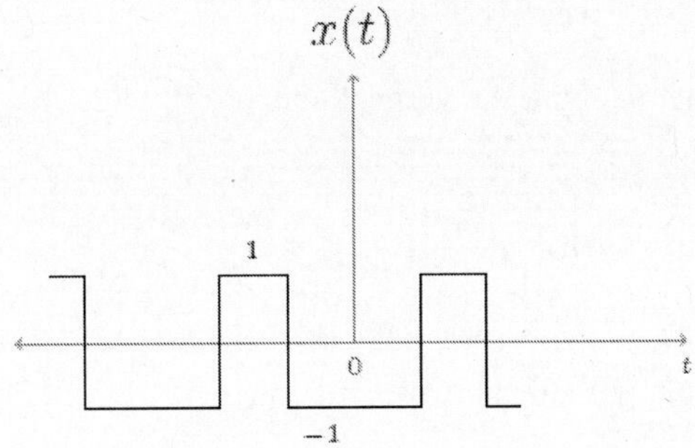

Digital continuous-time signal

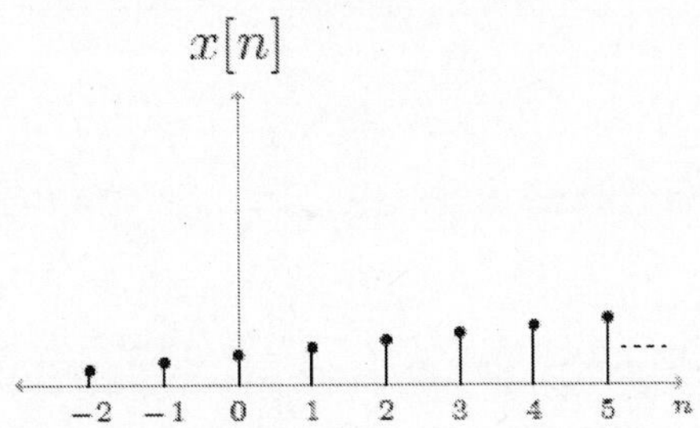

Analog discrete-time signal

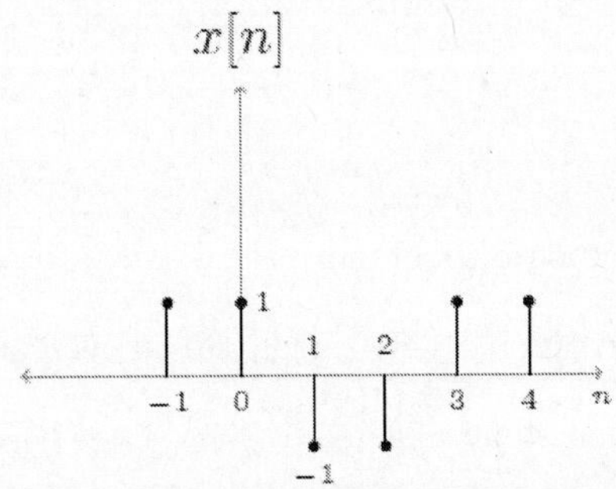

Digital discrete-time signal

3. Real and Complex Signal

- Definition: A signal is a real signal if its value is a real number
- Definition: A signal is a complex signal if its value is a complex number
- Continuous-time

and discrete-time

$x(t) = x_1(t) + j\,x_2(t)$

$x[n] = x_1[n] + j\,x_2[n],$

where $j = \sqrt{-1}$ and $x_1(.)$ and $x_2(.)$ are two real signals.

4. Even and Odd Signals

- Even signal

  $x(-t) = x(t)$ or

  $x[-n] = x[n]$

- Example: Graphical representation

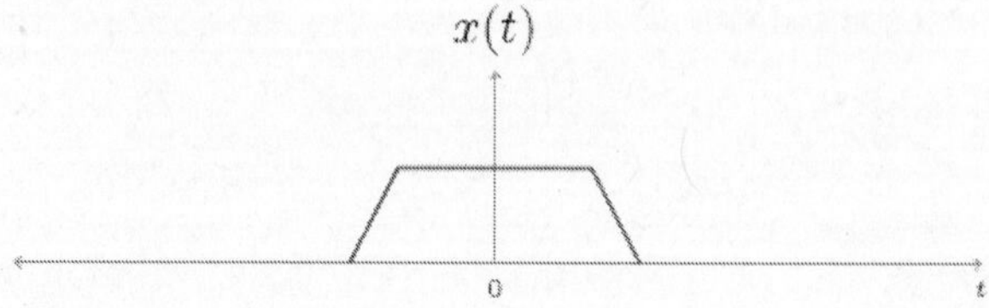

- Symmetric about the vertical axis or origin
- Odd signal

  $x(-t) = -x(t)$ or

  $x[-n] = -x[n]$

- Example: Graphical representation

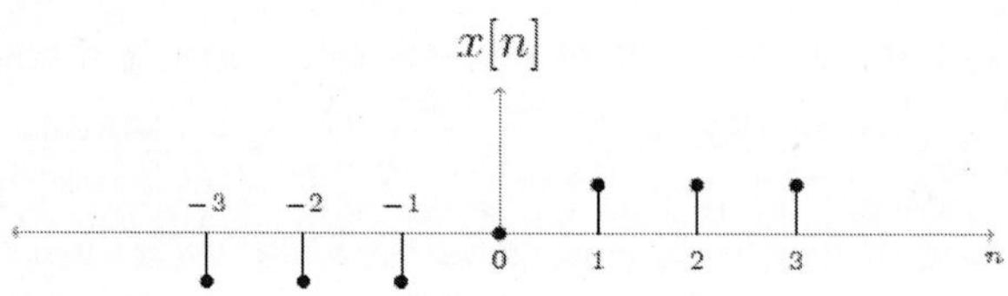

- Necessarily: $x(0) = 0$ or $x[0] = 0$
- Antisymmetric about the vertical axis or origin
- Decomposition of any signal into an even and odd part, i.e.
- Continuous-time signal

  $x(t) = Ev\{x(t)\} + Od\{x(t)\}$ where

  $$Ev\{x(t)\} = \frac{x(t) + x(-t)}{2}$$

- Discrete-time signal:

  $$x[n] = \text{Ev}\{x[n]\} + \text{Od}\{x[n]\}$$

  where

  $$\text{Ev}\{x[n]\} = \frac{x[n] + x[-n]}{2}$$

  and

  $$\text{Od}\{x[n]\} = \frac{x[n] - x[-n]}{2}$$

5. Energy and Power Signals:

- Often classification of signals according to energy and power
  - Terminology energy and power used for any signal *x(t), x[n]*
  - Need not necessarily have a physical meaning
- Signal energy
  - Energy of a possibly complex continuous-time signal *x(t)* in interval $t_1 \leq t \leq t_2$

$$E(t_1, t_2) = \int_{t_1}^{t_2} |x(t)|^2 dt$$

  - Energy of a possibly complex discrete-time signal *x[n]* in interval $n_1 \leq n \leq n_2$

- Total energy

$$E_\infty = E(-\infty, \infty) = \int_{-\infty}^{\infty} |x(t)|^2 dt(t)|^2 dt$$

$$E(n_1, n_2) = \sum_{n=n_1}^{n_2} |x[n]|^2$$

$$E_\infty = E(-\infty, \infty) = \sum_{n=-\infty}^{\infty} |x[n]|^2$$

Example 2.9.1 *Total energy of the discrete-time signal* $x[n] = \begin{cases} a^n, n \geq 0 \\ 0, n \leq 0 \end{cases}$ with $|a|<1$

$$E_\infty = \sum_{n=-\infty}^{\infty} |x[n]|^2 = \sum_{n=0}^{\infty} |a^n|^2 = \frac{1}{1-|a|^2}$$

<u>Signal Power:</u>

Consider the time-averaged signal power

- Average power of *x(t)* in interval $t_1 \leq t \leq t_2$

$$P(t_1, t_2) = \frac{1}{t_2 - t_1} \int_{t_1}^{t_2} |x(t)|^2 dt$$

- Average power of *x[n]* in interval $n_1 \leq n \leq n_2$

$$P(n_1, n_2) = \frac{1}{n_2 - n_1 + 1} \sum_{n=n_1}^{n_2} |x[n]|^2$$

- Analogously

$$P_\infty = P(-\infty, \infty) = \lim_{T \to \infty} \frac{1}{2T} \int_{-T}^{T} |x(t)|^2 dt$$

$$P_\infty = P(-\infty,\infty) = \lim_{N\to\infty} \frac{1}{2N+1} \sum_{n=-N}^{N} |x[n]|^2$$

- Classification of signals based on their energy and power

Signals with finite total energy, $0 < E_\infty < \infty$

* Zero average power $P_\infty = 0$

* Example: any signal with finite duration

Signals with finite average power, $0 < P_\infty < \infty$

* Infinite total energy $E_\infty = \infty$ if $P_\infty > 0$

* Example: periodic signals e.g. $x(t) = cos(t)$, $x[n] = sin(5n)$

Signals with infinite power $P_\infty = \infty$ and infinite energy $E_\infty = \infty$

* Not desirable in engineering applications

* Examples: $x(t) = e^t$, $x[n] = n^{10}$

Classification of signals based on their energy and power is mutuallyexclusive.

6. Periodic and Aperiodic Signals:

- Periodic continuous-time signal

$$x(t) = x(t + T),\ t \in (-\infty, \infty)$$

  - $T > 0$: period
  - $x(t)$ period with T

    $x(t)$ also periodic with mT, m is an integerconstant.
  - Smallest period of $x(t)$: Fundamental period T_0.

Example: $T_0 = T$

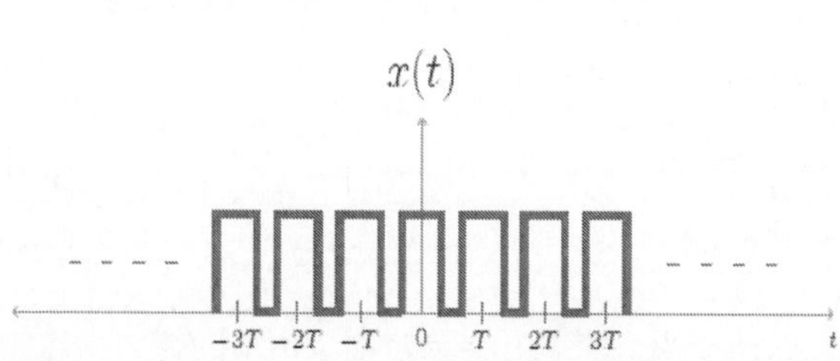

- Periodic discrete-time signal

$x[n] = x[n + N],\ n \in \{. . . -2, -1, 0, 1, 2, . . .\}$

  - Integer $N > 0$: period
  - $x[n]$ period with N $\Rightarrow$ $x[n]$ also periodic with mN, m is an integerconstant.
  - Smallest period of $x[n]$: Fundamental period N_0.
  - Example: $N_0 = 4$

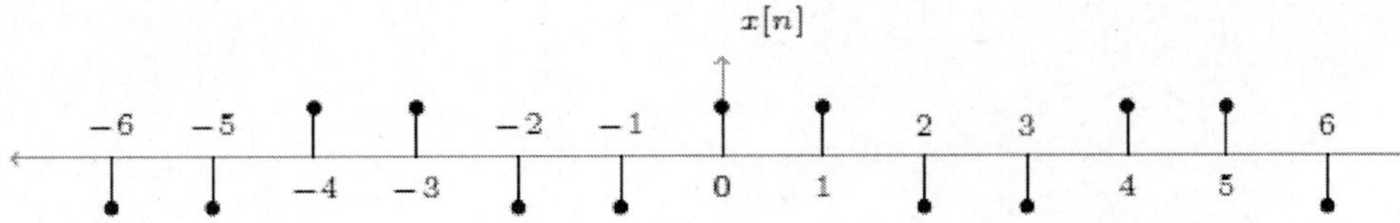

- A signal that is not periodic is referred to as aperiodic.

7. Deterministic and Random Signals:
    - A deterministic signal is a signal about which there is no uncertainty withrespect to its value at any time. Deterministic signals may be modeledas completely specified function of time.
    - By contrast, a random signal is a signal about which there is a uncertaintybefore it occurs.
    - Periodic and random signals are usually viewed as power signals
    - Aperiodic and deterministic are usually viewed as energy signals

2.10 SAMPLING AND RECONSTRUCTION OF THE CONTINUOUS TIME SIGNALS

Analog band-limited signal x(t) is sampled at the rate of $T = 1/F_s$ second. Max- imum analog signal frequency *is* $\Omega_{max} = 2\pi F_{max}$ rad, where F_{max} is the maximum frequencies in *Hz*. The signal sampling processes is illustrated in Fig. 2.18. The analog signal is multiplied by an impulse train *p(t)* as

$$y(t) = x(t)p(t) = x(t)\sum_{n=-\infty}^{\infty}\delta(t-nT)$$

$$y(t) = \sum_{n=-\infty}^{\infty} x(nT)\,\delta(t-nT)$$

We can write the Fourier series (FS) of the signal $\sum_{n=-\infty}^{\infty}\delta(t-nT) = \frac{1}{T}\sum_{k=-\infty}^{\infty} e^{j2\pi kt/T}$.

Take the Fourier transforms of both side, and we can have

$$Y(\Omega) = \frac{1}{2\pi}X(\Omega) * P(\Omega) = \frac{1}{T}\sum_{k=-\infty}^{\infty} X(\Omega - 2\pi kF_s)$$

Or $Y(F) = \frac{1}{T}\sum_{k=-\infty}^{\infty} X(\mathrm{F} - kF_s)$ Or, $Y(f) = \mathrm{F_s}\sum_{k=-\infty}^{\infty} X((\mathrm{f}-k)F_s)$

where $F = fF_s$. $-1/2 < f < 1/2$ and $-\infty < F < \infty$. Original signal frequencyspectrum is $X(F)$ or $X(\Omega)$ and it can be recovered from the $Y(f)$ passing througha lowpass filter (LPF) if $\Omega_s > 2\Omega_{max}$ or $F_s > 2F_{max}$, as shown in Fig. 2.19.

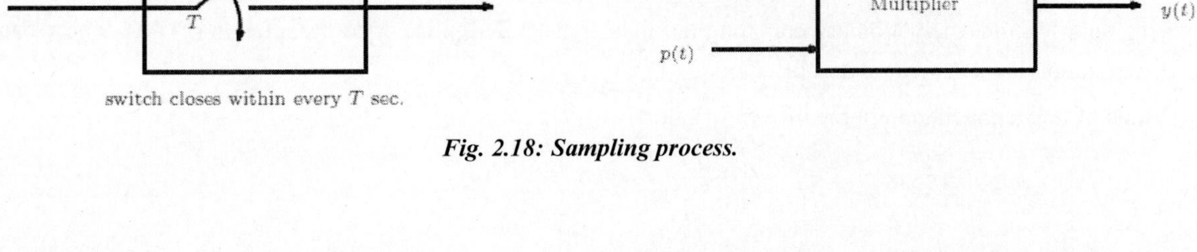

Fig. 2.18: Sampling process.

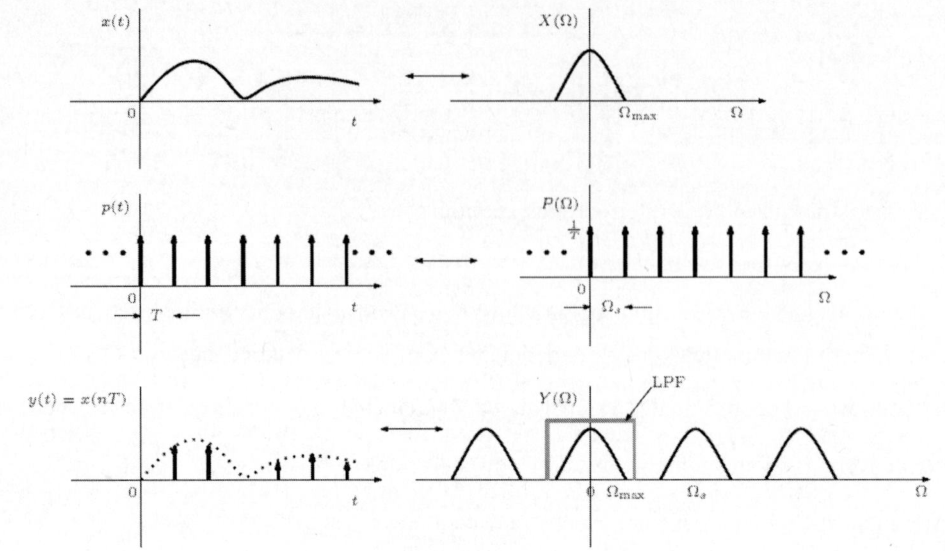

Fig. 2.19: Sampling of analog band-limited signal.

The Nyquist theorem states that in order to faithfully reconstruct a continuous- time signal from its samples, the sampling frequency must be at least twice the highest frequency component present in the signal. In other words, the sampling rate must be greater than or equal to twice the maximum frequency of the signal being sampled. Mathematically, the Nyquist theorem can be expressed as: $F_s > 2F_{max}$.

Analog signal can be recovered from the $y(t) = x(nT)$ as

$$\tilde{x}(t) = \sum_{n=-\infty}^{\infty} x(nT) \frac{sin(\pi/T)(t-nT)}{\pi/T(t-nT)} \tag{2.10}$$

2.11 ANALOG-TO-DIGITAL CONVERSION

Analog-to-digital (A/D) conversion, also known as digitization, involves several steps to convert continuous analog signals into discrete digital representations. The pro-cess typically consists of the following steps:

Sampling: The first step in A/D conversion is sampling, where the continuous-time analog signal is sampled at regular intervals. According to the Nyquist theorem, thesampling rate must be at least twice the highest frequency component of the analogsignal to avoid aliasing.

Quantization: Once sampled, the analog signal's amplitude values are quantized into discrete levels. This step involves mapping each sample's continuous ampli- tude value to the nearest discrete value in the quantization levels. The number of quantization levels determines the resolution of the digital signal and affects the signal-to-noise ratio (SNR) of the conversion process.

Encoding: After quantization, the quantized amplitude values are encoded into digital binary representations. This encoding process typically involves assigning abinary code to each quantization level. The most common encoding schemes includebinary encoding (straight binary) and pulse code modulation (PCM), where each quantization level is represented by a unique binary code word.

Steps of A/D conversion are mentioned in Fig. 2.20.

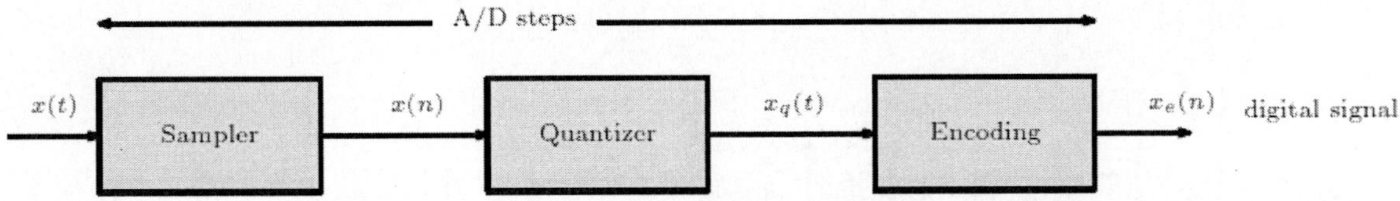

Fig. 2.20: A/D converter steps.

Example 2.11.1 *Signal and its corresponding frequency plots are shown in Fig.2.21for various stages of a system.*

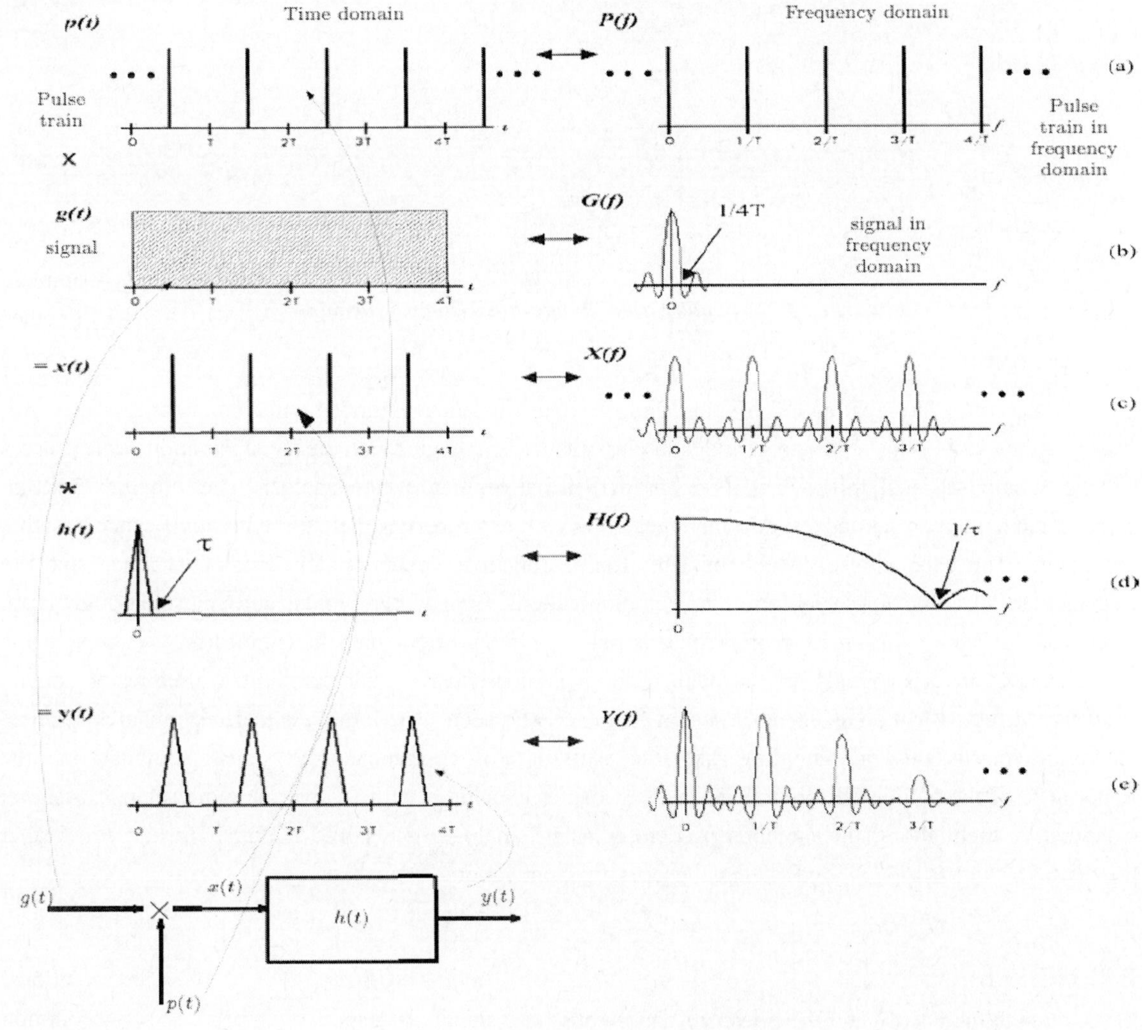

Fig. 2.21: Time and frequency domain signals[a].

[a]https://link.springer.com/chapter/10.1007/978 − 981 − 19 − 6549 − 4₂

Example 2.11.2 Impulse train and its Fourier series plots are shown in Fig.2.22.

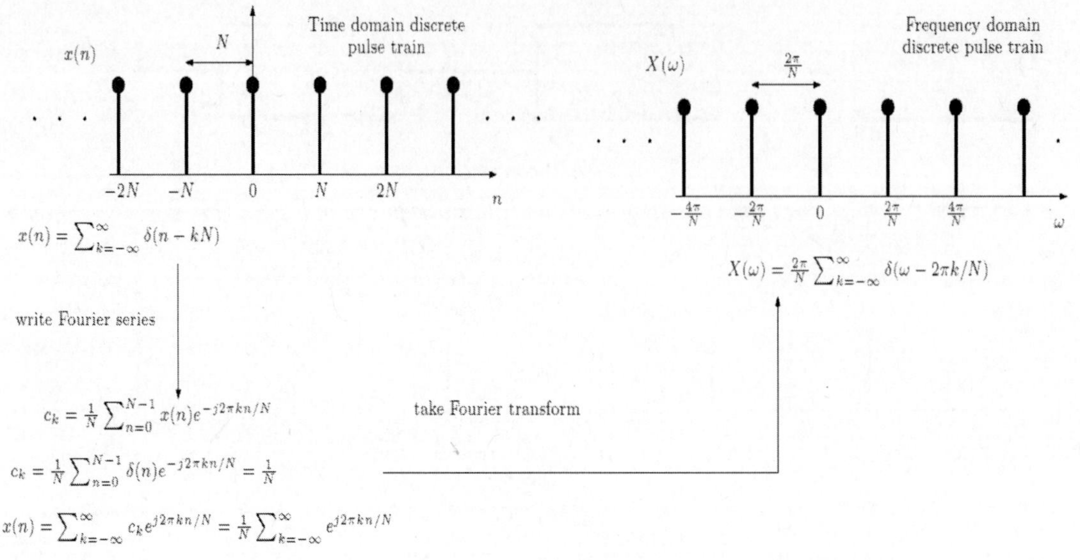

Fig. 2.22: Impulse train in time and frequency domain.

SUMMARY

The chapter on Classification of Signals and Systems introduces fundamental concepts essential for understanding various types of signals and their classifications. It begins with the Delta Function, which serves as an ideal impulse signal, followed by its key properties that facilitate system analysis. The Unit Step Function is presented next, representing a sudden change, along with its properties that define its significance in signal processing. The chapter also covers the Unit Ramp Function, which models gradual changes, and the Rectangular Pulse Signal, crucial for digital communications. Exponential Signals and Sinusoidal Signals are discussed for their widespread applications in both natural phenomena and engineering systems, while Complex Exponential Signals are introduced for a comprehensive understanding of frequency domain analysis. The classification of signals based on characteristics such as periodicity and determinism is detailed, leading to discussions on Sampling and Reconstruction of continuous-time signals, emphasizing the importance of the Nyquist theorem. Finally, the chapter concludes with an overview of Analog-to-Digital Conversion, highlighting the methods used to translate analog signals into a digital format for further processing, which is vital in modern signal processing applications.

EXERCISES

1. Compute the energy and the power of continuous-time signal $x(t) = e^{j4\pi t}$.
2. Find the energy of the signal $e^{-4t}u(t)$.
3. Find the exponential Fourier series for half wave rectified sine wave.
4. Find the output $y(t)$ of continuous-time system given as

$$\frac{dy(t)}{dt} + y(t) = \cos(2\pi t)$$

5. Find the output of the LTI system with impulse response $h(t) = e^{-2t}u(t)$ andthe input signal is $x(t) = e^{-t}u(t)$, where $u(t)$ is the unit step function.

6. Find the even and odd decomposition of the following signal

$$x(t) = \begin{cases} 4\sin(2t), \text{if } t > 0 \\ 0, \text{otherwise} \end{cases}$$

7. Find the period of signal $x(t) = 5\sin(100\pi t + \theta)\ \forall t$.

8. If signal $x(t)$ is

9. $$x(t) = \begin{cases} t + 2, \text{if } -2 \le t \le 0 \\ 2, 0 < t \le 2 \\ -(t-3), \text{if } -2 < t \le 3 \\ 0, \text{otherwise} \end{cases}$$

Find $x(t + 2)$, $x(t - 2)$, $x(2t)$, and $x(2t + 2)$.

10. Find the signals $2x(t)$, $x(t-1)$, $x(t + 2)$ and $x(2t-4)$ corresponding to signal $x(t)$ in Fig. 2.23.

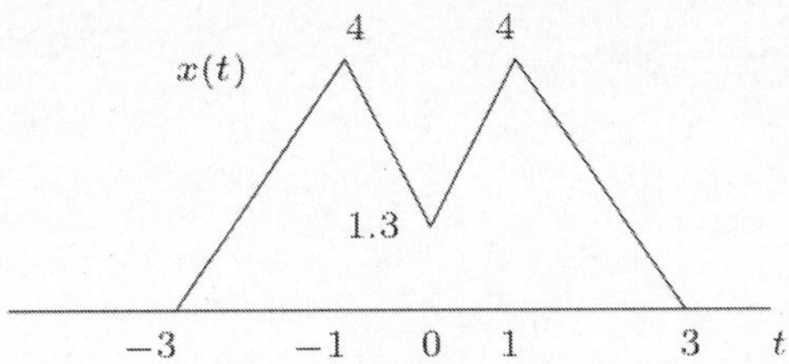

Fig. 2.23: Signal x(t).

Multiple Choice Questions

1. What is a continuous-time signal?

   A. A signal defined only at discrete points in time.

   B. A signal defined for every value of time.

   C. A signal that repeats itself after a certain period.

   D. A signal that has finite energy.

2. Which of the following is an example of a continuous-time signal?

   A. The daily closing price of a stock.

   B. Temperature variations over a day.

   C. A sequence of binary digits.

   D. A digital audio recording.

3. Which operation shifts a signal in time?

   A. Time Scaling

   B. Time Reversal

   C. Time Shifting

   D. Differentiation

4. If x(t) is a signal, what is the result of the time-reversal operation on this signal?

   A. x(−t)

   B. −x(t)

C. x(t)

D. 2x(t)

5. What is the effect of time scaling on the signal x(t) when a factor a>1 is used?

A. Compresses the signal in time.

B. Expands the signal in time.

C. Inverts the signal.

D. Shifts the signal in time.

6. What does the operation x(t) + x(−t) represent in signal processing?

A. Even part of the signal

B. Odd part of the signal

C. Time-reversed signal

D. Shifted signal

7. Which operation corresponds to y(t)=x(t−T)?

A. Time Scaling

B. Time Shifting

C. Amplitude Scaling

D. Time Reversal

8. If a signal x(t) is multiplied by a constant A, which operation is being performed?

A. Time Scaling

B. Time Shifting

C. Amplitude Scaling

D. Differentiation

9. The signal x(t)=cos(2πft) is an example of which type of signal?

A. Periodic

B. Aperiodic

C. Random

D. Continuous

10. What is the integral of a continuous-time signal x(t) with respect to time called?

A. Differentiation

B. Convolution

C. Integration

D. Sampling

ANSWERS

1	2	3	4	5	6	7	8	9	10
B	B	C	A	A	A	B	C	A	C

KNOW MORE

For more information related to this topic scan the QR code.

OR

Type this link in your browser

https://www.ece.uvic.ca/~frodo/sigsysbook/downloads/continuous_time_signals_and_systems-2.0.pdf

REFERENCES AND SUGGESTED READING

1. B. P. Lathi, "*Principles of Linear Systems and Signals*," *Oxford Second edition*,2009.
2. John G. Proakis, and Dimitris G. Manolakis "*Digital signal processing: principles, algorithms, and applications, 4/E*," *Pearson Education India*, 2007.
3. Alan V. Oppenheim, Alan S. Willsky, and S. Hamid Nawab "*Signals & Systems*," *Pearson Education India*, 1997.
4. P. Singh, A. Singhal, B. Fatimah, A. Gupta; S. Dutt Joshi "*Proper Definitions of Dirichlet Conditions and Convergence of Fourier Representations [Lecture Notes]*," *IEEE Signal Processing Magazine*, vol. 39, no. 5, pp. 77-84, 2022.
5. P. Singh, A. Gupta, and S. Dutt Joshi "*General Parameterized Fourier Trans- form: A Unified Framework for the Fourier, Laplace, Mellin and Z Transforms*," *IEEE Transactions on Signal Processing*, vol. 70, pp. 1295-1309, 2022.

Chapter 3: Discrete-time Signals and Systems

UNIT SPECIFICS

The discrete-time signals and systems chapter introduces the fundamental concepts and mathematical representations of signals and systems in the discrete-time domain. It covers the characterization and classification of discrete-time signals, such as periodic, aperiodic, and sampled signals. The chapter delves into linear time-invariant (LTI) systems, describing their behavior through convolution, difference equations, and impulse response.

RATIONALE

Discrete-time signals and systems chapter is to provide a fundamental understanding of how signals and systems function in the digital domain. In modern technology, most real-world signals are processed digitally, making it essential for students and professionals to grasp how discrete-time systems analyze, modify, and transmit information. This chapter bridges the gap between continuous signals and their discrete counterparts, equipping learners with tools like convolution, z-transforms, and Fourier analysis to handle practical applications in digital communication, control systems, and signal processing.

PRE-REQUISITE

Continuous time signals and systems

UNIT OUTCOMES

List of outcomes of this unit is as follows:

U3-O1: Different systems and their interconnections

U3-O2: Time domain system analysis

U3-O3: Constant coefficient differential equations for LTI systems

Unit-3 Outcomes	EXPECTED MAPPING WITH COURSE OUTCOMES (1- Weak Correlation; 2- Medium correlation; 3- Strong Correlation)					
	CO-1	CO-2	CO-3	CO-4	CO-5	CO-6
U3-O1	3	1	–	–	–	–
U3-O2	3	1	–	–	–	–
U3-O3	3	2	–	–	–	–

3.1 INTRODUCTION

In the realm of digital signal processing, discrete-time signals and systems stand as fundamental building blocks, essential for understanding and analyzing digital data in various applications. This chapter delves into the realm of discrete-time signals and systems, providing a comprehensive exploration of their characteristics, proper- ties, and mathematical representations. By examining the discrete nature of signals in the time domain, readers will gain insight into how discrete-time signals are sampled, quantized, and processed, distinguishing them from their continuous-time counterparts. Furthermore, this chapter delves into the analysis and manipulation of discrete-time systems, elucidating concepts such as convolution, difference equations, and system response. Through a blend of theoretical foundations, practical examples, and hands-on exercises, this chapter aims to equip readers with a solid understanding of discrete-time signals and systems, laying the groundwork for further exploration in the realm of digital signal processing.

A system has input x(n) and output y(n), as shown in Fig. 3.1. Output in terms of input is expressed as

$$y(n) = F[x(n)]$$

Here F(·) denotes a function. Input and output relation can also be expressed as

$$x(n) \xrightarrow{\mathcal{F}} y(n) \quad (3.1)$$

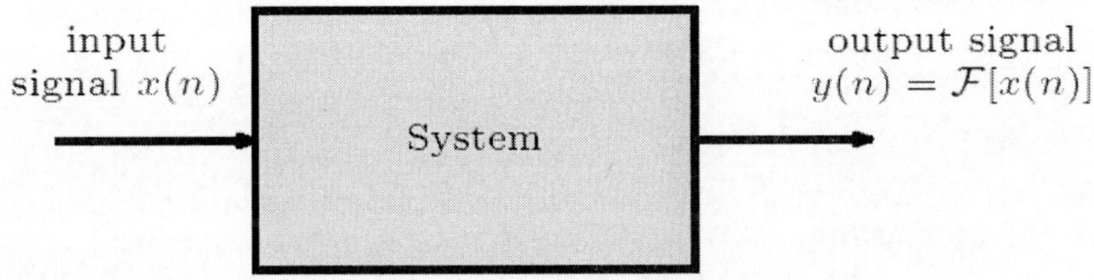

Fig. 3.1: System input and output relation.

Basic building block of discrete time system analysis are shown on Fig. 3.2.

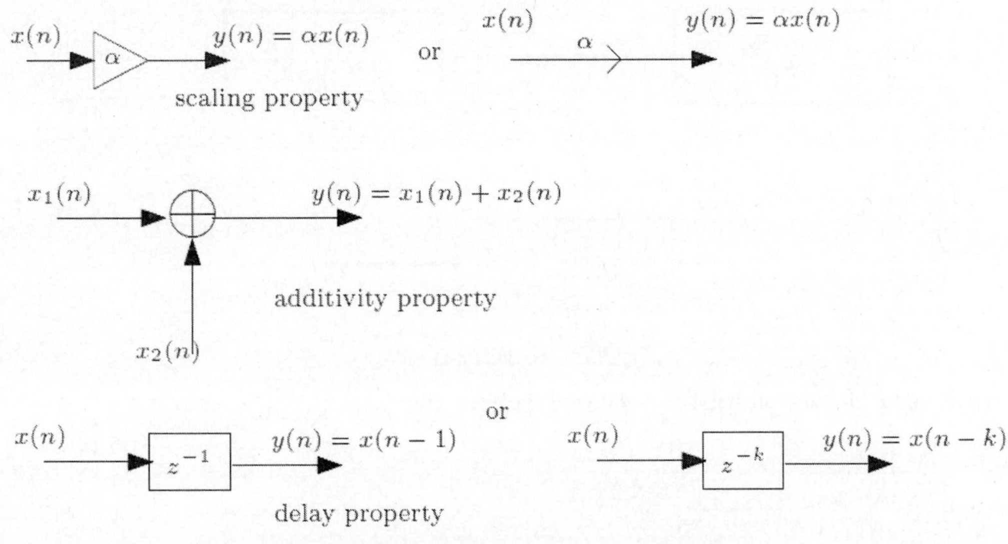

Fig. 3.2: Basic building block of discrete time system.

3.2 LINEAR TIME-INVARIANT (LTI) SYSTEMS

LTI systems are perhaps the most common type of discrete-time system encountered in digital signal processing. These systems satisfy two key properties: linearity and time-invariance. Linearity implies that the system obeys the principle of superposition, meaning that the response to a sum of inputs is equal to the sum of the responses to each input individually. Time-invariance means that the system's response does not change over time, i.e., its properties remain constant over time.

Despite the rarity of perfectly LTI systems in the physical world, many natural and engineered processes can be effectively approximated by LTI systems. By exhibit- ing properties of linearity and time-invariance, these approximations facilitate the modeling and analysis of a wide array of real-world phenomena, providing valuable insights and enabling practical solutions in various domains of science and engineering.

When a system is linear, it signifies that if an input applied to the system is multi- plied by a certain factor, the resulting output from the system is also scaled by the same factor as

$$\text{linearity} \quad x(n) \xrightarrow{\mathcal{F}} y(n) \quad \text{then} \quad ax(n) \xrightarrow{\mathcal{F}} ay(n). \tag{3.2}$$

Here *a* is the scaling factor

Further, if $x_1(n)$ and $x_2(n)$ signals generate the output signals $y_1(n)$ and $y_2(n)$, respectively. A linear system obeys the principle of superposition as

$$x_1(n) \xrightarrow{\mathcal{F}} y_1(n) \quad x_2(n) \xrightarrow{\mathcal{F}} y_2(n) \tag{3.3}$$

then

$$\text{superposition} \quad a_1x_1(n) + a_2x_2(n) \xrightarrow{\mathcal{F}} a_1y_1(n) + a_2y_2(n) \tag{3.4}$$

Here a_1 and a_2 are constants. If system satisfies both linearity and superposition is called LTI system. Two cascaded LTI systems and their equivalent are shown in Fig. 3.3.

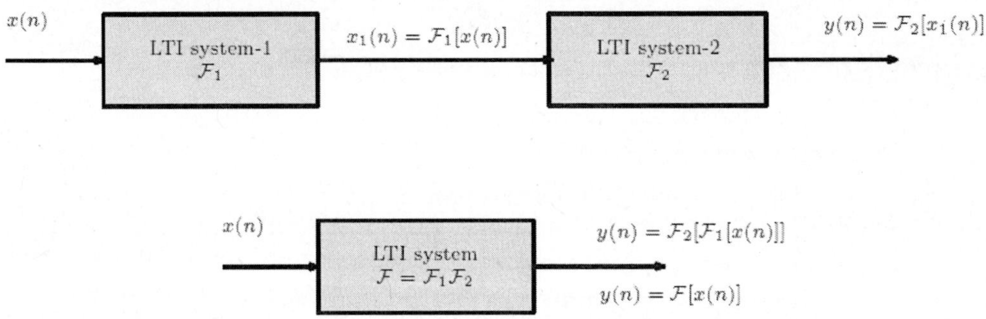

Fig. 3.3: Cascaded LTI systems.

Two parallel and their equivalent LTI systems are shown in Fig. 3.4.

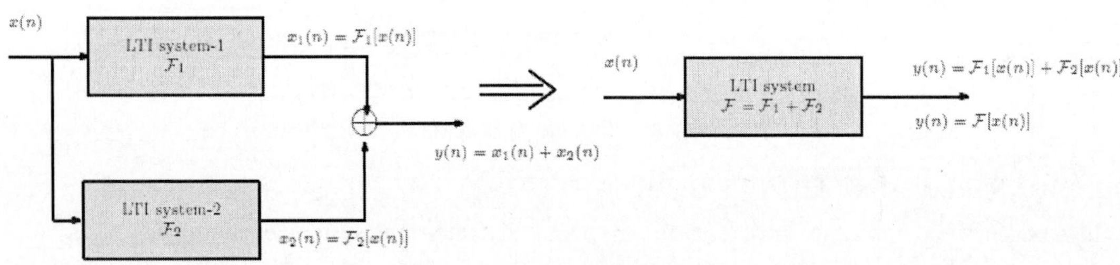

Fig. 3.4: Parallel LTI systems

LTI system is derived using the impulse response h(n) of the system as

$$h(n) = F[\delta(n)]$$

Any input signal x(n) can be decomposed in terms of weighted shifted impulses as

$$x(n) = \sum_{k=-\infty}^{\infty} x(k)\delta(n-k)$$

For an example, *x(n)* is written in terms of *δ(n)* in Fig. 3.5. Thus LTI system output for an arbitrary input signal *x(n)* is expressed as

$$y(n) = \mathcal{F}[x(n)] = \mathcal{F}[\sum_{k=-\infty}^{\infty} x(k)\delta(n-k)]$$

$$y(n) = \sum_{k=-\infty}^{\infty} \mathcal{F}[x(k)\delta(n-k)] = \sum_{k=-\infty}^{\infty} x(k)\underbrace{\mathcal{F}[\delta(n-k)]}_{h(n)}$$

$$y(n) = \sum_{k=-\infty}^{\infty} x(k)h(n-k) = x(n) * h(n) \quad (3.5)$$

Here ⋆ denotes the convolution between input signal *x(n)* and impulse response *h(n)*.

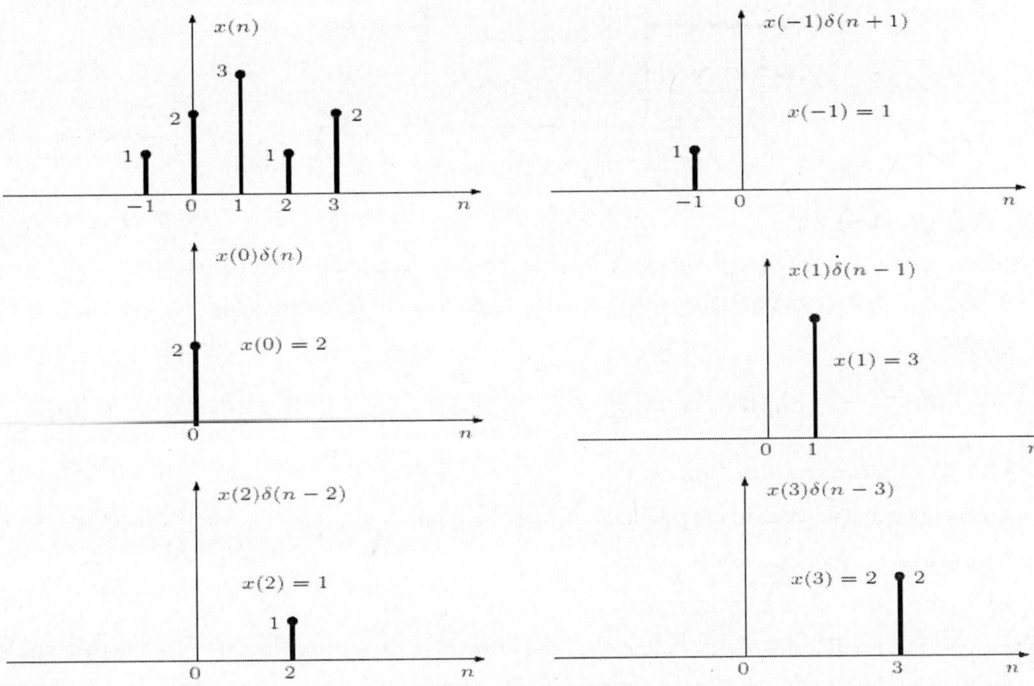

Fig. 3.5: $x(n)$ in terms of $\delta(n)$s.

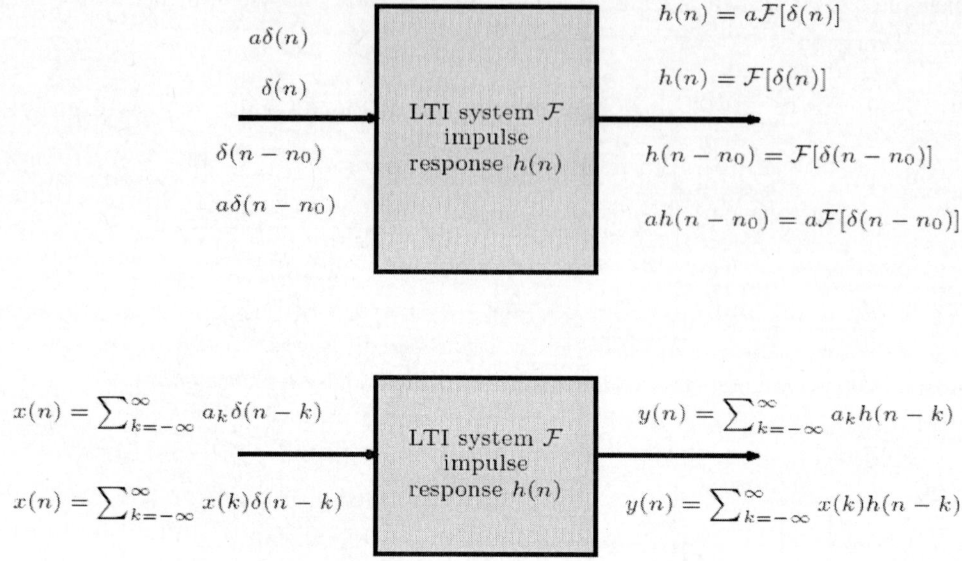

Fig. 3.6: Output calculation using the convolution in LTI system.

3.3 NONLINEAR SYSTEMS

Linear system means that if the input signals $x_1(n)$ and $x_2(n)$ generate the output signals $y_1(n)$ and $y_2(n)$, respectively, and if a_1 and a_2 are constants, then the input signal $a_1x_1(n) + a_2x_2(n)$ generates the output signal $a_1y_1(n) + a_2y_2(n)$.

$$a_1x_1(n) + a_2x_2(n) \xrightarrow{\mathcal{F}} a_1y_1(n) + a_2y_2(n)$$

Example 3.3.1 *$y(n) = 2x(n)$ is a linear system.*

A linear system is one that adheres to the principle of superposition, as given above. Some examples are

Example 3.3.2 $y(n) = x_1(n) + x_2(n)$ is a linear system.

Example 3.3.3 $y(n) = x(n - 3)$ is a linear system.

Unlike linear systems, nonlinear systems do not obey the principle of superposition. Instead, their output is a nonlinear function of their input. Nonlinear systems exhibit behaviors such as saturation, quantization, and distortion, making their analysis and characterization more complex compared to linear systems.

Example 3.3.4 $y(n) = 2x^2(n)$ is a nonlinear system.

Example 3.3.5 $y(n) = e^{x(n)}$ is a nonlinear system.

Example 3.3.6 $y(n) = \log_2[x(n)]$ is a nonlinear system.

3.4 TIME-VARYING SYSTEMS

Time-varying systems have parameters that change over time. Unlike time-invariant systems, where the system properties remain constant, time-varying systems' characteristics evolve as a function of time. Analyzing and designing time-varying systems often requires more sophisticated techniques compared to time-invariant systems.

A time-invariant system maintains a consistent characteristic wherein a specific input yields an identical output, regardless of when the input was introduced to the system, disregarding timing differences.

if $x(n) \rightarrow y(n)$ then $x(n - n_0) \rightarrow y(n - n_0)$. (3.6)

Here a_0 is a constant. $x(n-n_0)$ and $y(n-n_0)$ denote the shifted input and shifted output, respectively, as shown in Fig. 3.7.

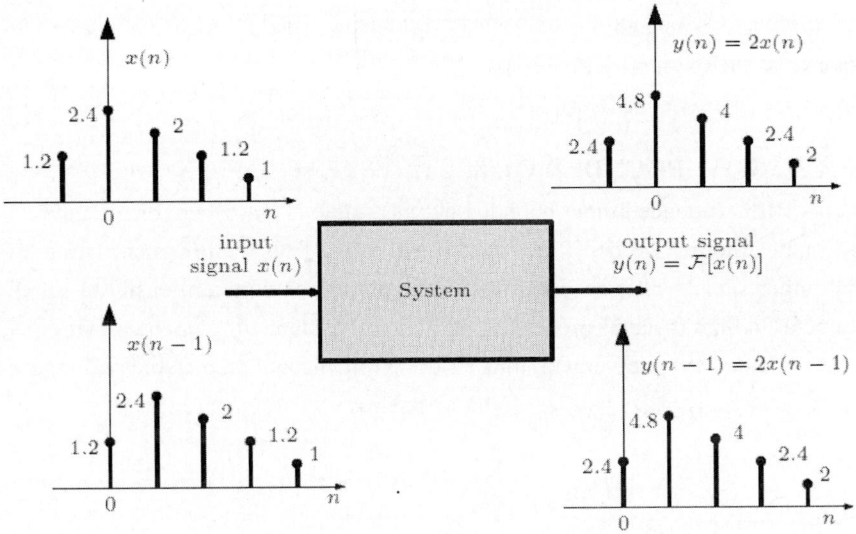

Fig. 3.7: System input and output relation

Example 3.4.1 $y(n) = x(n) + 1$ is a time invariant system.

If $y(n - n_0) \neq F[x(n - n_0)]$, then system is time variant system.

Example 3.4.2 $y(n) = nx(n)$ is a time variant system.

3.5 CAUSAL SYSTEMS

Causal systems are those whose output depends only on the present and past values of the input, not on future values. Mathematically, a system is causal if its impulse response is zero for negative time indices. Causal systems are prevalent in real-world applications, particularly in control systems and signal processing.

Example 3.5.1 $y(n) = x(n - n_0)$, $n_0 > 0$ is a causal system.

3.6 NON-CAUSAL SYSTEMS

Non-causal systems, in contrast to causal systems, can produce output that depends on future values of the input. While non-causal systems are theoretically possible, they are less common in practical applications due to their inherent challenges in implementation and causality violations.

Example 3.6.1 *$y(n) = x(n + 2)$ is a non-causal system.*

3.7 FINITE IMPULSE RESPONSE (FIR) SYSTEMS

FIR systems are characterized by a finite duration impulse response. In other words, the output of an FIR system is determined solely by the present and past values of the input. FIR systems are often preferred in applications where linear phase response and stability are crucial.

Impulse response of a FIR system is given as

$$(n) = \begin{cases} a^n, & \text{if } n = 0,1,\ldots, M-1 \text{ and } |a| < 1 \\ 0, & \text{otherwise} \end{cases}$$

3.8 INFINITE IMPULSE RESPONSE (IIR) SYSTEMS

Unlike FIR systems, IIR systems have an impulse response of infinite duration. This characteristic enables them to exhibit feedback, resulting in more compact system representations compared to FIR systems. IIR systems are commonly used in applications where compactness and efficiency are important factors.

Impulse response of a IIR system is given as

$h(n) + 0.2h(n-2) - 0.4h(n-1) + \delta(n) = 0.$

3.9 BOUNDED INPUT BOUNDED OUTPUT SYSTEM

A system that is BIBO (bounded input bounded output) stable is one where the output remains bounded for any bounded input. In other words, if the input signal to a BIBO stable system is limited in amplitude or duration, the output signal will also be limited in amplitude or duration, ensuring stability. This stability criterion is crucial in digital signal processing and control systems to guarantee that the system's response does not become unbounded or divergent, thus ensuring reliable and predictable performance.

BIBO system is characterized as if $|x(n)| = M_x < \infty \; \forall n$, then

$$|y(n)| = |\sum_{k=-\infty}^{\infty} h(k)x(n-k)| \leq M_y < \infty$$

Here $\sum_{k=-\infty}^{\infty} h(k)\,x(n-k)$ denotes the LTI system output in terms of input $x(n)$ and impulse response $h(n)$.

If LTI system is BIBO, impulse response is absolutely summable as

$$\sum_{n=-\infty}^{\infty} |h(n)| < \infty.$$

3.10 LINEAR CONSTANT-COEFFICIENT DIFFERENCE EQUATIONS

LTI systems are often represented by linear constant-coefficient difference equations. These equations describe the relationship between the input $x(n)$ and output $y(n)$ signals of an LTI system and are expressed in discrete-time domain. The general form of a linear constant-coefficient difference equation for an LTI system is

$$\sum_{k=0}^{N} a_k\, y(n-k) = \sum_{k=0}^{M} b_k\, x(n-k), a_0 = 1 \; (3.7)$$

Here, $\{a_k\}$s and $\{b_k\}$s are constant coefficients, described by the LIT systems. These parameters are independent of the input and output signal. Constant N and M are the order of the input and output difference equations, respectively.

Output of LTI system is expressed as

$$y(n) = \underbrace{-\sum_{k=1}^{N} a_k\, y(n-k)}_{previous\ output} + \underbrace{\sum_{k=0}^{M} b_k\, x(n-k)}_{input} \; (3.8)$$

Output of above relation, can be obtained using two step solutions: 1. zero input response or homogeneous solution $y_z(n)$ of difference equation, and 2. particular solution or zero initial conditions solution $y_p(n)$. Total output y(n) of LTI sys- tem expressed using Linear Constant-Coefficient Difference Equations (LCCDE) is written as

$$y(n) = y_z(n) + y_p(n) \tag{3.9}$$

3.10.1 Zero Input Response

The zero-input response of a LT system refers to the system's output when there is no input applied to it. In other words, it represents the response of the system solely due to its internal characteristics, such as its initial conditions or inherent dynamics. The zero-input response is often used to analyze the behavior of LTI systems in the absence of external stimuli and can provide insights into the system's stability, natural frequency, and transient behavior. Understanding the zero-input response is essential in system analysis, design, and control, as it complements the analysis of the system's response to input signals and helps predict its behavior in various scenarios.

Example 3.10.1 *Find the zero input response of the LTI system $y(n)+\alpha y(n-1) = x(n)$.*
$y(n)+\alpha y(n-1) = 0$ since $x(n) = 0$ for zero input response and assume that solution is $y_h(n) = \lambda^n$
So $\lambda^n + \alpha\lambda^{n-1} = 0$
$\lambda^{n-1}(\lambda + \alpha) = 0$, $\lambda = -\alpha$. Zero input response is expressed as $y_h(n) = C_0(-\alpha)^n$, where C_0 is a constant and can be determined using the system initial condition/s

3.10.2 Particular Response

The particular response of a LTI system refers to the system's output resulting from a specific input signal. Unlike the zero-input response, which considers the system's response in the absence of input, the particular response focuses on the output generated by applying a particular input signal to the system. This response is influenced by both the input signal and the system's characteristics, including its impulse response and transfer function. Analyzing the particular response allows engineers and researchers to understand how the system behaves under different input conditions and how it processes specific input signals to produce corresponding outputs. This understanding is crucial for designing and optimizing LTI systems for various applications, including signal processing, control systems, communication systems, and more.

Example 3.10.2 Find the zero-state response of a LTI system, which impulse re- sponse is $h(n) = \delta(n) + 3\delta(n-2) - u(n-3)$ and input is $x(n) = 2\delta(n) - 3\delta(n-2)$. Output is $y(n) = x(n) \star h(n) = [\delta(n) + 3\delta(n-2) - u(n-3)] \star [2\delta(n) - 3\delta(n-2)]$

$$y(n) = [\delta(n) + 3\delta(n-2) - u(n-3)] \star 2\delta(n) - [\delta(n) + 3\delta(n-2) - u(n-3)] \star 3\delta(n-2)$$

$$y(n) = 2\delta(n) + 6\delta(n-2) - 2u(n-3) - 3\delta(n-2) - 9\delta(n-4) + 3u(n-5)$$

$$y(n) = 2\delta(n) + 3\delta(n-2) - 9\delta(n-4) - 2u(n-3) + 3u(n-5)$$

Or output is expressed as

$$y(n) = \begin{cases} 0, & \text{if } n < 0 \\ 2, & \text{if } n = 0 \\ 0, & \text{if } n = 1 \\ 3, & \text{if } n = 2 \\ -2, & \text{if } n = 3 \\ -11, & \text{if } n = 4 \\ 1, & \text{if } n \geq 5 \end{cases}$$

Example 3.10.3 Given the difference equation $y(n) = 0.5y(n-1) + x(n),\ n \geq 0$ with $y(-1) = 0$. Determine the unit-impulse response.

$$\textit{Let}\ x(n) = \delta(n),\ h(n) = 0.5h(n-1) + \delta(n)$$

$$n = 0 \qquad h(0) = 0.5h(-1) + \delta(0) \rightarrow h(0) = 1$$

$$n = 1 \qquad h(1) = 0.5h(0) + \delta(1) \rightarrow h(1) = 0.5$$

$$n = 2 \qquad h(2) = 0.5h(1) + \delta(2) \rightarrow h(2) = 0.52$$

$$n = 3 \qquad h(3) = 0.5h(2) + \delta(3) \rightarrow h(3) = 0.53$$

Thus, impulse response is $h(n) = 0.5^n u(n)$.

3. 11 CROSS-CORRELATION AND AUTO-CORRELATION

The cross-correlation function is useful in various signal processing applications, such as pattern recognition, communication systems, and system identification, to analyze the relationship between two signals as a function of time lag. The cross- correlation shares similarities with the convolution of two functions. In an autocorrelation, which represents the cross-correlation of a signal with itself, a peak will consistently appear at a lag of zero, with its magnitude corresponding to the energy of the signal.

The cross-correlation between two finite energy signals is defined as

$$r_{xy}(l) = \sum_{n=-\infty}^{\infty} x(n)y(n-l),\ l = 0, \pm1, \pm2, \ldots \tag{3.11}$$

Index l serves as the time shift parameter, and the subscripts xy on the cross- correlation sequence $r_{xy}(l)$ denote the sequences undergoing correlation. If we can substitute, $n - l = n'$ and $n = n' + l$, the above expression is written as

$$r_{xy}(l) = \sum_{n'=-\infty}^{\infty} x(n'+l)y(n'),\ l = 0, \pm1, \pm2, \ldots \tag{3.12}$$

Therefore,

$$r_{xy}(l) = \sum_{n=-\infty}^{\infty} x(n+l)y(n),\ l = 0, \pm1, \pm2, \ldots \tag{3.13}$$

Therefore, by shifting x(n) (towards right) or y(n) (towards left) does not change the cross-correlation expression $r_{xy}(l)$.

Cross-correlation $r_{xx}(l)$:

$$r_{xy}(l) = \sum_{n=-\infty}^{\infty} x(n)y(n-l), \quad l = 0, \pm1, \pm2, \ldots$$

$$r_{xy}(l) = \sum_{n=-\infty}^{\infty} x(n+l)y(n), \quad l = 0, \pm1, \pm2, \ldots \tag{3.14}$$

By substituting $y(n) = x(n)$, cross-correlation is converted to auto-correlation $r_{xx}(l)$ and is expressed as

$$r_{xx}(l) = \sum_{n=-\infty}^{\infty} x(n)x(n-l),\ l = 0, \pm1, \pm2, \ldots \tag{3.15}$$

which is also expressed as

$$r_{xx}(l) = \sum_{n=-\infty}^{\infty} x(n+l)x(n), l = 0, \pm1, \pm2, ... \quad (3.16)$$

Auto-correlation $r_{xx}(l)$:

$$r_{xx}(l) = \sum_{n=-\infty}^{\infty} x(n)x(n-l), \quad l = 0, \pm1, \pm2, ...$$

$$r_{xx}(l) = \sum_{n=-\infty}^{\infty} x(n+l)x(n), \quad l = 0, \pm1, \pm2, ... \quad (3.17)$$

If we substitute, $l = 0$ in the $r_{xx}(l)$ as

$$r_{xx}(0) = \sum_{n=-\infty}^{\infty} x^2(n) = E_x \quad (3.18)$$

Represents the energy of a signal, and $r_{xx}(0) \geq 0$.

Example 3.11.1 Find the auto-correlation of the sequence x(n) = {−**1**, 2, 1}.

$$r_{xx}(l) = \sum_{n=-\infty}^{\infty} x(n)x(n-l)$$

$$r_{xx}(0) = \sum_{n=0}^{2} x(n)x(n) = 6$$

$$r_{xx}(1) = \sum_{n=0}^{2} x(n)x(n-1) = x(0)x(-1) + x(1)x(0) + x(2)x(1) = 0$$

$$r_{xx}(2) = \sum_{n=0}^{2} x(n)x(n-2) = -1$$

$$r_{xx}(3) = \sum_{n=0}^{2} x(n)x(n-3) = 0$$

$$r_{xx}(-1) = \sum_{n=0}^{2} x(n)x(n+1) = 0$$

$$r_{xx}(-2) = \sum_{n=0}^{2} x(n)x(n+2) = -1$$

$$r_{xx}(l) = \begin{cases} 6, & \text{if } l = 0 \\ 0, & \text{if } |l| \geq 3 \text{ or } l = \pm1 \\ -1, & \text{if } l = \pm2 \end{cases}$$

$r_{xx}(l)$ = {−1, **6**, 0, −1}. Plot of $r_{xx}(l)$ is shown in Fig. 3.8.

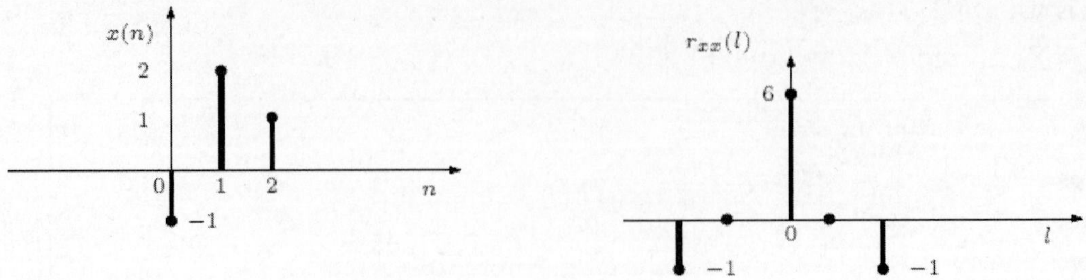

Fig. 3.8: Auto-correlation function plot.

Example 3.11.2 *Find the cross-correlation between* x(n) = {−3, 2, −1, 2} *and* y(n) = {−1, 0, −3, 2}. $r_{xy}(l) = \sum_{n=-\infty}^{\infty} x(n)y(n-l)$.

3.11.1 Properties of Cross-correlation and Auto-correlation

- The cross-correlation function is symmetric, meaning that $r_{xy}(l) = r_{yx}(-l)$.
- Cross-correlation is a linear operation. means $r_{ax+by,z} = ar_{xz}(l) + br_{yz}(l)$, where a and b are constants, and x(n), y(n) and z(n) are signals.
- Cross-correlation obeys scaling properties, where scaling one of the input sig- nals results in a scaled version of the cross-correlation function. This property is expressed as $r_{ax,y}(l) = ar_{xy}(l)$.
- Cross-correlation preserves the total energy of the signals involved. This prop- erty ensures that the integral of the cross-correlation function squared over all time is equal to the product of the energies of the two input signals.
- When two identical signals are cross-correlated, the resulting cross-correlation function exhibits a peak at zero lag, indicating perfect alignment between the signals.

$$|r_{xy}l| \le |r_{xy}(0)| \ \forall n \text{ Or } |r_{xx}l| \le r_{xx}(0) = E_x \ \forall n$$

- Normalized auto-correlation is defined as

$$\rho_{xx}(l) = \frac{r_{xx}(l)}{r_{xx}(0)}$$

- Similarly normalized cross-correlation is defined as

$$\rho_{xy}(l) = \frac{r_{xy}(l)}{\sqrt{r_{xx}(0)r_{yy}(0)}}$$

Thus $|\rho_{xy}(l)| \le 1$ and $|\rho_{xx}(l)| \le 1$.

- Cross-correlation can be computed using the convolution operation as

$$r_{xy}(l) = \sum_{n=-\infty}^{\infty} x(n)y(n-l) = x(n) * y(-n) \quad (3.20)$$

Similarity, auto-correlation can be computed using the convolution operation as

$$r_{xx}(l) = \sum_{n=-\infty}^{\infty} x(n)x(n-l) = x(n) * x(-n) \ (3.21)$$

SUMMARY

The chapter on Discrete-Time Signals and Systems delves into the fundamental concepts of signals that are defined at distinct time intervals, crucial for digital signal processing. It begins by introducing discrete-time signals, emphasizing their representation through sequences of numbers and their applications in various fields such as telecommunications and audio processing. The chapter covers essential operations on discrete-time signals, including time shifting, scaling, and inversion, which are fundamental for signal manipulation. It also explores discrete-time systems, which process these signals, outlining key characteristics such as linearity, time-invariance, and causality. Additionally, the chapter discusses the importance of convolution as a tool for understanding system behavior and response to input signals. Overall, the chapter provides a comprehensive foundation for understanding discrete-time signals and systems, setting the stage for more advanced topics in digital signal processing.

EXERCISES

1. Given a discrete-time unit step signal u(n), calculate the values of 4u(n)−u(n) for n = −3, −2, −1, 0, 1, 2, 3.
2. Calculate the first five values of the discrete-time sine wave x(n) = 5 sin(π/6n).
3. For the discrete-time impulse function δ(n), determine the values of 2δ(n) for n = −2, −1, 0, 1, 2, 3.
4. Given a 3-point moving average filter and the input signal x(n) ={1, 2, 3, 2, 1, 9, 0,-1}, compute the output y(n).
5. For the first-order difference equation y(n) = x(n) − 0.5x(n − 1) and the input signal x(n) = {4, 5, 6, 7, 8}, find the output y(n).
6. Given the impulse response h(n) = 0.5nu(n) and the input signal x(n) = {2, 1, 3, 1}, compute the output y(n) using convolution.
7. Write the signal $x(n) = \{-2,2,1,\underset{\uparrow}{-1},3,4,6,-2\}$ in terms of discrete-time impulse function δ(n).
8. Given the discrete-time signal 2u(n), where u(n) is the unit step function, calculate the autocorrelation $R_{uu}(k)$ for k = 0, 1, 2.
9. Given the finite-length discrete-time signal x(n) ={1, 1, 2, 3}, compute the autocorrelation $R_{xx}(k)$ for k = 0, 1, 2.
10. Given the discrete-time signals x(n) = {1, 2, 1} and y(n) = {2, 1}, compute the cross-correlation $R_{yx}(k)$ for k = 0, 1, 2, 3.
11 Find the signals 2x(n), x(n-1), x(n+2) and x(2n-4) corresponding to signal x(n) in Fig. 3.9.

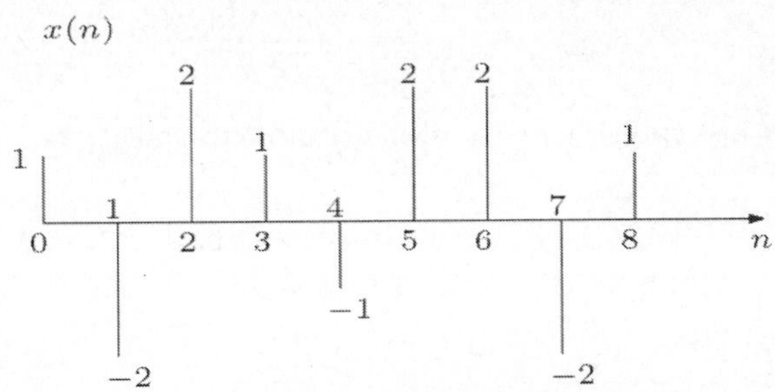

Fig. 3.9: Signal x(n).

Multiple Choice Questions

1. What is a discrete-time signal?

   A. A signal that is defined only at continuous points in time.

   B. A signal that is defined only at discrete points in time.

   C. A signal that is periodic.

   D. A signal that has infinite energy.

2. Which of the following is an example of a discrete-time signal?

   A. The voltage across a resistor over time.

   B. The number of visitors to a website each day.

   C. Temperature changes throughout a day.

   D. An analog sine wave.

3. What is the result of the time-reversal operation on a discrete-time signal $x[n]$?

   A. $x[n+1]$

   B. $-x[n]$

   C. $x[-n]$

   D. $x[n-1]$

4. In discrete-time signal processing, what does the operation $y[n]=x[n-k]$ represent?

   A. Time Reversal

   B. Time Scaling

   C. Time Shifting

   D. Amplitude Scaling

5. Which operation compresses the discrete-time signal $x[n]$ in time by a factor of 2?

   A. $x[2n]$

   B. $x[n/2]$

   C. $x[n+2]$

   D. $2x[n]$

6. What is the operation performed when a discrete-time signal $x[n]$ is multiplied by A?

   A. Time Scaling

   B. Amplitude Scaling

   C. Time Shifting

   D. Time Reversal

7. Which of the following operations is used to reverse a discrete-time signal?

   A. $x[n+1]$

   B. $x[-n]$

   C. $x[n-1]$

   D. $x[2n]$

8. In discrete-time signals, what is the Z-transform of the unit impulse signal δ[n]?

   A. 0

   B. 1

   C. z^{-1}

   D. Infinity

9. The convolution of two discrete-time signals x[n] and h[n] results in:

   A. Their sum

   B. Their product

   C. Their cross-correlation

   D. Their output response y[n]

10. If a discrete-time signal x[n] is periodic with period N, which of the following is true?

    A. x[n]=x[n+N]

    B. x[n]=x[n−N-1]

    C. x[n]=−x[n+N]

    D. x[n]=x[n+1]

11. Which operation on x[n] results in the signal being expanded in time by a factor of 2?

    A. x[2n]

    B. x[n/2]

    C. 2x[n]

    D. x[n−2]

12. What is the result of differentiating a discrete-time signal?

    A. Smoothing of the signal

    B. Delay of the signal

    C. Finding the difference between consecutive samples

    D. Reversing the signal

ANSWERS

1	2	3	4	5	6	7	8	9	10	11	12
B	B	C	C	A	B	B	B	D	A	A	C

KNOW MORE

For more information related to this topic scan the QR code.

OR

Type this link in your browser

https://www.pearsonhighered.com/assets/samplechapter/0/1/3/1/0131988425.pdf

REFERENCES AND SUGGESTED READING

1. B. P. Lathi, "*Principles of Linear Systems and Signals*," *Oxford Second edition*, 2009.
2. John G. Proakis, and Dimitris G. Manolakis "*Digital signal processing: principles, algorithms, and applications, 4/E*,"*Pearson Education India*, 2007.
3. Alan V. Oppenheim, Alan S. Willsky, and S. Hamid Nawab "*Signals & Systems*,"*Pearson Education India*, 1997.
4. P. Singh, A. Singhal, B. Fatimah, A. Gupta; S. Dutt Joshi "*Proper Definitions of Dirichlet Conditions and Convergence of Fourier Representations [Lecture Notes]*,"*IEEE Signal Processing Magazine*, vol. 39, no. 5, pp. 77-84, 2022.
5. P. Singh, A. Gupta, and S. Dutt Joshi "*General Parameterized Fourier Trans- form: A Unified Framework for the Fourier, Laplace, Mellin and Z Transforms*,"*IEEE Transactions on Signal Processing*, vol. 70, pp. 1295-1309, 2022.

Chapter 4: z-Transform

UNIT SPECIFICS

The z-Transform chapter focuses on the mathematical foundation and application of the z-transform in analyzing discrete-time signals and systems. It introduces the basic definition of the z-transform and its region of convergence (ROC), along with properties such as linearity, time-shifting, and convolution. The chapter explores the inverse z-transform methods, pole-zero analysis, and the significance of the z-plane in determining system stability and causality. Additionally, it delves into practical applications like system transfer functions, solving difference equations, and digital filter design. This unit provides essential tools for understanding and designing discrete-time systems in the digital domain.

RATIONALE

The z-transform chapter is to equip students and professionals with a powerful mathematical tool essential for analyzing discrete-time systems. The z-transform simplifies the study of linear time-invariant (LTI) systems by converting difference equations into algebraic equations, making system behavior easier to analyze and design. It also helps in determining system stability, frequency response, and inverse transformations, which are critical in digital signal processing, control systems, and communications. By understanding the z-transform, learners can solve complex problems more efficiently and apply these concepts in real-world applications involving digital filters, feedback control, and system modeling.

PRE-REQUISITE

Discrete time signals and systems

UNIT OUTCOMES

List of outcomes of this unit is as follows:

U4-O1: z transform definition

U4-O2: Properties of z transform

U4-O3: LTI system analysis using z transform

U4-O4: Inverse z transform

Unit-4 Outcomes	EXPECTED MAPPING WITH COURSE OUTCOMES (1- Weak Correlation; 2- Medium correlation; 3- Strong Correlation)					
	CO-1	CO-2	CO-3	CO-4	CO-5	CO-6
U4-O1	1	3	2	–	–	–
U4-O2	1	3	2	–	–	–
U4-O3	1	3	2	–	–	–

4.1 INTRODUCTION

Transform techniques like Fourier transform are used to analyze the linear-time variant systems. In this chapter, z-transform is introduced and its properties are discussed.

z-transform is an essential tool in digital signal processing and is used to analyze and manipulate discrete-time signals and systems.

z-transform is used for discrete-time signals as Laplace transform is used for continuous- time signals. Let x(n) be a discrete-time signal and its z-transform is defined as

$$X(z) = \sum_{n=-\infty}^{\infty} x(n)z^{-n}, \tag{4.1}$$

where z is a complex variable. Sometimes z-transform is denoted as

$X(z) \equiv Z\{x(n)\}$.

Relation between x(n) and X(z) can be written as

$x(n) \longleftrightarrow X(z)$

z transform of a signal can be calculated as shown in Fig. 4.1.

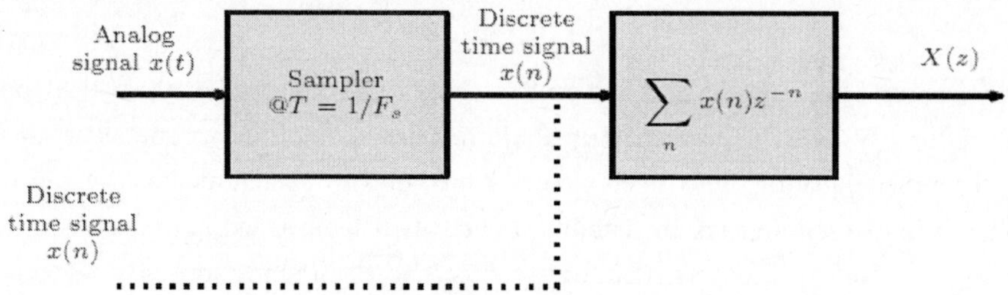

Fig. 4.1: z transform representation of a signal.

4.2 PROPERTIES OF Z-TRANSFORM

1. **Linearity**: The Z-transform is a linear transformation, which means that it satisfies the superposition principle. Let $x_1(n) \leftrightarrow X(z)$ and $x_2(n) \leftrightarrow X_2(z)$, then

$$ax_1(n) + bx_2(n) \longleftrightarrow aX_1(z) + bX_2(z).$$

Consider

$$\sum_{n=-\infty}^{\infty} x(n)z^{-n} = \sum_{n=-\infty}^{\infty} [ax_1(n)+bx_2(n)]z^{-n} = a\underbrace{\sum_{n=-\infty}^{\infty} x_1(n)z^{-n}}_{X_1(z)} + b\sum_{n=-\infty}^{\infty} x_2(n)z^{-n} \tag{4.2}$$

$$= aX_1(z) + bX_2(z) \tag{4.3}$$

2. **Time shifting**: The time-shifting property of the Z-transform is a fundamental characteristic that describes how the transform behaves when the signal is delayed or advanced in time.

If $x(n) \longleftrightarrow X(z)$ then

$x(n-k) \longleftrightarrow X(z)z^{-k}$ (4.4) Using the z transform formula

$$X(z) = \sum_{n=-\infty}^{\infty} x(n)z^{-n}$$

$$= \sum_{n=-\infty}^{\infty} x(n-k)z^{-n} = \underbrace{\sum_{n=-\infty}^{\infty} x(n)z^{-n}}_{X(z)} z^{-k} = z^{-k}X(z) \tag{4.5}$$

3. **Time reversal**: The time reversal property of the Z-transform is a funda- mental characteristic that describes how the transform behaves when the time sequence is reversed.

If x(n) ↔X(z) then

$x(-n) \leftrightarrow X(z^{-1}) = X(1/z)$ (4.6)

Using the z transform formula above equation can be derived.

4. **Time scaling**: The time scaling property of the z-transform relates to the effect of scaling or compressing a discrete-time sequence in the time domain on its z-transform. Let's consider a discrete-time sequence x(n) with z-transform X(z). The time scaling property is expressed as follows:

If x(n) ↔X(z) then

$x(an) \leftrightarrow X(z^{1/a})$. (4.7)

In other words, if you scale the time axis of a sequence by a factor of a, the z-transform of the scaled sequence is obtained by replacing z with $z^{1/a}$ in the z-transform of the original sequence.

Using z transform formula

$$\sum_{n=-\infty}^{\infty} x(an)z^{-n} = \sum_{n=-\infty}^{\infty} x(n)z^{-n/a}$$

$$\sum_{n=-\infty}^{\infty} x(n)(z^{1/a})^{-n} = X(z^{1/a}) \quad (4.8)$$

5. **Convolution**: The convolution property of the Z-transform is a fundamental characteristic that describes how the transform behaves when two sequences are convolved in the time domain.

If $x_1(n) \longleftrightarrow X_1(z)$ and $x_2(n) \longleftrightarrow X_2(z)$ then

$$y(n) = x_1(n) \star x_2(n) = \sum_{k=-\infty}^{\infty} x_1(k)x_2(n-k) \longleftrightarrow Y(z) = X_1(z)X_2(z), \quad (4.9)$$

where ⋆ denotes convolution between two sequences.

$$Y(z) = \sum_{n=-\infty}^{\infty} y(n)z^{-n} = \sum_{n=-\infty}^{\infty}\sum_{k=-\infty}^{\infty} x_1(k)x_2(n-k)z^{-n}$$

$$= \sum_{k=-\infty}^{\infty} x_1(k) \sum_{n=-\infty}^{\infty} x_2(n-k)z^{-n} = \sum_{k=-\infty}^{\infty} x_1(k) \underbrace{\sum_{n=-\infty}^{\infty} x_2(n)z^{-n}}_{X_2(z)} z^{-k}$$

$$= X_2(z) \sum_{k=-\infty}^{\infty} x_1(k)z^{-k} = X_1(z)X_2(z) \quad (4.10)$$

6. **Differentiation in Time**: If X(z) is the z-transform of x(n), then the z- transform of the sequence representing the first difference (derivative) of x(n), denoted as nx(n), is given by $-z\frac{dX(z)}{dz}$.

$$X(z) = \sum_{n=-\infty}^{\infty} x(n)z^{-n}$$

$$\frac{dX(z)}{dz} = \sum_{n=-\infty}^{\infty} x(n)\frac{dz^{-n}}{dz} = \sum_{n=-\infty}^{\infty} x(n) - nz^{-n}z^{-1}$$

$$-z^{1}\frac{dX(z)}{dz} = \sum_{n=-\infty}^{\infty} x(n)\frac{dz^{-n}}{dz} = \underbrace{\sum_{n=-\infty}^{\infty} [nx(n)]z^{-n}}_{\text{z transform of } nx(n)} \tag{4.11}$$

$$nx(n) \leftrightarrow -z\frac{dX(z)}{dz}.$$

7. **Correlation of two sequences**: The correlation of two sequences can be explored through the cross-correlation function. Let's consider two discrete sequences, x(n) and y(n), and denote their z-transforms as X(z) and Y (z), respectively as

If x(n) ⟷ X(z) and y(n) ⟷ Y (z) The cross-correlation function is

$$r_{xy}(k) = \sum_{n=-\infty}^{\infty} x(n)\,y(n-k)\,.$$

Then The z-transform of the cross-correlation function is the product of the z-transforms of the individual sequences as

$R_{xy}(z) = X(z)Y(z^{-1})$

Using the z transform formula as

$$R_{xy}(z) = \sum_{k=-\infty}^{\infty} r_{xy}(k)z^{-k} = \sum_{k=-\infty}^{\infty}\sum_{n=-\infty}^{\infty} x(n)y(n-k)z^{-k}$$

$$= \sum_{n=-\infty}^{\infty} x(n) \sum_{k=-\infty}^{\infty} y(n-k)z^{-k} = \sum_{n=-\infty}^{\infty} x(n) \underbrace{\sum_{k=-\infty}^{\infty} y(k)(z^{-1})^{-k}}_{Y(z^{-1})} z^{-n}$$

$$= Y(z^{-1}) \sum_{n=-\infty}^{\infty} x(n)z^{-n} = X(z)Y(z^{-1}) \tag{4.12}$$

This relationship between the z-transforms of the sequences and their cross- correlation function is useful when analyzing signals in the frequency domain using z-transform techniques.

8. **Multiplication of two sequences**: Multiplication of two sequences in the time domain corresponds to the convolution of their z-transforms. Specifically, if you have two sequences x(n) and y(n) with z-transforms X(z) and Y (z) respectively, then the z-transform of their convolution is the product of their individual z-transforms as

z-transform $[x_1(n) = x(n).y(n)] = X_1(z) = X(z) \star Y(z)$

Here, x(n).y(n) represents the multiplication of the sequences x(n) and y(n), and X(z) ⋆ Y (z) represents the convolution of their z-transforms. Using the z transform formula

$$X_1(z) = \sum_{n=-\infty}^{\infty} x_1(n) z^{-n} = \sum_{n=-\infty}^{\infty} x(n) y(n) z^{-n}$$

$$X_1(z) = \sum_{n=-\infty}^{\infty} \left[\frac{1}{2\pi j} \oint_C X(v) v^{n-1} dv \right] y(n) z^{-n} = \frac{1}{2\pi j} \oint_C X(v) \sum_{n=-\infty}^{\infty} y(n) z^{-n} v^{n-1} dv$$

$$= \frac{1}{2\pi j} \oint_C X(v) \underbrace{\sum_{n=-\infty}^{\infty} y(n)(z/v)^{-n}}_{Y(z/v)} v^{-1} dv \qquad (4.13)$$

So

$$X_1(z) == \frac{1}{2\pi j} \oint_C X(v) Y(z/v) v^{-1} dv = X(z) \star Y(z) \qquad (4.14)$$

9. **Parseval's relation**:

$$\sum_{n=-\infty}^{\infty} x_1(n) x_2^*(n) = \frac{1}{2\pi j} \oint_C X_1(v) X_2^*(1/v^*) v^{-1} dv \qquad (4.15)$$

Here $*$ denotes the conjugate of the sequence.

10. **Initial Value Theorem**: The initial value of x(n), denoted as x(0), is given by

$$x(0) = \lim_{z \to \infty} X(z)$$

If the sequence x(n) is causal

$$X(z) = \sum_{n=0}^{\infty} x(n) z^{-n} = x(0) + x(1) z^{-1} + x(2) z^{-2} + \ldots.$$

Consider $z \to \infty$, we can have

$$\lim_{z \to \infty} X(z) = x(0) + 0 + 0 + \ldots. = x(0) \qquad (4.16)$$

11. **Final Value Theorem**: The final value of a sequence x(n) as n approaches infinity is given

$$\lim_{n \to \infty} x(n) = \lim_{z \to 1} (1 - z^{-1}) X(z)$$

If the sequence x(n) is causal

$$z\left[x(n)\right] = \sum_{n=0}^{\infty} x(n)z^{-n} \quad \text{and} \quad z\left[x(n+1)\right] = \underbrace{\sum_{n=0}^{\infty} x(n+1)z^{-n}}_{\text{use dummy variable } n+1=n'}$$

$$z\left[x(n+1)\right] = \sum_{n=1}^{\infty} x(n)z^{-n} = \sum_{n=0}^{\infty} x(n)z^{-n}z - x(0)z = z\left[X(z) - x(0)\right]$$

$$z\left[x(n+1)\right] - z\left[x(n)\right] = z\left[X(z) - x(0)\right] - X(z) = (z-1)X(z) - x(0)z$$

Further,

$$\sum_{n=0}^{\infty}[x(n+1) - x(n)]z^{-n} = (z-1)X(z) - x(0)z$$

$$\lim_{z\to 1}\sum_{n=0}^{\infty}[x(n+1) - x(n)]z^{-n} = \lim_{z\to 1}(z-1)X(z) - x(0)z$$

$$\lim_{n\to\infty} x(n) - x(0) = \lim_{z\to 1}(z-1)X(z) - x(0)$$

$$\lim_{n\to\infty} x(n) = \lim_{z\to 1}(z-1)X(z) = \lim_{z\to 1}(1-z^{-1})X(z) \tag{4.17}$$

Example 4.2.1 *Find* x(∞) *if* X(z) *is*

$$X(x) = \frac{z^2}{(z-1)(z-3)}$$

$$x(\infty) = \lim_{n\to\infty} x(n) = \lim_{z\to 1}(z-1)X(z) = \frac{z^2}{(z-3)} = -\frac{1}{3} \tag{4.18}$$

Example 4.2.2 *Using the initial value theorem for z-transform, find the initial value of signal* x(n) *if*

$$X(z) = \frac{z^2 + z + 1}{(z+1)(z+3)}$$

$$x(0) = \lim_{z\to\infty} X(z) = \lim_{z\to\infty} \frac{z^2+z+1}{(z+1)(z+3)} x(0) \quad = \lim_{z\to\infty} \frac{1 + 1/z + 1/z^2}{(1+1/z)(1+3/z)} = 1$$

Example 4.2.3 *Find the z-transform of the signal* x(n) = n²u(n).

$$x(n) = u(n) \longleftrightarrow X(z) = \frac{z}{z-1}$$

$ROC = |z| > 1$

$$x_1(n) = nu(n) \longleftrightarrow X_1(z) = -z\frac{dX(z)}{dz} = \frac{z}{(z-1)^2}$$

$$x(n) = n^2u(n) \longleftrightarrow -z\frac{dX_1(z)}{dz} = \frac{-zd}{dz}\left[\frac{z}{(z-1)^2}\right]$$

$$x(n) = n^2u(n) \longleftrightarrow \frac{z(z+1)}{(z-1)^3}$$

$ROC = \{|z| > 1\} - \{\infty\}$

Relation between z transform $X(z)$ and Laplace transform $X(s)$: Sampled version of continuous time signal $x(t)$ is written as

$$x_s(t) = \sum_{n=-\infty}^{\infty} x(t)\delta(t - nT)$$

Laplace transform $X(s)$ is

$$X(s) = \int_{-\infty}^{\infty} x_s(t)e^{-st}dt \quad s = \sigma + j\omega$$

$$= \int_{-\infty}^{\infty} \sum_{n=-\infty}^{\infty} x(t)\delta(t - nT)e^{-st}dt$$

$$= \sum_{n=-\infty}^{\infty} \int_{-\infty}^{\infty} x(t)\delta(t - nT)e^{-st}dt$$

$$= \sum_{n=-\infty}^{\infty} x(nT)e^{-nsT} = \sum_{n=-\infty}^{\infty} x(nT)\left[e^{sT}\right]^{-n} = X(z)_{|z=e^{sT}} \tag{4.19}$$

Therefore, both the Laplace transform and z transform are related to each other through the sampling time interval T as $z = e^{sT}$.

Example 4.2.4 *Find the* z *transform of unit impulse sequence* δ(n).

Solution: *using the* z *transform formula*

$$X(z) = \sum_{n=-\infty}^{\infty} x(n)z^{-n}$$

$$= \sum_{n=-\infty}^{\infty} \delta(n)z^{-n} = z^0 = 1 \tag{4.20}$$

Since δ(n) is zero except n = 0. Further, X(z) converges for all the values of z, Hence ROC is entire z-plane.
ROC = ∀z

Example 4.2.5 *Find the* z *transform of unit sample sequence* u(n).

Solution: *using the* z *transform formula*

$$X(z) = \sum_{n=-\infty}^{\infty} x(n)z^{-n}$$
$$= \sum_{n=-\infty}^{\infty} u(n)z^{-n} = \sum_{n=0}^{\infty} z^{-n} = \frac{1}{1-z^{-1}} \tag{4.21}$$

Further, $X(z)$ converges for all the values of $|z| > 1$, Hence ROC is

ROC = |z| > 1

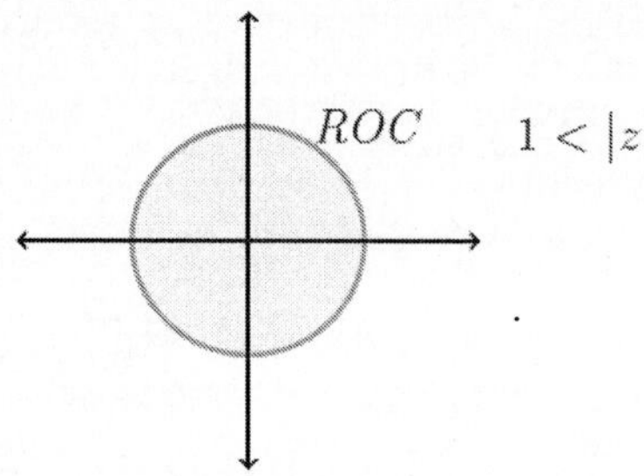

, and outside the unit circle, as shown below.

Example 4.2.6 *Find the* z *transform of unit sample sequence* u(-n).

Solution: *using the* z *transform formula*

$$X(z) = \sum_{n=-\infty}^{\infty} x(n)z^{-n}$$
$$= \sum_{n=-\infty}^{0} z^{-n} = \sum_{n=0}^{\infty} z^{n} = \frac{1}{1-z} = -\frac{z^{-1}}{1-z^{-1}} \tag{4.22}$$

Further, $X(z)$ converges for all the values of $|z| < 1$, Hence ROC is

ROC = |z| < 1

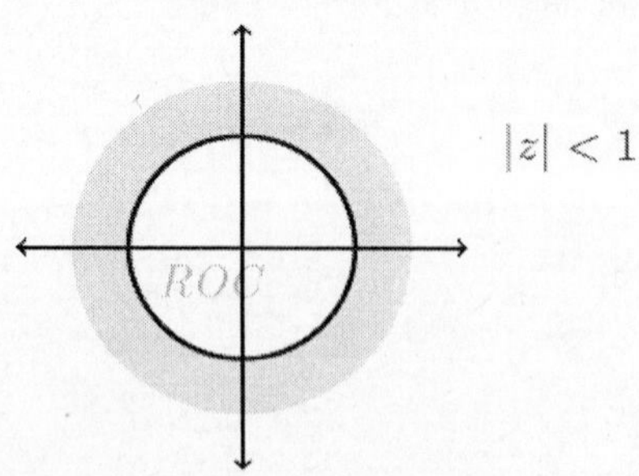

, and inside the unit circle, as shown below.

Example 4.2.7 *Find the* z *transform of signal* x(n) = {1, 2, 3, 4, −1}.

Solution: *using the* z *transform equation*

$$\begin{aligned} X(z) &= \sum_{n=-\infty}^{\infty} x(n)z^{-n} = \sum_{n=0}^{4} x(n)z^{-n} \\ &= 1 + 2z^{-1} + 3z^{-2} + 4z^{-3} - z^{-4} \end{aligned} \tag{4.23}$$

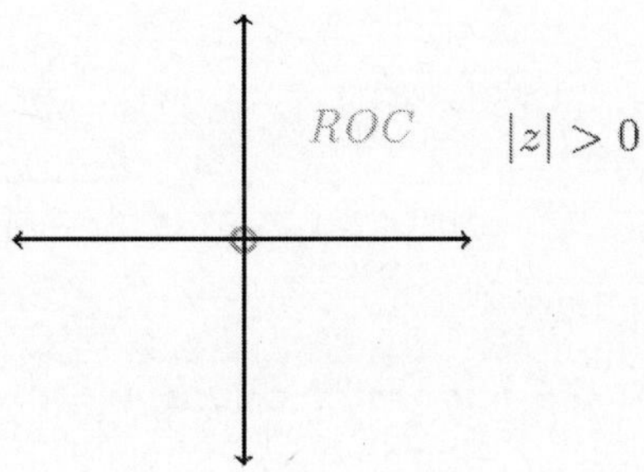

ROC is entire z plane except $z = 0$.

Example 4.2.8 *Find the* z *transform of signal* x(n) = {−1, 4, 3, 2, 1}.

Solution: *using the* z *transform equation*

$$\begin{aligned} X(z) &= \sum_{n=-\infty}^{\infty} x(n)z^{-n} \\ &= 1 + 2z^{1} + 3z^{2} + 4z^{3} - z^{4} \end{aligned} \tag{4.24}$$

ROC is entire z plane except $z = \infty$.

Example 4.2.9 *Find the* z *transform of signal* x(n) = {4, 3, 2, 1, 2, 3, 4}.

Solution: *using the* z *transform equation*

$$\begin{aligned} X(z) &= \sum_{n=-\infty}^{\infty} x(n)z^{-n} \\ &= 4z^{3} + 3z^{2} + 2z^{1} + 1 + 2z^{-1} + 3z^{-2} + 4z^{-3} \end{aligned} \tag{4.25}$$

ROC is entire z plane except $z = 0$ *and* $z = \infty$.

Example 4.2.10 *Find the z transform of the sequence* x(n) = $c^{|n|}$.

Solution: *using the z transform equation*

$$X(z) = \sum_{n=-\infty}^{\infty} x(n)z^{-n}$$

$$= \sum_{n=-\infty}^{-1} c^{-n}z^{-n} + \sum_{n=0}^{\infty} c^{n}z^{-n}$$

$$= \sum_{n=1}^{\infty} c^{n}z^{n} + \sum_{n=0}^{\infty} c^{n}z^{-n} = \sum_{n=0}^{\infty}(cz)^{n} - 1 + \sum_{n=0}^{\infty}(cz^{-1})^{n}$$

$$= \frac{1}{1-cz} - 1 + \frac{1}{1-cz^{-1}} = \frac{cz}{1-cz} + \frac{z}{z-c} \tag{4.26}$$

ROC is $|cz| < 1$ *and* $|cz^{-1}| < 1$, *hence* $|c| < |z| < \frac{1}{|c|}$.

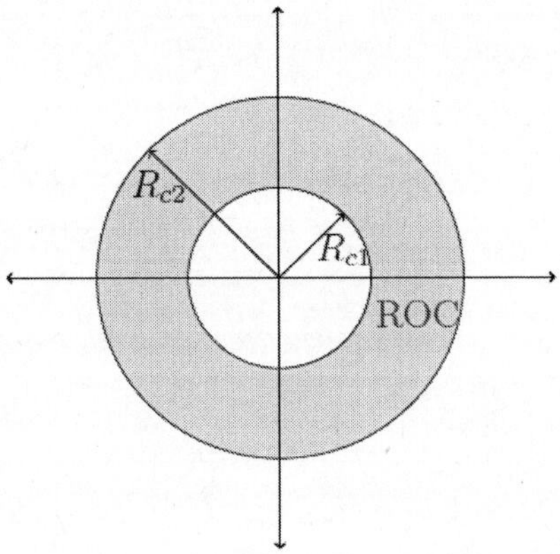

Fig. 4.2: ROC (Annular ring) plot of infinite duration bidirectional signal.

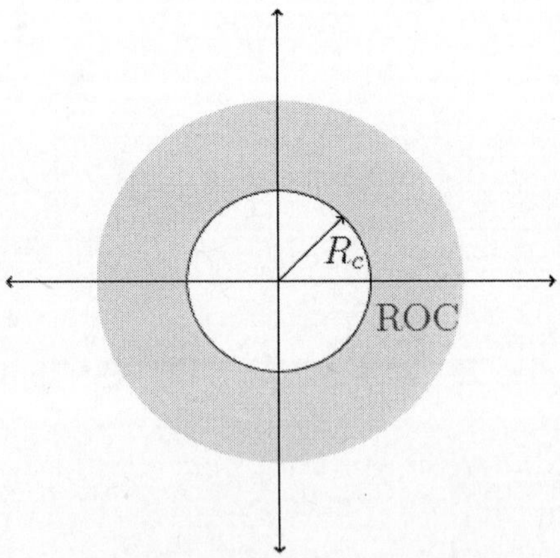

Fig. 4.3: ROC plot of infinite duration causal signal.

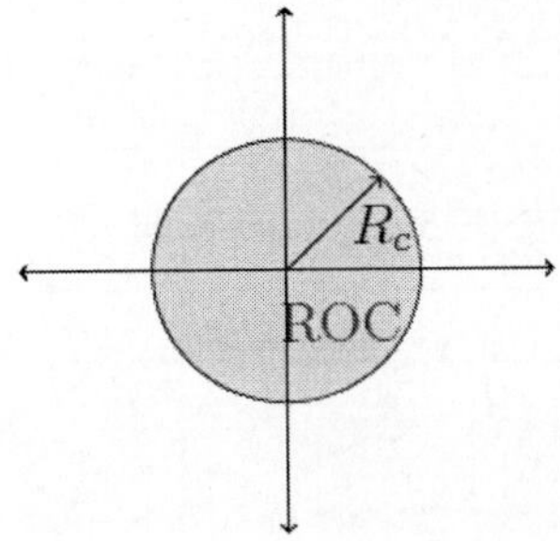

Fig. 4.4: ROC plot of infinite duration anti-causal signal.

Table 4.1: Types of signal sequences and their ROCs

Finite duration causal sequence	ROC: Entire z-plane except z = 0
Finite duration anticausal sequence	ROC: Entire z-plane except z = ∞
Finite duration bidirectional sequence	ROC: Entire z-plane except z = 0 and z = ∞
Infinite duration causal sequence	ROC: Outside a circle of some radius R_c
Infinite duration anticausal sequence	ROC: Inside a circle of some radius R_c
Infinite duration bidirectional sequence	ROC: Inform of ring of two circles with radius R_{c1} and R_{c2}

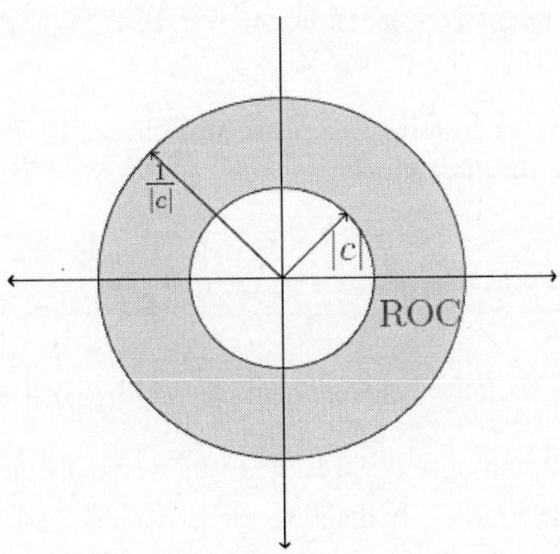

Fig. 4.5: ROC plot of X(z)

Table 4.2: z-Transform of Basic Signals

Signal $x(n)$	z-Transform $X(z)$	ROC
$\delta(n)$	1	Entire z plane
$u(n)$	$\frac{z}{z-1}$	$\lvert z\rvert > 1$
$u(-n-1)$	$-\frac{z}{z-1}$	$\lvert z\rvert < 1$
$\delta(n-k)$	z^{-k}	Entire z plane excerpt $z=0$ or $z=\infty$
$a^n u(n)$	$\frac{z}{z-a}$	$\lvert z\rvert > a$
$a^n u(-n-1)$	$-\frac{z}{z-a}$	$\lvert z\rvert < a$
$a^n \cos(\omega n)u(n)$	$\frac{1-az^{-1}\cos(\omega)}{1-2az^{-1}\cos(\omega)+a^2z^{-2}}$	$\lvert z\rvert > \lvert a\rvert$
$a^n \sin(\omega n)u(n)$	$\frac{az\sin(\omega)}{z^2-2az\cos(\omega)+a^2}$	$\lvert z\rvert > \lvert a\rvert$

ROC properties: The ROC defines the region in the complex z-plane for which the z-transform converges. The ROC is a crucial concept in understanding the stability and causality of discrete-time systems. The properties of the ROC for a discrete-time signal's z-transform are

- **ROC Determines Causality:** The ROC provides information about the causality of the signal. A signal is causal if the ROC includes the outer circle, excluding the inner circle of some radius.
- **ROC excludes Poles:** The ROC extends outward from the poles of the Z-transform. It does not include any poles, and the outer boundary of the ROC is determined by the poles farthest from the origin.
- **Two-Sided Signals ROC:** For two-sided signals (i.e., signals that are nonzero for both positive and negative time indices), the ROC is the region between the two circles defined by the poles.
- **Poles on the Unit Circle:** If poles lie on the unit circle, the ROC can extend up to but not include the unit circle.
- **Right-Sided Signals ROC:** For right-sided signals, the ROC includes the region outside the outermost pole.

4.2.1 Causality and Stability

A discrete-time system is causal if and only if the ROC of its z-transform includes the unit circle z = 1 in the z-plane and outside a circle of some radios. A discrete- time system is stable if and only if the ROC includes the unit circle z = 1 in the z-plane. Thus, if the ROC includes the unit circle and all the poles are inside the unit circle, the system is both causal and stable.

4.3 INVERSE Z-TRANSFORM

The inverse z-transform is a mathematical operation that transforms a given z- transform function X(z) back to the original sequence in the time domain x(n). The inverse z-transform is denoted by x(n), and it is obtained using techniques like partial fraction decomposition, contour integration, or table lookup methods.

The general expression for the inverse z-transform is given by:

$$x(n) = \frac{1}{2\pi j}\oint_C X(z)\, z^{n-1} dz$$

where C s a closed contour in the ROC that encircles all the poles of X(z) in the z-plane.

Above expression can be obtained as

$$X(z) = \sum_{n=-\infty}^{\infty} x(n) z^{-n}$$

$$\oint_C X(z) z^{k-1} dz = \oint_C \sum_{n=-\infty}^{\infty} x(n) z^{-n} z^{k-1} dz$$

$$\oint_C X(z) z^{k-1} dz = \sum_{n=-\infty}^{\infty} x(n) \oint_C z^{k-n-1} dz \tag{4.28}$$

Now using the Cauchy integral theorem, which states that

$$\oint_C z^{k-n-1} dz = \begin{cases} 2\pi j, & \text{if } n = k. \\ 0, & \text{otherwise.} \end{cases} \tag{4.29}$$

where C is any contour that encloses the origin in the z domain. Therefore,

$$\oint_C X(z) z^{k-1} dz = x(k) 2\pi j \Rightarrow x(k) = \frac{1}{2\pi j}\oint_C X(z) z^{k-1} dz \quad \text{or}$$

$$x(n) = \frac{1}{2\pi j}\oint_C X(z) z^{n-1} dz \tag{4.30}$$

Some common methods to find the inverse z-transform:

4.3.1 Partial Fraction Decomposition

Express the z-transform X(z) as a sum of partial fractions, each with a simple pole. The coefficients of the partial fractions are then used to find the corresponding inverse z-transform terms.

To ascertain the inverse z-transform of X(z) through the partial fraction expansion method, it is imperative that the denominator of X(z) is expressed in factored form. In this approach, we derive the partial fraction expansion of X(z) rather than X(z), as z-transforms of time-domain sequences inherently incorporate z in their numerators.

This method is exclusively applicable when X(z) represents a proper rational function, signifying that the order of its denominator exceeds that of its numerator. X(z)/z deviates from being a proper function, it becomes necessary to express it as a polynomial along with a proper function before applying the partial fraction method.

$$\frac{X(z)}{z} = \frac{b_0 + b_1 z^1 + b_2 z^2 + ... + b_m z^m}{a_0 + a_1 z^1 + a_2 z^2 + ... + a_n z^n} \tag{4.31}$$

If $m \geq n$, then $\frac{X(z)}{z}$ is not a proper function, then it is to be written as $m < n$

$$\frac{X(z)}{z} = A_0 + ... + A_m z^{n-m} + \text{proper rational function} \tag{4.32}$$

Further, if $\frac{X(z)}{z}$ has all distinct poles, then

$$\frac{X(z)}{z} = \frac{B_0}{z - p_0} + \frac{B_1}{z - p_1} + ... + \frac{B_n}{z - p_n} \tag{4.33}$$

where $B_0, B_1, ...B_n$ are constant and can be derived as

$$B_i = \left[(z - p_i) \frac{X(z)}{z} \right]_{z = p_i}, \quad i = 0, 1, ..., n \tag{4.34}$$

Example 4.3.1 *Find the inverse z transform of $X(z)$, where $X(z) = \frac{z}{2z^2 - 3z + 1}$ with ROC $|z| > 1$.*

$$\begin{aligned} \frac{X(z)}{z} &= \frac{1}{2z^2 - 3z + 1} = \frac{1}{2(z^2 - 3/2z + 1/2)} = \frac{1}{2(z-1)(z-1/2)} \\ \frac{1}{2(z-1)(z-1/2)} &= \frac{A}{z-1} + \frac{B}{z-1/2} \Rightarrow \frac{1}{z-1} - \frac{1}{z-1/2} \\ \frac{X(z)}{z} &= \frac{1}{z-1} - \frac{1}{z-1/2} \end{aligned} \tag{4.35}$$

So

$$X(z) = \frac{z}{z-1} - \frac{z}{z-1/2} \Rightarrow \frac{1}{1 - z^{-1}} - \frac{1}{1 - 1/2z^{-1}}$$

Due to the ROC of the provided ztransform being $|z| > 1$, it is established that both sequences must be causal. Consequently, upon performing the inverse z-transform, we obtain:

$$x(n) = u(n) - \left(\frac{1}{2}\right)^2 u(n) = \left(1 - \left(\frac{1}{2}\right)^2\right) u(n)$$

4.3.2 Power Series Expansion

Expand X(z) into a power series using methods like long division. This expansion is then inverse transformed to obtain x(n).

The method involves expressing the given z-transform in terms of a power series and then finding the coefficients of the power series to obtain the inverse Z-transform. The general form of the power series expansion is:

$$X(z) = \sum_{k=0}^{\infty} a_k z^{-k}$$

The inverse z-transform of X(z) is then given as

$$x(n) = \sum_{k=0}^{\infty} a_k \delta(n-k)$$

Here, a_n are the coefficients of the power series expansion, and δ(n k) is the discrete- time unit impulse function. The steps involved in the Power Series Expansion method are as follows:

Express the z-transform as a power series $X(z) = \sum_{k=0}^{\infty} a_k z^{-k}$

Identify the coefficients a_n

Write the inverse z-transform $x(n) = \sum_{k=0}^{\infty} a_k \delta(n-k)$

Example 4.3.2 *Find the inverse z transform of* $X(z) = z^2(1+2z^{-2})(1-1/2z^{-1})(1+z^{-1})$

X(z) is expressed as

$$X(z) = \frac{3}{2} - z^{-2} + z^{-1} + \frac{1}{2}z + z^2$$

So inverse z transform

$$x(n) = \frac{3}{2}\delta(n) - \delta(n-2) + \delta(n-1) + \frac{1}{2}\delta n + 1 + \delta(n+2)$$

or can be written as $x(n) = \{1, 1/2, \underset{\uparrow}{3/2}, 1, -1\}$

Example 4.3.3 *Fins the inverse z transform of* $X(z) = \log(1 + az^{-1})$, $|z| > |a|$.
ROC is $|z| > |a|$, *so it is a causal sequence.*
Using the power series expansion of log *function* $X(z) = \sum_{n=1}^{\infty} \frac{(-1)^{n+1} a^n z^{-n}}{n}$.
The inverse z transform is

$$x(n) = \begin{cases} \frac{(-1)^{n+1} a^n}{n}, & if\, n \geq 1 \\ 0, & if\, n \leq 0 \end{cases}$$

Example 4.3.4 *Find the inverse z transform of* $X(z) = \frac{1}{1-az^{-1}}$, $|z| > |a|$.
ROC is $|z| > |a|$, *so it is a causal sequence.*
Using the power series expansion in terms of z^{-1}

$$\begin{array}{l} \qquad 1 + az^{-1} + a^2z^{-2} + a^3z^{-3} + \dots \\ 1 - az^{-1} \,\overline{)\; 1} \\ \qquad 1 - az^{-1} \\ \qquad \overline{\qquad az^{-1}} \\ \qquad\quad az^{-1} - a^2z^{-2} \\ \qquad\quad \overline{\qquad a^2z^{-2}} \\ \qquad\qquad a^2z^{-2} - a^3z^{-3} \\ \qquad\qquad \overline{\qquad a^3z^{-3}} \end{array}$$

So $X(z) = \frac{1}{1-az^{-1}} = 1 + az^{-1} + a^2z^{-2} + a^3z^{-3} + \dots$
The inverse z transform is

$$x(n) = a^n u(n)$$

4.3.3 Contour Integration

Use contour integration techniques, such as the residue theorem, to evaluate the inverse z-transform. This involves integrating $X(z)z^{n-1}$ along a closed contour in the ROC.

Cauchy residue theorem: The Cauchy Residue Theorem is a fundamental result in complex analysis, providing a way to evaluate contour integrals of functions with isolated singularities. The theorem is named after the French mathematician Augustin-Louis Cauchy.

Let f(z) be a complex variable function of z, and let C represent a closed path in the complex plane. If the derivative df(z)/dz and if f(z) has no poles at $z = z_0$, then exists both on and within the contour C,

$$\frac{1}{2\pi j} \oint_C \frac{f(z)}{z - z_0} dz = \begin{cases} f(z_0), & \text{if } z_0 \text{ is inside } C \\ 0, & \text{if } z_0 \text{ is outside } C \end{cases}$$

In general, if the (k + 1)-order derivative of f(z) exists and f(z) has no poles at $z = z_0$, then

$$\frac{1}{2\pi j}\oint_C \frac{f(z)}{(z-z_0)^k}dz = \begin{cases} \frac{1}{(k-1)!}\frac{d^{k-1}f(z_0)}{dz^{k-1}}|_{z=z_0}, & \text{if } z_0 \text{ is inside } C \\ 0, & \text{if } z_0 \text{ is outside } C \end{cases}$$

The values on the right-hand side of above expressions are called the residues of the pole at $z = z_0$.

In the case of the inverse ztransform. we have $x(n)$ as

$$x(n) = \frac{1}{2\pi j}\oint_C X(z)z^{n-1}dz = \sum_{\text{all poles } z_i \text{ inside } C} [\text{residue of } X(z)z^{n-1} \text{ at } z = z_i]$$
$$= \sum_i (z - z_i)X(z)z^{n-1}|_{z=z_i} \tag{4.36}$$

Example 4.3.5 *Find the inverse z transform of* $X(z) = \frac{1}{1-az^{-1}}$, $|z| > |a|$ *using the complex inversion integral.*

$$x(n) = \frac{1}{2\pi j}\oint_C X(z)z^{n-1}dz = \frac{1}{2\pi j}\oint_C \frac{1}{1-az^{-1}}z^{n-1}dz = \frac{1}{2\pi j}\oint_C \frac{z^n}{z-a}dz \tag{4.37}$$

where C is a circle at radius greater than $|a|$. *We shall evaluate this integral using Cauchy residue theorem with* $f(z) = z^n$.
If $n \neq 0$, $f(z)$ *has only zeros and no poles inside C. Only pole inside C is* $z = a$, *hence*

$$x(n) = \frac{1}{2\pi j}\oint_C \frac{z^n}{z-a}dz = f(a) = a^n, \; n \neq 0 \tag{4.38}$$

If $n < 0$, $f(z)$ *has nth order poles at* $z = 0$, *which is also inside C and one pole inside C is* $z = a$, *hence contribution from both poles as*

$$x(-1) = \frac{1}{2\pi j}\oint_C \frac{1}{z(z-a)}dz = \frac{1}{z-a}|_{z=0} + \frac{1}{z}|_{z=a} = 0 \tag{4.39}$$

Further,

$$x(-2) = \frac{1}{2\pi j}\oint_C \frac{1}{z^2(z-a)}dz = \frac{d}{dz}\left[\frac{1}{z-a}\right]|_{z=0} + \frac{1}{z^2}|_{z=a} = 0 \tag{4.40}$$

So $x(n) = 0, \quad n < 0$, *Thus* $x(n) = a^n u(n)$.

Example 4.3.6 *Find inverse z transform of* $X(z) = \frac{1}{2-3z}$, *if* $|z| > 2/3$

$$x(n) = \frac{1}{2\pi j}\oint_C X(z)z^{n-1}dz = \frac{1}{2\pi j}\oint_C \frac{1}{2-3z}z^{n-1}dz = \frac{1}{2\pi j}\oint_C \frac{-1}{3}\frac{z^n}{z(z-2/3)}dz \tag{4.41}$$

where C is a circle at radius greater than $|2/3|$. *We shall evaluate this integral using Cauchy residue theorem.*

$$x(n) = \lim_{z \to 2/3} (z - 2/3) \frac{-1}{3} \frac{z^n}{z(z-2/3)} + \lim_{z \to 0} z \frac{-1}{3} \frac{z^n}{z(z-2/3)}$$

$$= \frac{-1}{3}(2/3)^{n-1} + \frac{1}{2} \quad (4.42)$$

Right side expression is evaluated for $n = 1$ *and other higher values of* n, *it is zero.* $x(0) = \frac{-1}{3}\frac{3}{2} + \frac{1}{2} = 0$, *thus,*

$$x(n) = \frac{-1}{3}(2/3)^{n-1}, n \geq 1 = \frac{-1}{3}(2/3)^{n-1}u(n-1)$$

Example 4.3.7 *Find inverse z transform of* $X(z) = \frac{z}{z-2}$, *if* $|z| < 2$

$$x(n) = \frac{1}{2\pi j} \oint_C X(z) z^{n-1} dz = \frac{1}{2\pi j} \oint_C \frac{z}{z-2} z^{n-1} dz = \frac{1}{2\pi j} \cdot \oint_C \frac{z^n}{(z-2)} dz \quad (4.43)$$

The closed contour C must lie inside the ROC, so for the ROC $|z| < 2$ *you have no poles (poles at* $z = 2, \infty$*) inside C for* $n \geq 0$, *hence* $x(n) = 0$, $n \geq 0$. *If* $n = -1$

$$x(-1) = \frac{1}{2\pi j} \oint_C \frac{1}{z(z-2)} dz = \frac{z}{z(z-2)}\Big|_{z=0} = -\frac{1}{2} \quad (4.44)$$

If $n = -2$

$$x(-2) = \frac{1}{2\pi j} \oint_C \frac{1}{z^2(z-2)} = \frac{1}{2\pi j} \oint_C \frac{f(z)}{z^2} dz = \frac{df(z)}{(2-1)!dz}\Big|_{z=0} = -\frac{1}{(z-2)^2}\Big|_{z=0} = -\frac{1}{2^2} \quad (4.45)$$

So $x(n) = -(\frac{1}{2})^n u(-n-1)$

4.3.4 Table of z-transforms

Refer to tables of z-transform pairs that provide known correspondences between X(z) and x(n). This is a straightforward method when dealing with standard transforms.

4.4 RELATIONSHIP BETWEEN Z-TRANSFORM AND DTFT

The relationship between the z-transform and the Discrete-Time Fourier Transform (DTFT) lies in their mathematical connection and application in signal processing.

Using z-transform equation

$$X(z) = \sum_{n=-\infty}^{\infty} x(n)z^{-n}, \text{ use } z = re^{j\omega}$$

$$X(z) = \sum_{n=-\infty}^{\infty} x(n)r^{n}e^{-j\omega n} \text{ use } r = 1 \tag{4.46}$$

$$X(z) = \sum_{n=-\infty}^{\infty} x(n)1e^{-j\omega n} \text{ assume signal is absolutely summable } \sum_{n=-\infty}^{\infty} |x(n)| < \infty \tag{4.47}$$

The DTFT can be obtained from the z-transform by evaluating the z-transform along the unit circle in the complex plane. This is known as the mapping from z to $e^{-j\omega}$. The z-transform has a ROC associated with it, which determines the values of z for which the transform converges. The DTFT does not have a formal ROC, but its convergence is implied within its definition for values of ω within the interval $-\pi < \omega \leq \pi$.

4.5 SYSTEM ANALYSIS USING Z-TRANSFORM

The transfer function of an LTI system is obtained from the z-transform of its impulse response. The transfer function H(z) relates the system's output Y (z) to its input X(z) as:

Y (z) = H(z)X(z) → H(z) = Y(z)/X(z)

The transfer function characterizes the system's response to different frequencies in the z-domain. Convolution in the time domain corresponds to multiplication in the z-domain. This property simplifies the analysis of system responses to complex input signals.

4.5.1 Pole-Zero Analysis:

The z-transform provides insights into the system's poles and zeros. The poles of H(z) are the values of z for which H(z) approaches infinity, indicating the system's natural response. Zeros of H(z) are the values for which H(z) equals zero, representing points where the system response is attenuated.

4.5.2 Frequency Response:

The frequency response of an LTI system is obtained by evaluating H(z) on the unit circle in the complex z-plane. This analysis provides information about how the system responds to different frequencies.

4.5.3 System Stability:

The stability of an LTI system can be analyzed by examining the location of poles in the z-plane. A system is considered stable if all poles lie within the unit circle.

Example 4.5.1 Pole-zero plot of causal and anti-causal signal is shown in Fig. 4.6. ROC is also highlighted in the z plane.

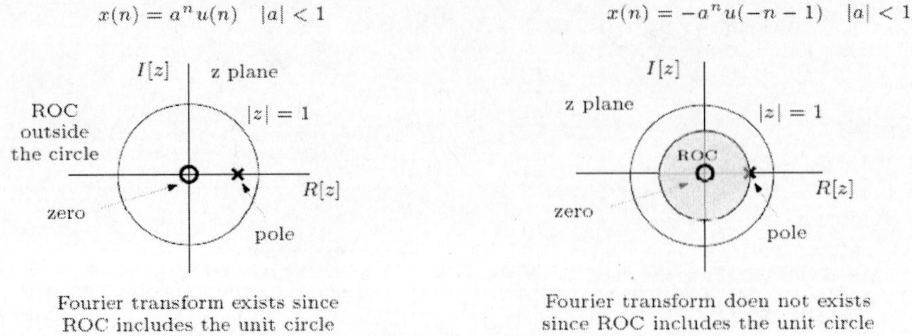

Fig. 4.6: Pole-zero plot of causal and anti-causal signal.

Example 4.5.2 Pole-zero plot of causal and anti-causal signal is shown in Fig. 4.71. ROC is also highlighted in the z plane. Time domain senescence is also expressed in 4.7.

1https://www.dsprelated.com/showarticle/993.php

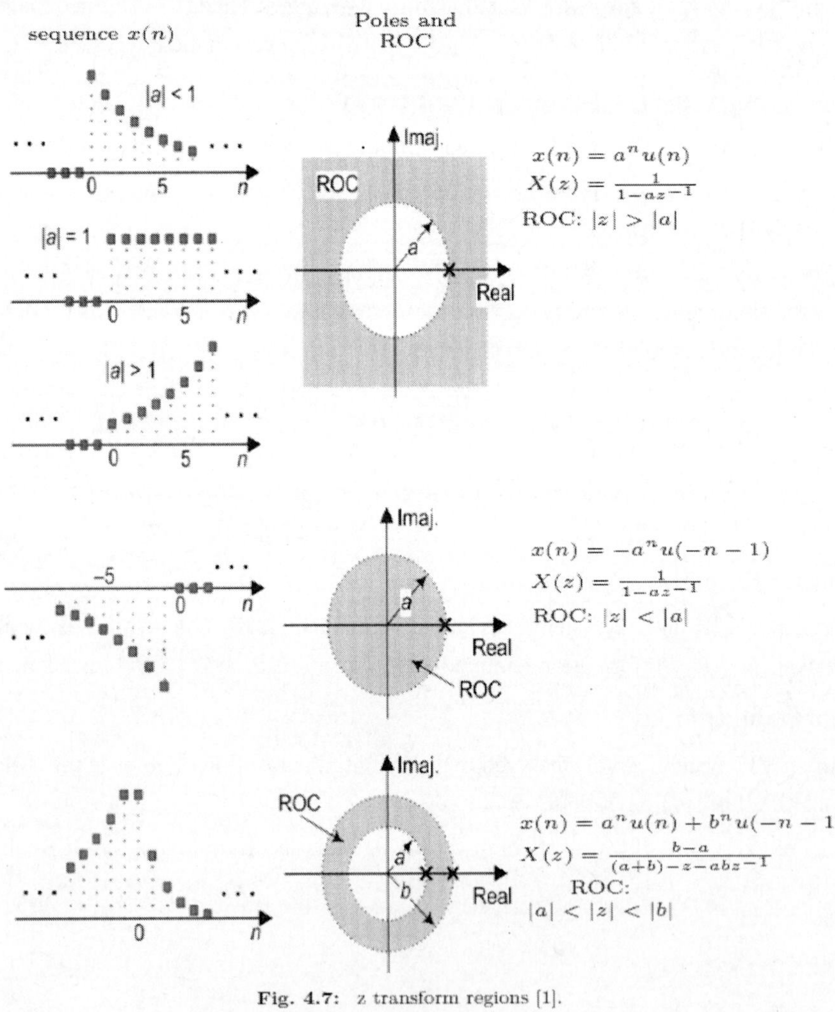

Fig. 4.7: z transform regions [1].

Example 4.5.3 *ROCs of finite and infinite duration signals are shown in Fig. 4.8 [1].*

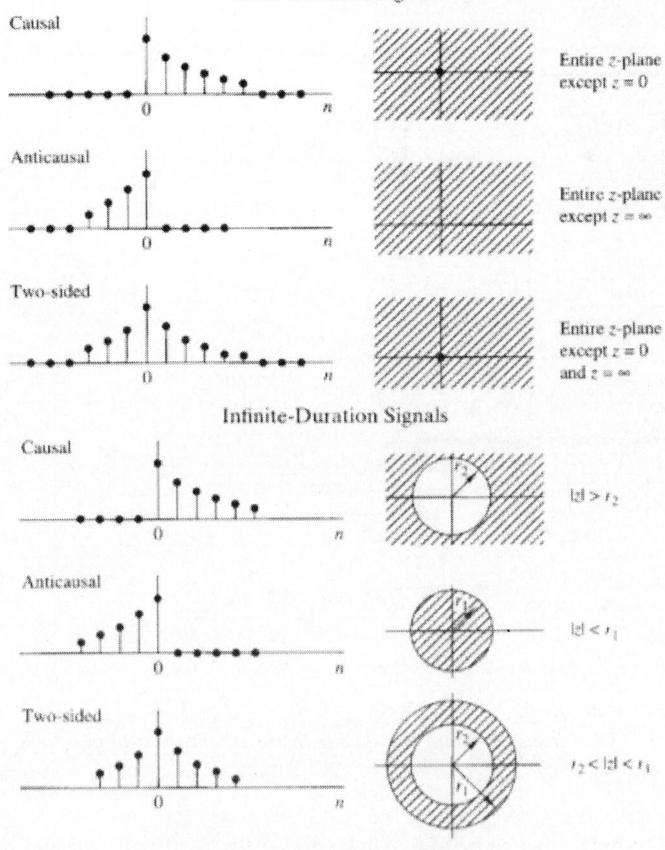

Fig. 4.8: Signals and their ROCs [1].

Example 4.5.4 Pole-zero plots and their corresponding time domain signals are shown in Fig. 4.9 [1].

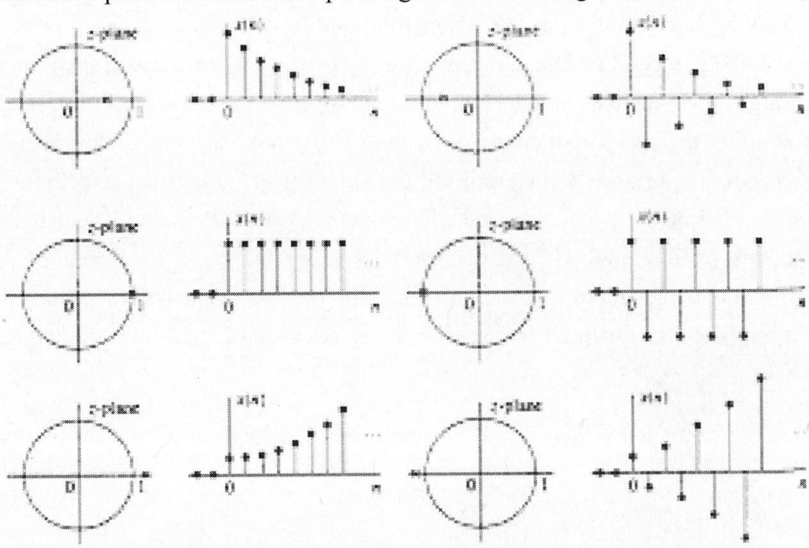

Fig. 4.9: Signals with their pole-zero plot [1].

Relation between Laplace transform and z transform is shown in Fig. 4.10. Analo- gous to z transform, Laplace transform is used for continuous time analog signals.

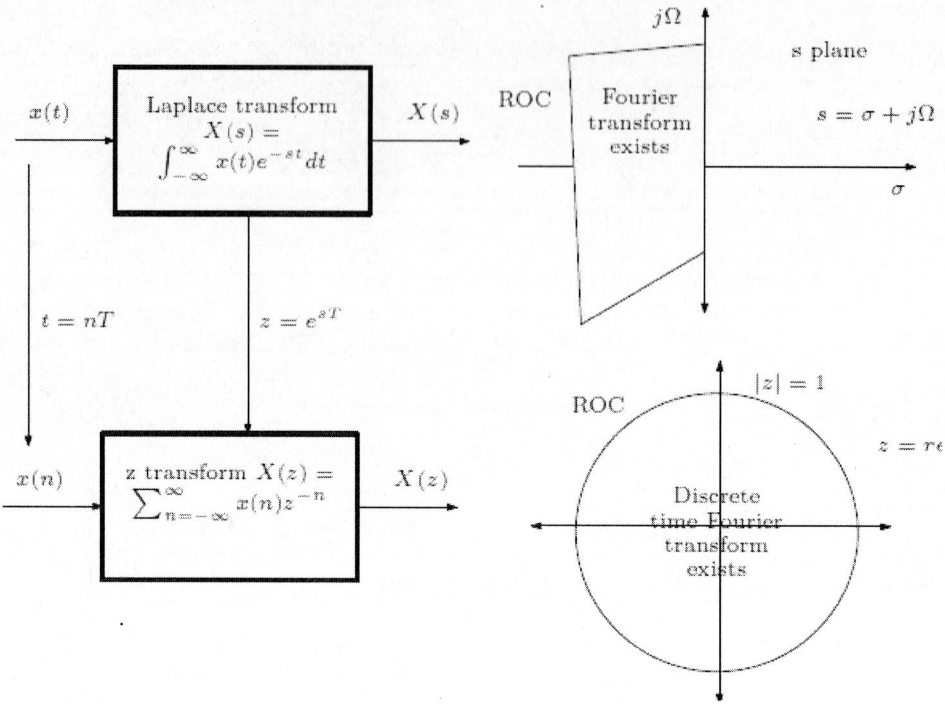

Fig. 4.10: z transform and Laplace transform representation of a signal.

SUMMARY

The chapter on z-Transform provides a comprehensive overview of this crucial mathematical tool used in the analysis and design of discrete-time signals and systems. The z-transform converts discrete-time signals into a complex frequency domain representation, facilitating the analysis of linear time-invariant (LTI) systems. The chapter begins with the definition of the z-transform and its mathematical formulation, emphasizing its significance in system stability and frequency response. Key properties of the z-transform, such as linearity, time shifting, scaling in the z-domain, and the convolution property, are thoroughly discussed, illustrating how these properties simplify the analysis of complex signals. The chapter also covers the region of convergence (ROC), highlighting its importance in determining the stability of the system and the existence of the z-transform. The inverse z-transform is introduced, along with various methods for its calculation, including the long division method, residue method, and the use of contour integrals. Each method is explained with examples to reinforce understanding. Overall, this chapter equips readers with a solid foundation in the z-transform and its applications, essential for tackling more advanced topics in digital signal processing and control systems.

EXERCISES

1. Find the z-transform of the discrete-time unit step signal $u(n)$ and $u(-n)$.
2. Given the finite-length sequence $x(n) = \{\underset{\uparrow}{1}, 2, 3, 4\}$, find its z-transform.
3. Find the inverse z-transform of $X(z) = \frac{2z}{z-0.5}$.
4. Determine the z-transform of the discrete-time exponential sequence $x(n) = a^n u(n)$, where $|a| < 1$.
5. Find the inverse z-transform of $X(z) = \frac{z^2}{z^2-0.5z+0.25}$.
6. Calculate the z-transform of $x(n) = \cos(\omega_0 n)u(n)$.
7. Given $X(z) = \frac{z^2+0.5z+0.25}{z^2-0.5z+0.25}$, determine the poles and zeros and sketch the pole-zero plot.
8. Find the z-transform of the shifted unit step signal $2u(n-4)$.
9. Given two sequences $x(n) = \{1, 2, 1\}$ and $h(n) = \{1, 1, 2\}$, use the z-transform to find their convolution $y(n) = x(n) \star h(n)$.
10. A discrete-time system has an impulse response $h(n) = \{1, -1, 2\}$. If the input to the system is $x(n) = \{1, 2, 1, 2\}$, find the output $y(n)$ using the z-transform.
11. Given the z-transform of the signal as $H(z) = \frac{1-4z^{-1}+z^2}{z^{-1}+\frac{5}{2}z^{-2}+z^{-3}}$.
    a. Plot all the poles and zeros with respect to the unit circle.
    b. Determine all the possible regions of convergence for $H(z)$
    c. Calculate the signal $h(n)$ corresponding to each region of convergence
    d. Is $H(z)$ an all-pass filter?
    e. Find the zero-input response of the system if initial conditions are $y(-3) = 0$, $y(-2) = 1$, and $y(-1) = 2$.
    f. Draw the input and output relation circuit diagram using Direct form-I for $H(z)$ and comment on the system complexity.

Multiple Choice Questions

1. The Z-transform of a discrete-time signal $x(n) = a^n u(n)$ is

   A. z/z−a

   B. z/z+a

   C. z/z−1

   D. z−a/z

2. What is the region of convergence (ROC) for the Z-transform of a right-sided sequence?

   A. Inside the unit circle

   B. Outside the unit circle

C. Entire z-plane except z=0

D. None of the above

3. The Z-transform is particularly useful for analyzing which type of systems?

A. Continuous-time linear systems

B. Discrete-time linear systems

C. Non-linear systems

D. Analog systems

4. Which property of the Z-transform states that $Z\{x[n-k]\}=z^{-k}X(z)$?

A. Linearity

B. Time Shifting

C. Scaling

D. Convolution

5. The inverse Z-transform of $1/(1-az^{-1})$ is:

A. $a^n u[n]$

B. $a^{-n}u[n]$

C. $-a^n u[-n-1$

D. $-a^{-n}u[-n-1]$

6. What is the Z-transform of the unit step function u[n]?

A. $1/1-z^{-1}$

B. $1/1+z^{-1}$

C. $z/z-1$

D. $z/z+1$

7. Which of the following is the convolution property of the Z-transform?

A. $Z\{x[n]*h[n]\}=X(z)+H(z)$

B. $Z\{x[n]*h[n]\}=X(z)-H(z)$

C. $Z\{x[n]*h[n]\}=X(z)H(z)$

D. $Z\{x[n]*h[n]\}=X(z)/H(z)$

8. What is the effect of scaling in the Z-transform, i.e., a^n x(n)?

A. X(z) is multiplied by a

B. X(z) is divided by a

C. X(z/a)

D. aX(z)

9. What is the Z-transform of a finite duration signal x[n] where x[n]=1 for n=0,1,2 and 0 otherwise?

A. $1+z^{-1}+z^{-2}$

B. $1-z^{-1}+z^{-2}$

C. $1+z^{-2}+z^{-3}$

D. $1-z^{-1}-z^{-2}$

10. For a signal x[n] with Z-transform X(z), if X(z) is given by $\frac{1+z^{-1}}{1-0.5z^{-1}}$, what is the corresponding difference equation?

A. y[n]−0.5y[n−1]=x[n]+x[n−1]

B. y[n]+0.5y[n−1]=x[n]−x[n−1]

C. y[n]−0.5y[n+1]=x[n]+x[n−1]

D. y[n]+0.5y[n+1]=x[n]−x[n−1]

ANSWERS

1	2	3	4	5	6	7	8	9	10
A	B	B	B	A	C	C	C	A	A

KNOW MORE

For more information related to this topic scan the QR code.

OR

Type this link in your browser

https://www.pearsonhighered.com/assets/samplechapter/0/1/3/1/0131988425.pdf

REFERENCES AND SUGGESTED READING

1. B. P. Lathi, "*Principles of Linear Systems and Signals*," *Oxford Second edition*, 2009.
2. John G. Proakis, and Dimitris G. Manolakis "*Digital signal processing: principles, algorithms, and applications, 4/E*,"*Pearson Education India*, 2007.
3. Alan V. Oppenheim, Alan S. Willsky, and S. Hamid Nawab "*Signals & Systems*,"*Pearson Education India*, 1997.
4. P. Singh, A. Singhal, B. Fatimah, A. Gupta; S. Dutt Joshi "*Proper Definitions of Dirichlet Conditions and Convergence of Fourier Representations [Lecture Notes]*,"*IEEE Signal Processing Magazine*, vol. 39, no. 5, pp. 77-84, 2022.
5. Barrie W. Jervis, and Emmanuel C. Ifeachor "*Digital Signal Processing: A Practical Approach*,"*Pearson Education India*, 2002.

Chapter 5: DTFT: Discrete Time Fourier Transform

UNIT SPECIFICS

The discrete-time Fourier transform (DTFT) chapter provides a comprehensive understanding of how to analyze discrete-time signals in the frequency domain. It begins with the definition of the DTFT and explores its relationship with discrete-time signals. Key properties such as linearity, time-shifting, and convolution in the frequency domain are covered in depth. The chapter also introduces the concepts of magnitude and phase spectra, which are crucial for understanding signal characteristics. Additionally, it discusses the inverse DTFT and how to use it for signal reconstruction.

RATIONALE

The discrete-time Fourier transform (DTFT) chapter is to provide a fundamental framework for analyzing discrete-time signals in the frequency domain, a crucial aspect of digital signal processing. The DTFT allows for the decomposition of signals into their frequency components, aiding in understanding signal behavior, filtering, and spectral analysis. By mastering the DTFT, students and professionals can analyze system responses, design digital filters, and perform frequency-based signal manipulations.

PRE-REQUISITE

Discrete time signal and systems, z-transform

UNIT OUTCOMES

List of outcomes of this unit is as follows:

U5-O1: Properties of DTFT

U5-O2: Auto-correlation and cross-correlation

U5-O3: Frequency based LTI system analysis

Unit-5 Outcomes	EXPECTED MAPPING WITH COURSE OUTCOMES (1- Weak Correlation; 2- Medium correlation; 3- Strong Correlation)					
	CO-1	CO-2	CO-3	CO-4	CO-5	CO-6
U5-O1	1	3	2	–	–	–
U5-O2	1	3	2	–	–	–
U5-O3	1	3	2	–	–	–

5.1 INTRODUCTION

The discrete-time Fourier transform (DTFT) serves as a cornerstone in the realm of signal processing, providing a powerful tool for analyzing the frequency content of discrete-time signals. This book chapter delves into the intricacies of the DTFT, offering a comprehensive exploration of its theoretical foundations, mathematical formulations, and practical applications. Beginning with a rigorous introduction to the DTFT definition and properties, the chapter navigates through key concepts such as periodicity, linearity, time shifting, and frequency shifting. Through detailed derivations and illustrative examples, readers gain a deep understanding of how the DTFT characterizes the frequency spectrum of discrete-time signals and facilitates their manipulation and analysis in both time and frequency domains. Furthermore, the chapter explores important topics including the convolution theorem, Fourier duality, and the relationship between the DTFT and other signal processing tools. By combining theoretical insights with practical insights, this chapter equips readers with the knowledge and skills needed to leverage the DTFT effectively in various applications.

DTFT of sequence x(n) is defined as

$X(\omega) = \sum_{n=-\infty}^{\infty} x(n)e^{-jnw}$

Here, we assume that X(ω) is converges and absolute value of sequence is finite, i.e., $X(\omega) = \sum_{n=-\infty}^{\infty} x(n)e^{-jn\omega}$. We denote the DTFT as DTFT[x(n)] =F[x(n)] = X(ω), where F is the DTFT of a sequence. The ω = 2πf is the digital signal frequency in rad/sample. The f is the digital frequency in the Hz/sample as f = F/F_s, where F is the analog frequency and F_s is the sampling frequency. DTFT representation of a signal is shown in Fig. 5.1.

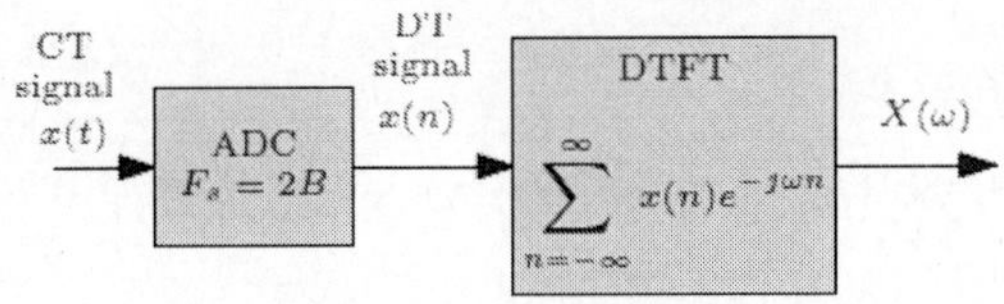

Fig. 5.1: DTFT representation of a signal x(t).

Exponential signal $x(n) = e^{j\omega_0 n}$ is the input of the LTI system, which has impulse response h(n). Output y(n) is expressed as

$y(n) = x(n) \star h(n) = e^{j\omega_0 n} \star h(n) = H(\omega_0)e^{j\omega_0 n}$, (5.1)

where ⋆ is the convolution operation. Here h(n) is the impulse response of the LTI system. DTFT of LTI system is

$$H(\omega) = \sum_{n=-\infty}^{\infty} h(n)\, e^{-jn\omega}$$

Input and output relation in a LTI system using the DTFT is illustrated in Fig. 5.2.

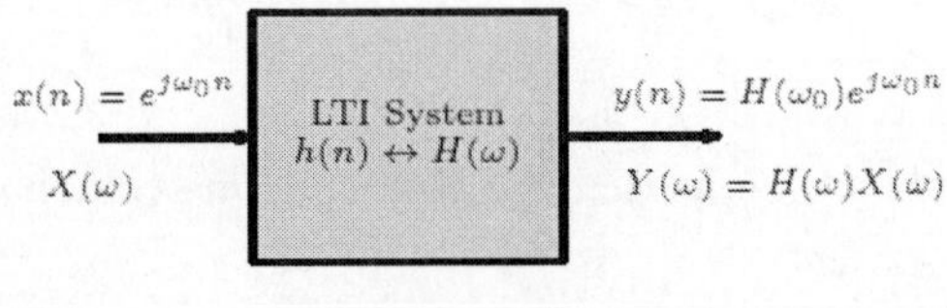

Fig. 5.2: LTI system

5.2 PROPERTIES OF DTFT

Some key properties of the DTFT are

Linearity: The DTFT is a linear operation. For any constants a and b and signals $x_1(n)$ and $x_2(n)$:

$$F[ax_1(n) + bx_2(n)] = aF[x_1(n)] + bF[x_2(n)] = aX_1(\omega) + bX_2(\omega)$$

Here, $X_1(\omega) = F[x_1(n)]$ and $X_2(\omega) = F[x_2(n)]$.

Time Shifting: A time-shifted signal x(nk) in the time domain results in a modulation by $e^{-j\omega k}$ in the frequency domain.

Using the DTFT equation

$\sum_{n=-\infty}^{\infty} x(n-k)\, e^{-jnw} = \sum_{n=-\infty}^{\infty} x(n)\, e^{-jnw} e^{-jkw}$, using dummy variable n-k=m

$=X(\omega)e^{-jk\omega}$

If $X(\omega) = F[x(n)]$ and $e^{-jk\omega}X(\omega) = F[x(n-k)]$.

Frequency Shifting: A frequency-shifted signal $e^{j\omega}0nx(n)$ in the time domain results in a modulation by $X(\omega - \omega_0)$ in the frequency domain.

Using the DTFT equation

$$F\left[x(n)e^{jw0n}\right] = \sum_{n=-\infty}^{\infty} x(n)\, e^{jw0n} e^{-jnw}$$

$$= \sum_{n=-\infty}^{\infty} x(n)\, e^{-jn(w-w0)}$$

$$= X(w - \omega_0)$$

Scaling: Scaling a signal x(an) in the time domain results in compression/stretching by a factor of |a| in the frequency domain.

Using the DTFT equation

$$F[x(an)] = \sum_{n=-\infty}^{\infty} x(an)\, e^{-jnw}, use\ an = m$$

$$= \sum_{m=-\infty}^{\infty} x(m)\, e^{-jm\left(\frac{w}{a}\right)}$$

$$= X(w/a)$$

Conjugate Property: The DTFT of the conjugate of a signal $x^*(n)$ is the complex conjugate of its DTFT.

Using the DTFT equation

$$\sum_{n=-\infty}^{\infty} x^*(n)\, e^{-jnw} = \sum_{n=-\infty}^{\infty} (x(n)e^{-jnw})^* = \sum_{n=-\infty}^{\infty} (x(n)e^{-jn(-w)})^*$$

$$= X^*(-w)$$

Time Reversal: The DTFT of the time-reversed signal x(n) is the complex conjugate of the DTFT of the original signal x(n).

Using the DTFT equation

$$\sum_{n=-\infty}^{\infty} x(-n)\, e^{-jnw} = \sum_{n'=-\infty}^{\infty} x(n')\, e^{-jn'w} = \sum_{n'=-\infty}^{\infty} x(n')\, e^{-jn'(-w)}$$

$$= X(-w)$$

So, if $X(\omega) = F[x(n)]$, then $X(-\omega) = F[x(-n)]$

Frequency Differentiation: $F[nx(n)] = jd/d\omega[\, X(\omega)]$

Using the DTFT equation

$$X(w) = \sum_{n=-\infty}^{\infty} x(n)\, e^{-jnw}, \frac{dX(w)}{dw} = \sum_{n=-\infty}^{\infty} -j\, nx(n)e^{-jwn} = -j \sum_{n=-\infty}^{\infty} n\, x(n)e^{-jnw} = -jF[nx(n)]$$

$$F[nx(n)] = j\frac{dX(w)}{dw}$$

Time Convolution: Convolution of two signal in the time domain is the multiplication of their DTFTs as $x_1(n) \star x_2(n) = X_1(\omega)X_2(\omega)$ Convolution of two signals is expressed as

$$y(n) = x_1(n) * x_2(n) = \sum_{k=-\infty}^{\infty} x_1(k)\, x_2(n-k) \ (5.2)$$

DTFT of y(n) is written as

$$Y(w) = \sum_{n=-\infty}^{\infty} y(n)\, e^{-jnw} = \sum_{n=-\infty}^{\infty} \left[\sum_{k=-\infty}^{\infty} x_1(k)\, x_2(n-k)\right] e^{-jnw} \ (5.3)$$

$$Y(w) = \sum_{k=-\infty}^{\infty} x_1(k) \sum_{n=-\infty}^{\infty} x_2(n-k)\, e^{-jnw}$$

Use n-k=m

$$Y(w) = \sum_{k=-\infty}^{\infty} x_1(k) \underbrace{\sum_{m=-\infty}^{\infty} x_2(m)e^{-jmw}}_{X2(w)} e^{-jkw}$$

$$Y(w) = X_2(w) \sum_{k=-\infty}^{\infty} x_1(k)\, e^{-jkw} = X_1(w)X_2(w)$$

Symmetry Properties: When a signal exhibits certain symmetry properties in the time domain, these characteristics impose specific symmetry conditions on its Fourier transform. Utilizing any symmetry features results in more straightforward formulas for both the direct and inverse Fourier transform.

$x(n) = x_R(n) + jx_I(n)\ X(\omega) = X_R(\omega) + jX_I(\omega)$ (5.4)

Using DTFT expression as

$$X(w) = \sum_{n=-\infty}^{\infty} x(n)e^{-jwn} = \sum_{n=-\infty}^{\infty} [x_R(n) + jx_1x(n)][cos(wn) - jsin(wn)]$$

$$= -j \sum_{n=-\infty}^{\infty} n\, x(n)e^{-jwn} = -jF[nx(n)]$$

$$F[nx(n)] = j\frac{dX(w)}{dw}$$

The correlation theorem: The DTFT correlation theorem states that the cor- relation in the time domain corresponds to multiplication in the frequency domain. Mathematically, if x(n) and y(n) are two sequences with DTFTs X(ω) and Y (ω) respectively, then the DTFT of their correlation x(n) ⋆ y(n) is given by the product of their individual DTFTs as

$F[x(n) \star y(-n)] = X(\omega)Y(-\omega) = S_{xy}(\omega)$.

Correlation is expressed as

$$r_{xy}(n) = \sum_{n=-\infty}^{\infty} x(k)y(k-n) = x(n) * y(-n)$$

Using DTFT expression as

$$\sum_{n=-\infty}^{\infty} r_{xy}(n)e^{-jwn} = \sum_{n=-\infty}^{\infty}[\sum_{k=-\infty}^{\infty} x(k)\,y(k-n)]e^{-jwn}$$

$$= \sum_{k=-\infty}^{\infty} x(k) \sum_{n=-\infty}^{\infty} y(k-n)\,e^{-jwn}\text{ , using dummy variable } k-n=n'$$

$$= \sum_{k=-\infty}^{\infty} x(k) \underbrace{\sum_{n=-\infty}^{\infty} y(n)e^{jwn}e^{-jkw}}_{Y(-w)}$$

$$\sum_{k=-\infty}^{\infty} x(k)e^{-jkw}Y(-w) = X(w)Y(-w) = S_{xy}(w)$$

The Wiener-Khintchine theorem: The Wiener-Khintchine theorem, also known as the power spectral density theorem, establishes a relationship between the auto- correlation function $r_{xy}(n)$ of a wide-sense stationary random process and its power spectral density (PSD) $S_{xy}(\omega)$. If x(n) be a real signal,

$$r_{xy}(n) \leftrightarrow S_{xy}(\omega).$$

This result holds significant importance, signifying that both the autocorrelation sequence and the energy spectral density of a signal carry identical information about the signal. However, as neither of these contains any phase information, the unique reconstruction of the signal from either the autocorrelation function or the energy density spectrum becomes impossible.

The modulation theorem: If signal $x(n) \leftrightarrow X(\omega)$, Then

$x(n)\cos(\omega_0 n) \leftrightarrow 2\,[X(\omega-\omega_0) + X(\omega+\omega_0)]$

$$x(n)cos(w_o n) = x(n)\frac{e^{jw_o n} + e^{-jw_o n}}{2}$$

$$= \frac{1}{2}x(n)e^{jw_o n} + \frac{1}{2}x(n)e^{-jw_o n}$$

Take DTFT

$$= \frac{1}{2}X(w-w_o) + \frac{1}{2}X(w+w_o)$$

DTFT of signal $\cos(\omega_0 n)$ is shown in Fig. 5.3.

$x(n) = \cos(\omega_0 n)$

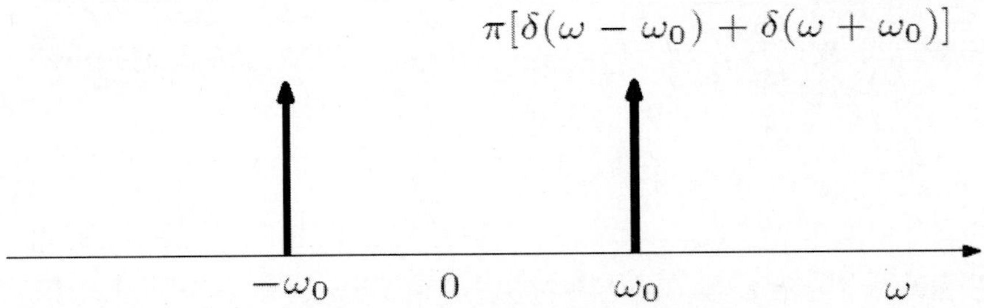

Fig. 5.3: DTFT of $\cos(\omega_0 n)$.

5.2.1 Steady-State and Transient Response to Sinusoidal Input Signals

In the context of sinusoidal inputs, the steady-state response represents the behavior of the system after a sufficient amount of time has passed, and the effects of any initial conditions or transients have decayed. For sinusoidal inputs, LTI systems exhibit steady-state sinusoidal responses at the same frequency as the input. The amplitude and phase of the steady-state response depend on the system's frequency response characteristics.

In the context of sinusoidal inputs, the transient response includes the time it takes for the system to settle down to its steady-state sinusoidal response.

Example 5.2.1 *LTI system is expressed using the first-order difference equation as*

$y(n) = ay(n-1) + x(n)$. *Its response to any input* $x(n)$ *applied at* $n = 0$ *is given by*

$y(0) = ay(-1) + x(0)$, $y(1) = ay(0) + x(1) \Rightarrow y(1) = a^2y(-1) + ax(0) + x(1)$ $y(2) = a^3y(-1) + a^2x(0) + ax(1) + x(2)$

Therefore,

$y(n) = a^{n+1}y(-1) + \sum_{k=0}^{n} a^k x(n-k), n \geqslant 0$

where $y(-1)$ *is the initial condition. Let consider* $x(n) = Be^{j\omega n}, n \geq 0$, *so*

$$y(n) = a^{n+1}y(-1) + \sum_{k=0}^{n} a^k Be^{jw(n-k)}$$

$$= a^{n+1}y(-1) + \sum_{k=0}^{n} a^k Be^{jwn}e^{-jwk}$$

$$y(n) = a^{n+1}y(-1) + Be^{iwn}\sum_{k=0}^{n}(ae^{-jw})^k$$

$$= a^{n+1}y(-1) + Be^{jwn}\frac{1-(ae^{-jw})^{n+1}}{1-(ae^{-jw})}$$

$$= a^{n+1}y(-1) + \frac{Be^{iwn}}{1-(ae^{-jw})} - \frac{Ba^{n+1}e^{-jw}}{1-(ae^{-jw})}, n \geqslant 0$$

If $|a| < 1$, system is BIBO system. Further, as $n \to \infty$, a^{n+1} approaches zero. Thus

$$a^{n+1}y(-1) - \frac{Ba^{n+1}e^{-j\omega}}{1-(ae^{-j\omega})} = y_{tr}(n)$$

is called the transient response of the system for $n \geq 0$. Term $y_{ss}(n) = \frac{Be^{j\omega n}}{1-(ae^{-j\omega})}$ is the the steady-state response of te system. Thus

$$\begin{aligned} y_{ss}(n) &= \lim_{n\to\infty} y(n) = \underbrace{\frac{1}{1-(ae^{-j\omega})}}_{H(\omega)} Be^{j\omega n} \\ &= H(\omega)Be^{j\omega n} \end{aligned}$$

In numerous practical scenarios, the transient response of a system is often considered unimportant, leading to its usual omission when analyzing the system's response to sinusoidal inputs.

Steady-State Response to Periodic Input Signals:
Consider a stable linear time-invariant system with a periodic signal $x(n)$ having a fundamental period N. Use of the Fourier series representation of the periodic signal as

$$x(n) = \sum_{k=0}^{N-1} \underbrace{c_k e^{\frac{j2\pi kn}{N}}}_{x_k(n)} = \sum_{k=0}^{N-1} x_k(n),\ k = 0, ..., .N-1$$

Response due to $x_k(n)$ is $y_k(n) = c_k H(\frac{2\pi kn}{N})x_k(n)$, where $H(\frac{2\pi kn}{N}) = H(\omega)|_{\omega=H(\frac{2\pi kn}{N})}$ is the system transfer function. Thus total output of the system due to periodic input signal is

$$y(n) = \sum_{k=0}^{N-1} y_k(n) = \sum_{k=0}^{N-1} c_k H(\frac{2\pi kn}{N})e^{\frac{j2\pi kn}{N}}$$

Hence, the linear system can change the shape of the periodlc input signal by scaling the amplitude and shifting the phase of the Fourier series components. However, it does not affect the period of the periodic input signal.

Example 5.2.2 *Consider a causal LTI system that is characterized by the difference equation*

$$y(n) - \frac{3}{4}y(n-1) + \frac{1}{8}y(n-2) = 2x(n)$$

What is the impulse response of this system? If the input to this system is $x(n) = (\underline{1})^n u(n)$*, what is the system response to this input signal?*

Take the DTFT of both side

$$Y(w) - \frac{3}{4}Y(w)e^{-jw} + \frac{1}{8}Y(w)e^{-j2w} = 2X(w)$$

$$H(w) = \frac{Y(w)}{X(w)} = \frac{2}{1 - \frac{3}{4}e^{-jw} + \frac{1}{8}e^{-j2w}} = \frac{2}{\left(1 - \frac{1}{2}e^{-jw}\right)\left(1 - \frac{1}{4}e^{-jw}\right)}$$

$$H(w) = \frac{4}{(1 - \frac{1}{2}e^{-jw})} - \frac{2}{(1 - \frac{1}{4}e^{-jw})}$$

$$h(n) = 4(\frac{1}{2})^n u(n) - 2(\frac{1}{4})^n u(n)$$

Output is Y(w)=H(w)X(w) so

$$Y(w) = \frac{2}{(1 - \frac{1}{2}e^{-jw})(1 - \frac{1}{4}e^{-jw})} \frac{1}{(1 - \frac{1}{4}e^{-jw})}$$

Using the partial-fraction expression, we can obtain

$$H(w) = -\frac{4}{(1 - \frac{1}{4}e^{-jw})} - \frac{2}{(1 - \frac{1}{4}e^{-jw})^2} + \frac{8}{(1 - \frac{1}{2}e^{-jw})}, taking\ IDTFT$$

$$h(n) = -4(\frac{1}{4})^n u(n) - 2(n+1)(\frac{1}{4})^n u(n) + 8(\frac{1}{2})^n u(n)$$

5.3 INPUT-OUTPUT CORRELATION FUNCTIONS AND SPECTRA

LTI system, which impulse response is h(n). Input and output are x(n) and y(n) respectively. Output correlation is expressed as

$$r_{yy}(n) = r_{hh}(n) \star r_{xx}(n) \quad r_{yx}(n) = h(n) \star r_{xx}(n)$$

where $r_{xx}(n)$ is the autocorrelation sequence of the input signal x(n), $r_{yy}(n)$ is the autocorrelation sequence of the output y(n), $r_{hh}(n)$ is the autocorrelation sequence of the impulse response h(n) and $r_{yx}(n)$ is the crosscorrelation sequence between the output and the input signals. Here ⋆ denotes the convolution operation. Input and output auto-correlations are shown in Fig. 5.4.

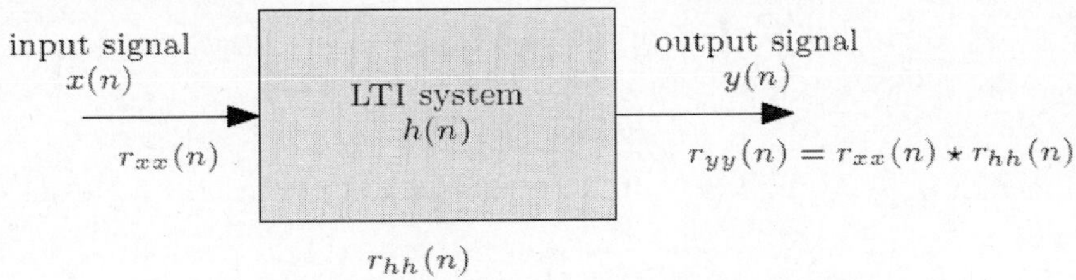

Fig. 5.4: LTI system's input and output

Taking the DTFT of both side

$$S_{yy}(\omega) = S_{hh}(\omega)S_{xx}(\omega) = H(\omega)H^*(\omega)S_{xx}(\omega) = |H(\omega)|^2 S_{xx}(\omega)$$

$$S_{yx}(\omega) = H(\omega)S_{xx}(\omega) = H(\omega)|X(\omega)|^2$$

Here $S_{yx}(\omega)$ is the cross-energy density spectrum of x(n) and y(n). $S_{yy}(\omega)$ is the en- ergy density spectrum (EDS) of the output signal. Thus, output energy is calculated as

$$E_y = \frac{1}{2\pi}\int_{-\pi}^{\pi} S_{yy}(w)dw = \frac{1}{2\pi}\int_{-\pi}^{\pi} |H(w)|^2 S_{xx}(w)dw$$

If input signal is flat in the frequency range $-\pi < \omega \leq \pi$ then

$$E_x = \frac{1}{2\pi}\int_{-\pi}^{\pi} S_{xx}(w)dw = constant$$

So, $S_{yx}(\omega) = H(\omega)E_x$, $h(n) = \frac{r_{yx}(n)}{E_x}$. The relationship in above equation implies that h(n) can be calculated by applying a spectrally flat signal x(n) as input to the system and then cross-correlating this input with the system's output. This approach proves valuable for determining the impulse response of an unfamiliar system.

5.3.1 System response due to random input signal

The response of a Linear Time-Invariant (LTI) system to a random input signal varies depending on the characteristics of the input signal and the system itself. Random input signals can include white noise, Gaussian noise, or other stochastic processes.

In general, when an LTI system is subjected to a random input signal, its response can be analyzed statistically. For instance, one might be interested in determining the mean response, variance, autocorrelation function, or power spectral density of the output signal. The specific behavior of the LTI system in response to a random input signal can be described using techniques from stochastic processes and linear system theory. These techniques allow for the characterization of how the system processes and modifies the statistical properties of the input signal to produce an output signal.

Input signal is random sequence then its mean is defined as $\mu_x = E[x(n)]$, where E is the expectation operator and denotes the statistical average of the signal. Output random signal is expressed as

$$y(n) = \sum_{k=-\infty}^{\infty} h(k)x(n-k)$$

Thus, the output mean is defined as

$$\mu_y = E[y(n)] = E[\sum_{k=-\infty}^{\infty} h(k)x(n-k)]$$

$$= \sum_{k=-\infty}^{\infty} h(k)\underbrace{E[x(n-k)]}_{\mu_x} = \mu_x = \mu_x \sum_{k=-\infty}^{\infty} h(k)$$

Further, $H(0) = \sum_{k=-\infty}^{\infty} h(k)$ is the system response at zero frequency (DC value).

Thus, $\mu_y = H(0)\mu_x$.

Output autocorrelation $\phi_{yy}(m)$ corresponding random real input signal is defined as

$$\phi_{yy}(m) = E[y(n)y(n+m)]$$

$$= E[\sum_{k=-\infty}^{\infty} h(k)x(n-k) \sum_{l=-\infty}^{\infty} h(l)x(n+m-l)]$$

Arranging the terms, we can have

$$\phi_{yy}(m) = \sum_{k=-\infty}^{\infty} \cdot \sum_{l=-\infty}^{\infty} h(k)h(l)E[x(n-k)x(n+m-l)]$$

Assuming a dummy variable n − k = n ′, we have

$$\phi_{yy}(m) = \sum_{k=-\infty}^{\infty} \sum_{l=-\infty}^{\infty} h(k)h(l) \underbrace{E[x(n')x(n'+k-l+m)]}_{\phi_{xx}(k-l+m)}$$

So

$$\phi_{yy}(m) = \sum_{k=-\infty}^{\infty} \sum_{l=-\infty}^{\infty} h(k)h(l)\phi_{xx}(k-l+m)$$

$$= \sum_{l=-\infty}^{\infty} r_{hh}(l)\phi_{xx}(m-l) = r_{hh}(m) \star \phi_{xx}(m)$$

Check it

If input signal is random white signal, then $S_{xx}(\omega) = \sigma_x^2$and $\phi_{xx}(m) = \sigma_x^2\delta(m)$

Then

$$\phi_{yy}(m) = \sigma_x^2 \sum_{k=-\infty}^{\infty} h(k)h(m+k)$$

Output signal power is $E_y = \phi_{yy}(0) = \sigma_x^2 \sum_{k=-\infty}^{\infty} |h(k)|^2. Using\ the\ Parseval's$

Theorem, $\sum_{k=-\infty}^{\infty} |h(k)|^2 = \frac{1}{2\pi}\int_{-\pi}^{\pi} |H(\omega)|^2 d\omega.$

Thus, $E_y = \sigma_x^2 \frac{1}{2\pi}\int_{-\pi}^{\pi} |H(\omega)|^2 d\omega.$

Taking the DTFT of the above equation, autocorrelation function in the frequency domain is

$$\Phi_{yy}(\omega) = \sum_{n=-\infty}^{\infty} \phi_{yy}(n)e^{-jn\omega}$$

$$= \sum_{n=-\infty}^{\infty} \sum_{k=-\infty}^{\infty} \sum_{l=-\infty}^{\infty} h(k)h(l)\phi_{xx}(k-l+n)e^{-jn\omega}$$

Take dummy variable k − l + n = n ′,

$$\Phi_{yy}(\omega) = \sum_{k=-\infty}^{\infty} \sum_{l=-\infty}^{\infty} h(k)h(l) \underbrace{\sum_{n=-\infty}^{\infty} \phi_{xx}(n)e^{-jn\omega}}_{\Phi_{xx}(\omega)} e^{-jl\omega} e^{-jk\omega}$$

Arranging the terms in the above equation, we can get

$$\Phi_{yy}(\omega) = H(\omega)H(-\omega)\Phi_{xx}(\omega) = |H(\omega)|^2\Phi_{xx}(\omega) = S_{hh}(\omega)\Phi_{xx}(\omega)$$

System is deterministic, hence, we are using energy spectral density of system as

$S_{hh}(\omega) = |H(\omega)|2$ with input energy spectral density $\Phi_{xx}(\omega) = \sum_{n=-\infty}^{\infty} \phi_{xx}(n)e^{-jn\omega}$.

For special case ω = 0,

$$E_y = \Phi_{yy}(0) = |H(0)|^2\Phi_{xx}(0) = |H(0)|^2 E_x$$

Example 5.3.1 Find the energy of the sinc signal x(n) = sin(ωcn)/ πn .

Signal energy in the time domain is

$$E_x = \sum_{n=-\infty}^{\infty} x^2(n) = \sum_{n=-\infty}^{\infty} (\frac{\sin(\omega_c n)}{\pi n})^2$$

So directly it is difficult tp evaluate the above expression, hence we use Parseval's theorem as

$$E_x = \frac{1}{2\pi}\int_{-\pi}^{\pi} |X(\omega)|^2 d\omega = \frac{1}{2\pi}\int_{-\omega_c}^{\omega_c} 1\, d\omega$$

A straightforward interpretation of this finding is that the energy is directly proportional to the bandwidth of the sinc signal.

5.4 DISCRETE TIME FOURIER SERIES

The Discrete-Time Fourier Series (DTFS) is a mathematical tool used to repre- sent periodic discrete-time signals in the frequency domain. It is analogous to the Continuous-Time Fourier Series (CTFS) for continuous-time signals but is applied to signals sampled at discrete intervals.

If signal x(n) is periodic with period N, i.e,

$$x(n + N) = x(n)\ \forall n$$

An arbitrary Discrete Time-periodic signal x(n) can be written as a linear combination of harmonic complex sinusoids $e^{j\frac{2\pi k}{N}}$ as

$$x(n) = \sum_{k=0}^{N-1} c_k\, e^{j\frac{2\pi kn}{N}} \text{ for } n = 0,1, \dots, N-1$$

where the c_ks the coefficients in the above series representation and is called DTFS coefficients.

By multiplying the $e^{\frac{-j2\pi kn}{N}}$ to both side and averaging over a period in the above equation.

$$\sum_{n=0}^{N-1} x(n)e^{-j\frac{2\pi ln}{N}} = \sum_{n=0}^{N-1}\sum_{k=0}^{N-1} c_k\, e^{j\frac{2\pi kn}{N}} e^{-j\frac{2\pi ln}{N}} = \sum_{k=0}^{N-1} c_k \sum_{n=0}^{N-1} e^{j\frac{2\pi(k-l)n}{N}}$$

We consider that

$$\sum_{n=0}^{N-1} e^{j\frac{2\pi(k-l)n}{N}} = \begin{cases} N, & \text{if } k-l = 0, \pm N, \pm 2N, \dots \\ 0, & \text{otherwise} \end{cases}$$

Thus

$$c_l = \frac{1}{N}\sum_{n=0}^{N-1} x(n)e^{-j\frac{2\pi ln}{N}}, l = 0,1, \dots, N-1$$

DTFS Summary

Synthesis equation:

$$x(n) = \sum_{k=0}^{N-1} c_k e^{j\frac{2\pi kn}{N}} \quad n = 0, 1, ...N-1$$

Analysis equation:

$$c_k = \frac{1}{N}\sum_{n=0}^{N-1} x(n) e^{-j\frac{2\pi kn}{N}} \quad k = 0, 1, ...N-1$$

1. c_ks form a periodic sequence in the frequency domain $c_k = c_{k+N}$

$$c_{k+N} = \frac{1}{N}\sum_{n=0}^{N-1} x(n) e^{-j\frac{2\pi(k+N)n}{N}} = \frac{1}{N}\sum_{n=0}^{N-1} x(n) e^{-j\frac{2\pi kn}{N}} \underbrace{e^{-j\frac{2\pi Nn}{N}}}_{1} = c_k$$

Thus $c_k = c_{k+N}$ ∀k

2. Both x(n) and c_k are periodic in nature with a period of N. The domain of both signals is also discrete in nature.
3. The Power Density Spectrum (PDS) of periodic signals describes the distri- bution of power across different frequencies in the frequency domain. Power is expressed as

$$P_x = \frac{1}{N}\sum_{n=0}^{N-1} |x(n)|^2$$

Using DTFT we can write

$$P_x = \frac{1}{N}\sum_{n=0}^{N-1} x(n)x^*(n) = \frac{1}{N}\sum_{n=0}^{N-1} [\sum_{k=0}^{N-1} c_k e^{j\frac{2\pi kn}{N}}][\sum_{l=0}^{N-1} c_l e^{j\frac{2\pi ln}{N}}]^*$$

$$= \sum_{k=0}^{N-1}\sum_{l=0}^{N-1} c_k c_l^* \sum_{n=0}^{N-1} e^{j\frac{2\pi(k-l)n}{N}}$$

So

$$P_x = \sum_{k=0}^{N-1} |c_k|^2 = \frac{1}{N}\sum_{n=0}^{N-1} |x(n)|^2$$

Similarly for energy signals

$$E_x = \sum_{k=0}^{N-1} |c_k|^2 = \frac{1}{N}\sum_{n=0}^{N-1} |x(n)|^2$$

4. If the signal x(n) is real, c*k = c–k.

$$c_k^* = \left(\frac{1}{N}\sum_{n=0}^{N-1} x(n)e^{-j\frac{2\pi kn}{N}}\right)^*$$

$$= \frac{1}{N}\sum_{n=0}^{N-1} \underbrace{x(n)}_{x(n)=x^*(n)} \ e^{j\frac{2\pi kn}{N}} = c_{-k}$$

Example 5.4.1 *Find the DTFS coefficients of the signal* x(n) = {..., 1, 2, 3, 4, 1, 2, 3, 4, 1, 2, 3, 4, ...}

FS

$$x(n) = \sum_{k=0}^{N-1} c_k e^{j\frac{2\pi kn}{N}}, n = 0,1, \ldots, N-1$$

$$x(n) = \sum_{k=0}^{3} c_k e^{j\frac{2\pi kn}{4}}$$

FS coefficients

$$c_k = \frac{1}{4}\sum_{n=0}^{3} x(n)e^{-j\frac{2\pi kn}{4}}, k = 0,1,2,3$$

$$c_0 = \frac{5}{2}, c_1 = \frac{-1+j}{2}, c_2 = -\frac{1}{2}, c_3 = \frac{-1-j}{2}$$

Thus

$$x(n) = \frac{5}{2} + \frac{-1+j}{2}e^{j\frac{2\pi n}{4}} + -\frac{1}{2}e^{j\frac{4\pi n}{4}} + \frac{-1-j}{2}e^{j\frac{6\pi n}{4}}$$

Signal and FS coefficients are plotted in Fig. 10.7.

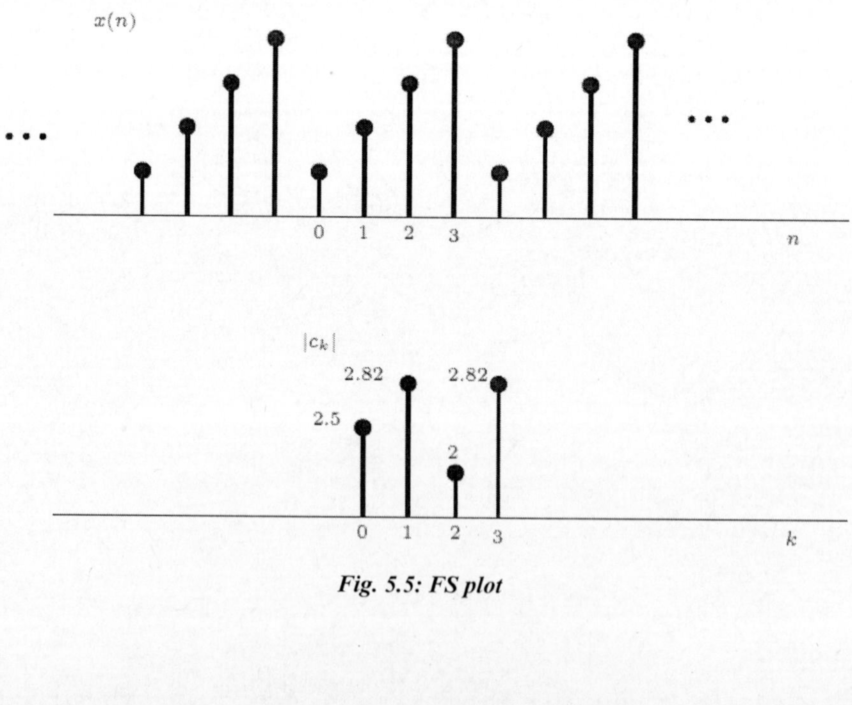

Fig. 5.5: FS plot

5.5 FILTERS SPECIFICATION

Filters are essential components in signal processing and communications systems, designed to selectively pass or reject certain frequency components of a signal.

Low-Pass Filter (LPF):

Allows frequencies below a certain cutoff frequency to pass through while attenuating higher frequencies, as shown in Fig. 5.6. Cutoff frequency $f_c = B$ below which the signal is passed with minimal attenuation. Filter order determines the steepness of the filter's transition between passband and stopband.

High-Pass Filter (HPF):

Allows frequencies above a certain cutoff frequency to pass through while attenuating lower frequencies, as shown in Fig. 5.6. Cutoff frequency $f_c = B$ above which the signal is passed with minimal attenuation.

Bandpass Filter:

Passes a specific range or band of frequencies while attenuating frequencies outside this band, as shown in Fig. 5.6.

Band-Reject Filter (Notch Filter):

Attenuates a specific range or band of frequencies while allowing frequencies outside this band to pass through, as shown in Fig. 5.6.

Ideal LPF filters do not exist due to their non-causal nature and infinite duration. Therefore, in practice, we can only realize approximations close to the ideal frequency response, as shown in Fig. 5.7. Practical LPF filters have passbands, transition bands, and stopbands, as illustrated in Fig. 5.7. A narrower bandwidth of the transition band necessitates a higher filter order design.

Example 5.5.1 *The plots of the DTFT of a signal are shown in Fig. 5.8, Fig. 5.9, and Fig. 5.10, considering three different lengths of the signal:* $L = 30, 100,$ *and* 500. *The signal contains five different frequency components, which may not be visible in Fig. 5.8 due to the shorter length of the signal.* However, as we increase the signal's length in the time domain, more frequency components are captured in its DTFT, as observed in Fig. 5.10.

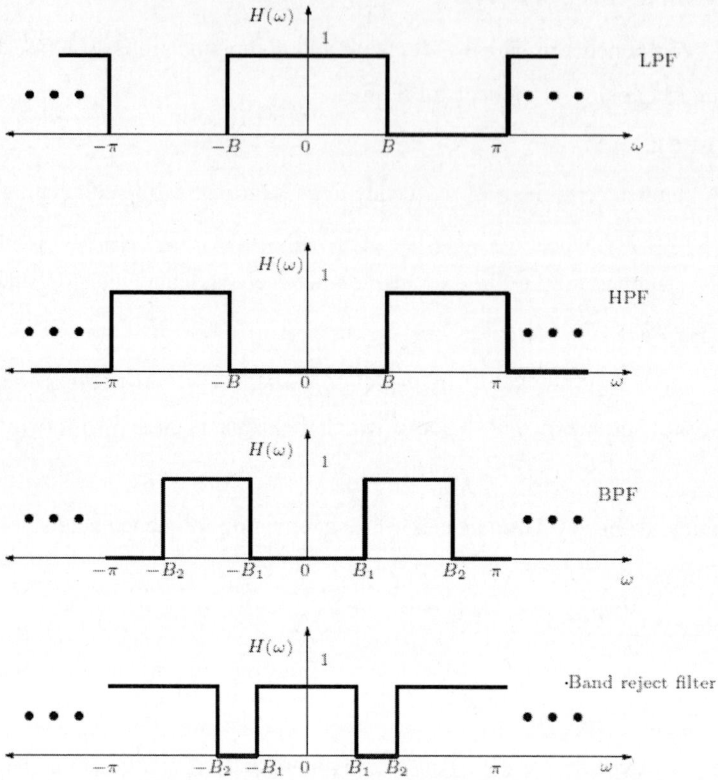

Fig. 5.6: Ideals digital filters

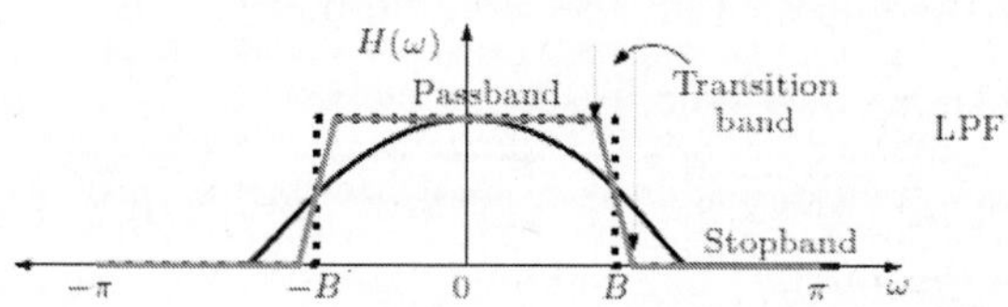

Fig. 5.7: Lowpass filter characterization

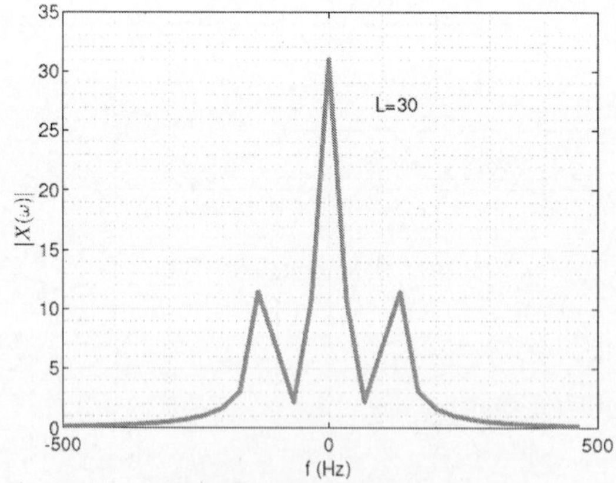

Fig. 5.8: DTFT plot for L = 30.

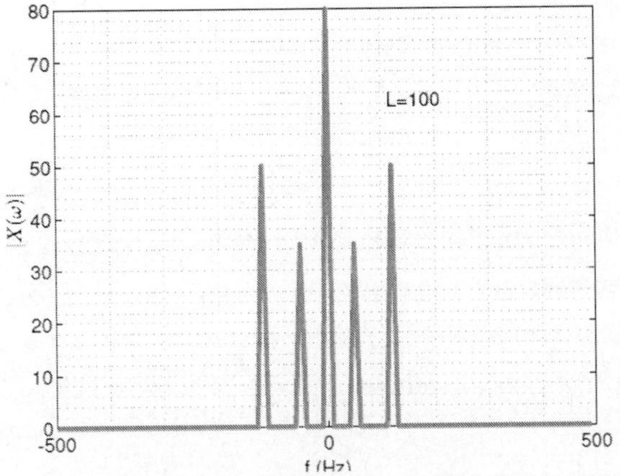

Fig. 5.9: DTFT plot for L = 100.

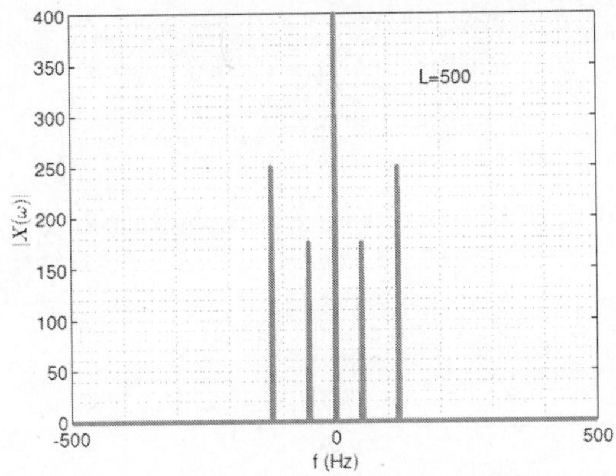

Fig. 5.10: DTFT plot for $L = 500$.

SUMMARY

The chapter on Discrete Time Fourier Transform (DTFT) explores the transformation of discrete-time signals into the frequency domain, enabling the analysis of their frequency content. It begins by defining the DTFT and providing its mathematical formulation, highlighting its utility in studying linear time-invariant (LTI) systems. The chapter details the relationship between discrete-time signals and their corresponding frequency spectra, emphasizing the periodic nature of the DTFT in the frequency domain. Key properties of the DTFT, including linearity, time shifting, frequency shifting, convolution, and duality, are thoroughly examined, showcasing how these properties facilitate signal processing tasks. The chapter also discusses the relationship between the DTFT and other transforms, such as the z-transform, clarifying their respective applications and contexts. Additionally, the concept of the sampling theorem is introduced, highlighting its importance in reconstructing continuous signals from discrete samples. The chapter concludes with practical examples and applications of the DTFT, illustrating its relevance in various fields such as communications, audio processing, and control systems, providing readers with a solid foundation for further studies in signal processing.

EXERCISES

1. Find the DTFT of the discrete-time unit impulse signal $2\delta(n)$.
2. Given the finite-length sequence x(n) ={1, 2, 3, 4} for n = 0, 1, 2, 3, compute its DTFT X(ω).
3. Find the inverse DTFT of $X(\omega) = 1 + 2e^{-j\omega} + e^{-j2\omega}$.
4. Determine the DTFT of the discrete-time complex exponential sequence $x(n) = e^{j2\omega 0n}$.
5. Calculate the DTFT of the rectangular pulse x(n) = 1 for n = 0, 1, 2, ..., N −1.
6. Given x(n) = {1, 2, 1}, compute the magnitude and phase of its DTFT 2X(ω).
7. Given the impulse response h(n) = {1,-1, 1}, determine the frequency response H(ω) of the system.
8. Given two sequences x(n) ={1, 2, 1} and h(n) ={1,-1} , use the DTFT to find their convolution y(n) = x(n) ⋆ h(n).
9. Find the DTFT of sequence $x(n) = a^n u(-n-1)$, where a is real number.
10. Find the DTFT of sequence $x(n) = (1/3)^n u(n-2)$.
11. Find the inverse DTFT of X(ω) as

$$X(\omega) = \frac{2-5/4e^{-j\omega}}{1/16e^{-j2\omega}-3/8e^{-j\omega}+1/2}.$$

Multiple Choice Questions

1. What is the fundamental period of the DTFT for a discrete-time signal x[n]?

   A. 2π

   B. π

   C. 1

   D. 0

2. The DTFT of a discrete-time signal x[n] is given by:

   A. $X(\omega) = \sum_{n=-\infty}^{\infty} x(n)\, e^{-jn\omega}$

   B. $X(\omega) = \int_{-\infty}^{\infty} x(n)\, e^{-jn\omega} d\omega$

   C. $X(\omega) = \sum_{n=-\infty}^{\infty} x(n)\, e^{jn\omega}$

   D. $X(\omega) = \int_{-\infty}^{\infty} x(n)\, e^{jn\omega} d\omega$

3. Which of the following is the inverse DTFT formula?

   A. $x(n) = \frac{1}{2\pi}\int_{-\infty}^{\infty} X(\omega)\, e^{-jn\omega} d\omega$

   B. $x(n) = \frac{1}{2\pi}\int_{-\pi}^{\pi} X(\omega)\, e^{-jn\omega} d\omega$

C. $x(n) = \int_{-\pi}^{\pi} X(\omega)\, e^{-jn\omega} d\omega$

D. $x(n) = \frac{1}{2\pi} \int_{-\pi}^{\pi} X(\omega)\, e^{jn\omega} d\omega$

4. Which property of DTFT states that if x[n] is real, then $X(e^{j\omega})$ satisfies:

   A. $X(e^{j\omega})=X(e^{-j\omega})$

   B. $X(e^{j\omega})=X^*(e^{-j\omega})$

   C. $X(e^{j\omega})=X(-e^{j\omega})$

   D. $X(e^{j\omega})=-X^*(e^{-j\omega})$

5. What is the DTFT of the unit impulse signal δ[n-1]?

   A. 1

   B. $e^{-j\omega}$

   C. $e^{j\omega}$

   D. δ(ω)

6. The DTFT of a shifted signal $x[n-n_0]$ is given by:

   A. $e^{-j\omega n0}X(e^{j\omega})$

   B. $e^{j\omega n0}X(e^{j\omega})$

   C. $X(e^{j\omega-n0})$

   D. $X(e^{j\omega+n0})$

7. What is the DTFT of $x[n]=a^n u[n]$, where $|a|<1$?

   A. $1/(1-ae^{-j\omega})$

   B. $1/(1+ae^{-j\omega})$

   C. $1/(1-ae^{j\omega})$

   D. $1/(1+ae^{j\omega})$

8. The DTFT of the signal $x[n]=\cos(\omega_0 n)$ is:

   A. $\pi[\delta(\omega-\omega_0)+\delta(\omega+\omega_0)]$

   B. $0.5[\delta(\omega-\omega_0)+\delta(\omega+\omega_0)]$

   C. $0.5[\delta(\omega-\omega_0)-\delta(\omega+\omega_0)]$

   D. $\delta(\omega_0)$

9. Which operation in the time domain corresponds to modulation in the frequency domain in DTFT?

   A. Multiplication

   B. Convolution

   C. Shifting

   D. Differentiation

10. What is the effect of time-domain convolution on the DTFT of two signals x[n] and h[n]?

   A. Addition of $X(e^{j\omega})$ and $H(e^{j\omega})$

   B. Multiplication of $X(e^{j\omega})$ and $H(e^{j\omega})$

C. Division of $X(e^{j\omega})$ by $H(e^{j\omega})$

D. Subtraction of $X(e^{j\omega})$ and $H(e^{j\omega})$

ANSWERS

1	2	3	4	5	6	7	8	9	10
A	A	D	B	B	A	A	B	A	B

KNOW MORE

For more information related to this topic scan the QR code.

OR

Type this link in your browser

https://www.google.co.in/books/edition/_/H_5SAAAAMAAJ?hl=en&gbpv=0

REFERENCES AND SUGGESTED READING

1. B. P. Lathi, "*Principles of Linear Systems and Signals*," *Oxford Second edition*, 2009.
2. John G. Proakis, and Dimitris G. Manolakis "*Digital signal processing: principles, algorithms, and applications, 4/E*,"*Pearson Education India*, 2007.
3. Alan V. Oppenheim, Alan S. Willsky, and S. Hamid Nawab "*Signals & Systems*,"*Pearson Education India*, 1997.
4. P. Singh, A. Singhal, B. Fatimah, A. Gupta; S. Dutt Joshi "*Proper Definitions of Dirichlet Conditions and Convergence of Fourier Representations [Lecture Notes]*,"*IEEE Signal Processing Magazine*, vol. 39, no. 5, pp. 77-84, 2022.
5. Barrie W. Jervis, and Emmanuel C. Ifeachor "*Digital Signal Processing: A Practical Approach*,"*Pearson Education India*, 2002.

Chapter 6: DFT: Discrete Fourier Transform

UNIT SPECIFICS

The discrete Fourier transform (DFT) chapter covers the fundamental concepts and mathematical foundations of transforming discrete-time signals from the time domain to the frequency domain. Unit specifics include the derivation and properties of the DFT, such as periodicity, symmetry, and linearity, which are essential for understanding signal behavior in the frequency domain. The chapter also explores practical aspects of DFT computation, including algorithmic implementation using matrix representation and the relationship between DFT and the continuous Fourier transform (CFT). Additionally, it discusses the limitations and challenges of DFT, like spectral leakage and resolution, and introduces techniques for mitigating these issues.

RATIONALE

The DFT chapter is crucial because it provides a fundamental tool for analyzing and processing discrete signals in the frequency domain. The rationale behind studying DFT is to enable the transformation of discrete-time signals into their frequency components, facilitating tasks such as filtering, spectral analysis, and signal reconstruction. DFT is widely used in various applications, including audio and image processing, telecommunications, and radar systems. Understanding the DFT allows for efficient implementation of algorithms like the Fast Fourier Transform (FFT), making it essential for both theoretical and practical aspects of digital signal processing.

PRE-REQUISITE

Discrete-time signals and systems, z transform, DTFT

UNIT OUTCOMES

List of outcomes of this unit is as follows:

U6-O1: Fundamentals of DFT and its properties

U6-O2: Circular convolution

U6-O3: DFT based signal filtering

U6-O4: DFT application in OFDM system

Unit-6 Outcomes	EXPECTED MAPPING WITH COURSE OUTCOMES (1- Weak Correlation; 2- Medium correlation; 3- Strong Correlation)					
	CO-1	CO-2	CO-3	CO-4	CO-5	CO-6
U6-O1	–	3	2	1	–	–
U6-O2	–	3	2	1	–	–
U6-O3	–	3	2	1	–	–
U6-O4	–	3	2	1	–	–

6.1 INTRODUCTION

The discrete Fourier transform (DFT) stands as a foundational pillar in signal pro- cessing, serving as a powerful tool for analyzing the frequency content of discrete- time signals. This book chapter embarks on an exploration of the theoretical under- pinnings, practical applications, and computational aspects of the DFT.

Beginning with a comprehensive introduction to the DFT definition and its mathematical formulation, the chapter navigates through key concepts such as the discrete-time Fourier series, the relationship between the DFT and the continuous Fourier Trans- form (CTFT), and the interpretation of DFT coefficients in the frequency domain. Through illustrative examples and intuitive explanations, readers gain insights into the fundamental principles underlying the DFT, including its role in spectral anal- ysis, filtering, and digital signal processing. By bridging theoretical concepts with real-world applications, this chapter aims to equip readers with a holistic under- standing of the DFT, empowering them to leverage its capabilities in solving com- plex signal processing challenges and advancing technological innovations.

6.2 DFT DEFINITION

DTFT of a discrete-time signal $x(n)$ in the previous chapter is expressed as

$$X(\omega) = \sum_{n=\infty}^{\infty} x(n)e^{-j\omega n}$$

Here, continuous spectra $X(\omega)$ is periodic with period 2π, i.e., $X(\omega + 2\pi) = X(\omega)$.Take N samples in the frequency range from 0 to 2π as $\omega = 2\pi k/N$, $k = 0, 1, 2, ..., N - 1$. Interval between two consecutive samples is 2π , as shown in Figure 6.1.

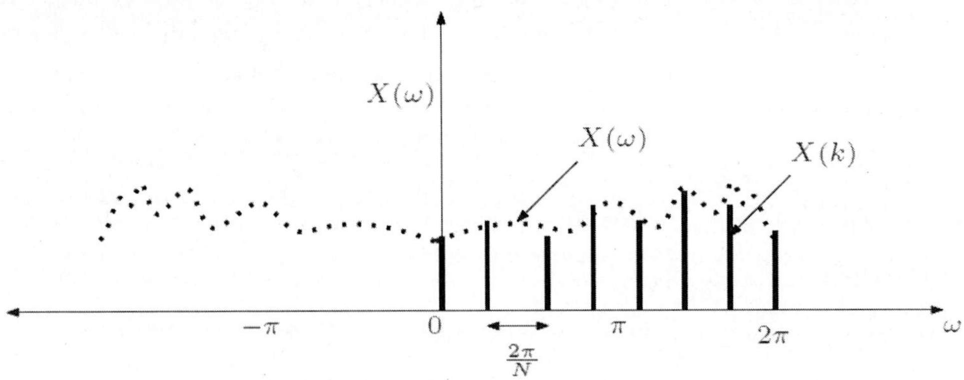

Fig. 6.1: Sampling illustration of X(ω)

Sampled sequence is written as

$$X(k) = X(\omega)|_{\omega=2\pi k/N} = \sum_{n=-\infty}^{\infty} x(n)e^{-\frac{j2\pi kn}{N}}, k = 0, 1, ..., N-1.$$

$$X(k) = ... + \sum_{n=-N}^{-1} x(n)e^{-\frac{j2\pi kn}{N}} + \sum_{n=0}^{N-1} x(n)e^{-\frac{j2\pi kn}{N}} + \sum_{n=N}^{2N-1} x(n)e^{-\frac{j2\pi kn}{N}} + ...$$

$$X(k) = \sum_{l=-\infty}^{\infty} \left[\sum_{n=lN}^{lN+N-1} x(n)e^{-\frac{j2\pi kn}{N}} \right]. \quad (6.1)$$

Substitute $n - lN = n'$ a dummy variable and change the order of summation, we get

$$X(k) = \sum_{n=0}^{N-1}\left[\sum_{l=-\infty}^{\infty} x(n-lN)\right] e^{-\frac{j2\pi kn}{N}} = \sum_{n=0}^{N-1} x_p(n) e^{-\frac{j2\pi kn}{N}}, \tag{6.2}$$

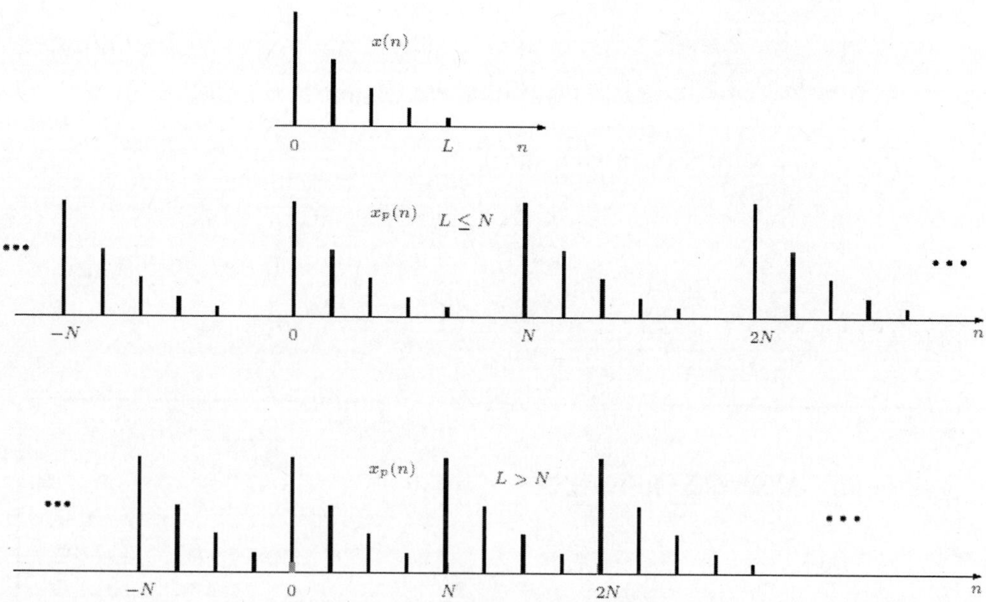

Fig. 6.2: relation between $x_p(n)$ and x(n)

where $x_p(n) = \sum_{l=-\infty}^{\infty} x(n-lN)$. $x_p(n)$

is the periodic extension of the signal $x(n)$ with time period N. *Let x(n) be the finite length sequence of the length L.* Therefore, $x_p(n)$ is generated using $x(n)$ with shifting it at $\pm lN$, as shown in Figure 6.2.

The $x(n)$ is nonzero in the interval $0 < n < L$ 1 for L length sequence, and $x(n) = x_p(n)$, $n = 0, 1, ..L - 1$ if $N \geq L$. Thus, $x(n)$ can be recovered from $x_p(n)$ without ambiguity. On the other hand, if $N < L$, it is not possible to recover from its periodic extension due to time domain aliasing. We conclude that the spectrum of an aperiodic discrete-time signal $x(n)$ with finite duration L can be exactly recovered from its samples at frequencies $\omega_k = 2\pi k/N$ if $N > L$.

Relation between $x(n)$ and $x_p(n)$ is expressed as

$$x(n) = \begin{cases} x_p(n), & \text{if } 0 \leq n \leq N-1 \\ 0, & \text{elsewhere.} \end{cases}$$

Therefore, $X(k)$ for a single time period signal ($x(n)$) is written as

$$X(k) = \sum_{n=0}^{N-1} x(n) e^{-\frac{j2\pi kn}{N}}, \quad k = 0, 1, ..., N-1.$$

and $X(k)$ is called N points DFT of signal $x(n)$.

Multiply DFT expression by $e^{j2\pi km/N}$ both sides and take average, i.e.,

$$\sum_{k=0}^{N-1} X(k)e^{\frac{j2\pi km}{N}} = \sum_{k=0}^{N-1}\sum_{n=0}^{N-1} x(n)e^{-\frac{j2\pi kn}{N}}e^{\frac{j2\pi km}{N}} = \sum_{n=0}^{N-1} x(n)\sum_{k=0}^{N-1} e^{-\frac{j2\pi k(n-m)}{N}}. \quad (6.4)$$

We can write

$$\sum_{k=0}^{N-1} e^{-\frac{j2\pi k(n-m)}{N}} = \begin{cases} N, & \text{if } n = m \\ 0, & \text{elsewhere.} \end{cases}$$

So

$$\sum_{k=0}^{N-1} X(k)e^{\frac{j2\pi km}{N}} = Nx(n)$$

$$x(n) = \frac{1}{N}\sum_{k=0}^{N-1} X(k)e^{\frac{j2\pi kn}{N}}, n = 0, 1, ..., N-1. \quad (6.5)$$

DFT:

$$X(k) = \sum_{n=0}^{N-1} x(n)e^{-\frac{j2\pi kn}{N}}, \quad k = 0, 1, ..., N-1$$

IDFT:

$$x(n) = \frac{1}{N}\sum_{k=0}^{N-1} X(k)e^{\frac{j2\pi kn}{N}}, \quad n = 0, 1, ..., N-1$$

6.3 RELATION BETWEEN DFT AND OTHER TRANSFORMS

$x_p(n)$ and $x(n)$: The periodic signal $x_p(n)$ is generated from $x(n)$ using the periodic extension of the signal $x(n)$, Hence, one time period $x_p(n)$ is written as

$$x_p(n) = \frac{1}{N}\sum_{k=0}^{N-1} X(k)e^{\frac{j2\pi kn}{N}}, n = 0, 1, ..N-1$$

Since $x\_p(n) = x(n)$.

DTFS and DFT: Periodic signal $x_p(n)$ using DTFS is expressed as

$$x_p(n) = \sum_{n=0}^{N-1} c_k e^{\frac{j2\pi kn}{N}}, n = 0, 1, ..., N-1$$

Fourier coefficients: $c_k = \frac{1}{N}\sum_{n=0}^{N-1} x_p(n)\, e^{\frac{-j2\pi kn}{N}}, k = 0, 1, \ldots, N-1$. For a single time period $X(k) = \sum_{n=0}^{N-1} x_p(n)\, e^{-\frac{j2\pi kn}{N}}$. Thus $c_k = \frac{1}{N}X(k)$ and $x_p(n) = \frac{1}{N}\sum_{k=0}^{N-1} X(k)\, e^{\frac{j2\pi kn}{N}}, n = 0, 1, ..N-1$. This relationship provides the reconstruction of the periodic signal $x\_p(n)$ from the samples of the spectrum $X(\omega)$, i.e., $X(k)$.

DTFT and DFT: DTFT $X(\omega)$ of a finite length (L, $L <= N$) senescence $x(n)$ is expressed as

$$X(\omega) = \sum_{n=0}^{N-1} x(n) e^{-j\omega n}$$

Further,

$$X(\omega) = \sum_{n=0}^{N-1} \left[\frac{1}{N} \sum_{k=0}^{N-1} X(k) e^{\frac{j2\pi kn}{N}} \right] e^{-j\omega n}$$

$$X(\omega) = \sum_{k=0}^{N-1} X(k) \left[\frac{1}{N} \sum_{n=0}^{N-1} e^{-j(\omega - \frac{2\pi kn}{N})} \right].$$

Let $P(\omega)$ be an interpolation function as

$$P(\omega) = \frac{1}{N} \sum_{n=0}^{N-1} e^{-j\omega n} = \frac{1}{N} \frac{1 - e^{-j\omega N}}{1 - e^{-j\omega}} = \frac{\sin(\omega N/2)}{N \sin(\omega/2)} e^{-j\omega(N-1)/2}.$$

Therefore,

$$X(\omega) = \sum_{k=0}^{N-1} X(k) P(\omega - 2\pi k/N), \quad N \geq L.$$

Given DFT samples $X(k)$, we can generate DTFT signal $X(\omega)$ after passing through a interpolation function $P(\omega - 2\pi k/N)$.

CTFT and DFT: First, we can get the DTFT signal from the DFT as

$$X(\omega) = \sum_{k=0}^{N-1} X(k) P(\omega - 2\pi k/N)$$

CTFT $X(\Omega)$ and DFT $X(\omega)$ are related as

$$X(\omega) = F_s \sum_{n=-\infty}^{\infty} X(\Omega - n2\pi F_s)$$

Here F_s is the sampling frequency of the continuous time signal. So $X(\Omega)$ is recovered form the $X(\omega)$ after passing through a lowpass filter, as shown in Fig. 6.3.

CTFS and DFT: Conterminous time periodic signal $x_p(t)$ with period $T_0 = 1/F_0$ has CTFS as

$$x_p(t) = \sum_{k=-\infty}^{\infty} c_k e^{j2\pi k F_0 t}, \quad t \in [0, T_0]. \tag{6.6}$$

c_k denotes the Fourier series coefficients. After sampling at a rate $F_s = NF_0$, $x_p(t)$ is expressed as

$$x_p(t = nF_s) = x(n) = \sum_{k=-\infty}^{\infty} c_k e^{j2\pi k F_0 \frac{n}{F_s}} = \sum_{k=-\infty}^{\infty} c_k e^{\frac{j2\pi kn}{N}}$$

$$= \ldots + \sum_{k=-N}^{-1} c_k e^{\frac{j2\pi kn}{N}} + \sum_{k=0}^{N-1} c_k e^{\frac{j2\pi kn}{N}} + \sum_{k=N}^{2N-1} c_k e^{\frac{j2\pi kn}{N}} + \ldots \tag{6.7}$$

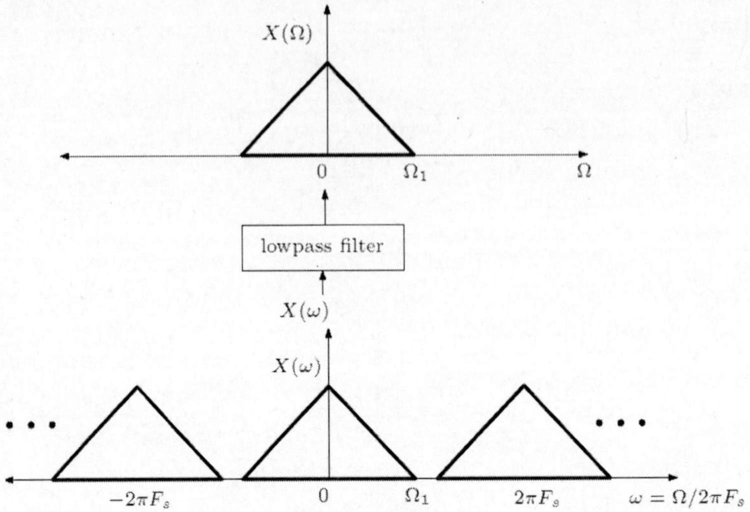

Fig. 6.3: DTFT and

CTFT plot

$$x(n) = \sum_{l=-\infty}^{\infty} \sum_{k=lN}^{lN-1} c_k e^{\frac{j2\pi kn}{N}}$$

$$= \sum_{k=0}^{N-1} \underbrace{\sum_{l=-\infty}^{\infty} c_{k-lN}}_{\tilde{c}_k} e^{\frac{j2\pi kn}{N}} = \sum_{k=0}^{N-1} \tilde{c}_k e^{\frac{j2\pi kn}{N}}. \quad \text{comparing to IDFT} \qquad (6.8)$$

$$\tilde{c}_k = X(k)\frac{1}{N} = \sum_{l=-\infty}^{\infty} c_{k-lN}\frac{1}{N}.$$

Here $\tilde{c}_k$ is the aliased version of c_k. If c_k has non-zero values less than the N, $\tilde{c}_k$ is the periodic extension of c_k only.

z-transform and DFT: *z*-transform of a finite length sequence *x*(*n*) is given as

$$X(z) = \sum_{n=0}^{N-1} x(n) z^{-n}$$

After substituting the value of *x*(*n*) in terms if *X*(*k*)

$$X(z) = \sum_{n=0}^{N-1} \left[\frac{1}{N} \sum_{k=0}^{N-1} X(k) e^{\frac{j2\pi kn}{N}} \right] z^{-n}$$

$$= \frac{1}{N} \sum_{k=0}^{N-1} X(k) \sum_{n=0}^{N-1} \left(z^{-1} e^{\frac{j2\pi k}{N}}\right)^n = \frac{1}{N} \sum_{k=0}^{N-1} X(k) \frac{1 - z^{-N} e^{\frac{j2\pi kN}{N}}}{1 - z^{-1} e^{\frac{j2\pi k}{N}}}. \qquad (6.9)$$

$$X(z) = \frac{1 - z^{-N}}{N} \sum_{k=0}^{N-1} \frac{X(k)}{1 - z^{-1} e^{\frac{j2\pi k}{N}}}. \qquad (6.10)$$

Further, z-transform is given as

$$X(z) = \sum_{n=-\infty}^{\infty} x(n) z^{-n}$$

If ROC includes the unit circle, substituting $z = e^{j\omega} = e$ N samples on the circle DFT is expressed as

$$X(k) = \sum_{n=-\infty}^{\infty} x(n) e^{\frac{-j2\pi kn}{N}}, \quad k = 0, 1, ..., N-1.$$

A summary of various transforms is given in Fig. 6.4, where we highlight that any transform can be derived from the DFT $X(k)$.

N and collecting

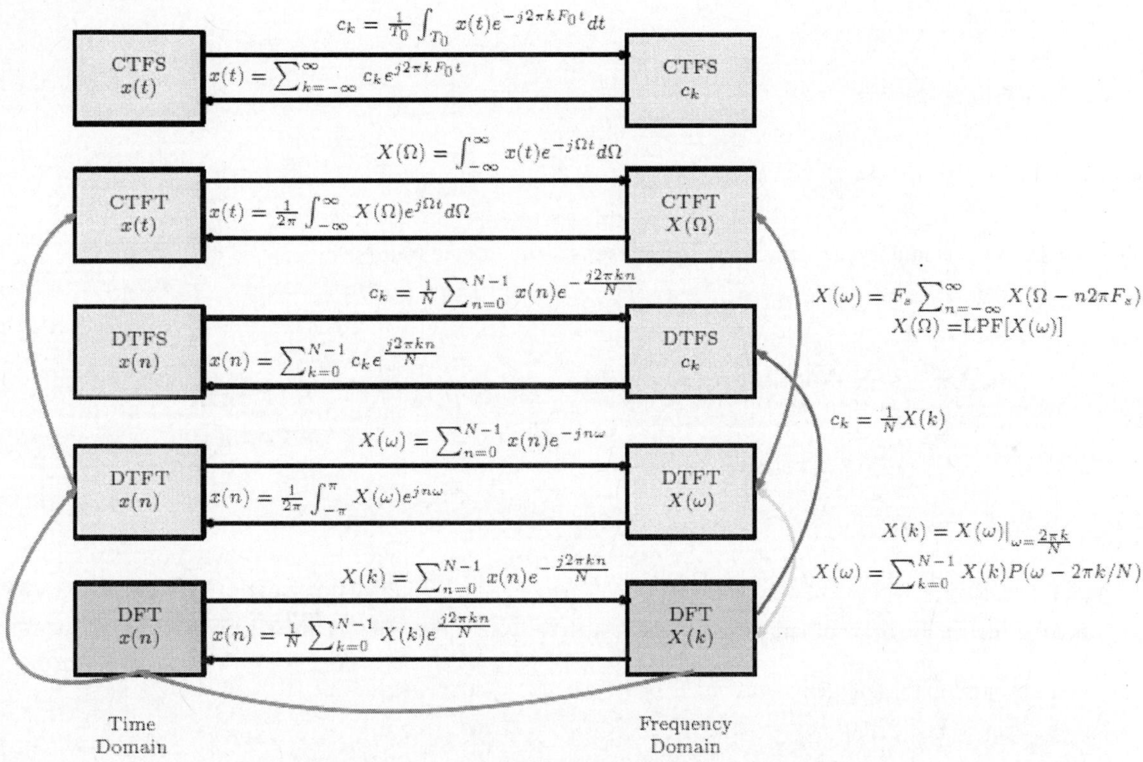

Fig. 6.4: Relation and summary of various transforms

6.3.1 DFT matrix

DFT matrix is a square matrix used to compute the DFT and its inverse efficiently. DFT matrix of size $N \times N$ is expressed as DFT matrix is expressed as

$$\mathbf{W}_N = \begin{bmatrix} W_N^{0.0} & W_N^{0.1} & \cdots & W_N^{0.(N-2)} & W_N^{0.(N-1)} \\ W_N^{1.0} & W_N^{1.1} & \cdots & W_N^{1.(N-2)} & W_N^{1.(N-1)} \\ W_N^{2.0} & W_N^{2.1} & \cdots & W_N^{2.(N-2)} & W_N^{2.(N-1)} \\ \cdots \\ W_N^{(N-2).0} & W_N^{(N-2).1} & \cdots & W_N^{(N-2).(N-2)} & W_N^{(N-2).(N-1)} \\ W_N^{(N-1).0} & W_N^{(N-1).1} & \cdots & W_N^{(N-1).(N-2)} & W_N^{(N-1).(N-1)} \end{bmatrix}_{N\times N}$$

$W_N = e^{\frac{-j2\pi}{N}}$, where *k*, *n* are indices ranging from 0 to $N-1$ for rows and columns, respectively.

The rows and columns of the DFT matrix are orthogonal to each other. For example, first row and second row are orthogonal, i.e.,

$$\begin{bmatrix}1 & 1 & 1 & 1\end{bmatrix} .* \begin{bmatrix}1 & -j & -1 & j\end{bmatrix} = 1 - j - 1 + j = 0$$

So we can write

$$\mathbf{W}_{N}^{m}, .* \mathbf{W}_N^{l} = \begin{cases} N, & \text{if } m = l \\ 0, & \text{if } m \neq l \end{cases}$$

The DFT matrix is unitary, meaning that its inverse is its conjugate transpose,

i.e.,

$$\mathbf{W}_N^{-1} = \frac{1}{N}\mathbf{W}_N^{\star}$$

$$\mathbf{W}_N\mathbf{W}_N^{\star} = \mathbf{W}_N^{\star}\mathbf{W}_N = N\mathbf{I}_N,$$

or

where $\mathbf{I}_N$ is an $N \times N$ identity matrix. Here $\mathbf{W}\star = \mathbf{W}^H$ denotes the conjugate transpose of $\mathbf{W}_N$. The eigenvalues of the DFT matrix are roots of unity, specifically, *N* th roots of unity. That is, the eigenvalues are of the form

$e^{\frac{-j2\pi(k)}{N}}$ example, $N = 4$, eigenvalues are 1, $-j$, $+j$, -1.

where $k = 0, 1, \ldots N-1$. For

The DFT matrix exhibits symmetry in its structure. Specifically, it can be partitioned into *N*/2 submatrices that are related by a certain permutation and scaling, depending on whether *N* is even or odd.

6.4 PROPERTIES OF DFT

Periodicity

The DFT exhibits periodicity in both the time and frequency domains due to the discrete nature of the sampled signals it operates on. Periodicity allows us to analyze signals efficiently by considering only one period of the signal or spectrum.

$$x(N+n) = x(n)\ \forall n \text{ and } X(N+k) = X(k)\ \forall k$$

$$X(k) = \sum_{n=0}^{N-1} x(n)e^{\frac{-j2\pi kn}{N}}$$

$$X(k+N) = \sum_{n=0}^{N-1} x(n)e^{\frac{-j2\pi(k+N)n}{N}} = \sum_{n=0}^{N-1} x(n)e^{\frac{-j2\pi kn}{N}} \underbrace{e^{\frac{-j2\pi kN}{N}}}_{1} = X(k) \quad (6.11)$$

$$x(n) = \frac{1}{N}\sum_{k=0}^{N-1} X(k)e^{\frac{j2\pi kn}{N}}$$

$$x(n+N) = \frac{1}{N}\sum_{k=0}^{N-1} X(k)e^{\frac{j2\pi k(n+N)}{N}} = \frac{1}{N}\sum_{k=0}^{N-1} X(k)e^{\frac{j2\pi kn}{N}} \underbrace{e^{\frac{j2\pi kN}{N}}}_{1} = x(n) \quad (6.12)$$

Linearity:

Let $x_1(n) \leftrightarrow X_1(k)$ and $x_2(n) \leftrightarrow X_2(k)$ are N point DFTs. Then

$a_1x_1(n) + a_2x_2(n) \leftrightarrow a_1X_1(k) + a_2X_2(k)$

Circular symmetries of a signal:

Circular shift of the signal $x'(n)$ can be represented as the index modulo N of original signal $x(n)$ as

$x'(n) = x((n-k)_N)$

For example, finite length N right side sequence $x(n)$ is represented by N points on the circle using anticlock wise direction as $x(n) = \{1, 2, 3, 4, 5, 6, 7, \underset{\uparrow}{8}\}$.

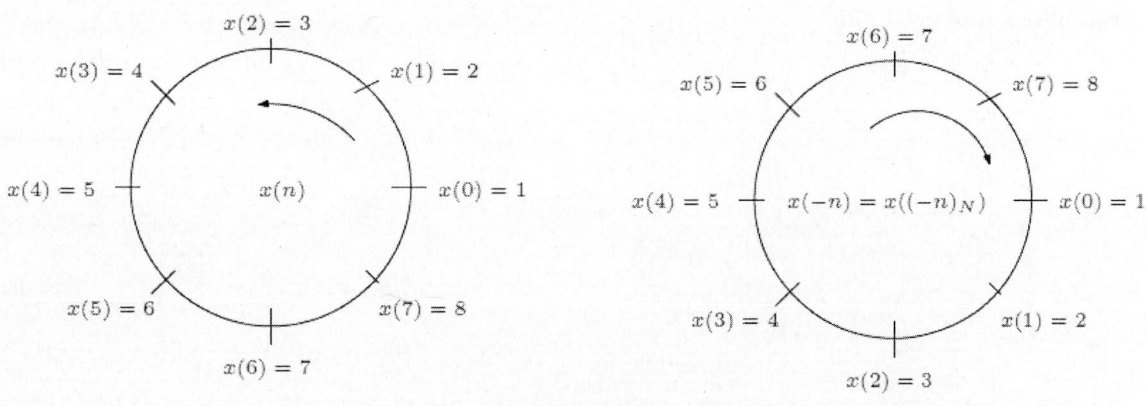

Fig. 6.5: Circular shift of a sequence.

Signal $x(n)$ is shown in Figure 6.5 by considering 8 points. The time reversal $x(-n)$ of the signal $x(n)$ is also shown in Figure 6.5, which is equivalent to $x(-n) = x((-n)_N)$.

Similarly, left sight sequence is represented by N points on the circle using clock wise direction as $x(n) = \{1, 2, 3, 4, 5, 6, 7, \mathbf{8}\}$. Left side sequence $x(n)$ is shown in Figure 6.6, and its left and right shift by unit one is also shown in Figure 6.6.

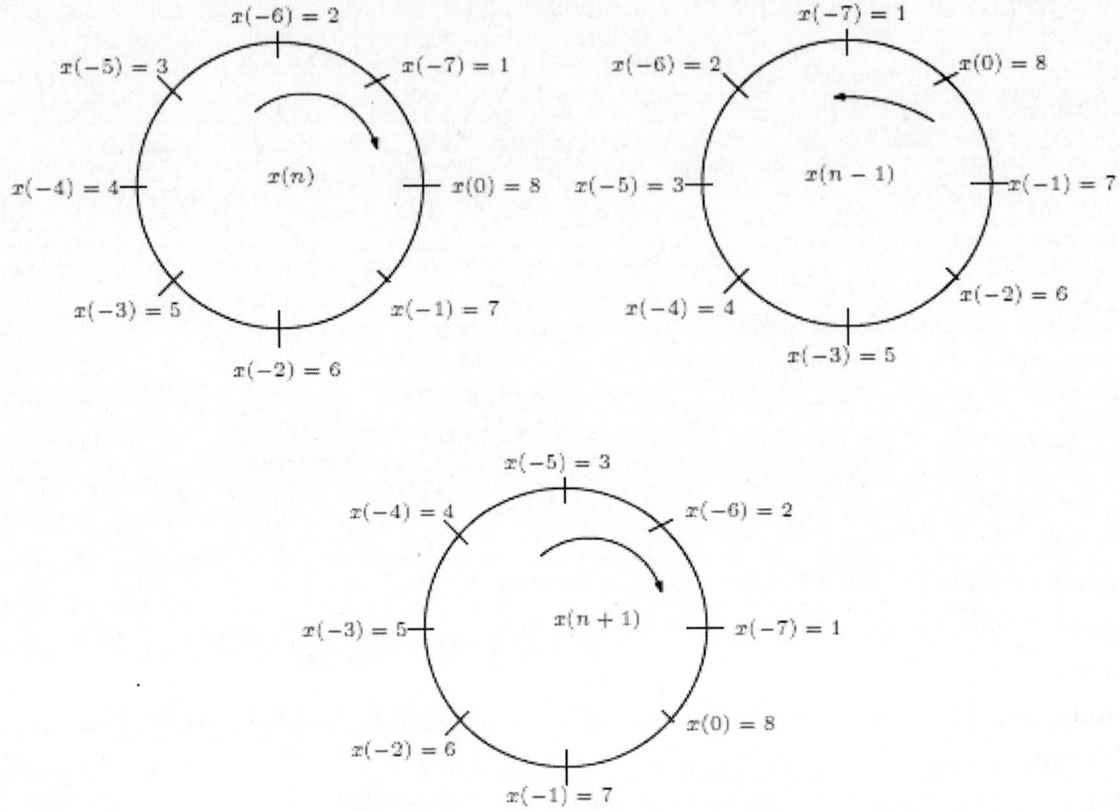

Fig. 6.6: Circular shift of a sequence.

Multiplication of two DFTs:

Let $x_1(n)$<-->$X_1(k)$ and $x_2(n)$<-->$X_2(k)$ are N point DFTs. Their multiplication is written as $X(k) = X_1(k)X_2(k)$, where

$$X_1(k) = \sum_{n=0}^{N-1} x_1(n)e^{-\frac{j2\pi kn}{N}}.$$

and

$$X_2(k) = \sum_{n=0}^{N-1} x_2(n)e^{-\frac{j2\pi kn}{N}}.$$

The IDFT of $X(k)$ is

$$x(m) = \frac{1}{N}\sum_{k=0}^{N-1} X(k)e^{\frac{j2\pi kn}{N}} = \frac{1}{N}\sum_{k=0}^{N-1} X_1(k)X_2(k)e^{\frac{j2\pi km}{N}}. \tag{6.13}$$

$$x(m) = \frac{1}{N}\sum_{k=0}^{N-1}\left[\sum_{n=0}^{N-1} x_1(n)e^{-\frac{j2\pi kn}{N}}\right]\left[\sum_{l=0}^{N-1} x_2(l)e^{-\frac{j2\pi kl}{N}}\right]e^{\frac{j2\pi km}{N}}$$

$$= \sum_{n=0}^{N-1} x_1(n)\sum_{l=0}^{N-1} x_2(l)\frac{1}{N}\sum_{k=0}^{N-1} e^{-\frac{j2\pi k(m-n-l)}{N}}. \qquad (6.14)$$

$\sum_{k=0}^{N-1} a^k = \begin{cases} N & \text{if } a = 1 \\ \frac{1-a^N}{1-a} & a \neq 1 \end{cases}$ Here $a = e^{-\frac{j2\pi k(m-n-l)}{N}}$, for $a = 1$, $(m-n-l)$ is multiple of N so $l = m - n + pN$, where $p \in \mathbb{Z}$.

$$x(m) = \sum_{n=0}^{N-1} x_1(n)\sum_{l=0}^{N-1} x_2(l)\underbrace{\frac{1}{N}\sum_{k=0}^{N-1} e^{-\frac{j2\pi k(m-n-l)}{N}}}_{1}$$

$$= \sum_{n=0}^{N-1} x_1(n)x_2(m-n+pN) = \sum_{n=0}^{N-1} x_1(n)x_2((m-n)_N),\ m = 0, 1, ..., N-1 \qquad (6.15)$$

This above expression is called circular convolution of two sequences $x_1(n)$ and $x_2(n)$. Circular convolution is used in various applications, including digital signal processing, communication systems, and filter design.

Circular convolution:

Circular convolution is a mathematical operation that combines two sequences to produce a third sequence. It's called "circular" because the operation as- sumes that the sequences repeat periodically.

If $x_1(n) \leftrightarrow X_1(k)$ and $x_2(n) \leftrightarrow X_2(k)$ are N point DFTs, then

$$x_1(n) \textcircled{N} x_2(n) \leftrightarrow X_1(k)X_2(k)$$

$$x_1(n) \textcircled{N} x_2(n) = \sum_{m=0}^{N-1} x_1(m)x_2((n-m)_N),\ n = 0, 1, ..., N-1 \qquad (6.16)$$

Here $x_1(n) \textcircled{N} x_2(n)$ denotes the circular convolution.

Time reversal:

If $x(n) \leftrightarrow X(k)$, $x((-n)_N) = x(N-n) \leftrightarrow X((-k)_N) = X(N-k)$
Therefore, reversing the N-point sequence in time is analogous to reversing the values of the DFT.

$$\text{DFT}[x((-n)_N)] = \sum_{n=0}^{N-1} x((N-n))e^{-\frac{j2\pi kn}{N}},\ k = 0, 1, ..., N-1$$

use dummy variable $N - n = m$

$$= \sum_{m=0}^{N-1} x(m)e^{-\frac{j2\pi(-k)m}{N}}\underbrace{e^{-\frac{j2\pi kN}{N}}}_{1}$$

$$= X((-k)_N) = X(N-k). \qquad (6.17)$$

Circular time shift: If $x(n) \leftrightarrow X(k)$, then

$$x((n-l)_N) \leftrightarrow X(k)e^{-\frac{j2\pi kl}{N}}.$$

$$\text{DFT}[x((n-l)_N)] = \sum_{n=0}^{N-1} x((n-l)_N)e^{-\frac{j2\pi kn}{N}}, \quad k = 0, 1, ..., N-1$$

replace modulo operation first

$$\sum_{n=l}^{N-1} x(n-l)e^{-\frac{j2\pi kn}{N}} + \underbrace{\sum_{n=0}^{l-1} x(n-l+N)e^{-\frac{j2\pi kn}{N}}}_{\text{this part we need to consider in modulo}} \tag{6.18}$$

Use dummy variable $n - l + N = m$

$$= \sum_{n=l}^{N-1} x(n-l)e^{-\frac{j2\pi kn}{N}} + \sum_{m=N-l}^{N-1} x(m)e^{-\frac{j2\pi k(l+m)}{N}} \underbrace{e^{\frac{j2\pi k(N)}{N}}}_{1}$$

use dummy variable $n - l = m$

$$= \sum_{m=0}^{N-l-1} x(m)e^{-\frac{j2\pi k(l+m)}{N}} + \sum_{m=N-l}^{N-1} x(m)e^{-\frac{j2\pi k(l+m)}{N}} = \sum_{m=0}^{N-l} x(m)e^{-\frac{j2\pi k(l+m)}{N}}. \tag{6.19}$$

$$= e^{-\frac{j2\pi kl}{N}} \sum_{m=0}^{N-l} x(m)e^{-\frac{j2\pi km}{N}} = X(k)e^{-\frac{j2\pi kl}{N}}. \tag{6.20}$$

Therefore,

$$x((n-l)_N) \leftrightarrow X(k)e^{-\frac{j2\pi kl}{N}}.$$

Circular time shift results in phase shift in the DFT.

Frequency convolution:

If $x_1(n) \leftrightarrow X_1(k)$ and $x_2(n) \leftrightarrow X_2(k)$, then

$$x_1(n)x_2(n) \leftrightarrow \tfrac{1}{N}X_1(k) \textcircled{N} X_2(k),$$

Here circle N denotes the N point circulation convolution.

$$X(k) = \text{DFT}[x_1(n)x_2(n)] = \sum_{n=0}^{N-1} x_1(n)x_2(n)e^{-\frac{j2\pi kn}{N}}, \quad k = 0, 1, ..., N-1$$

Substitute values of $x_1(n)$ and $x_2(n)$

$$= \sum_{n=0}^{N-1} \left[\frac{1}{N}\sum_{m=0}^{N-1} X_1(m)e^{\frac{j2\pi mn}{N}}\right]\left[\frac{1}{N}\sum_{l=0}^{N-1} X_2(l)e^{\frac{j2\pi ln}{N}}\right] e^{-\frac{j2\pi kn}{N}} \tag{6.21}$$

$$X(k) = \frac{1}{N^2}\sum_{m=0}^{N-1} X_1(m)\sum_{l=0}^{N-1} X_2(l)\underbrace{\sum_{n=0}^{N-1} e^{\frac{j2\pi k(m-n+l)}{N}}}_{N}$$

For $l = (n-m)$ or $l = (n-m)_N$

$$= \frac{1}{N}\sum_{m=0}^{N-1} X_1(m)X_2(n-l)_N = \frac{1}{N}X_1(k)\textcircled{N}X_2(k) \qquad (6.22)$$

Parseval's theorem:

$$\sum_{n=0}^{N-1} x(n)y^*(n) = \frac{1}{N}\sum_{k=0}^{N-1} X(k)Y^*(k).$$

or

$$\sum_{n=0}^{N-1} |x(n)|^2 = \frac{1}{N}\sum_{k=0}^{N-1} |X(k)|^2.$$

Circular correlation:

$x(n) \leftrightarrow X(k)$ and $y(n) \leftrightarrow Y(k)$, then

$$\tilde{r}_{xy}(l) = \sum_{n=0}^{N-1} x(n)y^*((n-l)_N) \leftrightarrow \tilde{R}_{xy}(k) = X(k)Y^*(k)$$

It can be proved using the circular convolution property as

$$\tilde{r}_{xy}(l) = \sum_{n=0}^{N-1} x(n)y^*((n-l)_N) = x(l)\textcircled{N}y^*(-l)$$

Take DFT of both side $\tilde{R}_{xy}(k) = X(k)Y^*(k)$.

DFT Properties are summarized in Table 6.1. Further, different transforms between time-frequency domain are briefed in Table 6.2.

6.5 FILTERING OF LONG DATA SEQUENCES USING DFT

Filtering of long data sequences using the DFT *overlap-save* and *overlap-add* meth- ods are commonly used techniques in digital signal processing to efficiently apply finite impulse response (FIR) filters to long input sequences. Both methods exploit the circular convolution theorem and the properties of the DFT to break down the filtering process into smaller, more manageable chunks.

Table 6.1: Summary of DFT Properties

Property	Time Domain	Frequency Domain
Periodicity	$x(N+n) = x(n)$	$X(N+k) = X(k)$
Linearity	$a_1x_1(n) + a_2x_2(n)$	$a_1X_1(k) + a_2X_2(k)$
Time reversal	$x(-n) = x(N-n)$	$X(-k) = X(N-k)$
Circular time shift	$x((n-l)_N)$	$e^{-\frac{j2\pi kl}{N}}X(k)$
Circular frequency shift	$e^{\frac{j2\pi nl}{N}}x(n)$	$X((k-l)_N)$
Circular convolution	$x_1(n) \circledN x_2(n)$	$X_1(k)X_2(k)$
Multiplication of two signals	$x_1(n)x_2(n)$	$\frac{1}{N}X_1(k) \circledN X_2(k)$
Parseval's theorem	$\sum_{n=0}^{N-1} x_1(n)x_2^*(n)$	$\frac{1}{N}\sum_{k=0}^{N-1} X_1(k)X_2^*(k)$
Modulation	$x(n)\cos((2\pi k_0/N)n)$	$\frac{1}{2}X(k-k_0) + \frac{1}{2}X(k+k_0)$
Complex conjugate	$x^*(n)$	$X^*(N-k)$
Circular correlation	$x_1(n) \circledN x_2^*(-n)$	$X_1(k)X_2^*(k)$

Table 6.2: Different transforms between time-frequency domain

Transform	Time Domain	Frequency Domain
CT Fourier Series (CTFS)	Continuous, Periodic	Discrete, Aperiodic
CT Fourier Transform (CTFT)	Continuous, Aperiodic	Continuous, Aperiodic
DTFT	Discrete,Aperiodic	Continuous, Periodic
DT Fourier Series (DTFS)	Discrete, Periodic	Discrete, Periodic
DFT	Discrete, Periodic	Discrete, Periodic

Output of the FIR filter is written as

$$Y(k) = H(k)X(k),\ k = 0, 1, \ldots, N-1.$$

Here N is the DFT size of the data and FIR filter response. However, we can not have very large value of N due to hardware constraint and algorithm complexity.

6.5.1 Overlap-Save Method

The input data sequence is divided into segments, with each segment being of length L. Impulse response of FIR filter has length M. Therefore, we consider DFT size $N = L+M-1$ by adding some zero samples in the each block data and filter impulse response. First we compute N point DFT of impulse response $h(n)$ by adding $L-1$ samples and stored in the memory as

$$H(k) = \sum_{n=0}^{N-1} h(n)\, e^{\frac{-j2\pi kN}{N}}, \quad k=0, 1, \ldots, N-1$$

In overlap-save method, data points are added in the beginning of the each block as

$$x_1(n) = \overbrace{\{\underbrace{0, 0, \ldots, 0}_{(M-1)\text{zeros}}, \underbrace{x(0), x(1), \ldots, x(L-1)}_{L \text{ points from } x(n)}\}}^{N \text{ points}}.$$

Second block of length N is created as

$$x_2(n) = \overbrace{\{\underbrace{x(L-M+1), x(L-M+2), \ldots, x(L-1)}_{(M-1)\text{points from } x_1(n)}, \underbrace{x(L), x(L+1), \ldots, x(2L-1)}_{L \text{ points from } x(n)}\}}^{N \text{ points}}.$$

Similarly, third block of length N is created as

$$x_3(n) = \overbrace{\{\underbrace{x(2L-M+1), x(2L-M+2), \ldots, x(2L-1)}_{(M-1)\text{points from } x_2(n)}, \underbrace{x(2L), x(2L+1), \ldots, x(3L-1)}_{L \text{ points from } x(n)}\}}^{N \text{ points}}.$$

The ith block DFT is computed as $X_i(k)$ and output correspond to it is expressed as

$$Y_i(k) = H(k)X_i(k), \; k = 0, 1, 2, \ldots, N-1 \tag{6.23}$$

IDFT of each output block is calculated as $y_i(n)$ and these blocks are combined to get the complete output corresponding data signal $x(n)$.

Combined output signal is

$$y(n) = y_1(M), y_1(M+1), \ldots, y_1(N1), y_2(M), y_2(M+1), \ldots, y_2(N1), \ldots . \tag{6.24}$$

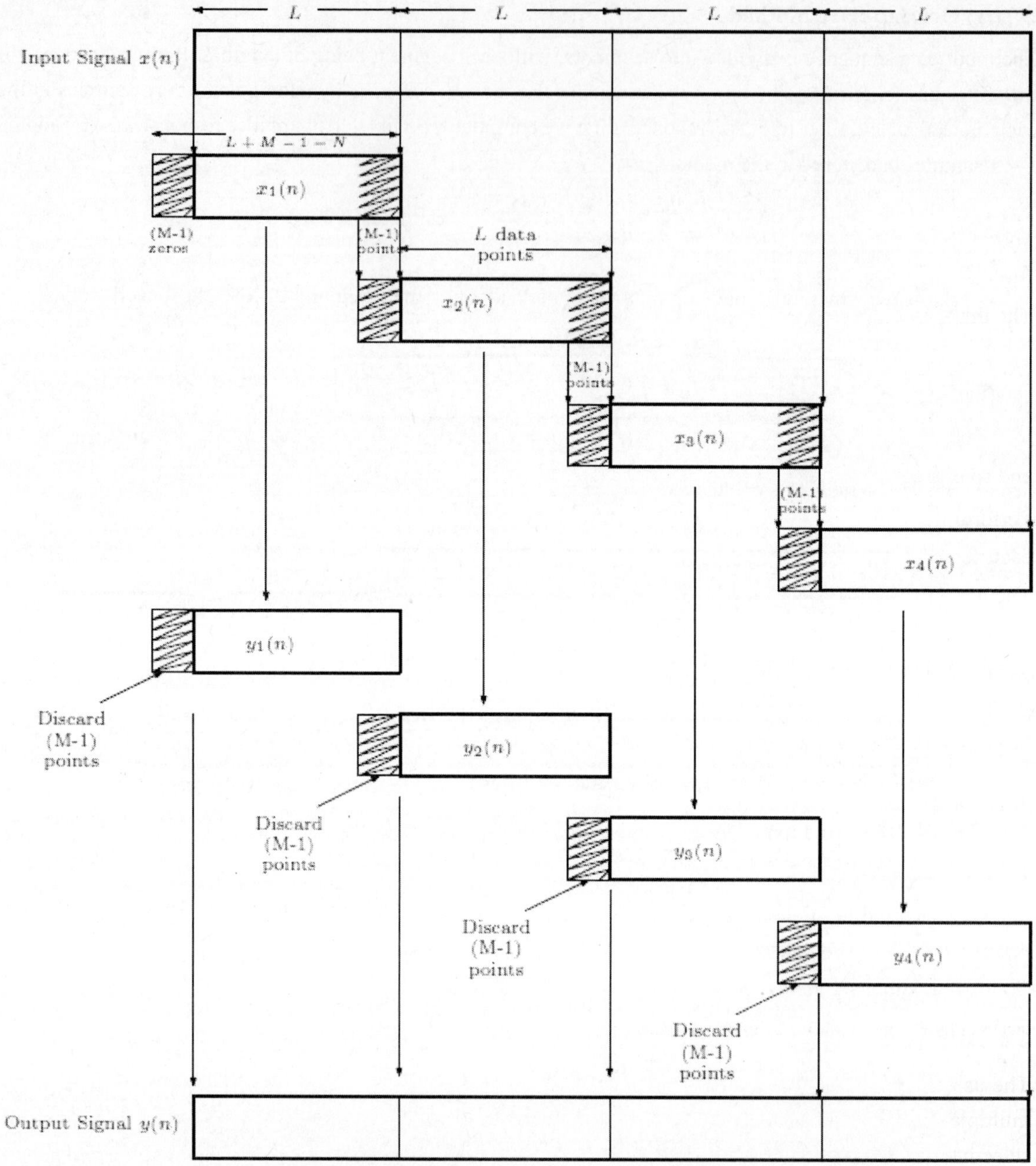

Fig. 6.7: Linear FIR filtering using the overlap-save method [1].

6.5.2 Overlap-Add Method

Similar to the overlap-save method, the input data sequence is segmented into over- lapping chunks, but with the addition of zero-padding to each segment to avoid aliasing.

First input data block of length $N = L + M - 1$ points is created as

$$x_1(n) = \{\underbrace{\overbrace{x(0), x(1), ..., x(L-1)}^{}}_{L \text{ points from x(n)}}, \underbrace{0, 0, ..., 0}_{(M-1)\text{zeros}}\}^{N \text{ points}}.$$

Here we have added (M1) zeros at the ending of the L data points. Similarly second block is created as

$$x_2(n) = \overbrace{\{\underbrace{x(L), x(L+1), ..., x(2L-1)}_{L \text{ points from x(n)}}, \underbrace{0, 0, ..., 0}_{(M-1)\text{zeros}}\}}^{N \text{ points}}.$$

The third block is created as

$$x_3(n) = \overbrace{\{\underbrace{x(2L), x(2L+1), ..., x(3L-1)}_{L \text{ points from x(n)}}, \underbrace{0, 0, ..., 0}_{(M-1)\text{zeros}}\}}^{N \text{ points}}.$$

and so on.

Perform the DFT of each zero-padded segment. After that multiply the frequency- domain representation of each segment by the frequency response of the FIR filter. Perform the inverse DFT on each filtered segment. The ith block DFT is computed as $X_i(k)$ and output correspond to it is expressed as

$$Y_i(k) = H(k)X_i(k),\ k = 0, 1, 2, ..., N-1 \tag{6.25}$$

IDFT of each output block is calculated as $y_i(n)$ and these blocks are combined to get the complete output corresponding data signal $x(n)$.

In the output side previous block's last $(M-1)$ points are added the to current block's first $(M-1)$ data points to get the combined output as

$$\begin{aligned} y(n) = \{&y_1(0), y_1(1), ..., y_1(L-1), y_1(L) + y_2(0), y_1(L+1) + y_2(1), ..., \\ &y_1(N-2) + y_2(M-2), y_1(N-1) + y_2(M-1), y_2(M), y_2(M+1), ..., y_2(L-1), \\ &y_2(L) + y_3(0), y_2(L+1) + y_3(1), ... \\ &y_2(N-2) + y_3(M-2), y_2(N-1) + y_3(M-1), y_3(M), y_3(M+1), ...\}. \end{aligned} \tag{6.26}$$

6.6 DFT IN OFDM

The use of DFT in OFDM systems enables efficient modulation and demodulation of data symbols across multiple orthogonal subcarriers. It allows for high spectral efficiency and robustness against frequency-selective fading channels. Additionally, the orthogonality between subcarriers minimizes inter-symbol interference (ISI) and simplifies equalization at the receiver. Overall, the DFT plays a crucial role in enabling the implementation and performance of OFDM systems.

The linear convolution can be converted into circular convolution by adding Cyclic Prefix (CP) in the OFDM architecture. The last L samples of the N-sample time- domain symbol and concatenates it to the front of the symbol to be transmitted.

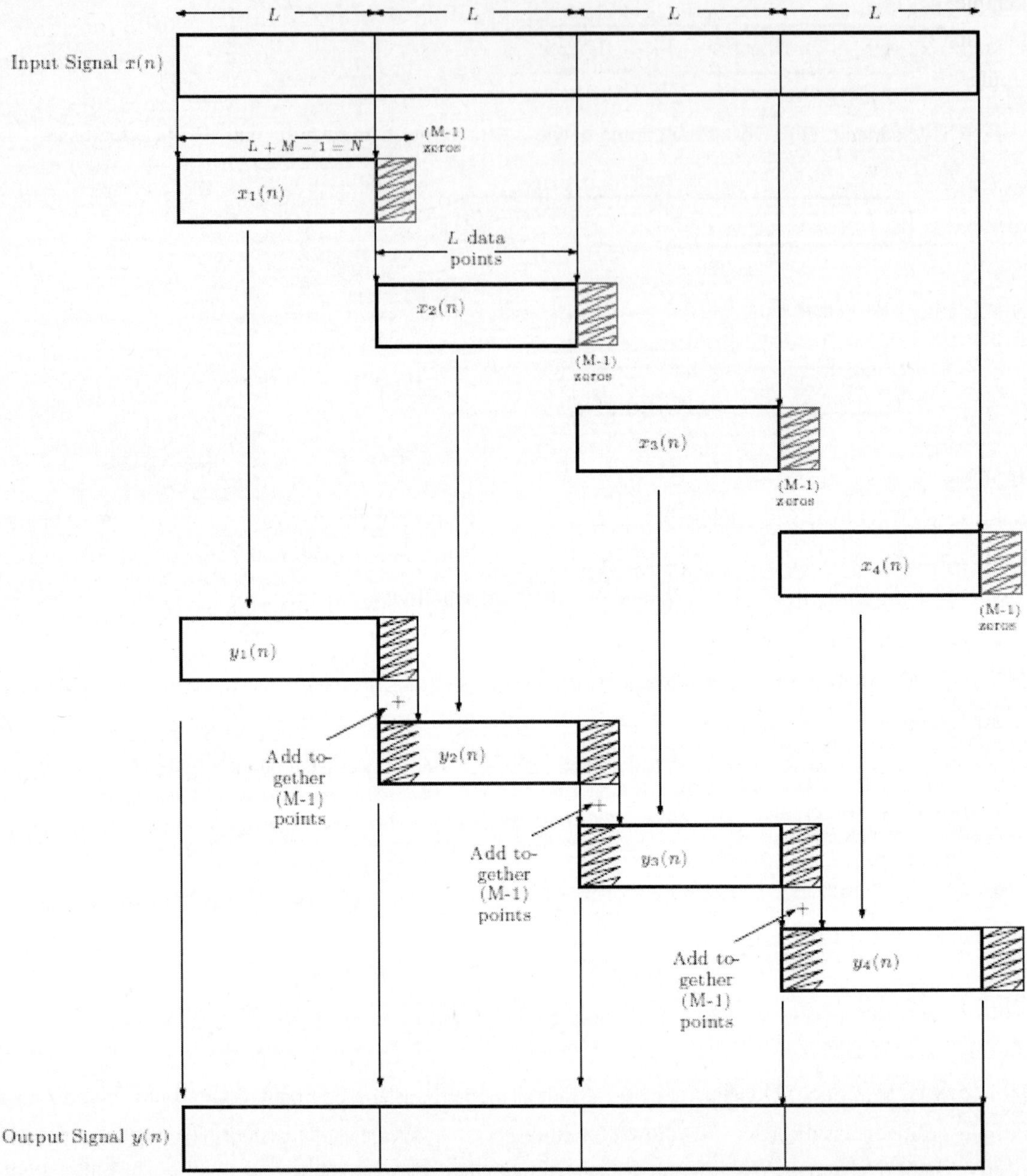

Fig. 6.8: Linear FIR filtering using the overlap-add method.

L-taps channel O/P:

$$y(n) = \sum_{l=0}^{L-1} h(l)x(n-l) = h(0)x(n) + h(1)x(n-1) + \ldots + h(L-1)x(n-L+1)$$

Here red color indicates the ISI in the signal $y(n)$.

Example: $[\mathbf{x}_1\mathbf{x}_2]=[x_1(0), x_1(1), ..., x_1(N1)\ x_2(0), x_2(1), ..., x_2(N1)]$ are two different symbols of OFDM system. Thus, first symbol interferes to the second symbols while passing through the multi path wireless channel.

Circular convolution:

$$y(n) = \textstyle\sum_{m=0}^{N-1} h(m)x((n-m)_N)\text{: we are interested}$$

- Tx symbols: $x(N-L), ..., x(N-2), x(N-1), x(0), x(1), ...x(N-1)$: blues are CP

- So

$$y(0) = h(0)x(0) + h(1)x(-1) + ... + h(L-1)x(-L+1)$$

$$= h(0)x(0) + h(1)x(N-1) + ... + h(L-1)x(N-L+1)$$

$$y(1) = h(0)x(1) + h(1)x(0) + ... + h(L-1)x(N-L+1)$$

$$y(2) = h(0)x(2) + h(1)x(1) + h(2)x(0) + ... + h(L-1)x(N-L+2)$$

$$y(3) = h(0)x(3) + h(1)x(2) + h(2)x(1) + h(3)x(0) ... + h(L-1)x(N-L+3)$$

$$y(N-1) = h(0)x(N-1) + h(1)x(N-2) + h(2)x(N-3) + ... + h(L-1)x(N-L)$$

Inputs: $[x(0), x(1), ..., x(N\ 1)]T$ outputs: $[y(0), y(1), ..., y(N\ 1)]T$ Thus, after adding CP to the transmitted symbols, linear convolution is converted to the circular convolution as shown above.

Circular Convolution: $\mathbf{y} = \mathbf{Cx}$ for example L taps channel

$$\mathrm{C} = \begin{bmatrix} h(0) & \cdots & & h(L-1) & h(L-2) & \cdots & h(1) \\ h(1) & h(0) & \cdots & & h(L-1) & \cdots & h(2) \\ \cdots & & & & & & \\ & & \cdots & & h(L-1) & h(1) & h(0) \end{bmatrix}_{N\times N}$$

$$\mathrm{y} = \begin{bmatrix} y(0) \\ y(1) \\ \cdots \\ y(N-1) \end{bmatrix}_{N\times 1} \qquad \mathrm{x} = \begin{bmatrix} x(0) \\ x(1) \\ \cdots \\ x(N-1) \end{bmatrix}_{N\times 1}$$

Matrix **C** is written as

C is a circulant matrix.

Circular convolution is expressed as product of circulant matrix (generated using the channel) and input signal vector **x**.

Diagonalization of circulant matrices using the DFT offers a powerful and efficient technique in various areas of signal processing and linear algebra. Circulant matrices possess a unique structure where each row is a cyclic shift of the preceding row, making them amenable to diagonalization via the DFT. By exploiting the properties of the DFT, circulant matrices can be decom- posed into a diagonal matrix containing the eigenvalues and a unitary ma- trix composed of the eigenvectors, facilitating efficient matrix manipulation and analysis. This diagonalization process significantly simplifies operations such as matrix multiplication, inversion, and solving linear systems, enabling streamlined algorithms with reduced computational complexity. Moreover, the connection between circulant matrices and the DFT underscores the profound link between time-domain and frequency-domain representations, facilitating insights into signal properties and spectral analysis. Overall, the utilization of the DFT for circulant matrix diagonalization exemplifies the synergy between mathematical theory and practical applications, offering elegant solutions to a wide range of problems in signal processing, communication systems, and beyond.

- $\mathbf{C} = \mathbf{U}_N \mathrm{diag}(\mathbf{F}_N \mathbf{c}) \mathbf{U}_N^*$, where $\mathbf{U}_N^* = \frac{e^{-j2\pi kn/N}}{\sqrt{N}}$, $\mathbf{U}_N = \frac{e^{j2\pi kn/N}}{\sqrt{N}}$, c is the first column of F
- $\mathbf{C} = \frac{\mathbf{F}_N^{-1} \mathrm{diag}(\mathbf{F}_N \mathbf{c}) \mathbf{F}_N}{N}$, $\mathbf{F}_N$: DFT matrix

Example: $L = 3,\ N = 6,\ y(n) = \sum_{k=0}^{2} h(k)x(n-k)$

$$x = [x(4), x(5), x(0), x(1), x(2), x(3), x(4), x(5)]$$

$$y(0) = h(0)x(0) + h(1)x(-1) + h(2)x(-2) = h(0)x(0) + h(1)x(5) + h(2)x(4)$$

$$y(1) = h(0)x(1) + h(1)x(0) + h(2)x(-1) = h(0)x(1) + h(1)x(0) + h(2)x(5)$$

$$y(2) = h(0)x(2) + h(1)x(1) + h(2)x(0)$$

$$y(3) = h(0)x(3) + h(1)x(2) + h(2)x(1)$$

$$y(4) = h(0)x(4) + h(1)x(3) + h(2)x(2)$$

$$y(5) = h(0)x(5) + h(1)x(4) + h(2)x(3)$$

$$\begin{bmatrix} y(0) \\ y(1) \\ y(2) \\ y(3) \\ y(4) \\ y(5) \end{bmatrix} = \begin{bmatrix} h(0) & 0 & 0 & 0 & h(2) & h(1) \\ h(1) & h(0) & 0 & 0 & 0 & h(2) \\ h(2) & h(1) & h(0) & 0 & 0 & 0 \\ 0 & h(2) & h(1) & h(0) & 0 & 0 \\ 0 & 0 & h(2) & h(1) & h(0) & 0 \\ 0 & 0 & 0 & h(2) & h(1) & h(0) \end{bmatrix} \begin{bmatrix} x(0) \\ x(1) \\ x(2) \\ x(3) \\ x(4) \\ x(5) \end{bmatrix}$$

OFDM output:

$$\mathbf{y} = \mathbf{C}\mathbf{x}$$

$$\underbrace{\begin{bmatrix} Y(0) \\ Y(1) \\ \cdots \\ Y(N-1) \end{bmatrix}}_{\mathbf{y}} = \underbrace{\begin{bmatrix} h(0) & 0 & 0 & 0 & h(2) & h(1) \\ h(1) & h(0) & 0 & 0 & 0 & h(2) \\ h(2) & h(1) & h(0) & 0 & 0 & 0 \\ 0 & h(2) & h(1) & h(0) & 0 & 0 \\ 0 & 0 & h(2) & h(1) & h(0) & 0 \\ 0 & 0 & 0 & h(2) & h(1) & h(0) \end{bmatrix}}_{\mathbf{C}} \underbrace{\begin{bmatrix} X(0) \\ X(1) \\ \cdots \\ X(N-1) \end{bmatrix}}_{\mathbf{x}}$$

Circulant matrix is diagonalazed as

$$\mathbf{C} = \mathbf{U}^{-1}\mathbf{\Lambda}\mathbf{U}$$

$$\mathbf{y} = \mathbf{U}^{-1}\mathbf{\Lambda}\mathbf{U}\mathbf{x}.$$

$$\mathbf{U}\mathbf{y} = \mathbf{U}\mathbf{U}^{-1}\mathbf{\Lambda}\mathbf{U}\mathbf{x}.$$

DFT domain:

$$\mathbf{Y} = \mathbf{\Lambda}\mathbf{X} \in \mathbb{C}^{N \times N}$$

the eigenvalues of $\mathbf{C}$ are the DFT coefficients of the channel $\mathbf{h}$.

OFDM system block diagram is shown in Fig. 6.9.

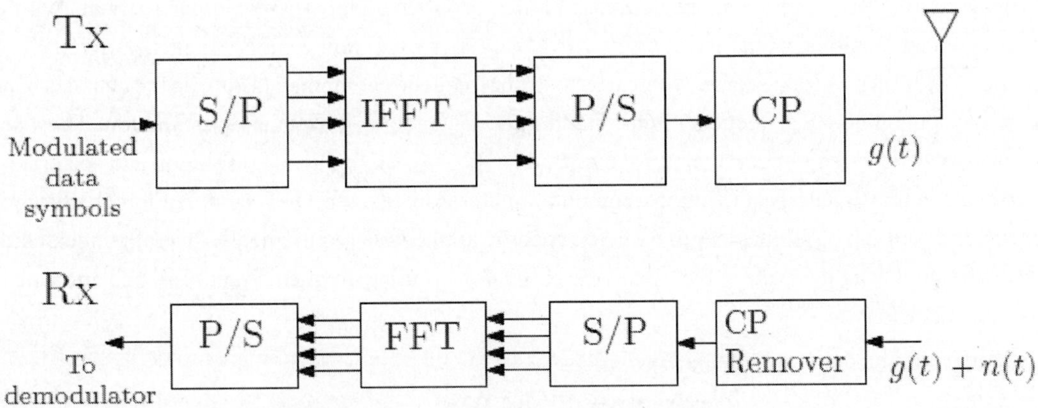

Fig. 6.9: OFDM system block diagram.

OFDM system steps:

The OFDM system employs a series of key steps depicted in its block diagram to enable efficient data transmission over wireless channels. At the core of the OFDM system lies the inverse fast Fourier transform (IFFT) block. The IFFT operation is responsible for mapping the modulated data symbols onto orthogonal subcarriers, which are distributed across the available bandwidth. This process allows for the simultaneous transmission of multiple data streams, each occupying a distinct frequency subcarrier. Following the IFFT operation, the system incorporates a CP insertion block. The CP is a guard interval inserted at the beginning of each OFDM symbol to mitigate the effects of multipath propagation and intersymbol interference (ISI). The CP ensures orthogonality between OFDM symbols and facilitates robust signal reception at the receiver.

Once the modulated OFDM symbols, including the CP, are transmitted over the wireless channel, they undergo propagation effects such as fading, attenuation, and noise distortion. These channel impairments introduce distortions that must be compensated for at the receiver to recover the transmitted data accurately.

At the receiver end, the first step involves the removal of the CP from the received signal. The CP removal block extracts the useful OFDM symbol from the received signal, discarding the guard interval. Subsequently, the received signal is subjected to the fast Fourier transform (FFT) operation. The FFT operation demodulates the received OFDM symbol, separating the individual subcarriers and converting them back into their original data symbols.

The received data symbols undergo equalization to compensate for channel distortions introduced during transmission. Equalization techniques aim to estimate and mitigate the effects of channel fading and frequency-selective impairments, ensuring accurate recovery of the transmitted data symbols. Various equalization algorithms, such as zero-forcing (ZF) or minimum mean square error (MMSE) equalization, may be employed depending on the channel characteristics and system requirements.

6.7 DFT-BASED FREQUENCY ANALYSIS OF SIGNALS

The impact of signal length on the DFT plot is a critical consideration in signal processing. The length of the signal directly affects the frequency resolution and spectral leakage observed in the DFT plot. In general, longer signals result in finer frequency resolution, allowing for better dis- crimination between closely spaced frequency components. This finer resolution is particularly beneficial when analyzing signals with distinct frequency components or when detecting narrow- band signals in noisy environments. Conversely, shorter signals may exhibit spectral leakage, where energy from frequency components outside the analysis bandwidth contaminates neighbor- ing frequency bins, leading to inaccuracies in frequency estimation. Thus, selecting an appropriate signal length is crucial to balance trade-offs between frequency resolution and spectral leakage. Moreover, longer signals require more computational resources for DFT computation, highlighting the importance of optimizing signal length based on specific application requirements. Overall, understanding the impact of signal length on the DFT plot is essential for accurate frequency analysis and informed signal processing decisions.

For example, a time domain signal is given as

$$x(t) = 0.8 + 0.7\sin(100\pi t) + \sin(240\pi t)$$

The plots of the DFT using the different length of the signal are shown in Fig. 6.10. We can clearly see the impact of DFT length N on the signal spectrum.

The frequency resolution of the DFT refers to the ability of the DFT to distinguish between different frequencies in a signal. It is determined by the number of samples used in the DFT computation and the duration of the signal. Generally, as the number of samples increases or the duration of the signal extends, the frequency resolution improves. The frequency resolution of the DFT is inversely proportional to the length of the signal in time domain, meaning that longer signals provide better frequency resolution. However, increasing the number of samples also leads to higher computational complexity. The frequency resolution can be calculated as the reciprocal of the total time duration of the signal being analyzed. Accurate frequency resolution is essential for applications such as spectral analysis, signal processing, and system identification, where precise frequency information is required to analyze and interpret the underlying signals effectively.

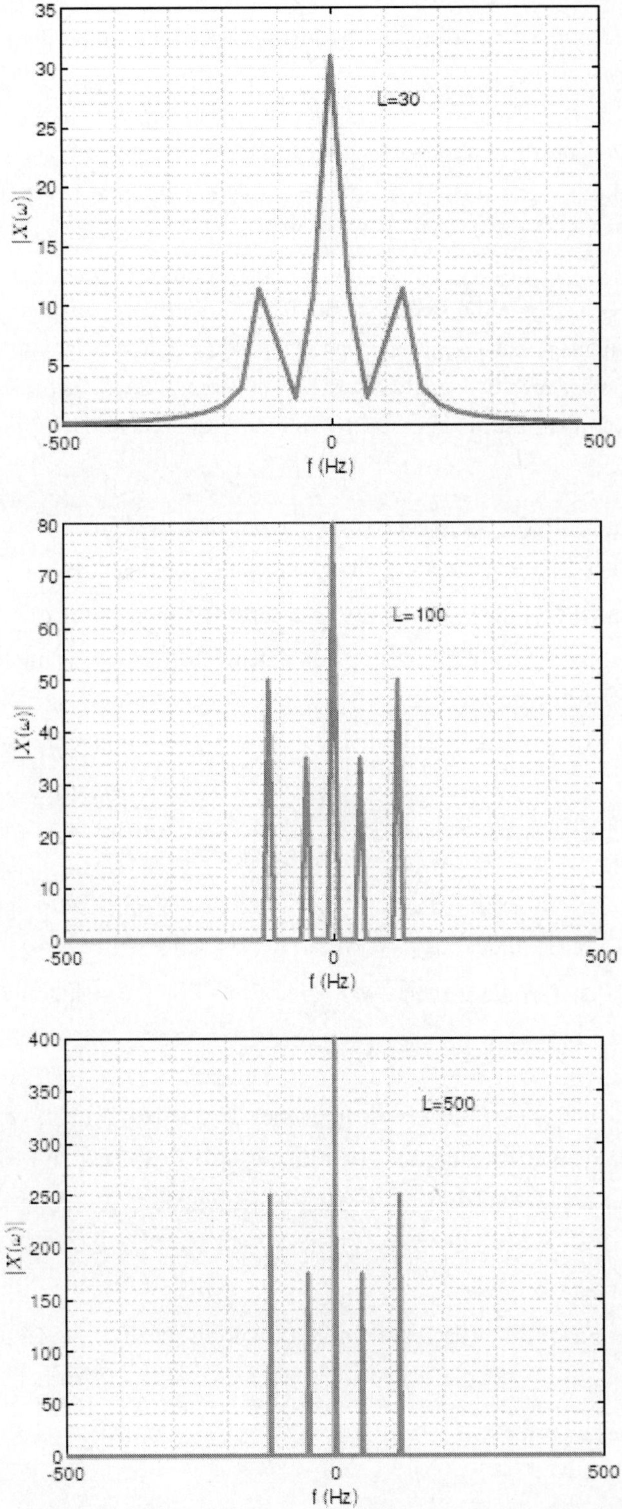

Fig. 6.10: Impact of length L.

SUMMARY

The chapter on Discrete Fourier Transform (DFT) focuses on transforming discrete-time signals into their frequency domain representation, facilitating the analysis and processing of digital signals. It begins by defining the DFT and presenting its mathematical formulation, emphasizing its application in analyzing finite-length sequences. The chapter discusses the relationship between the DFT and the Discrete Time Fourier Transform (DTFT), highlighting the DFT's ability to provide a discrete approximation of the continuous frequency spectrum. Key properties of the DFT are thoroughly examined, including linearity, periodicity, symmetry, time and frequency shifting, convolution, and the duality property, which collectively enhance the understanding of signal behavior in the frequency domain. Furthermore, the chapter discusses the impact of windowing on the DFT and its role in minimizing spectral leakage. Practical examples illustrate the application of the DFT in various fields, such as signal processing, telecommunications, and audio analysis, providing readers with a solid foundation for utilizing the DFT in real-world scenarios.

EXERCISES

1. Compute the 4-point DFT of the sequence $x(n) = \{1, 1, 1, 2\}$.
2. Given the 4-point DFT $X(k) = \{8, 0, 0, 0\}$, find the original sequence $x(n)$.
3. Compute the 8-point DFT of the sequence $x(n) = 2\cos(\pi/4n)$ for $n = 0, 1, ..., 7$.
4. Given the sequence $x(n) = \{1, 2, 3, 4, 3, 2, 1, 0\}$ compute the 8-point DFT and determine the magnitude and phase of each DFT coefficient.
5. Given two sequences $x(n) = \{1, 2, 1, 2\}$ and $h(n) = \{2, 2, 2, 2\}$, compute their circular convolution using DFT.
6. Compute the 4-point DFT of the sequence $x(n) = \{0, 1, 0, 0\}$. Then, find the DFT of the sequence $x((n - 1)_4)$.
7. Verify Parseval's theorem for the sequence $x(n) = \{1, 2, 3, 4\}$ using its 4-point DFT.
8. Compute the 4-point DFT of the sequence $x(n) = \{1 + j, 2 - j, 3 + 2j, 4 - 2j\}$.
9. Compute the 8-point DFT of the sequence $x(n) = \{1, 2, 3, 4\}$ by zero-padding it to 8 points. Compare the result with the 4-point DFT.
10. A discrete sequence is given by $x(n) = [1, 1, 0, 0, 1, 1]$. Find the DFT coefficients $X(k)$ of this sequence. Sketch its magnitude and phase. What is the impact of DFT length N on its computation?
11. Calculate the circular convolution between two signals $h(n) = \{1, 2, 3\}$ and $x(n) = \{1, 2, 2, 1\}$.
12. Can we compute linear convolution using circular convolution? If yes, how?

Multiple Choice Questions

1. What is the main purpose of the Discrete Fourier Transform (DFT) in signal processing?

   A) Time-domain analysis

   B) Frequency-domain analysis

   C) Amplitude modulation

   D) Phase shifting

2. The DFT of a sequence of length NNN produces how many frequency components?

   A) N/2

   B) 2N

   C) N

   D) N^2

3. Which of the following is a property of the DFT?

   A) Linearity

   B) Time-shifting

   C) Frequency-shifting

   D) All of the above

4. What is the primary computational disadvantage of the DFT?

   A) It requires high memory usage

   B) It is computationally expensive, with a complexity of $O(N^2)$

   C) It can only be used for real signals

   D) It does not provide phase information

5. Which algorithm is commonly used to reduce the computational complexity of the DFT?

   A) Fast Fourier Transform (FFT)

   B) Inverse Fourier Transform (IFT)

   C) Z-transform

   D) Laplace Transform

6. If x[n] is a real-valued sequence, what symmetry property does the DFT X[k] exhibit?

   A) Magnitude symmetry

   B) Phase symmetry

   C) Conjugate symmetry

   D) No symmetry

7. The DFT of a constant sequence (e.g., x[n]=1 for all n) results in:

   A) A constant in the frequency domain

   B) A delta function at k=0

   C) All zeros

   D) A linear function

8. What happens to the frequency resolution of the DFT as the length of the input sequence increases?

   A) Increases

   B) Decreases

   C) Remains the same

   D) Becomes unpredictable

9. In the context of DFT, what is spectral leakage?

   A) A phenomenon where signal power leaks into adjacent frequencies

B) Loss of energy in the frequency domain

C) Noise addition to the signal

D) Error in time-domain representation

10. The circular convolution of two sequences in the time domain is equivalent to what operation in the frequency domain?

    A) Addition of their DFTs

    B) Subtraction of their DFTs

    C) Multiplication of their DFTs

    D) Convolution of their DFTs

ANSWERS

1	2	3	4	5	6	7	8	9	10
B	C	D	B	A	C	B	A	A	C

KNOW MORE

For more information related to this topic scan the QR code.

OR

Type this link in your browser

https://www.robots.ox.ac.uk/~sjrob/Teaching/SP/l7.pdf

REFERENCES AND SUGGESTED READING

1. B. P. Lathi, "*Principles of Linear Systems and Signals*," *Oxford Second edition*, 2009.
2. John G. Proakis, and Dimitris G. Manolakis "*Digital signal processing: principles, algorithms, and applications, 4/E*,"*Pearson Education India*, 2007.
3. Alan V. Oppenheim, Alan S. Willsky, and S. Hamid Nawab "*Signals & Systems*,"*Pearson Education India*, 1997.
4. Steven W. Smith "*Digital Signal Processing: A Practical Guide for Engineers and Scientists*,"*California Technical Publishing*, 1999.
5. Barrie W. Jervis, and Emmanuel C. Ifeachor "*Digital Signal Processing: A Practical Approach*,"*Pearson Education India*, 2002.

Chapter 7: FFT: Fast Fourier Transform

UNIT SPECIFICS

The FFT chapter focuses on the principles and algorithms that make the computation of the discrete Fourier transform (DFT) more efficient. It introduces the basic concept of the FFT and explains how it reduces the computational complexity from O(N^2) to O(NlogN). The chapter covers various FFT algorithms, including the Cooley-Tukey algorithm and its different variants like radix-2, radix-4, and split-radix FFTs. It also discusses practical implementation aspects, such as in-place computation and bit-reversal, as well as applications in signal processing, filtering, and spectral analysis.

RATIONALE

The FFT chapter is crucial for understanding the efficient computation of the DFT, a fundamental operation in digital signal processing. The DFT is widely used in applications such as spectral analysis, filtering, and image processing, but its direct computation can be computationally intensive, especially for large datasets. The FFT algorithm significantly reduces this complexity, making real-time processing feasible and enabling the analysis and manipulation of signals in various practical applications.

PRE-REQUISITE

DFT and z transform

UNIT OUTCOMES

List of outcomes of this unit is as follows:

U7-O1: Radix-2 and Radix-4 FFT structures

U7-O2: Divide and Conquer algorithm

U7-O3: FFT computation complexity

Unit-7 Outcomes	EXPECTED MAPPING WITH COURSE OUTCOMES (1- Weak Correlation; 2- Medium correlation; 3- Strong Correlation)					
	CO-1	**CO-2**	**CO-3**	**CO-4**	**CO-5**	**CO-6**
U7-O1	–	3	2	–	–	–
U7-O2	–	3	2	–	–	–
U7-O3	–	3	2	–	–	–

7.1 INTRODUCTION

The Fast Fourier Transform (FFT) is an algorithm used to efficiently compute the Discrete Fourier Transform of a sequence or array of complex numbers. The FFT algorithm significantly reduces the computational complexity of the DFT, especially for large input sizes. While the standard DFT algorithm has a time complexity of O(N^2) for N input samples, the FFT algorithm achieves a complexity of O($Nlog_2N$), making it much faster for large N.

The FFT algorithm decomposes the DFT computation into smaller subproblems by exploiting the symmetry properties of complex roots of unity and the periodicity of the DFT. These smaller subproblems are then solved recursively, and the results are combined to obtain the final DFT.

There are several variations of the FFT algorithm, including the Cooley-Tukey algorithm, the Radix-2 FFT, and the Radix-4 FFT, each suited to different input sizes and hardware architec- tures. Additionally, various optimizations such as bit-reversal permutation and memory-efficient implementations further improve the performance of the FFT algorithm.

The FFT algorithm is widely used in various applications, including digital signal processing, audio and image processing, communications, scientific computing, and many others, due to its efficiency and versatility in computing Fourier transforms.

Direct computation of the DFT is inherently inefficient due to its failure to leverage the symmetry and periodicity properties of the phase factor W_N. These properties include:

$$\begin{aligned} &\text{Symmetry property} \quad W_N^{k+N/2} = -W_N^k \\ &\text{Periodicity property} \quad W_N^{k+N} = W_N^k \end{aligned} \tag{7.1}$$

7.2 RADIX-2 FFT

Radix-2 FFT is particularly efficient for input sizes that are powers of 2, such as 2, 4, 8, 16, etc. In general $N = 2^v$, where v is any positive integer. It computes separately the DFTs of the even- indexed inputs ($x(0)$, $x(2)$, $x(4)$, ...) and of the odd-indexed inputs ($x(1)$, $x(3)$, $x(5)$, ...), and then combines those two results to produce the DFT of the whole sequence.

N point DFT is written as

$$X(k) = \sum_{n=0}^{N-1} x(n)e^{-\frac{j2\pi kn}{N}}, k = 0,1,2, \dots N-1$$

$$X(k) = \sum_{n=0}^{N/2-1} \underbrace{x(2n)}_{\text{even samples}} e^{-\frac{j2\pi k2n}{N}} + \sum_{n=0}^{N/2-1} \underbrace{x(2n+1)}_{\text{odd samples}} e^{-\frac{j2\pi k(2n+1)}{N}} \tag{7.2}$$

Type equation here.

$$X(k) = \sum_{n=0}^{N/2-1} x_e(n)e^{-\frac{j2\pi kn}{N/2}} + \sum_{n=0}^{N/2-1} x_o(n)e^{-\frac{j2\pi kn}{N/2}} e^{-\frac{j2\pi k}{N}} = \underbrace{\sum_{n=0}^{N/2-1} x_e(n)W_{N/2}^{kn}}_{\text{N/2 point DFTE }(k)} + W_N^k \underbrace{\sum_{n=0}^{N/2-1} x_o(n)W_{N/2}^{kn}}_{\text{N/2 point DFTO }(k)}. \tag{7.3}$$

$X(k) = E(k) + W_N^k O(k), k = 0,1, \dots N-1.$ (7.4)

Since $E(k + N/2) = E(k)$ and $O(k + N/2) = O(k)$. Here we have used the periodicity of $O(k)$ and $E(k)$ to translate the index k. Therefore, $X(k)$ is also written as

$$X(k) = \begin{cases} E(k) + \quad W_N^k O(k), & \text{if } k = 0,1, \dots N/2-1 \\ E(k-N/2) + W_N^k O(k-N/2), & \text{if } k = N/2, N/2+1, \dots N-1 \end{cases}$$

Here $W_N^k = e^{-\frac{j2\pi k}{N}}$ is called the twiddle factor and $W_N^{k+\frac{N}{2}} = -W_N^k$. Thus we can write $X(k)$ as

$$X(k) = \begin{cases} E(k) + W_N^k O(k), & \text{if } k = 0,1,..N/2-1 \\ E(k) - W_N^k O(k), & \text{if } k = N/2, N/2+1,..N-1 \end{cases}$$

Inherent structure of twiddle factor is exploited in Fig. 7.1 for $N = 8$. For example, $W_N^5 = -W_N^1$, which can be used to reduce the DFT complexity.

Further, $N/2$ DFT can be factored into $N/4$ size DFTs, and $N/4$ DFT can be factored into $N/8$ size DFTs, and so on. Basic 2 point DFT butterfly structure is shown in Fig. 7.2. Basic butterfly has one complex multiplication and two complex additions.

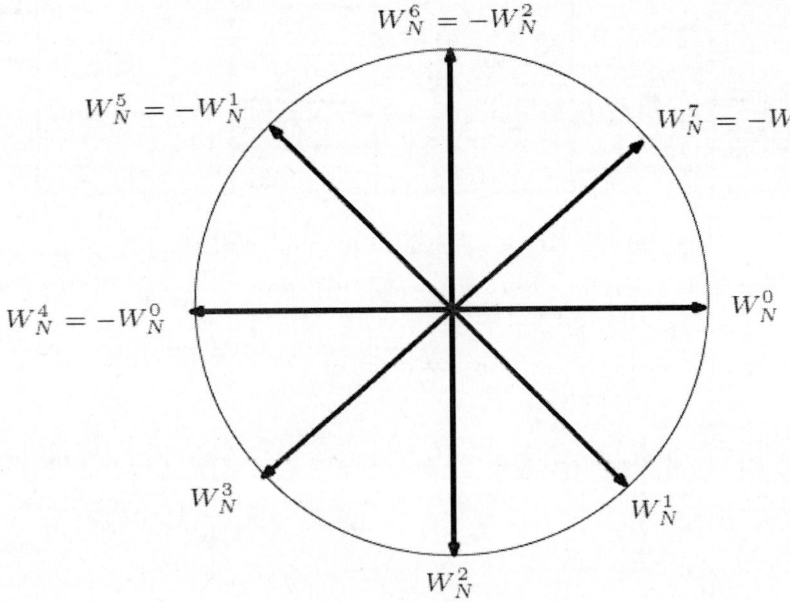

Fig. 7.1: Inherent structure of twiddle factor.

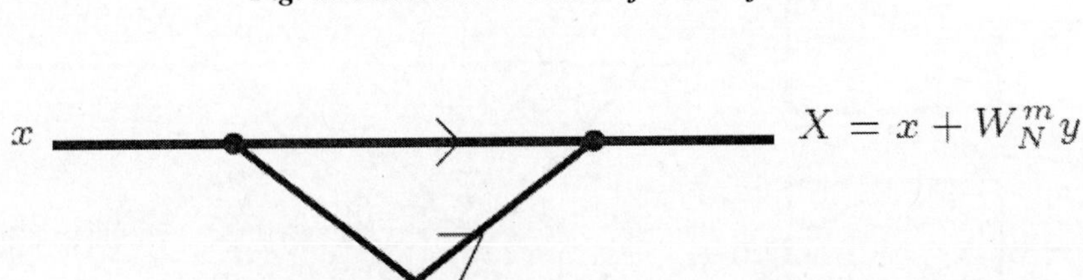

Fig. 7.2: Basic butterfly computation for decimation-in-time FFT for samples x and y.

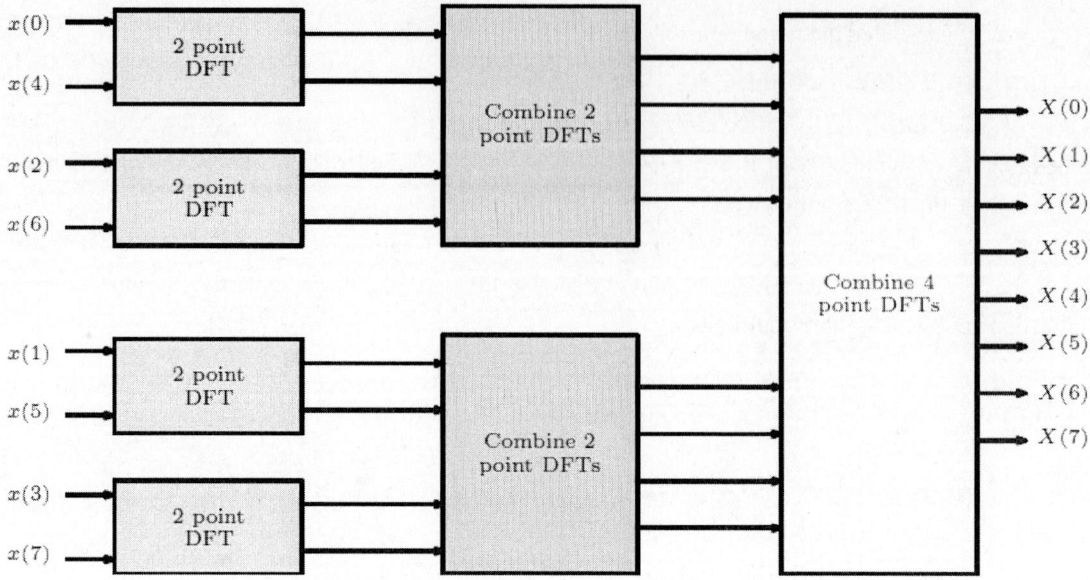

Fig. 7.3: Three stages computation of an N = 8 DFT.

Example 7.2.1 *$N = 8$ point DFT computation using two points DFTs is shown in Fig. 7.3. Here, we start from 2 point DFTs and we get 8 points in the output side.*

Let first compute 8 point DFT using two 4 point DFTs as in Fig. 7.4.

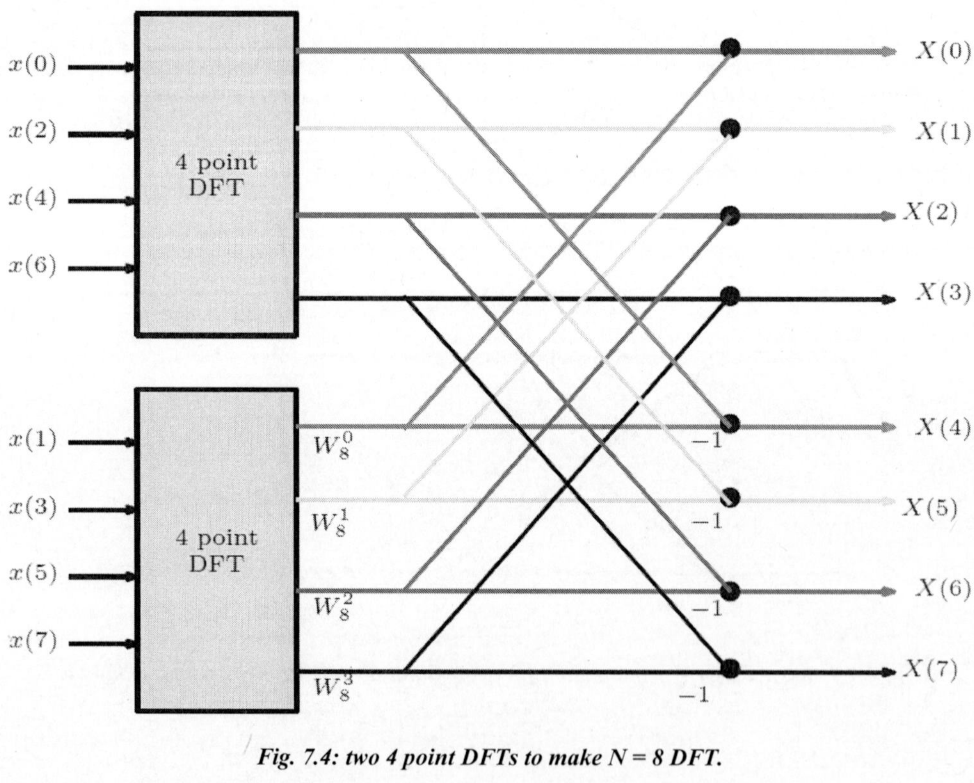

Fig. 7.4: two 4 point DFTs to make N = 8 DFT.

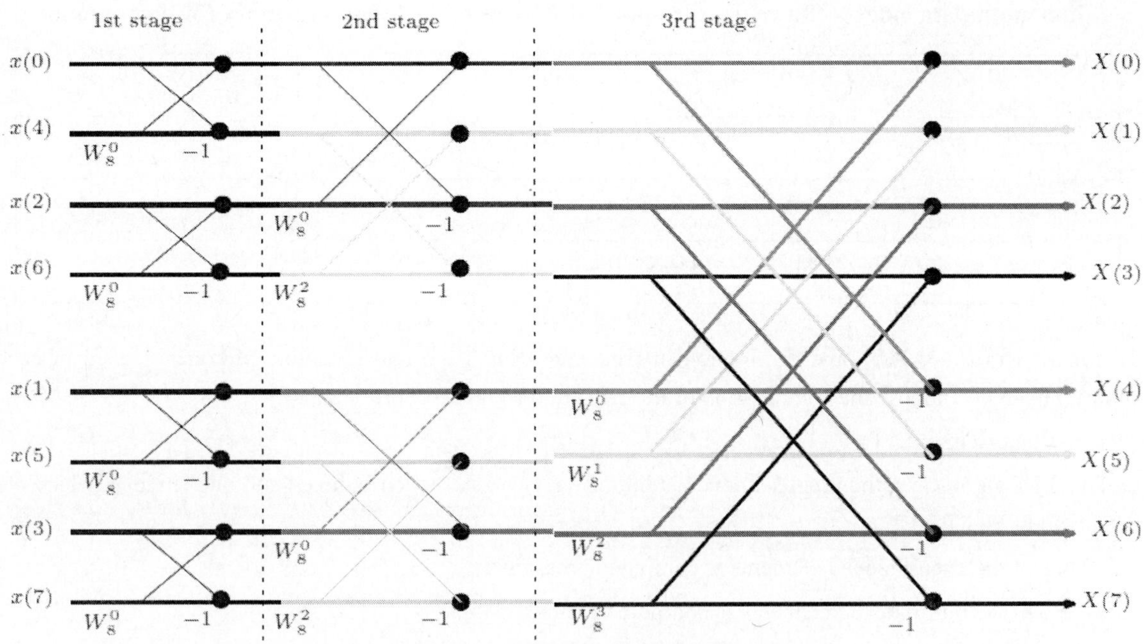

Fig. 7.5: Three stages computation of an N = 8 DFT.

7.2.1 FFT Computational complexity

Basic 2 point butterfly has complexity of one complex multiplication and two complex additions. For *N* point DFT we need $\log_2(N)$ stages and each stage needs *N/2* butterflies (as seen in Fig. 7.5). Therefore, complex multiplications in *N* point DFT is

No. of stages × No. of butterflies in each stage × multiplication in a butterfly

$$log_2(N).\frac{N}{2}.1 = \frac{N}{2}log_2(N) = O(N\ log_2(N))$$

Similarly, the complex additions are

$$log_2(N).\frac{N}{2}.2 = N\ log_2(N) = O(N\ log_2(N))$$

Thus FFT algorithm has complexity order $O(N\ log_2(N)$, unlike the direct computational complexity of DFT $O(N^2)$.

Table 7.1: Shuffling of the input data x(n) and bit reversal.

Initial input data index	Bit representation	Bit reversal	Input data index for computation
0	000	000	0
1	001	100	4
2	010	010	2
3	011	110	6

Initial input data index	Bit representation	Bit reversal	Input data index for computation
4	100	001	1
5	101	101	5
6	110	011	3
7	111	111	7

Decimation in time (DIT) and decimation in frequency (DIF) are two common approaches used in FFT algorithms to decompose the computation of the DFT into smaller subproblems.

Decimation in Time (DIT):

In DIT FFT algorithms, the input sequence is initially divided into even-indexed and odd- indexed elements as shown in Fig. 7.5.

The DFT of the even-indexed elements is computed recursively.

The DFT of the odd-indexed elements is computed recursively.

The results of the even and odd DFTs are combined using twiddle factors to obtain the final DFT of the entire sequence.

The Cooley-Tukey algorithm is a well-known DIT FFT algorithm, commonly implemented in FFT libraries.

Decimation in Frequency (DIF): DIF is an alternate way of developing the FFT algorithm. It is different from DIT in its development, although it leads to a very similar structure. The input data $x(n)$ follows the natural order, whereas the output DFT follows a bit-reversed order. Additionally, it's important to note that computations are performed in-place. However, it's feasible to modify the DIF algorithm such that the input sequence is in bit-reversed order while the output DFT is in natural order. Moreover, if we relax the requirement for in-place computations, it's also possible to have both the input data and the output DFT in natural order.

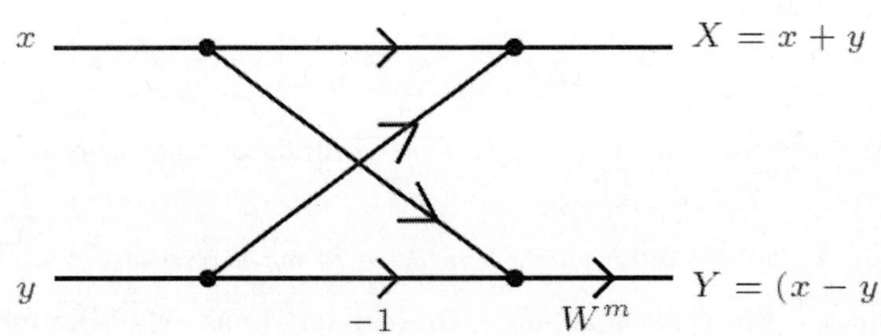

Fig. 7.6: Butterfly Structure: DIF.

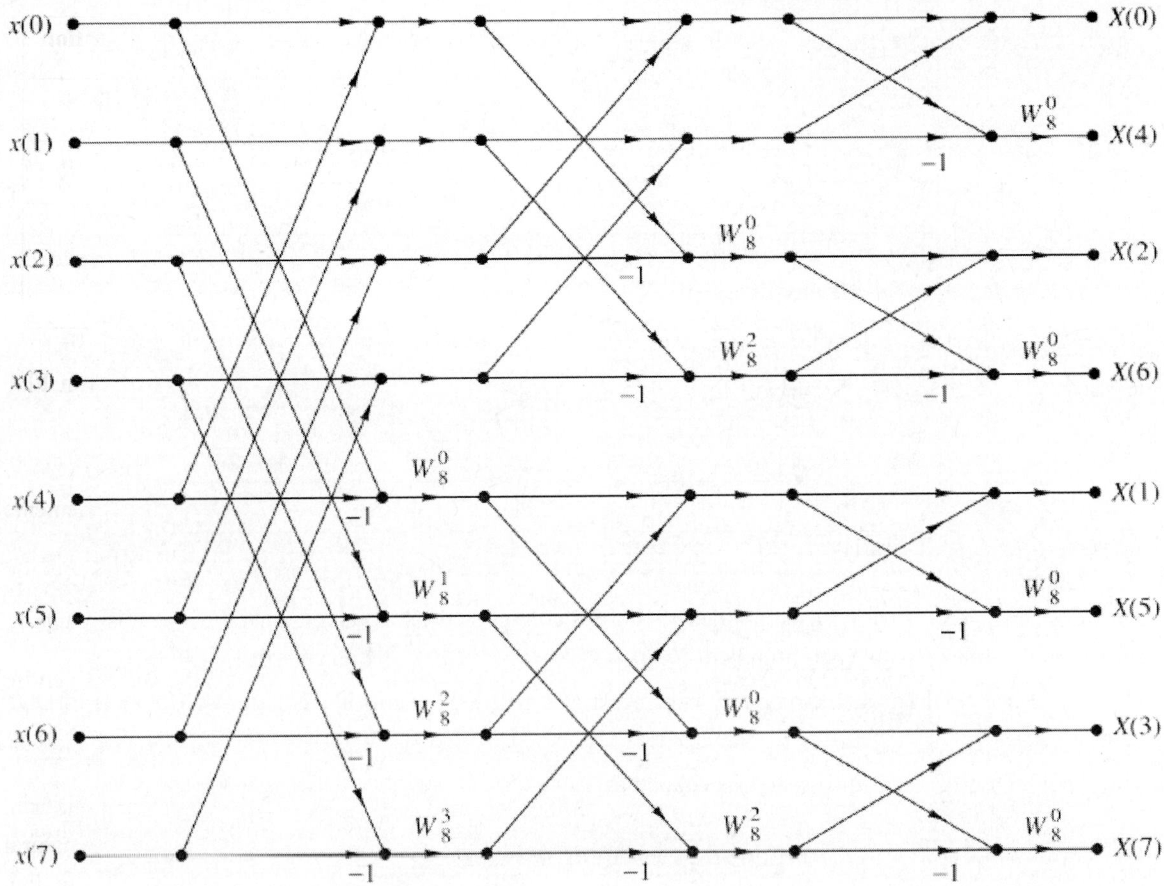

Fig. 7.7: Three stages computation of an N = 8 DFT using DIF. DFT values are in bit reversed order.

7.3 DIVIDE & CONQUER APPROACH

The divide and conquer approach in the FFT algorithm involves recursively dividing the input sequence into smaller subproblems, computing the Fourier transform of each subproblem separately, and then combining the results to obtain the final Fourier transform of the entire sequence.

Let's explore the computation of an N -point DFT, where N can be expressed as the product of two integers as $N = LM$. The sequence $x(n)$ can be stored either in a one-dimensional array indexed by $n = 0, 1, ..., N-1$ or as a two-dimensional array indexed by $l = 0, 1, ..., L-1$ and $m = 0, 1, ..., M-1$. l and m indexes denote the row and column of the matrix, respectively, and n is mapped to (l, m).

$n = Ml + m$ denotes the row wise data entry int the matrix from the vector of length N as

$$\begin{array}{c} l=0 \\ l=1 \\ l=2 \\ \vdots \\ l=L-1 \end{array} \begin{bmatrix} \overbrace{x(0)}^{m=0} & \overbrace{x(1)}^{1} & \overbrace{x(2)}^{2} & \ldots & \overbrace{x(M-1)}^{M-1} \\ \hline x(M) & x(M+1) & x(M+2) & \ldots & x(2M-1) \\ \hline \vdots & \vdots & \vdots & \ddots & \vdots \\ \hline x((L-1)M) & x((L-1)M+1) & x((L-1)M+2) & \ldots & x(ML-1) \end{bmatrix} \quad (7.5)$$

$n = Lm + l$ denotes the column wise data entry int the matrix from the vector of length N as

$$\begin{array}{c} l=0 \\ l=1 \\ l=2 \\ \vdots \\ l=L-1 \end{array} \begin{bmatrix} \overbrace{x(0)}^{m=0} & \overbrace{x(L)}^{1} & \overbrace{x(2L)}^{2} & \ldots & \overbrace{x((M-1)L)}^{M-1} \\ \hline x(1) & x(L+1) & x(2L+1) & \ldots & x((M-1)L+1) \\ \hline \vdots & \vdots & \vdots & \ddots & \vdots \\ \hline x(L-1)) & x(2L-1) & x(3L-1) & \ldots & x(ML-1) \end{bmatrix} \quad (7.6)$$

A similar arrangement can also be applied to store the computed DFT values. Specifically, this mapping associates the index k with a pair of indices (p, q), where $p = 0, 1, \ldots, L-1$ and $q = 0, 1, \ldots M-1$.

If $k = Mp + q$, the DFT is stored on a row-wise basis. If $k = Lq + p$, results in a column-wise storage of DFT values.

The N point DFT of a sequence $x(n)$ is calculated as

$$X(k) = \sum_{n=0}^{N-1} x(n) W_N^{kn}, \; k = 0,1,\ldots,N-1$$

$$X(p,q) = \sum_{l=0}^{L-1} \sum_{m=0}^{M-1} x(l,m) W_N^{(Mp+q)(mL+l)} \quad (7.7)$$

Phase factor can be written as $W_N^{(Mp+q)(mL+l)} = \underbrace{W_N^{M\,Lpm}}_{1} W_N^{M\,pl} W_N^{Lmq} W_N^{lq}$. Further, $W_N^{M\,pl} = W_{N/M}^{pl} = W_L^{pl}$ and $W_N^{Lmq} = W_{N/L}^{mq} = W_M^{mq}$. $X(p,q)$ is written as

$$X(p,q) = \sum_{l=0}^{L-1} \left(W_N^{lq} \underbrace{\left[\sum_{m=0}^{M-1} x(l,m) W_M^{mq} \right]}_{P(l,q)M \text{ point DFT}} \right) W_L^{lp} \quad (7.8)$$

We can write $P(l,q) = \sum_{m=0}^{M-1} x(l,m) W_M^{mq}$, and

$$X(p,q) = \sum_{l=0}^{L-1} \underbrace{\left(W_N^{lq} P(l,q) \right)}_{G(l,q)} W_L^{lp} \quad (7.9)$$

Further, above equation is expressed as

$$X(p,q) = \underbrace{\sum_{l=0}^{L-1} G(l,q) W_L^{lp}}_{L \text{ point DFT}} \ , q = 0,1, \ldots, M-1, p = 0,1, \ldots, L-1 \quad (7.10)$$

Computational Complexity:
The initial step entails computing L DFTs, each consisting of M points. Thus, this phase necessitates LM^2 complex multiplications and $LM(M-1)$ complex additions. The subsequent step involves LM complex multiplications. Lastly, the third step demands ML^2 complex multiplications and $ML(L-1)$ complex additions. Consequently, the computational complexity is
Complex multiplications: $LM^2 + LM + ML^2 = LM(M+L+1) = N(M+L+1)$
Complex additions: $LM(M-1) + ML(L-1) = ML(M-1+L-1) = N(M+L-2)$

As an illustration, consider $N = 10000$, with $L = 2$ and $M = 5000$ chosen. Instead of conducting 108 complex multiplications required by direct DFT computation, this method necessitates 5003 X 104 complex multiplications. This reflects a reduction of approximately half. Similarly, the number of additions is also halved.

Example 7.3.1 $N = 18$ *point DFT using* $L = 6$ *and* $M = 3$ *is shown in Fig. 7.8. Data is entered into a matrix as*

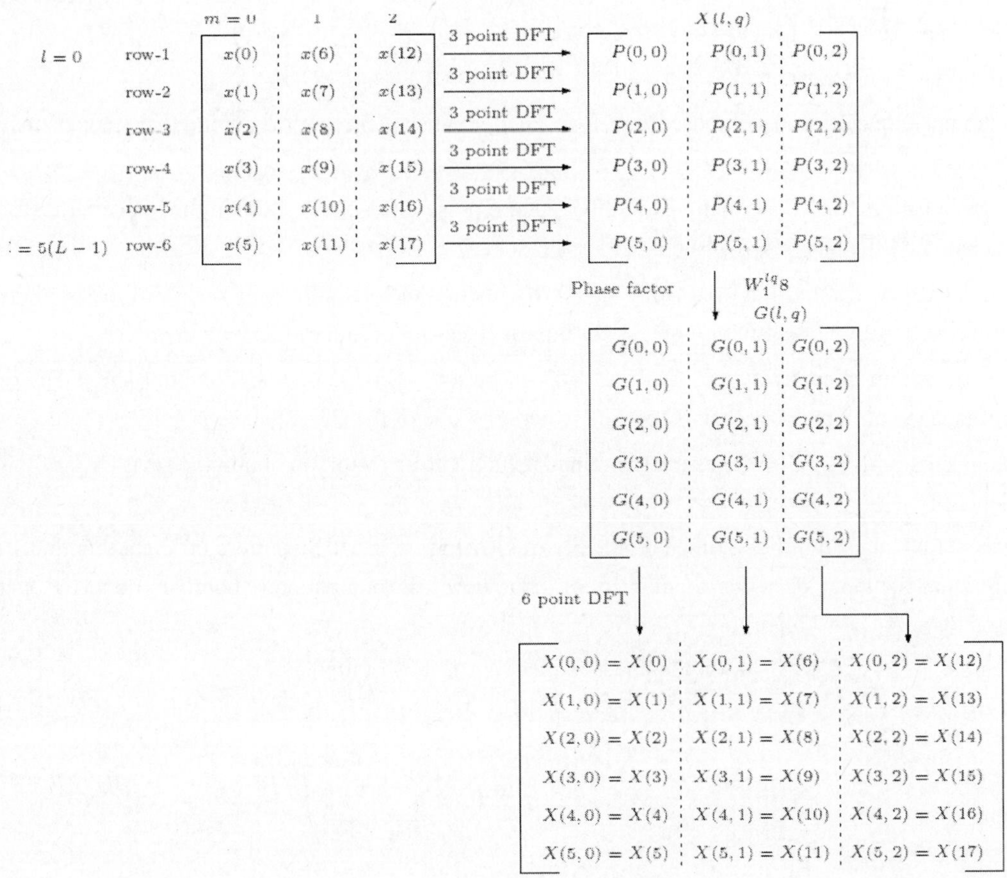

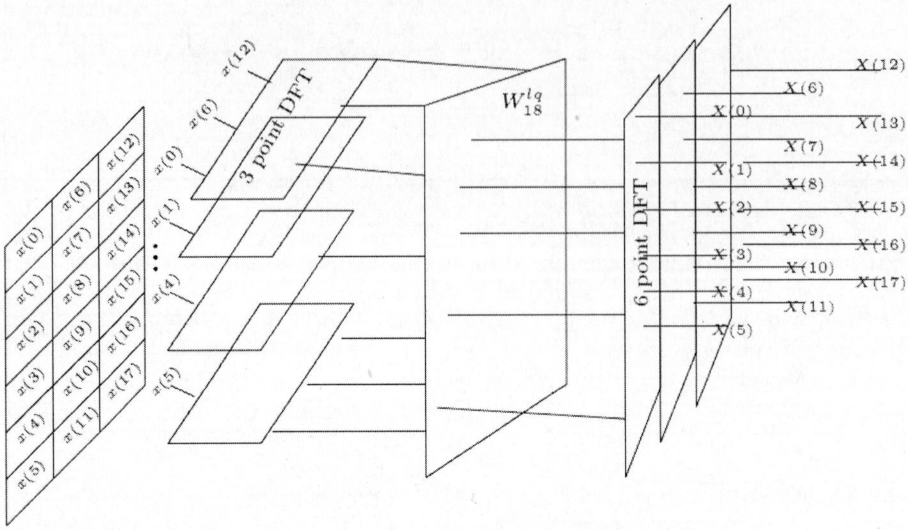

Fig. 7.8: Computation of N = 18 point DFT using L = 6 and M = 3 point DFTs.

7.4 RADIX-4 FFT

The radix-4 FFT algorithm is a variation of the FFT algorithm that decomposes the DFT computation into smaller subproblems using radix-4 (base-4) decomposition. This algorithm is particularly efficient for input sizes that are powers of 4, i.e., $N = 4^r$.

Steps in radix-4 FFT algorithm:

- The input sequence is decomposed into four smaller subsequences by grouping every four consecutive elements.
- Twiddle factors, which are complex numbers that represent the phase shifts in the Fourier transform, are precomputed for each stage of the FFT.
- The radix-4 FFT algorithm uses radix-4 butterfly operations to combine the results of the smaller DFTs. A radix-4 butterfly operation involves four input values and produces four output values.
- The algorithm recursively applies the radix-4 butterfly operations to compute the DFT of each subsequence until the base case is reached, where the size of the subsequence is 4 or less.
- The results of the smaller DFTs are combined using twiddle factors to obtain the final DFT of the entire sequence.

The radix-4 FFT algorithm has a time complexity of O($N \log_4 N$), which is more efficient than the standard FFT algorithm for input sizes that are powers of 4. However, it requires more complex butterfly operations compared to radix-2 FFT algorithms.

For example, $L = 4$ and $M = N/4$, divide-and-conquer approach is written as

$$X(p,q) = \sum_{l=0}^{L-1}\left(W_N^{lq} \underbrace{\left[\sum_{m=0}^{M-1} x(l,m) W_M^{mq}\right]}_{P(l,q)M\ point\ DFT} \right) W_L^{lp} \tag{7.11}$$

$$P(l,q) = \sum_{m=0}^{\frac{N}{4}-1} x(l,m)\, W_{N/4}^{mq}, l = 0,1,2,3, q = 0,1,\dots,\frac{N}{4}-1$$

Thus DFT is $X(p,q) = \sum_{l=0}^{3}(W_N^{lq}\, P(l,q))\, W_4^{lp}, p = 0,1,2,3$ (7.12)

Data is divided as

$$x(l,m) = x(4m+l), X(p,q) = X\left(\frac{N}{4}p + q\right).$$

Combining the $N/4$-point DFTs defines a radix-4 DIT butterfly, which can be represented in matrix form as

$$\begin{bmatrix} X(0,q) \\ X(1,q) \\ X(2,q) \\ X(3,q) \end{bmatrix} = \underbrace{\begin{bmatrix} 1 & 1 & 1 & 1 \\ 1 & -j & -1 & j \\ 1 & -1 & 1 & -1 \\ 1 & j & -1 & -j \end{bmatrix}}_{4\ point\ DFT\ matrix} \begin{bmatrix} W_N^0 P(0,q) \\ W_N^{1q} P(1,q) \\ W_N^{2q} P(2,q) \\ W_N^{3q} P(3,q) \end{bmatrix} \tag{7.13}$$

Radix-4 butterfly is shown in Fig. 7.9, which as has three complex multiplications ($W_N^q, W_N^{2q}, W_N^{3q}$) and 12 complex additions. Therefore, radix-4 FFT has complexity as following

Complex multiplications : $3 \times \underbrace{N/4}_{no.of\ butterflies} \times \underbrace{\log_4(N) = \frac{\log_2(N)}{2}}_{no.of\ stages} \approx O(N\log_2(N))$

Complex additions : $12 \times \frac{N}{4} \times \log_2(N)/2 = \frac{3N}{2}\log_2(N) \approx O(N\log_2(N))$

$N = 16$ point DFT computation using radix-4 FFT is shown in Fig. 7.10 using DIF approach.

Example 7.4.1 *Compute the FFT of the signal x(n) = {1, 2, 3, 4, 5, 6, 7.8} using the radix-2 FFT algorithms. Divide the data into 2 point data segments as [x(0), x(4)], [x(2), x(6)], [x(1), x(5)] and [x(3), x(7)]. Compute 2-points DFTs and combine them. Steps are shown in Fig. 7.11.*

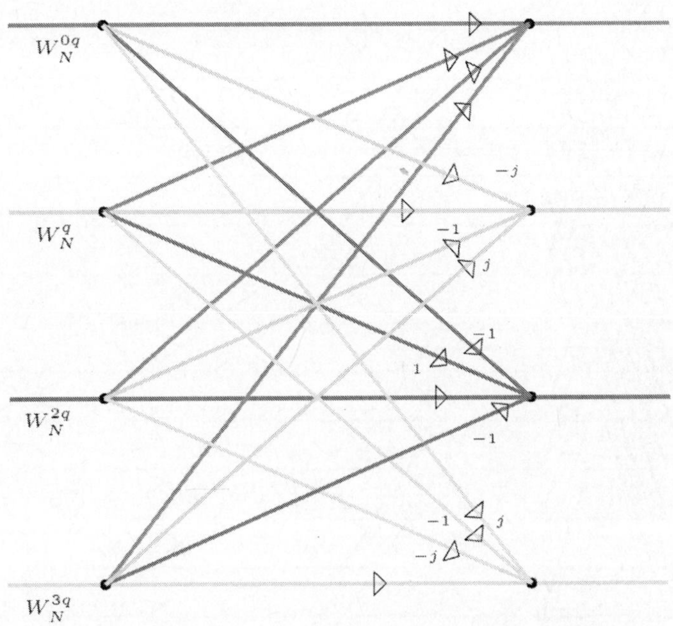

Fig. 7.9: Basic butterfly computation in a radix-4 FFT algorithm.

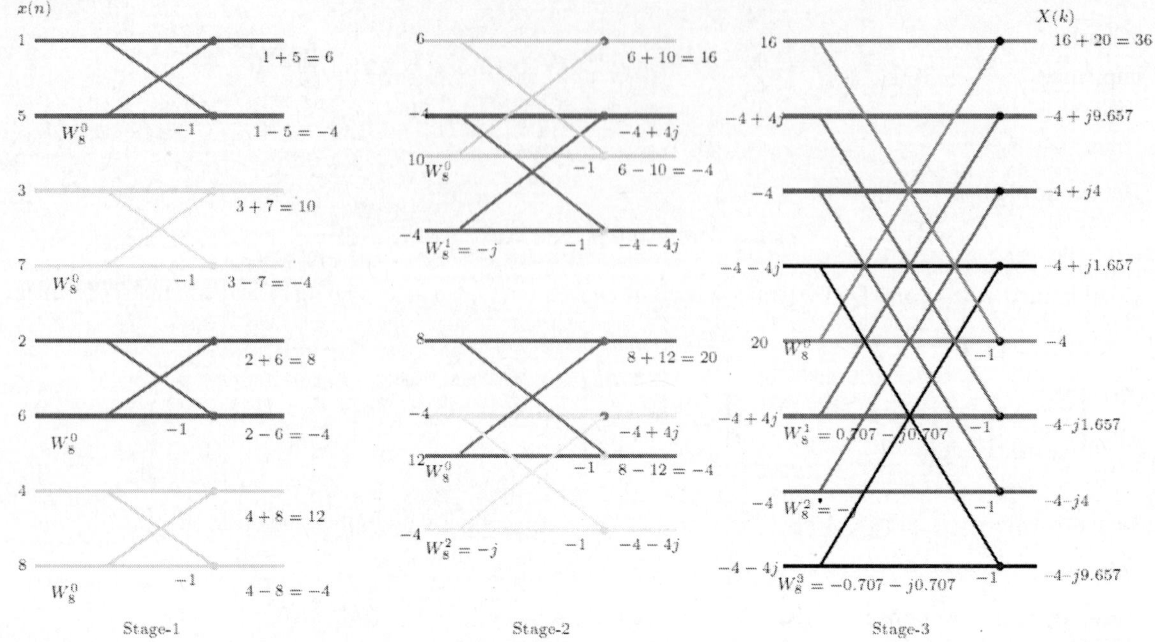

Fig. 7.10: FFT example.

Example 7.4.2 *Composite signal generation using the fundamental frequency f_0 Hz is shown in Fig. 7.12. Signal x(t) is generated using the sum of three different sinusoids. Shape of signal is different than the sinusoid.*

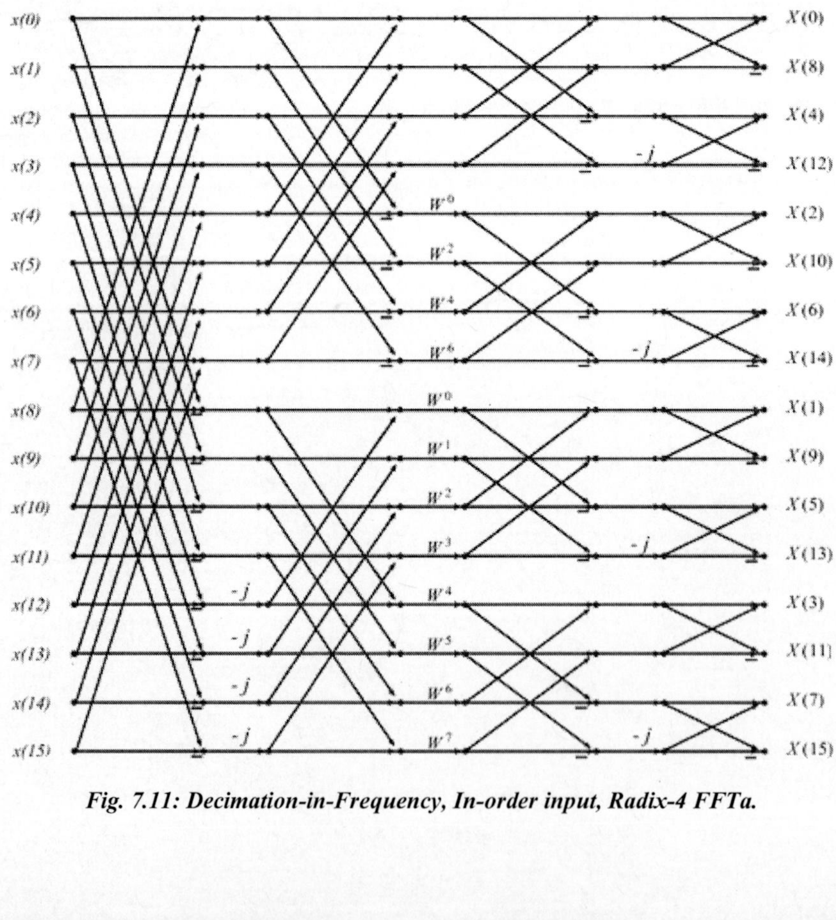

Fig. 7.11: Decimation-in-Frequency, In-order input, Radix-4 FFTa.

*a*Charles Sidney Burrus and Thomas W. Parks,"DFT/FFT and convolution algorithms: Theory and implementation", 1991, John Wiley & Sons, Inc. NY, USA

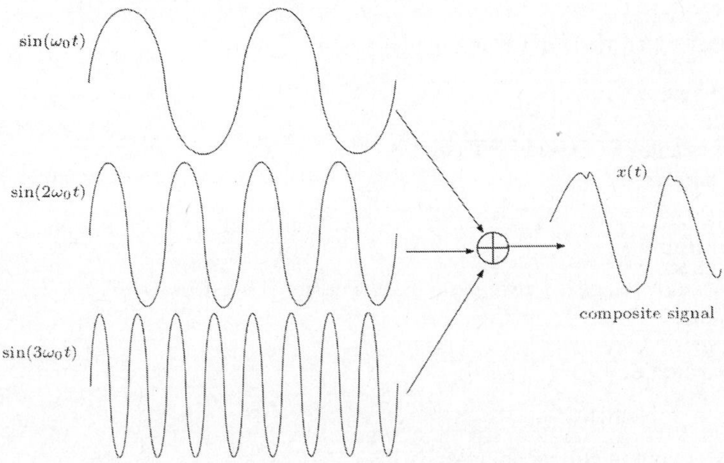

Fig. 7.12: Composite signal.

SUMMARY

The chapter on Fast Fourier Transform (FFT) provides an in-depth exploration of this efficient algorithm for computing the Discrete Fourier Transform (DFT) and its inverse, significantly enhancing the speed of Fourier analysis. It begins by explaining the necessity of the FFT in digital signal processing, particularly in handling large datasets, and contrasts the FFT with the direct computation of the DFT, which is computationally intensive. The chapter details the Cooley-Tukey algorithm, the most widely used FFT algorithm, which reduces the complexity from $O(N^2)$ to O(NlogN), making it feasible to process large signals in real-time applications. Key properties of the FFT, including linearity, periodicity, symmetry, and the convolution theorem, are discussed, emphasizing how these properties facilitate efficient computations. The chapter also covers various FFT implementations, such as the decimation-in-time and decimation-in-frequency approaches, along with practical considerations for choosing the appropriate FFT algorithm based on the signal characteristics. Additionally, the chapter addresses the effects of windowing and zero-padding on the FFT, highlighting their importance in improving frequency resolution and reducing spectral leakage.

EXERCISES

1. Write FFT algorithm to compute the DFT of a signal $x(n)$ using radix-2.
2. Given the impulse response of a system $h(n) = \{1,-1, 1,-1\}$, compute the 4-point FFT to determine the frequency response $H(k)$ of the system.
3. Given the input sequence $x(n) = \{1, 2, 3, 4\}$ and the impulse response $h(n) = \{1,-1, 1,-2\}$, use the FFT to find the output $y(n)$ of the system.
4. Explain with an example, how we can compute linear convolution using the FFT algorithm.
5. Given the frequency response $H(k) = \{2, -1, 0, 1\}$, use the inverse FFT to find the corresponding impulse response $h(n)$.
6. Given a signal $x(n) = \cos(2\pi/8n) + \cos(\pi n)$ for $n = 0, 1, \ldots, 7$, use the FFT to estimate the frequency components present in the signal.

7. Given the sequence $x(n) = \{1, 0, 1, 0, 1, 0, 2\}$, use the FFT to find the dominant frequency component.
8. Given the signal $x(n) = 2\cos(\pi/6n)$ for $n = 0, 1, ..., 15$, use the FFT to identify the harmonic frequencies and their amplitudes.
9. Compute the given signal $x(n)$ DFT using the radix-2 FFT structure.

   $x(n) = \{\underset{\uparrow}{1}, 2, 3, 4, 5, 6, 7, 8\}$

   Compare the direct and FFT-based DFT complexities.
10. Write the radix-4 FFT structure and its complexity.

Multiple Choice Questions

1. What is the main advantage of using the Fast Fourier Transform (FFT) over the Discrete Fourier Transform (DFT)?

   A) FFT is more accurate

   B) FFT is easier to implement

   C) FFT has a lower computational complexity

   D) FFT can handle larger datasets
2. What is the computational complexity of the FFT for a sequence of length N?

   A) O(N)

   B) $O(N^2)$

   C) O(NlogN)

   D) O(logN)
3. The FFT algorithm is based on the principle of:

   A) Divide and conquer

   B) Dynamic programming

   C) Greedy algorithm

   D) Backtracking
4. The Cooley-Tukey algorithm is a common implementation of which transform?

   A) Laplace Transform

   B) Fast Fourier Transform (FFT)

   C) Inverse Fourier Transform

   D) Z-Transform
5. For the FFT to work efficiently, the length of the input sequence should ideally be:

   A) A prime number

   B) A power of 2

   C) An odd number

   D) A perfect square
6. Which variant of the FFT is used when the input sequence length is not a power of 2?

   A) Cooley-Tukey FFT

B) Bluestein's FFT

C) Radix-2 FFT

D) Radix-4 FFT

7. What is the radix-2 FFT algorithm?

A) An FFT algorithm for sequences of any length

B) An FFT algorithm optimized for sequences of length 2^n

C) An FFT algorithm that uses base-2 logarithms

D) An FFT algorithm that operates in $O(N^2)$ time

8. The FFT is often used in digital signal processing to:

A) Smooth a signal

B) Convert a signal from the frequency domain to the time domain

C) Filter noise from a signal

D) Convert a signal from the time domain to the frequency domain

9. Which technique does the FFT utilize to improve the computational efficiency of the DFT?

A) Windowing

B) Convolution

C) Symmetry and periodicity properties

D) Interpolation

10. Which of the following applications can benefit from the use of the FFT?

A) Audio signal processing

B) Image compression

C) Communication systems

D) All of the above

ANSWERS

1	2	3	4	5	6	7	8	9	10
C	C	A	B	B	B	B	D	C	D

KNOW MORE

For more information related to this topic scan the QR code.

OR

Type this link in your browser

https://www.google.co.in/books/edition/_/H_5SAAAAMAAJ?hl=en&gbpv=0

REFERENCES AND SUGGESTED READING

1. B. P. Lathi, "*Principles of Linear Systems and Signals*," *Oxford Second edition*, 2009.
2. John G. Proakis, and Dimitris G. Manolakis "*Digital signal processing: principles, algorithms, and applications, 4/E*,"*Pearson Education India*, 2007.
3. Alan V. Oppenheim, Alan S. Willsky, and S. Hamid Nawab "*Signals & Systems*,"*Pearson Education India*, 1997.
4. Steven W. Smith "*Digital Signal Processing: A Practical Guide for Engineers and Scientists*,"*California Technical Publishing*, 1999.
5. Barrie W. Jervis, and Emmanuel C. Ifeachor "*Digital Signal Processing: A Practical Approach*,"*Pearson Education India*, 2002.

Chapeter-8: Design of Digital Filters

UNIT SPECIFICS

The design of digital filters chapter delves into the fundamental concepts and methodologies used to create digital filters for signal processing applications. It covers key topics such as the classification of filters into FIR (Finite Impulse Response) and IIR (Infinite Impulse Response) types, along with their respective design techniques. The chapter includes step-by-step procedures for filter design, including windowing methods, frequency sampling, and optimization techniques like the Parks-McClellan algorithm. Practical considerations such as filter stability, phase response, and computational efficiency are also discussed, providing a comprehensive understanding of how to design filters that meet specific performance criteria.

RATIONALE

This chapter serves as a crucial foundation in digital signal processing. It provides insights into how digital filters can be used to selectively enhance or suppress specific parts of a signal, which is essential for numerous applications such as noise reduction, signal separation, and data analysis. Understanding digital filter design is key to developing efficient systems in communications, audio processing, and control systems. This chapter equips readers with the theoretical background and practical techniques necessary to design, analyze, and implement digital filters effectively, ensuring optimal performance in real-world scenarios.

PRE-REQUISITE

DTFT, DFT, FTT, and analog filter design

UNIT OUTCOMES

List of outcomes of this unit is as follows:

U8-O1: Fundamentals of digital filter design

U8-O2: FIR filters design and analysis

U8-O3: IIR filters design and analysis

U8-O4: Frequency bands conversions for filter design

Unit-8 Outcomes	EXPECTED MAPPING WITH COURSE OUTCOMES (1- Weak Correlation; 2- Medium correlation; 3- Strong Correlation)					
	CO-1	CO-2	CO-3	CO-4	CO-5	CO-6
U8-O1	–	3	1	3	–	–
U8-O2	–	3	1	3	–	–
U8-O3	–	3	1	3	–	–

8.1 INTRODUCTION

In the process of designing frequency-selective filters, we specify the desired filter characteristics in the frequency domain, outlining the desired magnitude and phase response. During the filter design phase, we calculate the coefficients of a causal Finite Impulse Response (FIR) or Infinite Impulse Response (IIR) filter that closely approximates the specified frequency response criteria. The decision of whether to design an FIR or IIR filter depends on the nature of the problem at hand and the specifics of the desired frequency response specifications. A filter typically consists of passband, transition band, and stopband regions in its frequency response $H(\omega)$. An ideal filter has a transition band width equal to zero and zero gain in the stopband region, as shown in Fig. 8.1. The ω_c denotes the cutoff frequency of the lowpass filter.

8.2 GENERAL CONSIDERATIONS IN FILTER DESIGN

Let's consider an ideal low-pass filter (LPF) and its frequency response characteristic is defined as

$$H(\omega) = \begin{cases} 1, \text{if } |\omega| \leq \omega_c \\ 0, \text{otherwise} \end{cases}$$

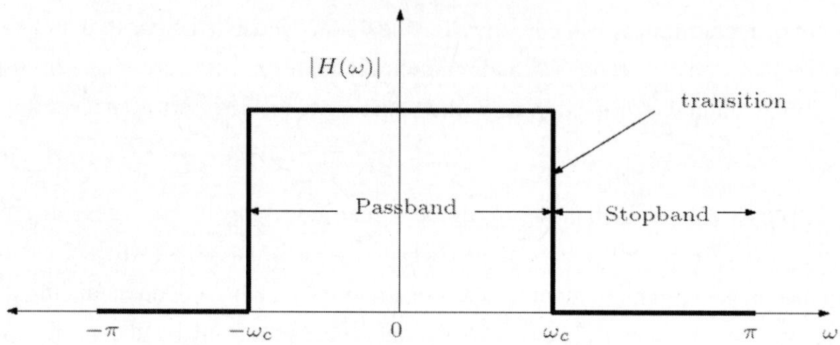

Fig. 8.1: Illustration of an ideal LPF.

Here $H(\omega)$ represents the filter's DTFT and $\omega \in [-\pi, \pi]$. Impulse response $h(n)$ of ideal LPF is expressed as

$$h(n) = \frac{1}{2\pi}\int_{-\omega_c}^{\omega_c} H(\omega)\, e^{j\omega n} d\omega = \frac{\omega_c}{\pi}\frac{\sin(\omega_c n)}{\omega_c n} \tag{8.1}$$

Further $h(n)$ can also be written as

$$h(n) = \begin{cases} \dfrac{\omega_c}{\pi}, \text{if n} = 0 \\ \dfrac{\sin(\omega_c n)}{\omega_c n}, \text{n} \neq 0 \end{cases}$$

Plot of $h(n)$ is shown in Fig. 8.2 for $\omega_c = \pi/3$ and n varies from -30 to 30. It's evident that the ideal lowpass filter, being noncausal, cannot be practically implemented.

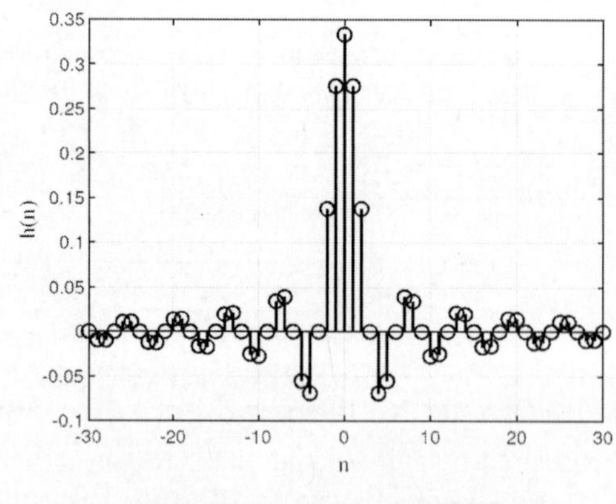

Fig. 8.2: Impulse response of ideal LPF.

The noncausal response $h(n)$ can be converted to causal response by shifting the $h(n)$ towards to right by n_0 time units. However, shifting will result in the phase change of the impulse response of the LPF $h(n)$. Further, $h(n)$ duration can be restricted by multiplying a finite time duration window $w(n)$. Therefore, practically realizable LPF impulse response $h_p(n)$ can be expressed as

$h_p(n) = h(n - n_0)w(n)$ Here, $h(n)$ is the ideal LPF response.

Paley-Wiener Theorem:

It is a fundamental result in the theory of Fourier transforms and complex analysis. It states that if a function in the time or frequency domain has exponential decay, then it must have compact support in the other domain. If impulse response is causal ($h(n) = 0$ for $n < 0$), then frequency response $H(\omega)$ should satisfy a condition that

$$\int_{-\pi}^{\pi} | \ln(|H(\omega)|)| d\omega < \infty \tag{8.2}$$

The Paley-Wiener condition suggests that no causal filter can have its frequency response $H(\omega)$ equal to zero over a finite frequency band. While $H(\omega)$ may be zero at certain frequencies, it cannot be zero over a continuous range of frequencies.

If system is causal, then even and odd part of $h(n)$ can also be expressed as

$h(h) = h_e(n) + h_o(n),\ n \geq 0$

$$h_e(n) = \frac{h(n) + h(-n)}{2}, and h_o(n) = \frac{h(n) - h(-n)}{2}.$$

If $h(n)$ is causal, it is possible to recover $h(n)$ from its even part $h_e(n)$ for $n = 0, 1, , ...$ or from its odd component $h_o(n)$ for $1 \leq n < \infty$, and it can be written as

$2h_e(n)u(n) = h(n)u(n) + h(-n)u(n) \rightarrow h(n) = 2h_e(n)u(n) - h_e(0)\delta(n),\ n \geq 0$

$h(n) = 2h_o(n)u(n) + h(0)\delta(n),\ n \geq 1.$

Therefore, $h_0(n)$ and $h_e(n)$ are related to each other, and are equal for $n \geq 1$.

Further, for absolutely summable $h(n)$, its frequency response is $H(\omega) = H_R(\omega) + jH_I(\omega)$. Thus

$h_e(n) \leftrightarrow H_R(\omega)$

$h_o(n) \leftrightarrow H_I(\omega)$.

Thus, $H_R(\omega)$ and $H_I(\omega)$ are related to each other, which suggests that magnitude $H(\omega)|$ and phase $\angle H(\omega)$ are related to each other in a causal system. The connection between the real and imaginary parts of the Fourier transform of an absolutely summable, causal, and real sequence can

be readily determined as follows:

$$H(\omega) = H_R(\omega) + jH_I(\omega) = \frac{1}{2\pi}\int_{-\pi}^{\pi} 2H_R(\omega) * U(\omega) d\omega - h_e(0)$$

$$H(\omega) = \frac{1}{\pi}\int_{-\pi}^{\pi} H_R(\lambda)\, U(\omega - \lambda) d\lambda - h_e(0)$$

Here ⋆ denotes the convolution operation. Further, $U(\omega) = \pi\delta(\omega) + \frac{1}{1-e^{jw}} = \pi\delta(\omega) + \frac{1}{2} - \frac{j}{2}cot(\frac{\omega}{2})$

for the range$-\pi \geq \omega\pi$. Thus,

$$H(\omega) = \frac{1}{\pi}\int_{-\pi}^{\pi} [\pi H_R(\omega) + \frac{1}{2}H_R(\omega) - \frac{j}{2}H_R(\lambda)cot(\frac{\omega - \lambda}{2})d\lambda] - h_e(0)$$

$$H(\omega) = H_R(\omega) - \frac{j}{2\pi}\int_{-\pi}^{\pi} H_R(\lambda)\, cot(\frac{\omega - \lambda}{2}) d\lambda$$

Comparing above two equations, we get

$$H_I(\omega) = -\frac{1}{2\pi}\int_{-\pi}^{\pi} H_R(\lambda)\, cot(\frac{\omega - \lambda}{2}) d\lambda$$

Thus, either time domain or frequency domain odd part of the signal is determined from the even part of the signal for a causal signal. Thus, magnitude and phase response of the *H(ω)* are dependent to each other.

In summary, causality holds significant implications in the design of frequency-selective filters, such as 1. The frequency response *H(ω)* cannot be zero except at a finite number of points in the frequency domain. 2. The magnitude |*H(ω)*| cannot remain constant within any finite range of frequencies, and the transition from passband to stopband cannot be infinitely sharp. This limitation arises from the Gibbs phenomenon, which stems from the truncation of *h(n)* to ensure causality. 3. The real and imaginary components of *H(ω)* are interconnected and governed by

the convolution relation

$$H_I(\omega) = -\frac{1}{2\pi}\int_{-\pi}^{\pi} H_R(\lambda)\, cot(\frac{\omega - \lambda}{2}) d\lambda$$

Consequently, the magnitude |*H(ω)*| and phase *Θ(ω)* = ∠*H(ω)* of *H(ω)* cannot be arbitrarily chosen.

8.2.1 Filter selection

- Clearly define the desired filter characteristics, including the passband ripple, stopband attenuation, transition bandwidth, and frequency response shape. These specifications will guide the design process and determine the appropriate filter type and order.
- Choose the appropriate filter type based on the application requirements and specifications. Consider whether a FIR or IIR filter is better suited for the desired frequency response and implementation constraints.
- Decide whether to design the filter in the frequency domain or time domain. Frequency domain design involves specifying the desired frequency response directly, while time domain design focuses on designing the filter impulse response to meet the desired specifications.
- Ensure that the designed filter is stable and causal to prevent unstable behavior or signal distortion. This is particularly important for IIR filters, which can become unstable for certain coefficient values.
- Determine whether a linear phase response is necessary for the application. Linear phase filters preserve the shape of input signals without introducing phase distortion and are often preferred in applications such as audio and image processing.
- Consider the computational resources available for filter implementation. Higher-order fil- ters and complex frequency response specifications may require more computational re- sources, which can impact real-time processing and hardware implementation.
- Determine the appropriate filter length based on the desired frequency response characteris- tics and computational constraints. Longer filter lengths may be necessary to achieve sharp cutoffs or steep transition bands but can increase computational complexity and memory requirements.

- Evaluate the feasibility of implementing the designed filter in hardware or software. Consider factors such as processing speed, memory requirements, and available resources for filter implementation.

8.2.2 Filter parameters

As discussed, ideal filters are non-causal, making them impractical for real-time signal processing applications. Causality dictates that the frequency response characteristic $H(\omega)$ of the filter cannot be zero, except at a finite set of points in the frequency range. Furthermore, $H(\omega)$ cannot exhibit an infinitely sharp cutoff from the passband to the stopband; in other words, it cannot drop abruptly from unity to zero.

The passband is the range of frequencies where the filter allows signals to pass through with minimal attenuation. In other words, it is the range of frequencies where the filter's gain is relatively high or non-zero. In Fig. 8.3, $\omega \in [0, \omega_p]$ denotes the passband of the LPF. Signals within the passband are preserved by the filter, while signals outside this range are attenuated.

The stopband is the range of frequencies where the filter attenuates or rejects incoming signals. It is the range of frequencies where the filter's gain is significantly reduced or zero. In Fig. 8.3, ω *in* $[\omega_s, \pi]$ denotes the stopband of the LPF. Signals within the stopband are effectively suppressed or filtered out by the filter.

The transition band is the frequency range between the passband and stopband where the filter's response transitions from its passband characteristics to its stopband characteristics. In Fig. 8.3, $\omega \in [\omega_p, \omega_s]$ denotes the transition of the LPF.

In Fig. 8.3, δ_1 and δ_2 are the passband ripple and stopband ripple, respectively. For ideal filter, $\delta_1 = 0$ and $\delta_2 = 0$, and transition band approaches $\omega_s - \omega_p \rightarrow 0$. Consequently, the ripple in the passband is $20 \log_{10}(\delta_1)$ decibels, and that in the stopband is $20 \log_{10}(\delta_2)$ since we use magnitude $H(\omega)$ for a filter specifications. In every filter design scenario, we can define the following parameters: The maximum allowable passband ripple, the maximum allowable stopband ripple, the passband edge frequency, denoted as ω_s, and the stopband edge frequency, denoted as ω_s.

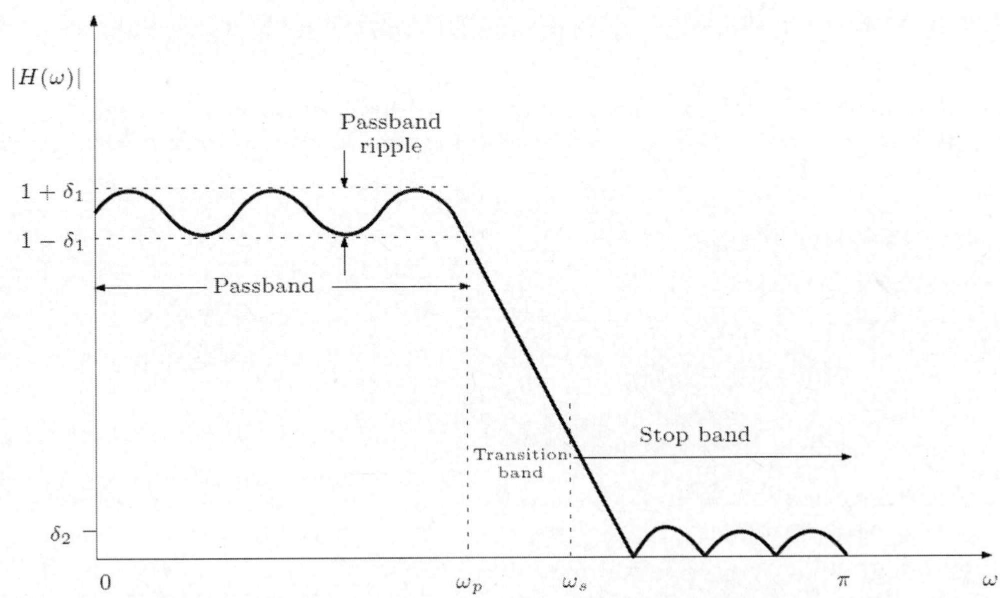

Fig. 8.3: Realizable LPF characteristics

8.3 FIR FILTERS

FIR filters are characterized by a finite impulse response, meaning that their output response to an impulse input eventually decays to zero.

In general, LTI causal and stable system is characterized using the difference equation

$$y(n) = -\sum_{k=1}^{N} a_k\, y(n-k) + \sum_{k=0}^{M-1} b_k\, x(n-k).$$

The z transform of the above equation is

$$H(z) = \frac{Y(z)}{X(z)} = \frac{\sum_{k=0}^{M-1} b_k z^{-k}}{\sum_{k=0}^{N} a_k z^{-k}}, a_0 = 1 \quad (8.3)$$

Evaluating the x-transform at the unit circle, we can write the DTFT of the system as

$$H(\omega) = \frac{\sum_{k=0}^{M-1} b_k e^{-j\omega k}}{1+\sum_{k=1}^{N} a_k e^{-j\omega k}} \quad (8.4)$$

The FIR filters are characterized using only the input and previous inputs, and system difference equation of the M length coefficients is expressed as

$$y(n) = b_0 x(n) + b_1 x(n-1) + \ldots + b_{M-1} x(n-(M-1)) = \sum_{k=0}^{M-1} b_k\, x(n-k).$$

System is characterized using the coefficients *{b_k}s* and comparing with causal and M length LTI system convolution output $\sum_{k=0}^{M-1} h(k)\, x(n-k)$, we can write $h(k) = b_k, k = 0, 1, \ldots, M-1$.

The direct form I signal flow graph for the FIR filter *H(z)* is shown in Fig. 8.4.

Thus FIR filter can be characterized as

$$H(z) = \frac{Y(z)}{X(z)} = \sum_{n=0}^{M-1} h(n) z^{-k}. \quad (8.5)$$

An FIR filter exhibits linear phase if its unit sample response meets the condition:

$h(n) = \pm h(M-1-n),\ n = 0, 1, \ldots M-1$

If h(n) = h(M-1-n) filter is called symmetric and h(n) = -h(M-1-n) filter is called anti-symmetric.

M-odd and h(n) Symmetric: Filter x transform is expressed as

$H(z) = h(0) + h(1)z^{-1} + h(1)z^{-1} + \ldots + h(M 2-1) + h(M-2)z^{M-2} + h(M-1)z^{M-1}$

$h(0) = h(M-1),\ h(1) = h(M-2), \ldots$ (8.6)

We can write above equation as

$$H(z) = z^{-(M-1)/2}[h(\frac{M-1}{2}) + \sum_{n=0}^{\frac{M-3}{2}} h(n)\,(z^{\frac{M-1-k}{2}} + z^{-\frac{M-1-k}{2}})]$$

Evaluating at the unit circle, DTFT is expressed as

$$H(\omega) = e^{-\frac{j\omega(M-1)}{2}}\left[h\left(\frac{M-1}{2}\right) + \sum_{n=0}^{\frac{M-3}{2}} 2\, h(n) cos\left(\omega\left(\frac{M-1-2n}{2}\right)\right)\right] = H_r(\omega) e^{j\theta(\omega)} \quad (8.7)$$

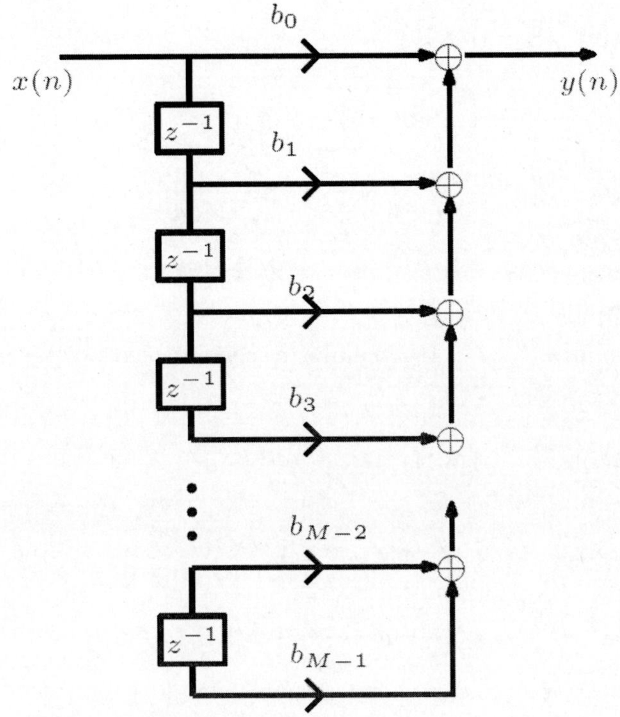

Fig. 8.4: Direct form I signal flow graph for FIR filter H(z).

Thus, H(ω) has linear phase and amplitude as a real function of frequency, i.e., $H_r(\omega)$

$$H_r(\omega) = h\left(\frac{M-1}{2}\right) + 2\sum_{n=0}^{\frac{M-3}{2}} h(n)\cos\left(\omega\left(\frac{M-1-2n}{2}\right)\right) \tag{8.8}$$

And

$$\theta(\omega) = \begin{cases} -\omega\dfrac{M-1}{2}, \text{if } H_r(\omega) \geq 0 \\ -\omega\dfrac{M-1}{2} + \pi, \text{if } H_r(\omega) < 0 \end{cases}$$

<u>M-odd and h(n) anti-symmetric</u>:

In this case h(n) =-h(M-1-n) for n = 0, 1, ...M-1 and filter response is expressed as

$H(\omega) = H_r(\omega)e^{j\Theta(\omega)}$ with

$$H_r(\omega) = 2\sum_{n=0}^{\frac{M-3}{2}} h(n)\sin(\omega(\frac{M-1-2n}{2})) \tag{8.8}$$

$$\text{And } \theta(\omega) = \begin{cases} \frac{\pi}{2} - \omega\frac{M-1}{2}, \text{if } H_r(\omega) \geq 0 \\ \frac{\pi}{2} - \omega\frac{M-1}{2} + \pi, \text{if } H_r(\omega) < 0 \end{cases}$$

<u>*M*-even and *h(n)* symmetric:</u>

In this case *h(n) = h(M-1-n)* for *n = 0, 1, ...M-1* and filter response is expressed as

$H(\omega) = H_r(\omega)e^{j\Theta(\omega)}$ with

$H_r(\omega) = 2\sum_{n=0}^{\frac{M}{2}-1} h(n)cos(\omega(\frac{M-1-2n}{2}))$ (8.10)

And

$$\theta(\omega) = \begin{cases} -\omega\frac{M-1}{2}, \text{if } H_r(\omega) \geq 0 \\ -\omega\frac{M-1}{2} + \pi, \text{if } H_r(\omega) < 0 \end{cases}$$

In this case h((M-1)/2)=0.

<u>M-even and *h(n)* anti-symmetric</u>:

In this case *h(n) = h(M-1-n)* for *n = 0, 1, ...M-1* and filter response is expressed as

$H(\omega) = H_r(\omega)e^{j\Theta(\omega)}$ with

$H_r(\omega) = 2\sum_{n=0}^{\frac{M}{2}-1} h(n)sin(\omega(\frac{M-1-2n}{2}))$ (8.11)

And

$$\theta(\omega) = \begin{cases} \frac{\pi}{2} - \omega\frac{M-1}{2}, \text{if } H_r(\omega) \geq 0 \\ \frac{\pi}{2} - \omega\frac{M-1}{2} + \pi, \text{if } H_r(\omega) < 0 \end{cases}$$

So symmetric or anti-symmetric case filter response is expressed as

$$H(\omega) = H_r(\omega)e^{j\theta(\omega)}$$

For even M case, filter response $H_r(\omega = 0) = 0$ and $H_r(\omega = \pi) = 0$. Thus it is not suitable for lowpass and highpass filter design.

Further, we can write

$$H(z) = z^{-(M-1)/2}[h(\frac{M-1}{2}) + \sum_{n=0}^{\frac{M-3}{2}} h(n)\,(z^{\frac{M-1-k}{2}} + z^{-\frac{M-1-k}{2}})]$$

$$H(z^{-1})z^{-(M-1)} = \pm H(z)$$

So roots of H(z) and $H(z^{-1})$are reciprocal to each other. Therefore, H(z) has reciprocal roots, as shown in Fig. 8.5. If zero at $z=z_2$, then complex conjugate at $z = z_2^*$. Further due to symmetry zeros at $z = 1/z_2^*$ and $z = 1/z_2$, as shown Fig. 8.5

8.3.1 FIR filter design using windows

Let $H_d(\omega)$ be the desired frequency response of the filter. Impulse response $h_d(n)$ is expressed as

$$h_d(n) = \frac{1}{2\pi}\int_{-\pi}^{\pi} H_d(\omega)e^{jn\omega}d\omega$$

Now impulse response $h_d(n)$ is multiplied by a window *w(n)* since ideal filter $h_d(n)$ has infinite duration. Window is defined as

$$\omega(n) = \begin{cases} non-zero, for\ n = 0,1,\dots,M-1 \\ 0, otherwise \end{cases}$$

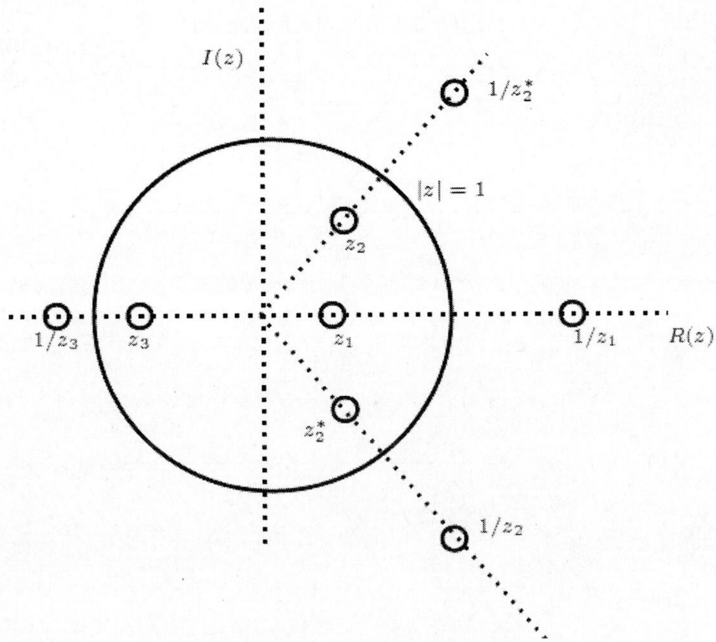

Fig. 8.5: Symmetry of zero locations for a linear-phase FIR fitter H(z).

For example, rectangular window to length M is defined as

$$\omega(n) = \begin{cases} 1, for\ n = 0,1,\dots, M-1 \\ 0, otherwise \end{cases}$$

Practical filter impulse response after windowing is defined

$h(n) = h_d(n)w(n)$.

or $h(n) = \begin{cases} h_d(n), for\ n = 0,1,\dots, M-1 \\ 0, otherwise \end{cases}$

Frequency domain filter response is defined as

$H(\omega) = 2\pi\ H_d(\omega) * W(\omega)$ Here $\star$ denotes the convolution, and

$$H(\omega) = \frac{1}{2\pi}\int_{-\pi}^{\pi} H_d(\lambda)W(\omega-\lambda)d\lambda$$

The desired frequency response is convolved with window frequency response. Thus, smearing effect appears in the practical filter response. Window in frequency domain is defined as

$$W(\omega) = \sum_{n=0}^{M-1} w(n)e^{-j\omega n} = e^{-\frac{j\omega(M-1)}{2}}\frac{sin(\omega M/2)}{sin(\omega/2)}. \qquad (8.13)$$

Window magnitude and phase are expressed as

$|W(\omega)| = \frac{|sin\left(\frac{\omega M}{2}\right)|}{|sin\left(\frac{\omega}{2}\right)|}, -\pi < \omega < \pi$ (8.14)

and

$$\angle W(\omega) = \theta(\omega) = \begin{cases} -\omega\frac{M-1}{2}, \text{if } \sin(\omega M/2) \ge 0 \\ -\omega\frac{M-1}{2} + \pi, \text{if } \sin(\omega M/2) < 0 \end{cases}$$

Table 8.1: Window Functions

Name of window	Time domain sequence $h(n)$ for $n = 0, 1, ..., M-1$
Rectangular	$h(n) = 1,\ n = 0, 1, ...M-1$
Bartlett (Triangular)	$h(n) = 1 - \frac{2\lvert n - \frac{M-1}{2}\rvert}{M-1},\ n = 0, 1, ...M-1$
Blackman	$h(n) = 0.42 - 0.5\cos(\frac{2\pi n}{M-1}) + 0.08\cos(\frac{4\pi n}{M-1})$
Hamming	$h(n) = 0.54 - 0.46\cos(\frac{2\pi n}{M-1}),\ n = 0, 1, ...M-1$
Hanning	$h(n) = 0.5\left[1 - \cos(\frac{2\pi n}{M-1})\right],\ n = 0, 1, ...M-1$
Kaiser	$h(n) = \frac{I_0\left[\alpha\sqrt{\left(\frac{M-1}{2}\right)^2 - \left(n - \frac{M-1}{2}\right)^2}\right]}{I_0\left[\alpha\left(\frac{M-1}{2}\right)\right]},\ n = 0, 1, ...M-1$
Tukey	$h(n) = 0.5\left[1 + \cos(\frac{n - (1+\alpha)(M-1)/2}{(1-\alpha)(M-1)/2}\pi)\right],$ $\alpha(M-1)/2 \le \lvert n - (M-1)/2\rvert \le (M-1)/2$

* $I_0(\cdot)$ is the zeroth-order modified Bessel function of the first kind.

Table 8.2: Frequency domain characteristics of some window functions

Name of window	Approximate width of the mainlobe	Peak sidelobe (dB) (relative to mainlobe)
Rectangular	$\frac{4\pi}{M}$	-13
Bartlett (Triangular)	$\frac{8\pi}{M}$	-25
Blackman	$\frac{12\pi}{M}$	-57
Hamming	$\frac{8\pi}{M}$	-41
Hanning	$\frac{8\pi}{M}$	-31

* M is the length of window in the time domain.

8.3.2 Design of FIR filters using frequency sampling method

In the frequency sampling method for FIR filter design, we define the desired frequency response $H_d(\omega)$ at a series of evenly spaced frequencies as

$$H_d(\omega) = \begin{cases} \frac{2\pi}{M}(k+\alpha), if k = 0,1,\ldots,\frac{M-1}{2} \; M\, odd \\ 0, if k = 0,1,\ldots,\frac{M}{2}-1 \; M\, even \end{cases}$$

$\alpha = 0$ or $1/2$. To minimize sidelobes, it is preferable to refine the frequency specifications within the transition band of the filter. First, we collect M samples in the frequency domain of the desired frequency response as $H(k+\alpha) = H_d(\omega = \frac{2\pi}{M}k)$, $k = 0, 1, \ldots, M-1$.

$$H(k+\alpha) = H_d(w = \frac{2\pi}{M}k), k = 0,1,\ldots,M-1$$

Therefore, time domain sequence is written as

$$h(n) = \frac{1}{M}\sum_{k=0}^{M-1} H(k+\alpha)\, e^{j\frac{2\pi(k+\alpha)n}{M}}, n = 0,1,\ldots,M-1$$

Further, if $h(n)$ is real then $H(k) = H^*(M-1-k)$. This frequency symmetry can also be combined with time domain symmetry to reduce the filter specifications, and highlighted below in Table 8.3 and Table 8.4. linear phase FIR filter is expressed as $H(\omega) = H_r(\omega)e^{j[\omega(M-1)/2+\pi/2]}$ (anti-symmetric) or $H(\omega) = H_r(\omega)e^{j[\omega(M-1)/2]}$ (symmetric) . Here $H_r(\omega)$ denotes the amplitude part of the filter response.

Table 8.3: Unit sample response h(n) for symmetric case

$\alpha = 0$	$H(k) = G(k)e^{j\pi k/M}, k = 0, 1, ..M-1$ $G(k) = (-1)^k H_r(2\pi k/M), G(k) = -G(M-k)$ $h(n) = \frac{1}{M}\left[G(0) + 2\sum_{k=1}^{U} G(k)\cos[\frac{2\pi k}{M}(n+1/2)]\right]$ $U = \begin{cases}(M-1)/2, & \text{if } M \text{ odd} \\ (M/2-1), & \text{if } M \text{ even}\end{cases}$
$\alpha = 1/2$	$H(k+1/2) = G(k+1/2)e^{-j\pi/2}e^{j\pi(2k+1)/2M}$ $G(k) = (-1)^k H_r(2\pi(k+1/2)/M), G(k+1/2) = -G(M-k-1/2)$ $h(n) = \frac{2}{M}\left[\sum_{k=0}^{U} G(k+1/2)\sin[\frac{2\pi(k+1/2)}{M}(n+1/2)]\right]$ $U = \begin{cases}(M-1)/2, & \text{if } M \text{ odd} \\ (M/2-1), & \text{if } M \text{ even}\end{cases}$

Parks-McClellan algorithm

The Parks-McClellan algorithm, also known as the Remez exchange algorithm, is a method used for designing FIR filters with specified frequency response characteristics. Here's an overview of the Park-McClellan method: Define the desired frequency response characteristics of the filter, such as passband ripple, stopband attenuation, and transition bandwidth. The Parks-McClellan algorithm is an iterative algorithm that finds the optimal filter coefficients by alternating between two steps: *Chebyshev approximation*: Initially, the algorithm computes an initial guess for the filter coefficients using the Chebyshev approximation, which minimizes the maximum absolute error between the desired and actual frequency responses.

Remez exchange: Then, it applies the Remez exchange algorithm to iteratively refine the filter coefficients. This involves finding the optimal filter coefficients by iteratively placing equiripple error bands in the frequency response.

The iterative process continues until the desired convergence criteria are met, such as the maximum number of iterations or the desired level of approximation error. The algorithm converges to a set of filter coefficients that provide the best approximation to the desired frequency response while meeting the specified constraints. Once the filter coefficients are determined, they can be used to implement the FIR filter using standard techniques such as convolution.

Table 8.4: Unit sample response h(n) for anti-symmetric case

$\alpha = 0$	$H(k) = G(k)e^{j\pi/2}e^{j\pi k/M}, k = 0, 1, ..M-1$ $G(k) = (-1)^k H_r(2\pi k/M), G(k) = G(M-k)$ $h(n) = -\frac{2}{M}\left[\sum_{k=1}^{(M-1)/2} G(k)\sin[\frac{2\pi k}{M}(n+1/2)]\right] \quad (M \text{ odd})$ $h(n) = \frac{1}{M}\left[(-1)^{n+1}G(M/2) - 2\left[\sum_{k=1}^{M/2-1} G(k)\sin[\frac{2\pi k}{M}(n+1/2)]\right]\right] \quad (M \text{ even})$
$\alpha = 1/2$	$H(k+1/2) = G(k+1/2)e^{j\pi(2k+1)/2M}, k = 0, 1, ..M-1$ $G(k+1/2) = (-1)^k H_r(2\pi(k+1/2)/M), G(k+1/2) = -G(M-k-1/2)$ $, G(M/2) = 0(\text{M odd})$ $h(n) = \frac{2}{M}\left[\sum_{k=0}^{V} G(k+1/2)\cos[\frac{2\pi(k+1/2)}{M}(n+1/2)]\right]$ $V = \begin{cases} \frac{M-3}{2}, & \text{if } M \text{ odd} \\ (M/2-1), & \text{if } M \text{ even} \end{cases}$

8.3.3 Steps of FIR filter design

Specification: Define the desired frequency response characteristics of the filter, including passband ripple, stopband attenuation, transition band width, and cutoff frequencies.

Select Window Function: Choose an appropriate window function based on the desired filter characteristics and design constraints. Common window functions include the Hamming, Hanning, Blackman, and Kaiser windows.

Determine Filter Length: Determine the length of the FIR filter based on the desired fre- quency response specifications and the characteristics of the selected window function. The filter length should be sufficient to meet the specified design requirements.

Calculate Impulse Response: Compute the ideal impulse response of the desired filter using frequency domain techniques such as the Fourier series expansion or the inverse Fourier transform.

Apply Window Function: Apply the selected window function to the ideal impulse response to shape it into the desired FIR filter response. This involves element-wise multiplication of the window function coefficients with the ideal impulse response.

Normalize Filter Coefficients: Normalize the filter coefficients to ensure that the frequency response meets the desired specifications and that the filter has unity gain in the passband.

Optional Optimization: If necessary, iteratively adjust the filter length, window function parameters, or other design parameters to optimize the filter performance while meeting the specified requirements.

Implementation: Implement the designed FIR filter in hardware or software using standard digital signal processing techniques. This may involve convolving the input signal with the filter coefficients in real-time or offline processing applications.

8.3.4 Examples: FIR filter designs

Example 8.3.1 *Determine the coefficients of a linear-phase FIR filter of length* M = 15 *which has a symmetric unit sample response and a frequency response that satisfies the conditions*

$$H_r\left(\frac{2\pi k}{M}\right) = \begin{cases} 1, k = 0,1,2,3 \\ 0.5, k = 4 \\ 0\ , 5,6,7 \end{cases}$$

If h(n) *is real,* H(k+α) = H*(M-k-α), *and* H(0+α) = H*(M-α) *or* H(1+α) = H*(M-1-α). *Then specification reduces from M points to (M+1)/2 or M/2.*

Since h(n) *is symmetric and the frequencies are selected to correspond to* α = 0, *as* $H(\omega) = H_r(\omega)e^{j[\omega(M-1)/2]}$ *with* $G(k) = (-1)^k H_r(2\pi k/15)$, k = 0, , 1, ..., 7 *and* G(k) = −G(M − k), k = 8, ...14 $G(0) = H_r(0) = 1$, $G(1) = -H_r(1) = -1$, $G(2) = H_r(2) = 1$, $G(3) = -H_3(3) = -1$, $G(4) = H_r(4) = 0.5$, $G(5) = -H_r(5) = 0$, $G(6) = H_r(6) = 0$, $G(7) = -H_r(7) = 0$. G(8) = −G(15 − 8) = −G(7) = 0, G(9) = 0, ...

Impulse response is

$$h(n) = \frac{1}{M}\left[G(0) + 2\sum_{k=1}^{U} G(k)\cos[\frac{2\pi k}{M}(n+1/2)]\right]$$

$$h(n) = \frac{1}{15}\left[G(0) + 2\sum_{k=1}^{7} G(k)\cos[\frac{2\pi k}{15}(n+1/2)]\right].$$

$$\begin{bmatrix} h(0) = h(14) \\ h(1) = h(143) \\ h(2) = h(12) \\ h(3) = h(11) \\ h(4) = h(10) \\ h(5) = h(9) \\ h(6) = h(8) \\ h(7) \end{bmatrix} = \begin{bmatrix} -0.0052 \\ -0.0127 \\ 0.0333 \\ 0.0244 \\ -0.0873 \\ -0.0311 \\ 0.3119 \\ 0.5333 \end{bmatrix} \quad (8.15)$$

Example 8.3.2 *Rectangular window in time and frequency domain is shown in Fig.* 8.6 *by considering window length* M = 51.

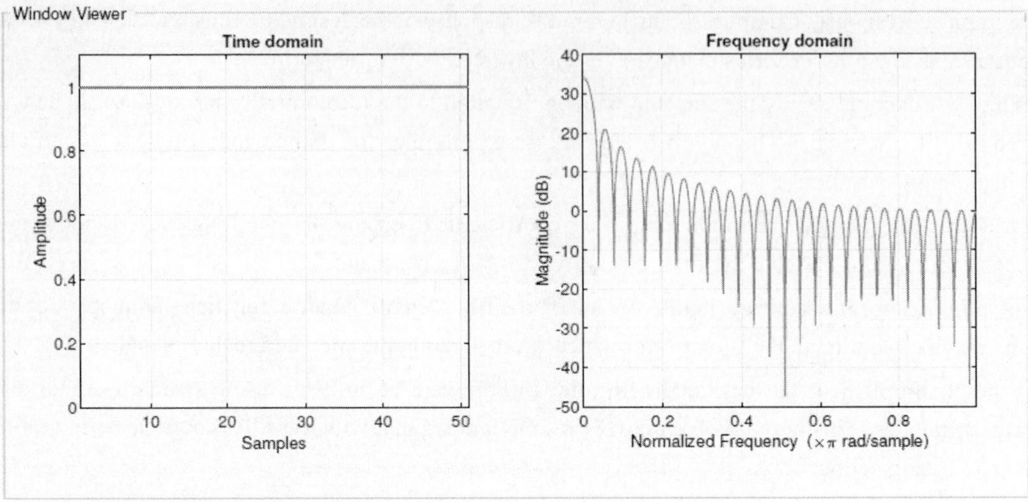

Fig. 8.6: Rectangular window function w(n).

Example 8.3.3 *Hanning window in time and frequency domain is shown in Fig.* 8.7 *by considering window length* M = 51.

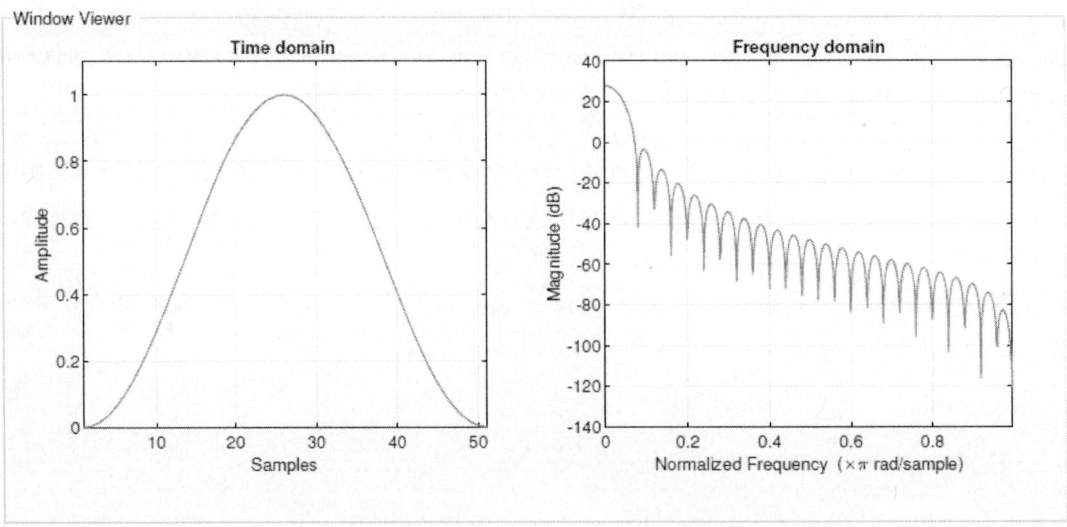

Fig. 8.7: Hanning window function w(n).

Example 8.3.4 *Hamming window in time and frequency domain is shown in Fig. 8.8 by considering window length* M = 51.

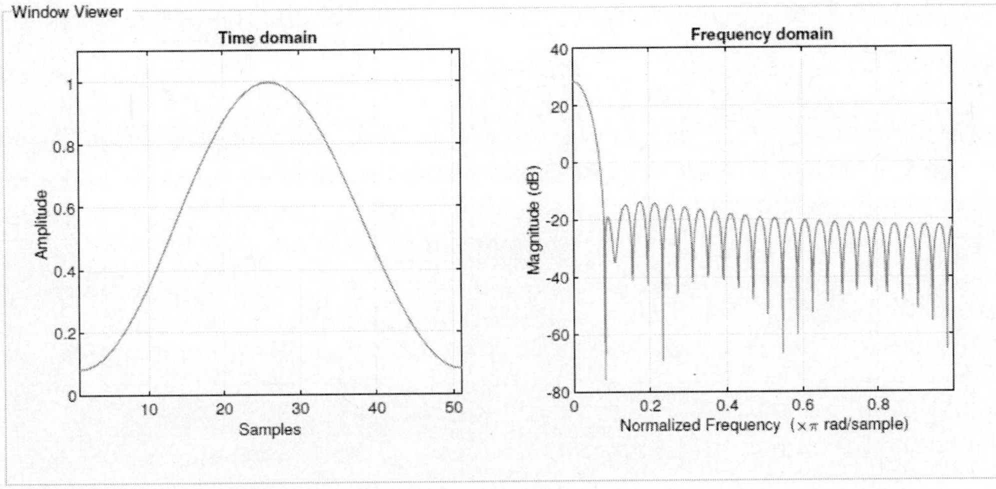

Fig. 8.8: Hamming window function w(n).

Example 8.3.5 Kaiser window in time and frequency domain is shown in Fig. 8.9 by considering window length M = 51.

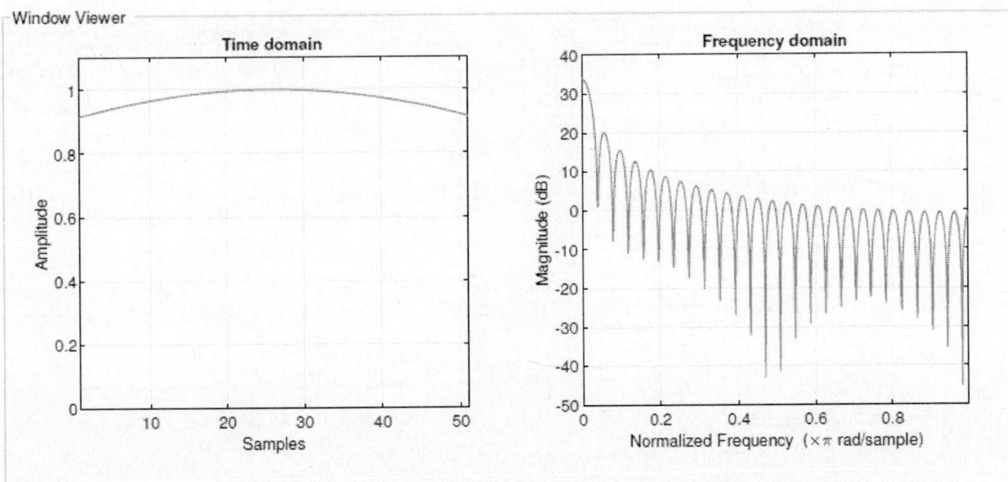

Fig. 8.9: Kaiser window function w(n).

Example 8.3.6 *Tukey window in time and frequency domain is shown in Fig.* 8.10 *by considering window length* M = 51.

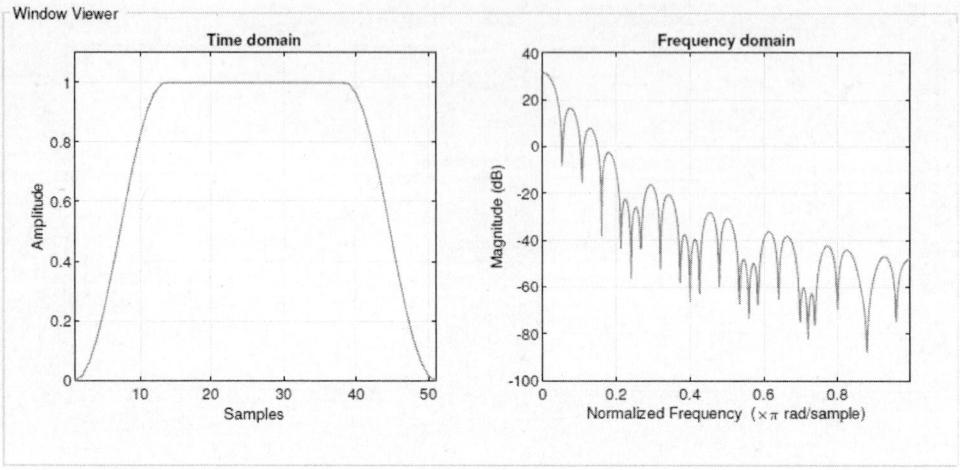

Fig. 8.10: Tukey window function w(n).

Example 8.3.7 *Blackman window in time and frequency domain is shown in Fig.* 8.11 *by considering window length* M = 51.

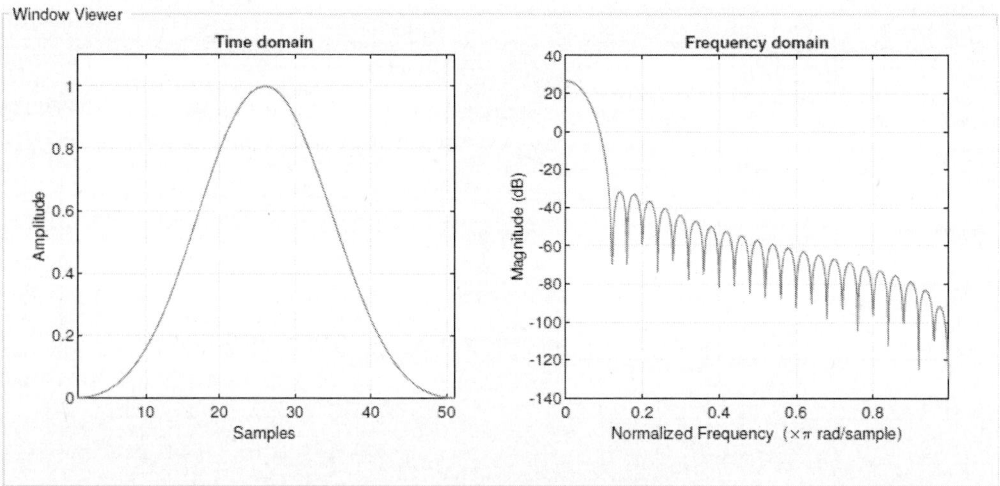

Fig. 8.11: Blackman window function w(n).

Example 8.3.8 *Bartlett window in time and frequency domain is shown in Fig. 8.12 by considering window length* M = 51.

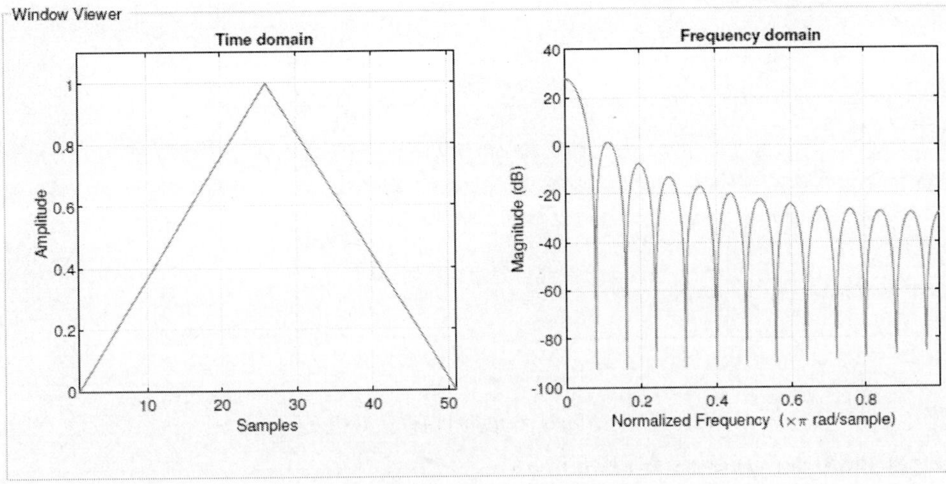

Fig. 8.12: Bartlett window function w(n).

Example 8.3.9 *Hilbert transform is designed in this example. Hilbert transform is expressed as*

$$H_d(\omega) = \begin{cases} -j, if\ 0 \le \omega \le \pi \\ j, if\ -\pi < \omega < 0 \end{cases}$$

Correspond impulse response in the time domain is written as

$$h_d(n) = \frac{1}{2\pi}\int_{-\pi}^{\pi} H_d(\omega)e^{jn\omega}d\omega$$

So

$$h_d(n) = \begin{cases} \frac{2}{\pi}\frac{\sin^2(\pi n/2)}{n}, if\ n \neq 0 \\ 0, \text{if n} = 0 \end{cases}$$

Magnitude and phase responses are plotted in Fig. 8.13

```
N = { 'mineven ', 18 } ; % Minimum even−order , start order estimate at 18
F = [ 0.1 0.9 ] ; % Frequency vector
A = [ 1 1 ] ; % Magnitude vector
R = 0.1 ; % Deviation ( ripple )
b = firgr (N,F,A,R, 'hilbert' ) ;
freqz ( b , 1 , ' whole ' )
```

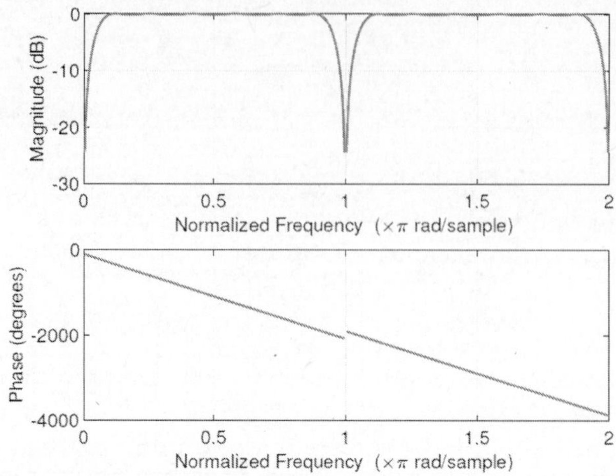

Fig. 8.13: Hilbert transform filter design

8.3.5 Advantages and Disadvantages of FIR Filters

Linear Phase Response: FIR filters can achieve linear phase response, which preserves the shape of input signals without introducing phase distortion. This property is crucial in applications where phase linearity is essential, such as in audio and image processing.

Stability: FIR filters are inherently stable, regardless of the filter order or coefficients. This stability makes FIR filters easier to design and implement compared to IIR filters, which may become unstable for certain coefficient values.

Arbitrary Frequency Response: FIR filters can approximate arbitrary frequency response characteristics with high precision, making them suitable for applications that require specific passband ripple, stopband attenuation, and transition band steepness.

Ease of Implementation: FIR filters can be implemented using direct convolution or fast convolution algorithms, which are straightforward to understand and implement. Additionally, FIR filters are well-suited for parallel processing architectures, enabling efficient hardware implementation.

Disadvantages

High Computational Complexity: FIR filters typically require a larger number of filter coefficients to achieve similar frequency response characteristics compared to IIR filters. As a result, FIR filters may have higher computational complexity, especially for high-order designs.

Longer Filter Length: FIR filters with sharp transition bands or narrow stopbands may re- quire long filter lengths to meet the desired specifications. Longer filter lengths can increase memory requirements and computational overhead, particularly in real-time applications.

Limited Frequency Selectivity: While FIR filters can achieve arbitrary frequency response characteristics, they may require a higher filter order to achieve sharp cutoffs or steep transition bands compared to IIR filters. This limitation can lead to increased design complexity and computational requirements.

No Feedback Path: FIR filters lack a feedback path, which limits their ability to adapt to changes in the input signal or to implement recursive filtering techniques. This limitation may be disadvantageous in certain adaptive filtering applications.

Large storage requirements: For the implementation of FIR filter complex computational techniques are required It is hard to implementation than IIR. Expensive due to large order, require more memory, and time-consuming process.

8.4 IIR FILTERS

IIR filters have an infinite impulse response, meaning that their output response to an impulse input continues indefinitely. Designing IIR filters primarily focuses on the magnitude response of the filter, considering the phase response as secondary. The prevalent approach for digital IIR filter design involves creating an analog IIR filter and subsequently converting it into an equivalent digital filter.

There exist several classes of analog low-pass filters, among which the Butterworth, Chebyshev, and Elliptic filters are prominent. These filters vary in their pole placement and exhibit distinct magnitude and phase responses. Fig. 8.14 depicts their frequency responses. The Butterworth filter maintains monotonicity across all frequencies, with no local maxima or minima. It is also referred to as a maximally flat magnitude filter. In contrast, the Chebyshev filter exhibits mono- tonicity in the stop-band and equiripple behavior in the pass-band. Meanwhile, the Elliptic filter demonstrates equiripple characteristics across all bands.

An analog filter can be described by its system function in the Laplace domain as

$$H_a(s) = \frac{\sum_{k=0}^{M-1} \beta_k\, s^k}{1 + \sum_{k=1}^{N-1} \alpha_k\, s^k}$$

where β_k and α_k are the filter coefficients. The Laplace transform is defined as

$$H_a(s) = \int_{-\infty}^{\infty} h_a(t)\, e^{-st} dt$$

Here $h_a(t)$ is the impulse response of the filter in the time domain and $s = \sigma + j\Omega$ is the com- plex variable. Further, the analog filter can be also described by the linear constant-coefficient differential equation as

$$\sum_{k=0}^{N-1} \alpha_k \frac{d^k y(t)}{dt^k} = \sum_{k=0}^{M-1} \beta_k \frac{d^k x(t)}{dt^k}$$

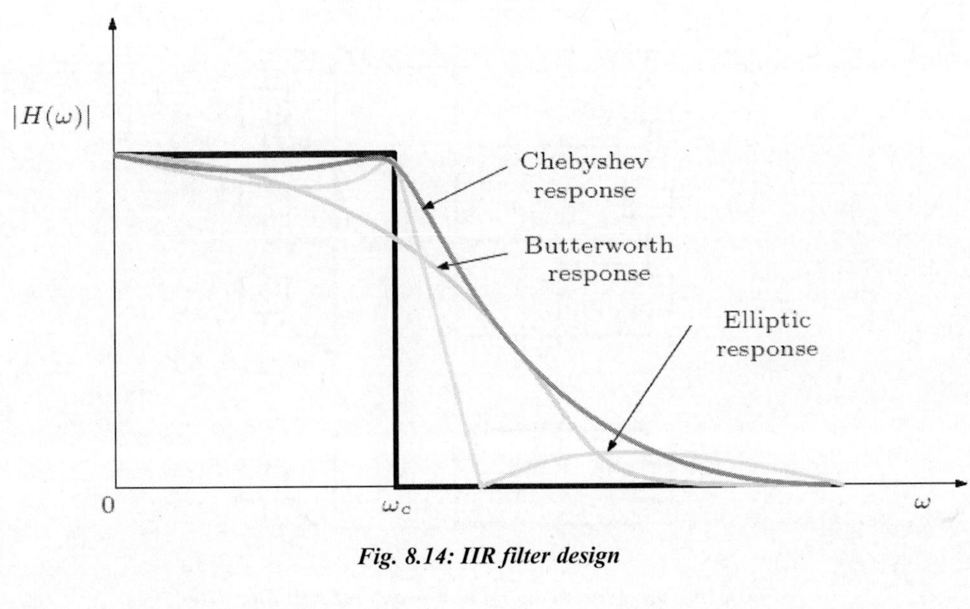

Fig. 8.14: IIR filter design

IIR filter difference equation is expressed as

$$y(n) = -\sum_{k=1}^{N} a_k\, y(n-k) + \sum_{k=0}^{M-1} b_k\, x(n-k)$$

Here a_ks and b_ks are specified the IIR filter response. By changing the coefficients, we can change the frequency response of the filter.

The direct form I signal flow graph for the IIR filter H(x) is shown in Fig. 8.15.

8.4.1 Approximation of derivatives for IIR filter design

One common approach is to approximate derivatives using finite difference methods or polynomial interpolation techniques. These methods involve estimating the derivative of the desired frequency response at various frequencies to determine the coefficients of the IIR filter. The choice of approximation method depends on factors such as the desired filter characteristics, the complexity of the filter, and computational considerations.

For the derivative $\frac{dy(t)}{dt}$ at time t = nT can be approximated as

$$\frac{dy(t)}{dt} = \frac{y(nT) - y(nT - T)}{T}$$

$$\frac{dy(t)}{dt}\Big|_{t=nT} = \frac{y(n) - y(n-1)}{T}$$

In this context, *T* denotes the sampling interval, and *y(n)* represents *y(nT)*. The analog differentiator, producing the output, is characterized by the system function *H(s)* = *s*. Conversely, the digital system, generating the output $[y(n) - y(n-1)]/T$, is described by the system function $H(z) = (1 - z^{-1})/T$. This establishes the frequency-domain equivalence for the relationship.

$$s = \frac{1 - z^{-1}}{T}$$

Time and frequency relation of a Differentiator is also given in Fig. 8.16.

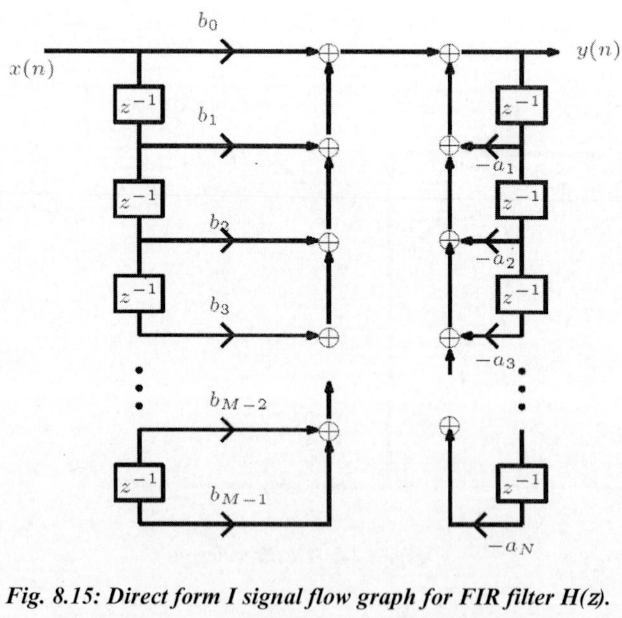

Fig. 8.15: Direct form I signal flow graph for FIR filter H(z).

The double derivative is approximated as

$$\frac{dy^2(t)}{dt} = \frac{dy(t)}{dt}\left[\frac{y(nT)-y(nT-T)}{T}\right] = \frac{y(nT)-y(nT-T)-y(nT-T)-y(nT-2T)}{T^2}$$

$$= \frac{y(nT)-y(nT-T)-y(nT-T)-y(nT-2T)}{T^2}$$

$$\frac{dy^2(t)}{dt}\Big|_{t=nT} = \frac{y(n)-2y(n-1)-y(n-2)}{T^2}, \quad (8.18)$$

Thus frequency domain equivalent is

$$s^2 = \frac{1-2z^{-1}+z^{-2}}{T^2} \rightarrow \left(\frac{1-z^{-1}}{T}\right)^2, \quad (8.19)$$

In general we can write

$$s^k = \left(\frac{1-z^{-1}}{T}\right)^k \quad (8.20)$$

Digital filter transfer is obtained by approximated the differential equation as

$H(z) = H_a(s)|s= \underline{1-z^{-1}}$. (8.21)

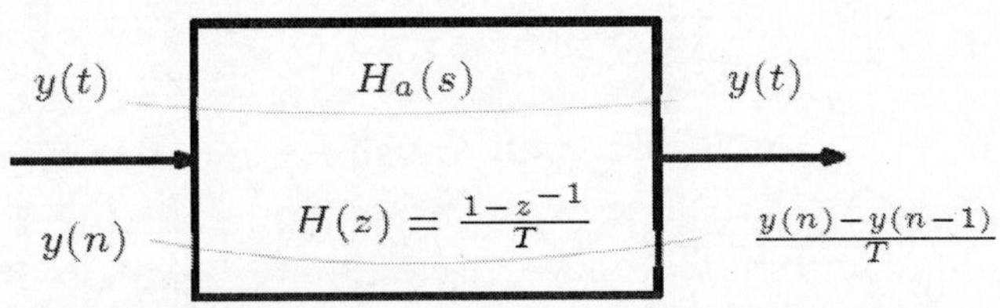

Fig. 8.16: analog and discrete time relation.

Thus analog filter is converted to digital filter using

$$\frac{1-z^{-1}}{T}$$

and digital filter is converted to analog as

$$z = \frac{1}{1-sT} \quad (8.22)$$

Evaluating at s = jΩ

$$z = \frac{1}{1-j\Omega T} = \frac{1+j\Omega T}{1+\Omega^2T^2}$$

$$re^{j\omega} = \frac{1}{1+\Omega^2T^2} + j\frac{\Omega}{1+\Omega^2T^2} \quad (8.23)$$

We can also write

$$z = \frac{1}{1-(\sigma+j\Omega)T} = \frac{1}{1-\sigma T-j\Omega T} = \frac{1-\sigma T+j\Omega T}{(1-\sigma T)^2+(\sigma T)^2}$$

$$x = \frac{1-\sigma T}{(1-\sigma T)^2+(\sigma T)^2}, y = \frac{\Omega T}{(1-\sigma T)^2+(\sigma T)^2} \quad (8.24)$$

Let $x^2+y^2 = (\frac{1-\sigma T}{(1-\sigma T)^2+(\sigma T)^2})^2 + (\frac{\Omega T}{(1-\sigma T)^2+(\sigma T)^2})^2$, write $x^2+y^2 = \frac{(1-\sigma T)^2+(\Omega T)^2}{((1-\sigma T)^2+(\Omega T)^2)^2} = \frac{1}{((1-\sigma T)^2+(\Omega T)^2)}$

Further, let $\sigma = 0, x^2+y^2 = x, x^2-x+y^2 = 0, (x-1/2)^2+y^2 = 1/4$ since $x = \frac{1}{1+(\Omega T)^2}$. Thus, circle at centre (1/2,0) and radius = ½.

As Ω varies from 0 to, the∞corresponding locus of points in the z-plane forms a circle with a radius of 1/2 and a center at $x = 1/2$.

Further, we can understand mapping as if $\Omega \to 0$, then $z = \frac{1}{1+\Omega^2 T^2} + j\frac{\Omega}{1+\Omega^2 T^2} \to 1$. DC to DC mapping, if $\Omega \to \infty$, then $z = \frac{1}{1-j\Omega T} \to 0$. So high frequency maps to zero, which is ambiguous.

The mapping described in $s = \frac{1-z-1}{T}$ readily illustrates in Fig. 8.17 how points located in the Left Half-Plane (LHP) of the s-plane are transformed to points within a designated circle in the z-plane, while points from the Right Half-Plane (RHP) of the s-plane are mapped outside this circle. Consequently, this mapping exhibits the advantageous trait of converting a stable analog filter into a stable digital filter. However, it's important to note that the potential positions of the digital filter's poles are limited to relatively lower frequencies (inside small circle only in Fig. 8.17). Consequently, this mapping is primarily suitable for designing lowpass and bandpass filters with modest resonant frequencies. Notably, it's impractical to convert a highpass analog filter into an equivalent highpass digital filter using this method.

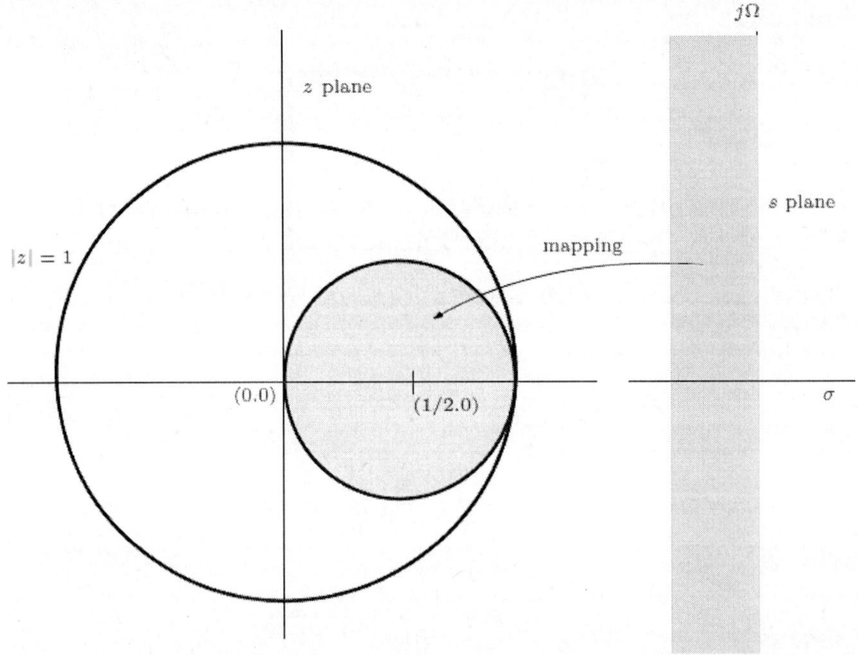

Fig. 8.17: Mapping as $z = \frac{1}{1-sT}$ *or* $s = \frac{1-z^{-1}}{T}$

8.4.2 The Bilinear *z*-transform

The bilinear transformation can be associated with the trapezoidal formula used in numerical integration. For instance, let's examine an analog linear filter with the system function as

$$H_a(s) = \frac{b}{s+a}$$

Here a and b are constants. This transfer is a differential equation as $\frac{dy(t)}{dt} = -ay(t) + bx(t)$.

Rather than replacing the derivative with a finite difference, consider integrating the derivative and approximating the integral using the trapezoidal formula. Hence,

$$y(t) = \int_{t_0}^{t} \frac{dy(\tau)}{d\tau} d\tau + y(t_0),$$

where $y(t_0)$ is the initial value of $y(t)$ at $t = t_0$. We can write using $t = nT$ and $t_0 = nT - T$ as

$$y(nT) = \frac{T}{2}[y'(nT) - y'(nT - T)] + y(nT - T),$$

Differential equation as

$$y'(nT) = -ay(nT) + bx(nT).$$

Thus substituting above equation as

$$y(nT) = \frac{T}{2}[-ay(nT) + bx(nT) - (-ay(nT - T) + bx(nT - T))] + y(nT - T)$$

$$y(nT)(1 + aT/2) - (1 - aT/2)y(nT - T) = \frac{bT}{2}[x(nT) + x(nT - T)]$$

$$y(nT)(1 + aT/2) - (1 - aT/2)y(n - 1) = \frac{bT}{2}[x(n) + x(n - 1)]$$

Taking z transform

$$Y(z)(1 + aT/2) - Y(z)z^{-1}(1 - aT/2) = X(z)(1 + z^{-1})\frac{bT}{2}$$

$$H(z) = \frac{Y(z)}{X(x)} = \frac{(1 + z^{-1})\frac{bT}{2}}{(1 + aT/2) - z^{-1}(1 - aT/2)}. \quad (8.26)$$

Thus $H(z) = \frac{b}{\frac{2(1-z^{-1})}{T(1+z^{-1})} + a}$

By comparing $H_a(s)$, we can write

$$s = \frac{2}{T}\frac{(1 - z^{-1})}{(1 + z^{-1})}$$

This is called the bilinear transformation for IIR filter design.

Using $z = re^{j\omega}$ and $s = \sigma + j\Omega$, we can write

$$s = \frac{2}{T}\frac{z - 1}{z + 1} = \frac{2}{T}\frac{z = re^{j\omega} - 1}{z = re^{j\omega} + 1}$$

$$\frac{2}{T}\frac{r\cos(\omega) - 1 + jr\sin(\omega)}{r\cos(\omega) + 1 + jr\sin(\omega)}$$

$$\sigma + j\Omega = \frac{2}{T}\frac{r^2 - 1}{1 + r^2 + 2r\cos(\omega)} + j\frac{2}{T}\frac{2r\sin(\omega)}{1 + r^2 + 2r\cos(\omega)}. \quad (8.27)$$

Thus

$$\sigma = \frac{2}{T}\frac{r^2 - 1}{1 + r^2 + 2r\cos(\omega)}$$

and

$$\Omega = \frac{2}{T}\frac{2r\sin(\omega)}{1 + r^2 + 2r\cos(\omega)}.$$

Initially, it's important to observe that when $r < 1$, $\sigma < 0$, and when $r >$, $\sigma > 0$. This results in the LHP in the s-plane mapping inside the unit circle in the x-plane, while the RHP in the s-plane maps outside the unit circle. Moreover, when $r = 1$, $\sigma = 0$.

Thus, it is a nonlinear mapping, as shown Fig. 8.18. $\Omega = \infty$ maps to $\omega = \pi$ and $\Omega = -\infty$ maps to $\omega = -\pi$. Further, small, Ω mapping can be approximated as linear mapping.

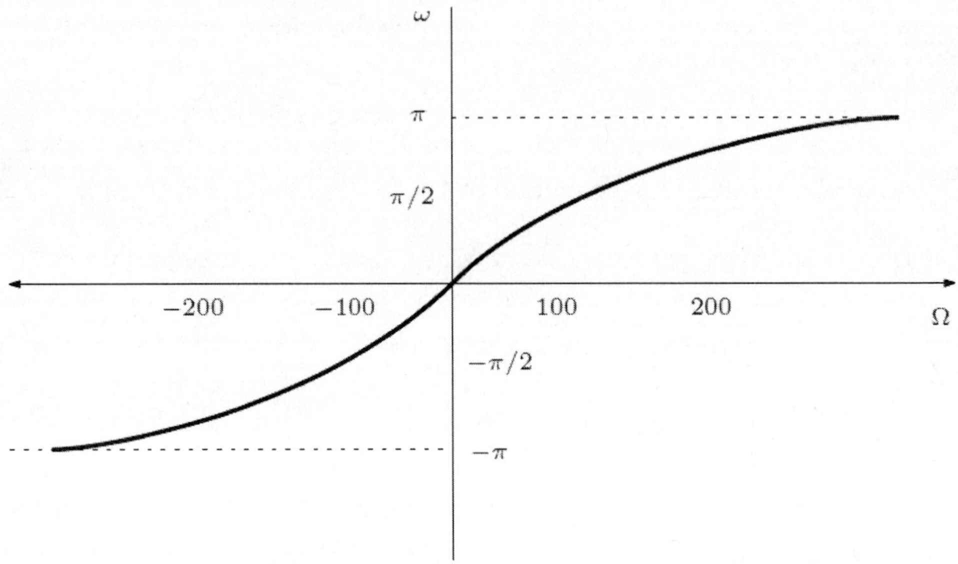

Fig. 8.18: Mapping as ω = tan−1(ΩT/2).

8.4.3 Impulse Invariance method

An IIR filter is designed to have a unit sample response, denoted as h(n), which directly corresponds to the sampled version of the impulse response of the analog filter as

$h(n) = h_a(t)|_{t=nT}, \; n = 0, 1, \ldots$

Frequency response $H(\omega)$ of digital filter is expressed as

$$H(\omega) = F_s \sum_{k=-\infty}^{\infty} H_a((\omega - 2\pi k)F_s) = F_s \sum_{k=-\infty}^{\infty} H_a(\omega - 2\pi k F_s) \tag{8.29}$$

where $F_s = 1/T$ is the sampling frequency and $H_a(\Omega)$ denotes the analog filter frequency response. Above equation can also be written as

$$H(\omega T) = F_s \sum_{k=-\infty}^{\infty} H_a(\omega - 2\pi k F_s) \tag{8.30}$$

It's evident that the digital filter, characterized by its frequency response H(ω), mirrors the frequency response traits of the corresponding analog filter when the sampling interval T is chosen adequately small, effectively preventing or minimizing aliasing effects. However, it's also apparent that the impulse invariance method is unsuitable for designing highpass filters because of the spectrum aliasing introduced by the sampling procedure.

The x transform H(x) of h(n) is expressed as

$$H(z)|_{z=e^{sT}} = \sum_{n=0}^{\infty} h(n)\, z^{-n}$$

$H(z)|_{z=e^{sT}} = \sum_{n=0}^{\infty} h(n)\, z^{-snT}$ (8.31)

Let's examine the mapping of points from the s-plane to the z-plane as indicated by the relation as

$z = e^{sT}$

$$rej\omega = e^{\sigma T}\, e^{j\Omega T}$$

$r = e^{\sigma T} \quad and\ \omega = \Omega T$ (8.32)

As a result, when σ suggests that 0 < r < 1, and σ > 0 indicates that r > 1. When σ = 1, r = 1. Hence, the LHP in s-plane is transformed within the unit circle in z-plane, while the RHP in s is shifted outside the unit circle in x-plane.

Moreo¥er, the jΩ-axis undergoes mapping onto the unit circle in x plane as described earlier. However, this mapping of the jΩ-axis onto the unit circle isn't one-to-one. Since ω is unique within the range (–π, π), the mapping ω = ΩT = Ω/F_s implies that the interval – π/T ≤ Ω ≤ π/T corresponds to values within ω (–π, π). Additionally, the frequency interval π/T ≤ Ω ≤ 3π/T also corresponds to the interval ω (–π, π), and generally, so does the interval (2k – 1)π/T Ω ≤ (2k + 1)π/T, where k denotes an integer, as shown in Fig. 8.19. Consequently, the mapping from the analog frequency Ω to the frequency variable ω in the digital domain is many-to-one, simply reflecting the effects of aliasing caused by sampling.

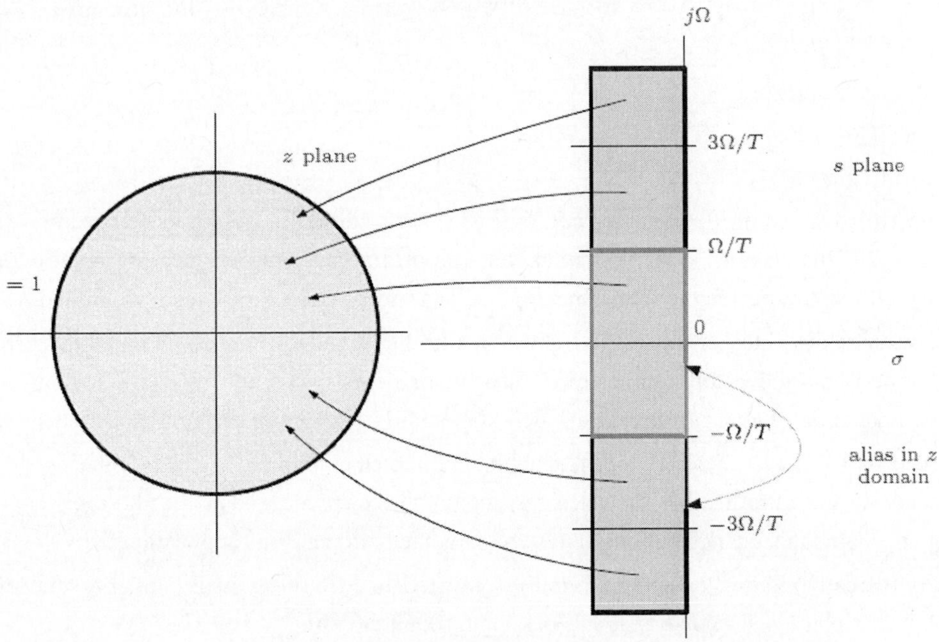

Fig. 8.19: Mapping as $x = e^{sT}$

Assuming that the N poles of the analog filter are distinct, we can express this as

$$H_a(s) = \sum_{l=1}^{N} \frac{c_l}{s - p_l}$$

Here p_l is the location of poles, and c_l is the coefficient. Time domain impulse response is expressed as $H_a(t) = \sum_{l=1}^{N} c_l\, e^{p_l t}, t \geq 0$

Discrete impulse response is expressed as

$$h(n) = H_a(t)|_{t=nT} = \sum_{l=1}^{N} c_l\, e^{p_l t}, t \geq 0, \text{n} = 0,1,2,... \tag{8.33}$$

z transform is expressed as

$$\begin{aligned} H(z) = \sum_{n=0}^{\infty} h(n)z^{-n} &= \sum_{n=0}^{\infty} h(n) \sum_{l=1}^{N} c_l e^{p_l T n} z^{-n} \\ &= \sum_{l=1}^{N} c_l \sum_{n=0}^{\infty} (e^{p_l T} z^{-1})^n \\ &= \sum_{l=1}^{N} c_l \frac{1}{1 - e^{p_l T} z^{-1}}. \end{aligned} \tag{8.34}$$

So digital filter has poles at $z = e^{p_l T}, l = 1, 2, ...N$.

Summary of IIR Filters Design

Approximation of derivatives:

$$s = \frac{1 - z^{-1}}{T}$$

Impulse invariance :

$$h(n) = h(t)|_{t=nT}, \quad \omega = \Omega T$$

Bilinear:

$$s = \frac{2}{T}\frac{1 - z^{-1}}{1 + z^{-1}}, \quad \omega = 2\tan^{-1}(\Omega T/2)$$

Some advantages of IIR filters

IIR filters typically require fewer filter coefficients compared to FIR filters to achieve sim- ilar filtering characteristics. This leads to lower computational complexity and reduced memory requirements, making them more efficient, especially for real-time applications and embedded systems with limited resources.

IIR filters can achieve steeper roll-off characteristics in the frequency domain compared to FIR filters with the same order. This allows for more selective filtering, particularly in applications where rapid attenuation of unwanted frequency components is crucial, such as in audio equalization or communication systems.

IIR filters can incorporate feedback loops, enabling the implementation of recursive filtering structures. This property allows for more flexible filter designs, including recursive or adaptive filtering techniques, which can adapt to changing signal conditions or system parameters in real-time applications.

IIR filters typically exhibit lower group delay compared to FIR filters with similar frequency responses, resulting in less phase distortion for signals passing through the filter.

IIR filters can closely approximate the characteristics of analog filters, making them suitable for converting analog filter designs into digital implementations using techniques like bilinear transformation or frequency warping. This property is beneficial when translating existing analog filter designs into digital domain applications.

8.5 CHARACTERISTICS OF ANALOG FILTERS

Analog filters exhibit various common characteristics or responses, each suited for different filtering applications. Some of the most common analog filter responses are as follows

8.5.1 Butterworth filters

Butterworth filters are known for their maximally flat frequency response in the passband and a gradual roll-off in the stopband. They offer a smooth transition between the passband and stopband with no ripples in the passband. Butterworth filters are commonly used in audio applications and signal conditioning where a flat passband response is desired.

Filter magnitude response is specified as

$$|H(\Omega)|^2 = \frac{1}{1+(\Omega/\Omega_c)^{2M}} = \frac{1}{1+\epsilon^2(\Omega/\Omega_p)^{2M}} \quad (8.35)$$

where M is the filter order. Ω_c is its -3 dB frequency usually called the cutoff frequency. Ω_p is the passband edge frequency, and $\frac{1}{1+\epsilon^2}$ is the bandedge value of response $|H(\Omega)|^2$. Laplace domain filter response is written as

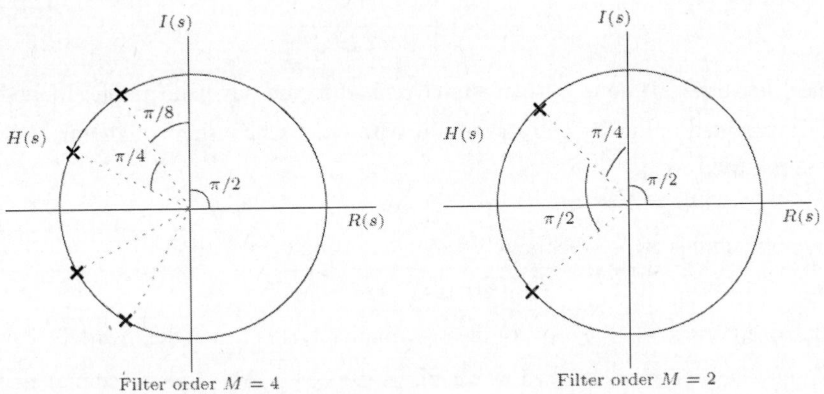

Fig. 8.20: Pole locations of Butterworth filters.

The frequency response characteristics of Butterworth filters are depicted in Fig. 8.20 for various values of M. It's observed that the response is maximally smooth in both the passband and stopband. Determining the filter order necessary to achieve a specific attenuation dB at a given frequency Ω_s. Thus at $\Omega = \Omega_s$ we can write as in Fig. 8.21

$$\frac{1}{1+\epsilon^2(\Omega_s/\Omega_p)^{2M}} = \delta_2^2 \quad (8.37)$$

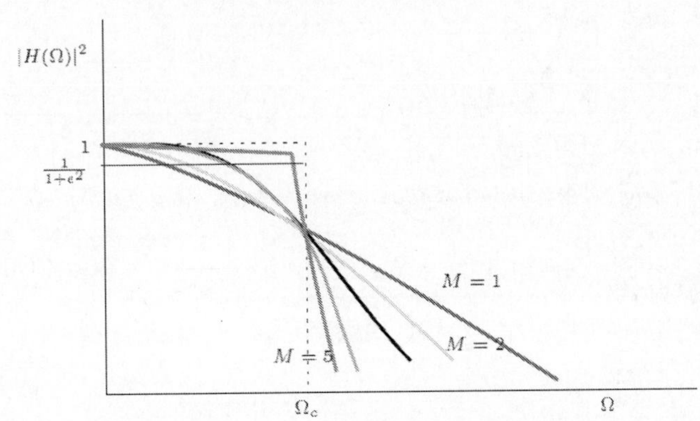

Fig. 8.21: Pole locations of Butterworth filters.

Filter order can be written as

$$M = \frac{log(\delta/\epsilon)}{log(\Omega_s/\Omega_p)} = \frac{log((1/\delta_2^2)-1)}{2log(\Omega_s/\Omega_c)},$$

where $\delta = \frac{1}{\sqrt{1+\delta_2^2}}$. A Butterworth filter is specified by M, δ, ϵ and Ω_s/Ω_c.

8.5.2 Chebyshev filters

Chebyshev filters provide steeper roll-off characteristics in the stopband compared to Butterworth filters. They achieve this by allowing ripples in either the passband or stopband, depending on the filter type (Type I or Type II). Chebyshev filters are often used in applications requiring sharper cutoffs, such as communication systems and instrumentation.

Filter magnitude response is specified as

$$|H(\Omega)|^2 = \frac{1}{1+\epsilon^2 T_M(\Omega/\Omega_p)},$$

where M is the filter order. Here ϵ is a parameter related to the passband ripple. Magnitude response of Chebyshev filter is plotted in Fig. 8.22. $T_M(x)$ is the Mth-order Chebyshev polynomial defined as $T_M(x) = \begin{cases} \cos(M\cos^{-1})(x), \text{if } |x| \leq 1 \\ \cosh(M\cosh - 1(x)), |x| > 1 \end{cases}$

The Chebyshev polynomials can be recursively generated using the equation

$$T_{M+1}(x) = 2xT_M(x) - T_{M-1}(x).$$

Here $T_0(x) = 0$ and $T_1(x) = x$. All the roots of the polynomial $T_M(x)$ lies in the interval $-1 \leq x \leq 1$.

We note that Chebyshev filters are defined by the parameters M, ϵ, δ_2 (stopband ripple), and the ratio Ω_s/Ω_p. Given a specific set of specifications on ϵ, δ_2 and Ω_s/Ω_p, we can ascertain the filter order using the equation:

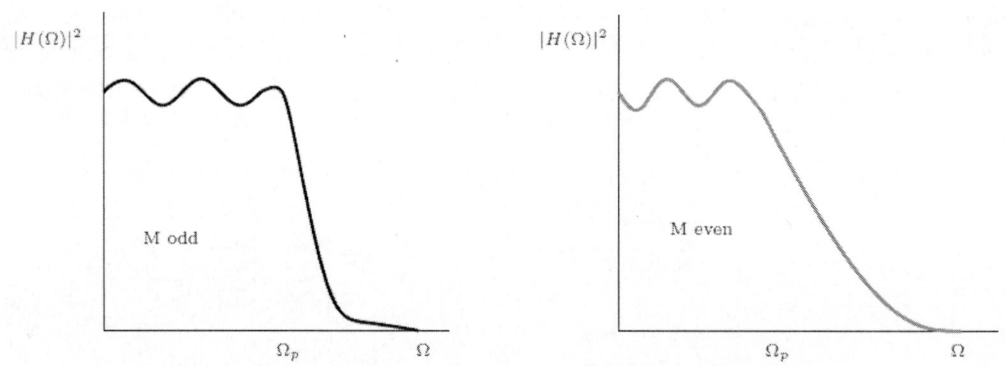

Fig. 8.22: Chebyshev filter characteristics (magnitude plot).

$$M = \frac{\log_{10}[((\sqrt{1-\delta_2^2}) + \sqrt{1-\delta_2^2(1+\epsilon^2)})/\epsilon\delta_2]}{\log_{10}[(\Omega_s/\Omega_p) + \sqrt{(\Omega_s/\Omega_p)^2 - 1}]} = \frac{\cosh^{-1}(\delta/\epsilon)}{cosh^{-1}(\Omega_s/\Omega_p)}. \tag{8.39}$$

Here $\delta_2 = 1/\sqrt{1+\delta^2}$.

8.6 ELLIPTIC FILTERS

Elliptic filters, also known as Cauer filters, offer the steepest roll-off characteristics among analog filters. They achieve this by allowing ripples in both the passband and stopband, resulting in a sharper transition between the two regions. Elliptic filters are commonly used in applications where extremely sharp cutoffs are required, such as in high-frequency communication systems and radar.

Filter magnitude response is specified as

$$|H(\Omega)|^2 = \frac{1}{1+\epsilon^2 U_M(\Omega/\Omega_p)}, \tag{8.40}$$

where M is the filter order. Here U_M(.) is the Jacobian elliptic function of order M, and ϵ is a parameter related to the passband ripple.

8.7 FILTER FREQUENCY TRANSFORMATION

The previous section we discuss the design of lowpass IIR or FIR filters. However, if we aim to design a highpass, bandpass, or bandstop filter, we can easily achieve this by starting with a lowpass prototype filter (such as Butterworth, Chebyshev, elliptic, or Bessel) and applying a frequency transformation.

One option is to conduct the frequency transformation in the analog domain and then convert the analog filter into a corresponding digital filter through a mapping of the s-plane into the z-plane. Alternatively, we can initially convert the analog lowpass filter into a lowpass digital filter and then transform it into the desired digital filter using a digital transformation.

Generally, these two approaches result in different designs, except for the bilinear transformation, where the resulting filter designs are identical.

For example lowpass filter edge frequency Ω_p is converted to another frequency $\Omega'p$ as

$s = \frac{\Omega_p}{\Omega'_p} s$ lowpass to lowpass conversion from Ω_p to $\Omega_p{}'$

The new filter response is written as

$$H(\Omega_p) \to H(\Omega'_p) = H(s)\Big|_{s=\frac{\Omega_p}{\Omega'_p}s} \tag{8.41}$$

We aim to convert a lowpass filter with edge frequency Ω_p into a highpass filter with a passband edge frequency $\Omega'p$ transformation is written as

$$s \to \frac{\Omega_p \Omega'_p}{s} \text{ LPF to HPF}$$

Analog LPF with pass-band edge frequency Ω_c is converted to BPF with lower pass-band edge frequency Ω_l and the upper-band edge frequency edge frequency Ω_u, we can achieve this by initially converting the lowpass filter into another LPF with a band edge frequency $\Omega'p = 1$. Subsequently, we can write the transformation as

$$s \to \frac{s^2 + \Omega_l \Omega_u}{s(\Omega_u - \Omega_l)} \quad LPF\ to\ BPF$$

Or in the single step we can write above transformation as

$$s \to \Omega_p{}' \frac{s^2 + \Omega_l \Omega_u}{s(\Omega_u - \Omega_l)} \quad LPF\ toBPF$$

Ultimately, if we intend to transform a lowpass analog filter with a band edge frequency Ω_p into a bandstop filter, the transformation is merely the inverse of BPF, with the added factor of Ω_p to normalize for the lowpass filter's band edge frequency. Consequently, the transformation is

$$s \rightarrow \Omega_p \frac{s(\Omega_u - \Omega_l)}{s^2 + \Omega_l \Omega_u} \text{ LPF to band stop filter}$$

Here we have used Ω_l: lower band edge frequency, Ω_u: upper band edge frequency. filter conversion is highlighted in Fig. 8.23.

Frequency transformation in filter design is summarized in Table 8.5 and Table 8.6.

As the option to conduct a frequency transformation exists in both the analog and digital domains, filter designers possess flexibility in their approach. However, caution should be taken, depending on the filter types under consideration. Notably, methods like impulse invariance and derivative mapping are unsuitable for designing highpass and many bandpass filters due to aliasing issues. Consequently, employing an analog frequency transformation followed by conversion into the digital domain using these mappings is discouraged. Instead, a more effective strategy involves mapping from an analog lowpass filter to a digital lowpass filter using either of these methods, followed by conducting the frequency transformation in the digital domain. This approach mitigates aliasing concerns.

In the case of the bilinear transformation, where aliasing isn't problematic, the choice between analog and digital domain for frequency transformation is inconsequential. Remarkably, in this scenario alone, both approaches yield identical digital filters.

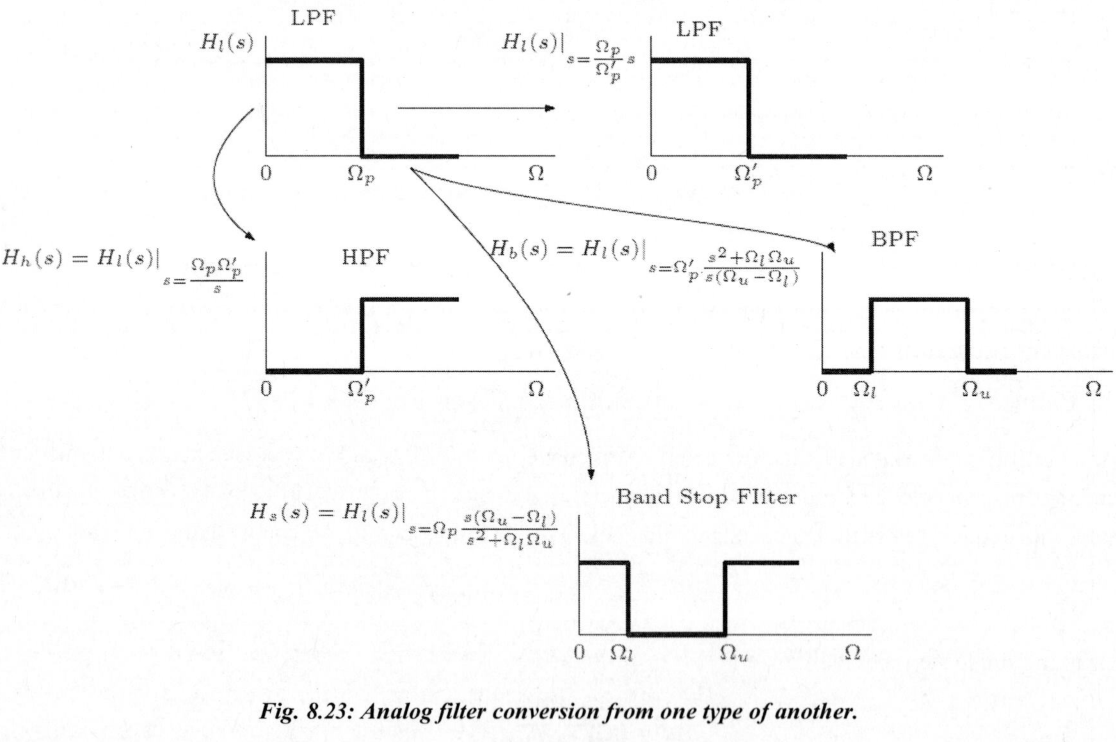

Fig. 8.23: Analog filter conversion from one type of another.

Table 8.5: Summary of LPF to other filters conversion in analog domain

Type of transformation	Transformation	Band edge frequencies of new filter
Lowpass	$s \to \frac{\Omega_p}{\Omega'_p} s$	Ω'_p
Highpass	$s \to \frac{\Omega_p \Omega'_p}{s}$	Ω'_p
Bandpass	$s \to \Omega'_p \frac{s^2 + \Omega_l \Omega_u}{s(\Omega_u - \Omega_l)}$	Ω_l, Ω_u
Bandstop	$s \to \Omega_p \frac{s(\Omega_u - \Omega_l)}{s^2 + \Omega_l \Omega_u}$	Ω_l, Ω_u

Example 8.7.1 *Design a 20th-order bandpass FIR filter with lower cutoff frequency 400 Hz and higher cutoff frequency 450 Hz. The sample rate is 2000 Hz.*

We use the MATLAB toolbox do design this filter. Magnitude and phase response are shown in Fig. 8.24. IIR filter has lower side lobes as compared to FIR filter for the same orcer of the filter as observed in Fig. 8.24 and Fig. 8.25

Table 8.6: Frequency transformation from LPF with passband edge frequency ω_p to other filters

Type of transformation	Transformation	Filter Parameters
Lowpass	$z^{-1} \to \frac{z^{-1} - a}{1 - az^{-1}}$	ω'_p edge frequency of the new filter, $a = \frac{\sin((\omega_p - \omega'_p)/2)}{\sin((\omega_p + \omega'_p)/2)}$
Highpass	$z^{-1} \to -\frac{z^{-1} + a}{1 + az^{-1}}$	ω'_p edge frequency of the new filter, $a = -\frac{\cos((\omega_p + \omega'_p)/2)}{\cos((\omega_p - \omega'_p)/2)}$
Bandpass	$z^{-1} \to -\frac{z^{-2} - a_1 z^{-1} + a_2}{a_2 z^{-2} - a_1 z^{-1} + 1}$	ω_l and ω_u edge frequencies of the new filter, $a_1 = -2\alpha\beta/(\beta + 1)$, $a_2 = (\beta + 1)/(\beta + 1)$. Here $\alpha = \frac{\cos((\omega_u + \omega_l)/2)}{\cos((\omega_u - \omega_l)/2)}$, $\beta = \cot(\frac{\omega_u - \omega_l}{2}) \tan(\omega_p/2)$
Bandstop	$z^{-1} \to -\frac{z^{-2} - a_1 z^{-1} + a_2}{a_2 z^{-2} - a_1 z^{-1} + 1}$	ω_l and ω_u edge frequencies of the new filter, $a_1 = -2\alpha\beta/(\beta + 1)$, $a_2 = (1 - \beta)/(\beta + 1)$. Here $\alpha = \frac{\cos((\omega_u + \omega_l)/2)}{\cos((\omega_u - \omega_l)/2)}$, $\beta = \tan(\frac{\omega_u - \omega_l}{2}) \tan(\omega_p/2)$

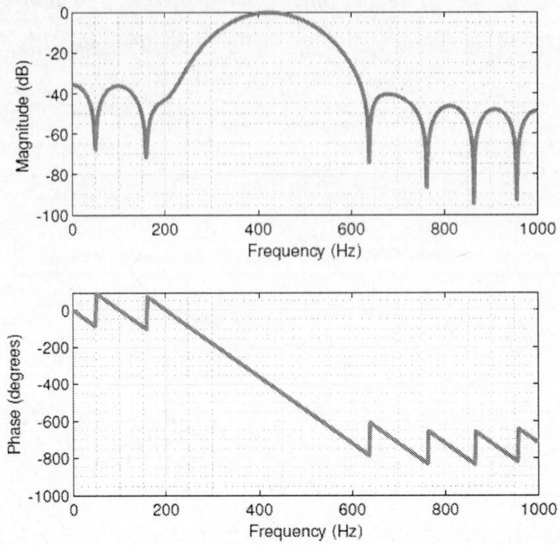

Fig. 8.24: Magnitude and phase response of FIR BPF.

Example 8.7.2 *Design a 20th-order bandpass IIR filter with lower 3-dB frequency 400 Hz and higher 3-dB frequency 450 Hz. The sample rate is 2000 Hz.*

We use the MATLAB toolbox do design this filter. Magnitude and phase response are shown in Fig. 8.25.

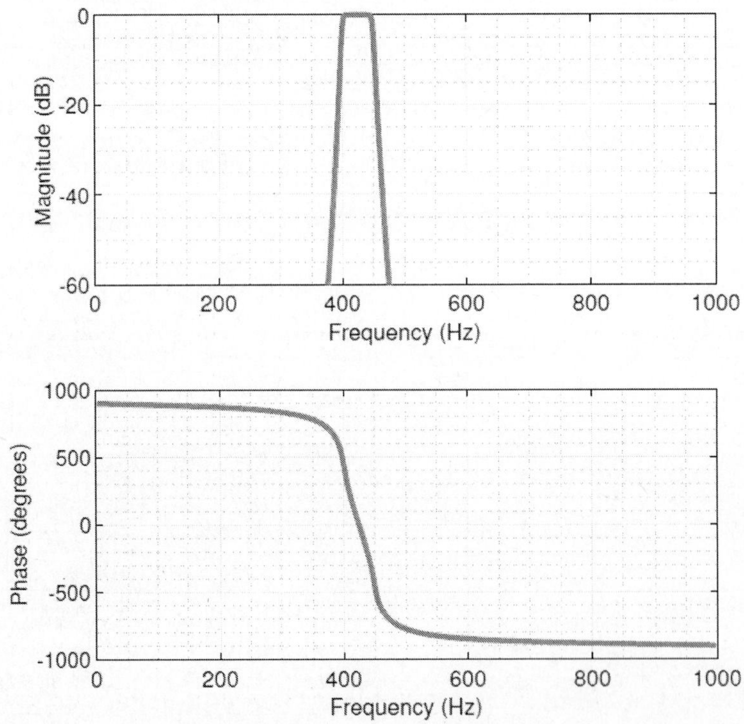

Fig. 8.25: Magnitude and phase response of IIR BPF.

Example 8.7.3 *We can design IIR filter using the the MATLAB toolbox as following: This ex- ample uses the first specification set from the table for the LPF design.*

Magnitude and phase response is plotted in Fig. 8.26. IIR filter has non-linear phase as shown in Fig. 8.26.

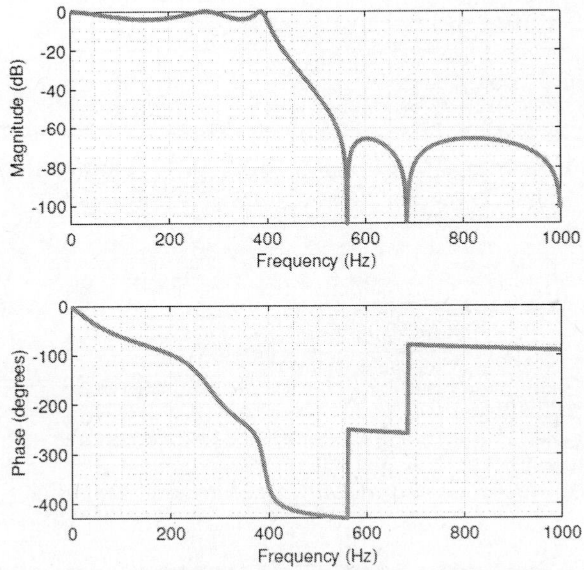

Fig. 8.26: Magnitude and phase response of IIR LPF.

Example 8.7.4 *Create a digital low-pass Butterworth filter with a 3dB cutoff frequency set at 2kHz and a minimum attenuation of 30dB at 4.25kHz, considering a sampling rate of 10kHz.*

Sampling frequency Fs = 10 *KHz, sampling interval* T = 10−4 *sec, passband frequency* F_p = 2 *KHz, stopband frequency* F_s = 4.25 *KHz*

Digital frequency are calculated as ω = tan−1 ΩT/2

Order of filter is calculated as

$$N = \frac{log(\delta/\epsilon)}{log(\Omega_s/\Omega_p)} = \frac{log((1/\delta_2^2) - 1)}{2log(\Omega_s/\Omega_c)}$$

$\delta = 1/\sqrt{1+\delta_2^2}$. Attenuation is 30 dB so $\delta_2 = 0.0316 = 10^{-30/20}$ and $\delta = \frac{1}{\sqrt{1+\delta_2^2}} = 0.9995$

Filter order N = 4.5826a ≈ 5

The pole positions are $s_k = \Omega_c e^{j\pi/2} e^{j(2k+1)\pi/2N}$, k = 0, 1, ..., N − 1

$s_0 = 4000\pi e^{j\pi/2} e^{j(2k+1)\pi/10}$ = −3.8832e + 03 + 1.1951e + 04i, s_1 = −1.0166e + 04 + 7.3863e + 03i

s_2 =-1.2566e + 04 + 1.5389e-12i, s_3 =-1.0166e + 04-7.3863e + 03i, s_4 =-3.8832e + 03 1.1951e + 04i

Example 8.7.5 *Design a digital filter equivalent to a 2nd-order Butterworth low-pass filter with a cutoff frequency* F_c = 100 *Hz and a sampling frequency* F_s = 1000 *samples/sec. Obtain the finite difference equation and illustrate the realization structure of the filter.*

Sampling frequency Fs = 10 *KHz, sampling interval* T = 10−4 *sec, Second order Butterworth filter is* $H_a(s) = 1/ s^2 + 2s + 1$

Digital frequency is given as $\omega_c = 2 * pi * F_s/F_s = 20 * 100/1000 = 0.628$ *Now determine the equivalent analogue filter cut-off frequency using the pre-warping function as*

$$\Omega_c = 2/T \tan(\omega/2) = 2/T * 0.3247 \ rad$$

Transform the frequency as $s \to \frac{\Omega_p}{\Omega'_p} s = s/(2/T * 0.3247)$ *So*

$$H_a(s) = \frac{1}{s^2/(2/T * 0.3247)^2 + 2s/(2/T * 0.3247) + 1}$$

Convert to z domain using $z = \frac{2}{T}\frac{1-z^{-1}}{+-z^{-1}}$ *and* $2/T = 1$ *can be considered since both terms will be cancel out.*

$$H(z) = \frac{1}{(s/0.3247)^2 + 2(s/0.3247) + 1} = \frac{1}{1/0.3247^2(\frac{1-z^{-1}}{+-z^{-1}})^2 + 2/0.3247 * \frac{1-z^{-1}}{+-z^{-1}} + 1}$$

H(z) can be approximated as $H(z) = \frac{0.067+0.135z^{-1}+0.067z^{-2}}{1-1.429z^{-1}+0.4127z^{-2}}$

Corresponding different equation is

$y(n) - 1.429y(n-1) + 0.4127y(n-2) = 0.067x(n) + 0.135x(n-1) + 0.067x(n-2)$

Direct realization for a 2nd order Butterworth equivalent filter is given in Fig. 8.27.

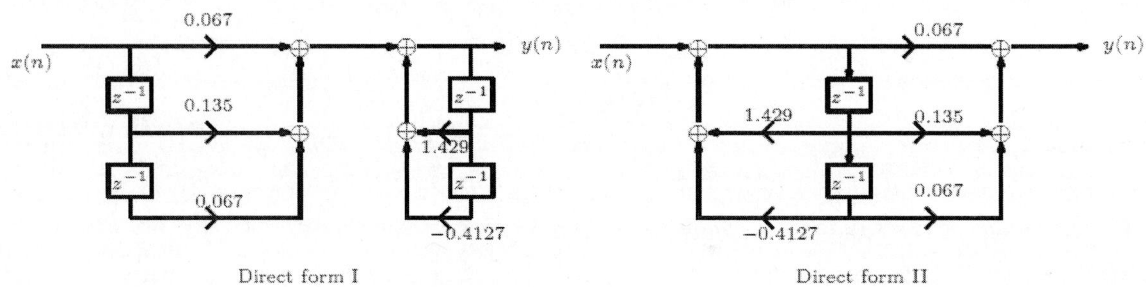

Fig. 8.27: Filter realization

Example 8.7.6 *Design a low-pass filter with* $\omega_p = 0.4\pi$ *and* $\omega_p = 0.6\pi$ *which exhibits a minimum attenuation greater than 50dB in the stop-band.*

Let cutoff frequency $\omega_c = \frac{\omega_p+\omega_s}{2} = 0.5\pi$. *Transition band width* $\omega_s - \omega_p = 0.2\pi$ *rad/sample. Stop band attenuation: 50dB, therefore, we can select* ***Hamming window*** *with length* M + 1

$$w(n) = \begin{cases} 0.54 - .46\cos(2\pi n/M), if\ 0 \le n \le M \\ 0, \text{otherwise} \end{cases}$$

Main lobe width of the Hamming window is 8π/M, M *roughly can be used by considering transition band width, Therefore,* 8 π/M = 0.2 π, M = 40. *Ideal low-pass filter* $h_d(n) = (\omega/\pi).sinc(w_c n/\pi) = 0.5sinc(n/2)$. Apply a time shift of M/2 (to make causal filter) and multiply $h_d(n)$ by window w(n).

$h(n) = h_d(n)w(n - M/2) = [0.54 - .46\cos(2\pi n/M)]0.5sinc(n - 20/2), 0 \le n \le M$

The h(n) *denotes the impulse response of the designed FIR filter*

Magnitude response is plotted in Fig. 8.28.

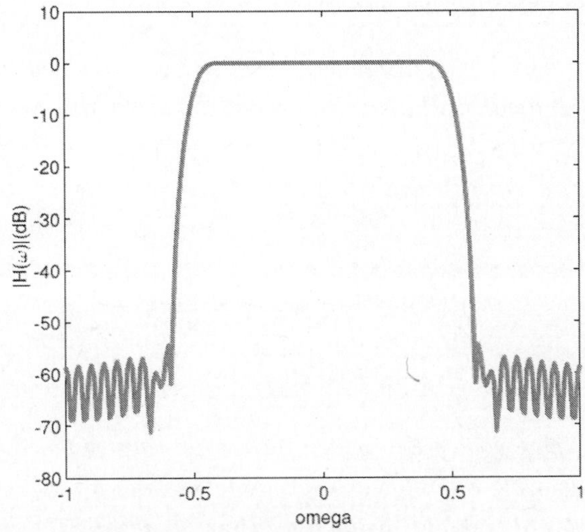

Fig. 8.28: Low-pass filter design

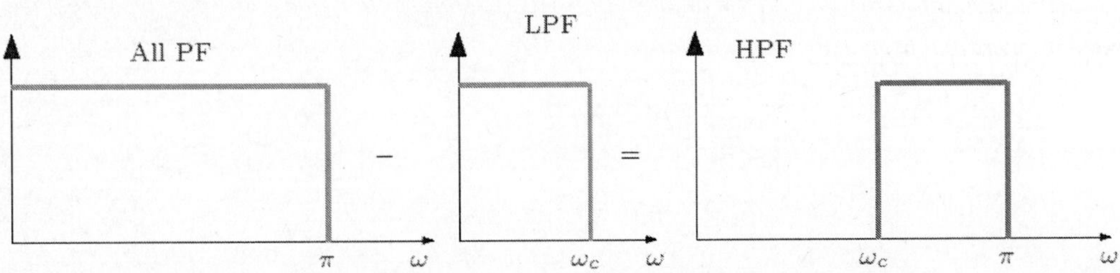

Fig. 8.29: High-pass filter

Apply a time shift of $M/2$ *(to make causal filter) and multiply* $h_d(n)$ *by window* $w(n)$.

$h(n) = h_d(n)w(n - M/2) = [0.5 - .5\cos(2\pi n/48)].[sinc(n - 24) - 0.415 sinc(0.415(n - 24))]\ 0 \le n \le M = 48.$

The $h(n)$ *denotes the impulse response of the designed high-pass FIR filter.*

Magnitude response is plotted in Fig. 8.29.

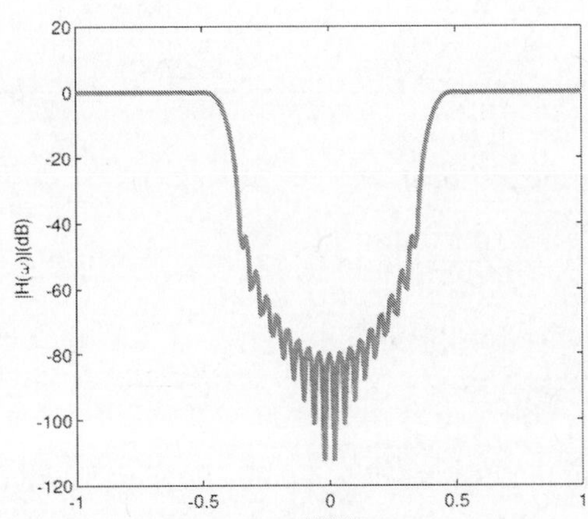

Fig. 8.30: High-pass filter

Example 8.7.8 *A continuous time filter has frequency response* $H(F) = \frac{1}{1+\frac{j2\pi F}{1000}}$ *Determine the passband and stopband frequencies in Hz, assuming a passband ripple of 1dB a*0 and *attenuation of 40dB in the stopband. Also determine the half power frequency* F$_c$ *(also called 3 dB bandwidth).*

$Let\ pass - band\ ripple\ \delta_1, 1-\delta_1 \le |H(F)| \le 1+\delta_1 20log_{10}(1+\delta_1) = 1dB, \rightarrow \delta_1 = 0.12. Passband$

Stop-band attenuation = 40 dB, $-20log_{10}|H(F)| = 40, \rightarrow\ |H(F)| = 0.01,$ *which results in* F = 915 *Hz. Half-power frequency,*

$$|H(F)| = \frac{1}{\sqrt{1+(2\pi F/1000)^2}} = \frac{1}{2}$$

which results in F = 488 *Hz.*

Example 8.7.9 *We aim to approximate the analog filter with transfer function* H(s) = $\frac{2s+1}{s^2+s+1}$ *using a discrete-time approach, employing the Bilinear transformation with a sampling frequency* F$_s$ = 10 *Hz. a) Calculate the zeros and poles of both the analog filter* H(s) *and the discrete-time implementation* H(x)*. b) Determine the Linear Difference Equation of the discrete-time implementation. c) Plot the frequency responses of the digital filter* H(ω) *and the analog filter* H(Ω)*. Confirm that one can be derived from the other through the appropriate frequency transformation.*

$$s = \frac{2}{T}\frac{1-z^{-1}}{1+z^{-1}}$$

$$z = -\frac{s+2/T}{s-2/T}$$

So zeros are

$$z = -\frac{-1/2+2*10}{-1/2-2*10} = 0.9512, -\frac{\infty+2*10}{\infty-2*10} = -1$$

Poles at

$$z = -\frac{e^{j2\pi/3}+2/T}{e^{j2\pi/3}-2/T} = 0.948+j0.0822, 0.948-j0.0822$$

System transfer function can be written as

$$H(z) = K\frac{(z+1)(z-0.9512)}{(z-0.948-j0.0822)(z-0.948+j0.0822)}$$

K can be determined by comparing two equations for $s = 0$ *and* $z = 1$ *as*

$$H(s) = \frac{2s+1}{s^2+s+1}|_{s=0} = H(z)|_{z=1} \rightarrow K = 0.098$$

We can also write the system difference equation.

Impact of finite register length:

The effect of finite register length in FIR filter design primarily impacts the filter's numerical accuracy and dynamic range such as

Finite register length introduces quantization noise, which arises from representing continuous- valued filter coefficients and signal samples with a limited number of bits. This noise can degrade the filter's performance, especially for low-order filters or filters with sharp transition bands.

Quantization of filter coefficients can lead to coefficient truncation errors, altering the filter's frequency response and magnitude characteristics. Higher-order filters are particularly sensitive to coefficient quantization, as small errors in coefficients can significantly affect filter performance.

Quantization of filter coefficients and input samples can cause frequency response distortion, leading to deviations from the desired filter characteristics. This distortion is more pronounced in filters with narrow transition bands or high stopband attenuation requirements.

Finite register length imposes limits on the dynamic range of filter coefficients and signal samples. As a result, signals with large dynamic ranges may experience signal clipping or overflow, leading to distortion and loss of signal fidelity.

Finite register length introduces roundoff errors during arithmetic operations, such as multiplication and accumulation, performed in the filter implementation. These errors can accumulate and affect the filter's accuracy, particularly in high-gain or high-resolution applications.

To mitigate the effects of finite register length in FIR filter design, techniques such as coefficient scaling, filter optimization, and noise shaping can be employed. Additionally, increasing the word length of registers or using higher precision arithmetic can improve numerical accuracy and reduce quantization errors.

Summary of digital filters design is given in Fig. 8.31, where we have highlighted different methods of FIR and IIR filter design.

First we design filters in the analog domain then convert to digital domain

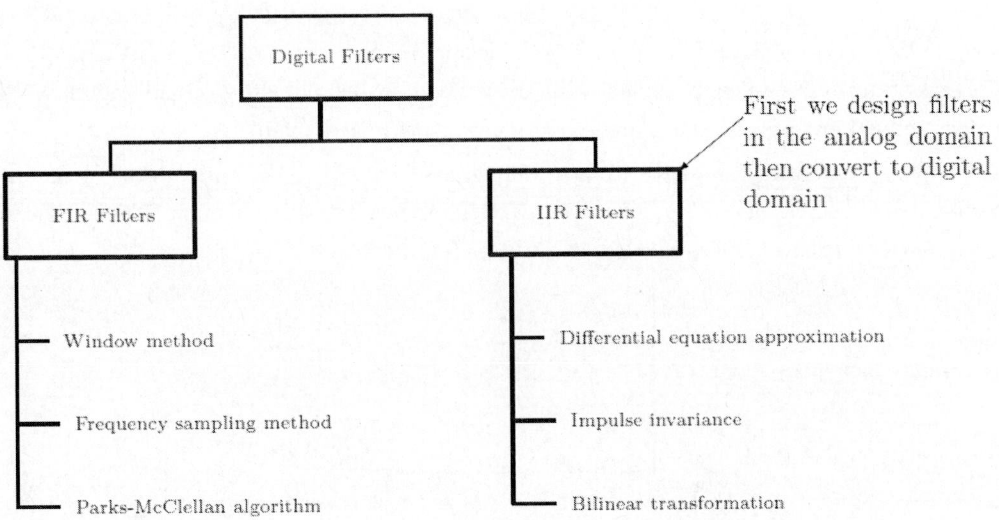

Fig. 8.31: Summary of filter designs.

SUMMARY

The chapter on Design of Digital Filters delves into the essential principles and methodologies for creating digital filters, which are vital components in signal processing systems. It begins by distinguishing between different types of digital filters, such as finite impulse response (FIR) and infinite impulse response (IIR) filters, and outlines their respective advantages and applications. The chapter covers the fundamental concepts of filter specifications, including passband, stopband, ripple, and attenuation, which guide the design process to meet specific performance criteria. Various design methods are discussed, including windowing techniques for FIR filters, which involve applying a window function to the ideal impulse response, and analog-to-digital transformation methods for designing IIR filters based on analog prototypes. The chapter also explores the role of frequency response and stability in filter design, emphasizing the importance of ensuring that filters are both effective and robust. Additionally, practical considerations, such as quantization effects, filter realization, and implementation challenges, are addressed, providing insights into the trade-offs involved in digital filter design.

EXERCISES

1. Given the signal x(n) = {1, 2, 3, 4, 5, 6, 7, 8} , design a low-pass filter using FFT to remove frequencies higher than π/4 and apply it to the signal.
2. Given the signal x(n) = {1, 1, 1, 1, 0, 0, 0, 0, 0} , design a high-pass filter using FFT to remove frequencies lower than π/4 and apply it to the signal.
3. We aim to implement an analog filter with the transfer function $H(s) = 3s+1/s^2+s+1$ through
4. discrete-time approximation, employing the Bilinear transformation. We will use a sampling frequency F_s = 50Hz. Determine zeros and poles of both the analog filter H(s) and the discrete time implementation H(z).
5. Why do IIR filters not have linear phases? Why is approximation of derivatives method not suitable for high-pass filter design? Kindly explain your answer with the help of equations and figure. Further, how can we convert low-pass filter to a high-pass filter in the digital domain?
6. The impulse response of an analog filter is shown in Figure 8.32. Let $h(n) = h_a(nT)$, be the impulse response of a discrete time filter, where T = 2. Determine the system function H(z) and the frequency response H(ω) for this FIR filter. Is H(z) a linear phase filter? Sketch |H(ω)|.

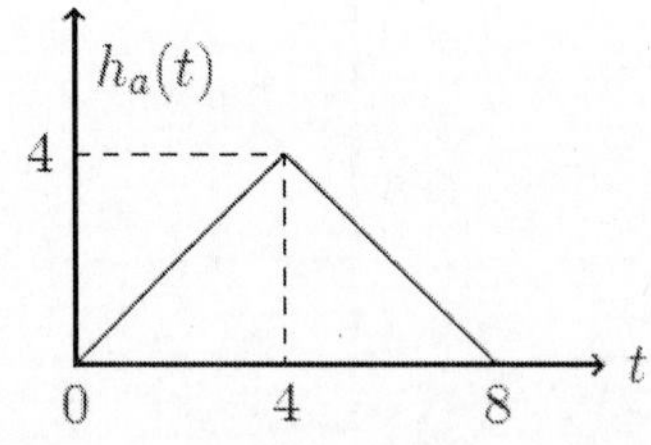

Fig. 8.32: Plot of impulse response $h_a(t)$

7. Design a 5-tap FIR filter with the following impulse response: h(n) = {0.2, 0.2, 0.2, 0.2, 0.1}. Apply this filter to the input sequence x(n) = {1, 2, 3, 4, 5, 6, 7, 8} and find the output y(n).
8. Design a low-pass FIR filter with a cutoff frequency of π/4 using the window method with a Hamming window. Use a filter length of 7 and apply it to the sequence x(n) ={1, 2, 3, 4, 5, 6, 7, 8}.

9. Given the input sequence x(n) = {2, 2, 2, 2, 2, 2, 2, 2, 2} and the IIR filter defined by the difference equation y(n) = 0.5y(n − 1) + x(n), compute the output sequence y(n).
10. Design a simple high-pass IIR filter with a cutoff frequency of π/2 and apply it to the sequence x(n) = {1, 2, 3, 4, 5, 6, 7, 8}. Use the filter difference equation y(n) = x(n) − 0.5x(n − 1) + 0.5y(n − 1).
11. For the IIR filter defined by the difference equation y(n)-1.2y(n 1) + 0.36y(n-2) = x(n), determine if the filter is stable by analyzing its poles.

Multiple Choice Questions

1. Which of the following is a characteristic of an Infinite Impulse Response (IIR) filter?
   A) It has a finite duration of the impulse response.
   B) It can only be designed using the windowing method.
   C) It can have poles and zeros in its transfer function.
   D) It cannot be used for real-time processing.
2. What is the primary advantage of a Finite Impulse Response (FIR) filter over an IIR filter?
   A) FIR filters are always stable.
   B) FIR filters have a higher computational complexity.
   C) FIR filters can realize any frequency response exactly.
   D) FIR filters have infinite duration responses.
3. Which design method is commonly used for FIR filters?
   A) Bilinear transform
   B) Windowing method
   C) Z-transform
   D) Inverse Chebyshev
4. Which window function has the best frequency resolution for FIR filter design?
   A) Hamming
   B) Hanning
   C) Blackman
   D) Rectangular
5. In digital filter design, what does the term "transition band" refer to?
   A) The range of frequencies that are passed by the filter.
   B) The range of frequencies that are completely attenuated.
   C) The region between the passband and stopband.
   D) The region of maximum ripple in the passband.
6. What is the main drawback of using the bilinear transform method in IIR filter design?
   A) It cannot be used for low-pass filters.
   B) It introduces aliasing.

C) It warps the frequency response.

D) It is computationally intensive.

7. Which of the following IIR filter design methods directly maps analog filter poles and zeros to the digital domain?

A) Impulse invariance

B) Bilinear transform

C) Windowing method

D) Frequency sampling

8. For a Chebyshev Type I filter, what is a key characteristic of its passband?

A) Linear phase response

B) No ripples in the passband

C) Equal ripples in the passband

D) No ripples in the stopband

9. In FIR filter design, the length of the filter (N) primarily determines which of the following?

A) The stability of the filter

B) The cutoff frequency

C) The width of the main lobe in the frequency response

D) The type of filter (low-pass, high-pass)

10. Which of the following is NOT an advantage of FIR filters?

A) Always stable

B) Can have exact linear phase

C) Requires less memory for implementation

D) No feedback is required

11. Which filter design method provides a filter that has exactly zero phase delay?

A) Butterworth

B) Chebyshev

C) Rectangular window FIR

D) Inverse Chebyshev

12. In the design of digital filters, which of the following defines the "order" of the filter?

A) The number of delays in the filter

B) The length of the impulse response

C) The number of poles in the transfer function

D) The complexity of the filter algorithm

ANSWERS

1	2	3	4	5	6	7	8	9	10	11	12
C	A	B	D	C	C	A	C	C	C	C	C

KNOW MORE

For more information related to this topic scan the QR code.

OR

Type this link in your browser

https://www.dsprelated.com/freebooks/filters/

REFERENCES AND SUGGESTED READING

1. B. P. Lathi, "*Principles of Linear Systems and Signals*," *Oxford Second edition*, 2009.
2. John G. Proakis, and Dimitris G. Manolakis "*Digital signal processing: principles, algo- rithms, and applications, 4/E*,"*Pearson Education India*, 2007.
3. Alan V. Oppenheim, Alan S. Willsky, and S. Hamid Nawab "*Signals & Systems*,"*Pearson Education India*, 1997.
4. Steven W. Smith "*Digital Signal Processing: A Practical Guide for Engineers and Scientists*,"*California Technical Publishing*, 1999.
5. Barrie W. Jervis, and Emmanuel C. Ifeachor "*Digital Signal Processing: A Practical Approach*,"*Pearson Education India*, 2002.

Chapter 9: Multirate Digital Signal Processing

UNIT SPECIFICS

The multirate digital signal processing chapter focuses on techniques for changing the sampling rates of digital signals to optimize processing efficiency and performance. Key topics include decimation (downsampling) and interpolation (upsampling), which involve reducing and increasing the sampling rate of signals while managing issues like aliasing. The chapter also delves into polyphase decomposition for efficient filter implementation and the design of filters suited for multirate systems. Additionally, it covers multistage multirate systems to reduce computational complexity and fractional sampling rate conversion techniques for non-integer rate changes.

RATIONALE

This chapter is to provide a comprehensive understanding of how varying sampling rates can optimize digital signal processing tasks. In many applications, such as communications, audio, and image processing, signals need to be processed at different rates to balance performance and computational efficiency. Multirate techniques like decimation and interpolation enable this flexibility, reducing the computational load and memory requirements while maintaining signal quality. By exploring polyphase structures, multistage implementations, and fractional sampling rate conversion, the chapter aims to equip readers with the tools and knowledge to design efficient systems that can handle diverse signal processing challenges in modern digital applications.

PRE-REQUISITE

Knowledge of discrete-time signals and systems, which provides the basis for understanding how signals are manipulated in the digital domain. Familiarity with the z-transform and discrete-time Fourier transform (DTFT) is essential for analyzing systems and signals in the frequency domain. A background in digital filter design, including FIR and IIR filters, is crucial for grasping the filtering operations involved in multirate processing.

UNIT OUTCOMES

List of outcomes of this unit is as follows:

U9-O1:Decimation and interpolation fundamentals

U9-O2:Efficient FIR filter structure design

U9-O3:Polyphase filter structures

U9-O4:Sampling rate conversion

Unit-9 Outcomes	EXPECTED MAPPING WITH COURSE OUTCOMES (1- Weak Correlation; 2- Medium correlation; 3- Strong Correlation)					
	CO-1	CO-2	CO-3	CO-4	CO-5	CO-6
U9-O1	–	1	–	2	3	1
U9-O2	–	1	–	2	3	1
U9-O3	–	1	–	2	3	1

9.1 INTRODUCTION

Multirate Digital Signal Processing (DSP) is a technique used to process digital signals at multiple sampling rates. It involves manipulating the sampling rate of a signal to achieve various objectives such as reducing computational complexity, improving efficiency, or extracting specific frequency bands of interest.

Multirate DSP often involves converting the sampling rate of a digital signal from one rate to another. This can be achieved through processes such as upsampling (increasing the sampling rate), downsampling (decreasing the sampling rate), or interpolation/decimation (combining or removing samples).

Filter banks are a key component of Multirate DSP systems. They consist of a set of filters designed to divide the signal into multiple frequency bands or channels. Each filter operates at a different sampling rate, allowing for efficient processing of specific frequency components.

Polyphase filters are used in Multirate DSP to implement efficient filter banks. They exploit the properties of periodicity and symmetry in the filter coefficients to reduce computational complexity.

Polyphase filters are commonly used in applications such as audio coding, digital communications, and image processing.

Multirate DSP finds applications in various fields, including telecommunications, audio and video processing, medical imaging, and radar systems. It allows for efficient processing of digital signals while meeting the specific requirements of each application.

Decimation and interpolation are fundamental operations used in sampling rate conversion, which involves changing the sampling rate of a digital signal.

It becomes evident that the continuous time signal $x(t)$ can undergo sampling with any sampling period $T=1/F_s$. Nevertheless, to ensure a singular correspondence between the continuous signal $x(t)$ and the discrete sequence $x(n)$, as shown in Fig.9.1, it is imperative to select the sampling period T in accordance with the criteria stipulated by the Nyquist sampling theorem.

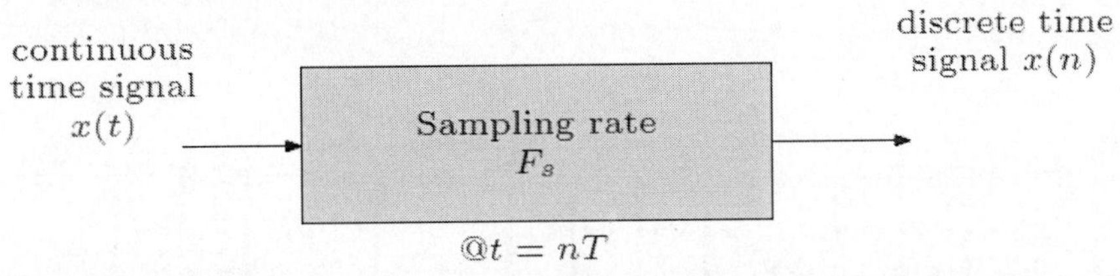

Fig.9.1: continuous to discrete time signal conversion at sampling rate $F_s \geq 2F_m$.

The procedure of altering the sampling rate of a signal from an initial-rate $F_s=F_x$ to a different rate $F_s= F_y$ is termed as sampling rate conversion. When the new sampling rate surpasses the original sampling rate, i.e.,

$$F_x < F_y \quad \text{or } T_x > T_y$$

The operation is commonly referred to as interpolation since it involves generating additional samples of the original physical process from a diminished set of samples.

Conversely, the process of digitally reducing the sampling rate of a signal form a given rate $F_s=F_x$

To a lower rate $F_s=F_y$ is termed as decimation. Indecimation

$$F_x > F_y \quad or\ T_x < T_y$$

Decimation and interpolation of signals are complementary processes. Sampling rate conversion is depicted in Fig.9.2.

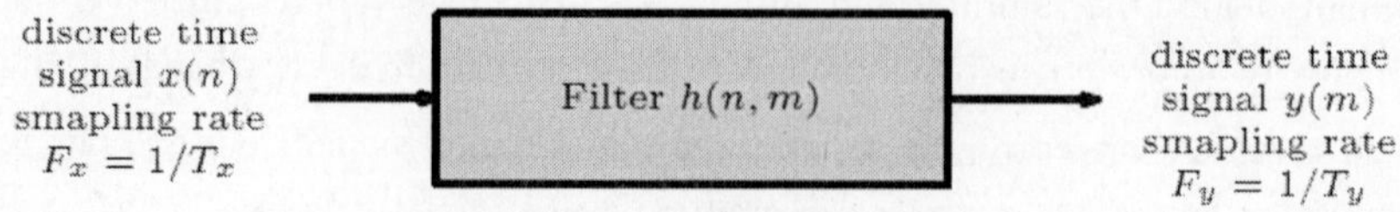

Fig.9.2: Sampling rate conversion.

9.2 DECIMATION

Decimation is the process of reducing the sampling rate of a signal by discarding some of its samples. It is often used to decrease the data rate of a signal while maintaining its essential characteristics.

In decimation, every *Dth* sample is retained, while the rest are discarded, where D is the decimation factor. For example, if the original sampling rate is F_x and the decimation factor is D, the new sampling rate after decimation is F_x/D.

Let's contemplate the act of diminishing the sampling rate of $x(n)$ by an integer factor D. Subse- quently, the resulting new sampling rate is denoted as $F_y=F_x/D$. Let's suppose $x(n)$ represents a full-band signal, meaning its spectrum exhibits non-zero values across all frequencies f within the range $|f| < F_x/2$.

To prevent aliasing, it is imperative to first limit the bandwidth of $x(n)$ to $F_{\max} = F_x/2D$ or, equivalently, to $\omega_{\max} = \pi/D$. Subsequently, down sampling by D can be performed, thereby circumventing aliasing issues. Anti-aliasing filter impulse response is $h(n)$ with bandwidth as

$$H_D(\omega) = \begin{cases} 1, & \text{if } |\omega| \leq \pi/D \\ 0, & \text{otherwise.} \end{cases}$$

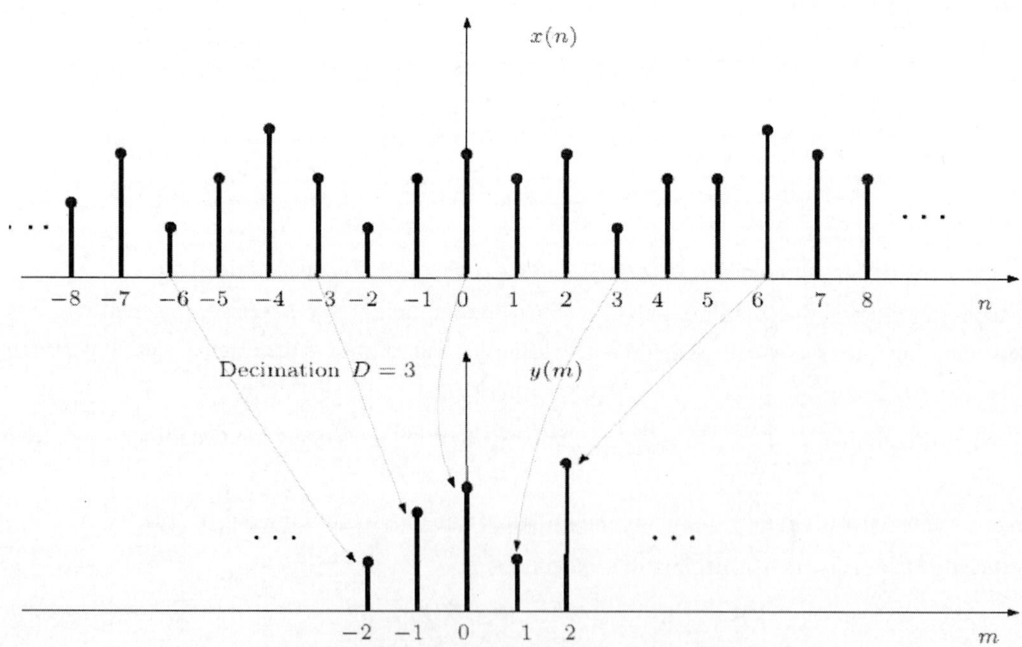

Fig.9.3: Time domain input and output signals.

Filter output $v(n)$ is expressed as

$$v(n) = \sum_{k=0}^{\infty} h(k)\, x(n-k).\ (9.1)$$

Filter output is down sampled by the factor D to produce decimated output $y(m)$ (as shown in Fig. 9.3) as

$$y(m) = v(mD) = \sum_{k=0}^{\infty} h(k)\, x(mD-k)\ (9.2)$$

While the filtering process applied to $x(n)$ remains linear and time-invariant, the down sampling operation in conjunction with filtering yields a time-variant system. This can be readily confirmed.

Despite $x(n)$ generating $y(m)$, it is important to note that $x(n - n_d)$ does not necessarily yield $y(n - n_d)$ unless n_d is a multiple of D. Consequently, the collective linear process (linear filtering followed by down sampling) applied to $x(n)$ is not time-invariant. Decimation operation is illustrated in Fig. 9.4.

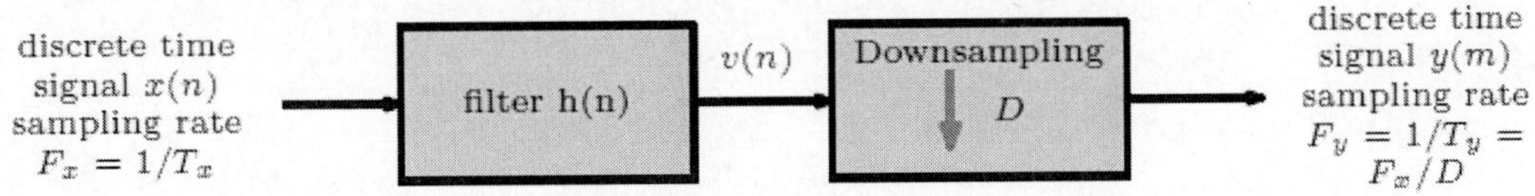

Fig.9.4: Decimation by a factor D.

Decimation operation in frequency domain can be written as

$$Y(z) = \sum_{m=-\infty}^{\infty} y(m)\, z^{-m}.\ (9.3)$$

Here $y(m)$ has every Dth sample of the input signal $v(n)$ can be expressed as

$$\tilde{v}(n) = \begin{cases} v, if\ n = 0, \pm D, \pm 2D, \dots \\ 0, otherwise \end{cases}$$

Thus, $\tilde{v}(n)$ is obtained by multiplying $v(n)$ by an impulse train $I(n)$ of period D. The discrete Fourier series of impulse train is written as

$$I(n) = \frac{1}{D}\sum_{k=0}^{D-1} e^{j\frac{2\pi kn}{D}}.\ (9.4)$$

Thus $\tilde{v}(n) = v(n)I(n)$ and final output is

$y(m) = \tilde{v}(mDn) = v(mD)I(mD) = v(mD).$ (9.5)

Further,

$$Y(z)=\sum_{m=-\infty}^{\infty}\underbrace{\tilde{v}(mD)}_{\text{use } mD=m}\ z^{-m}=\sum_{m=-\infty}^{\infty}\tilde{v}(m)z^{-m/D}$$

$$=\sum_{m=-\infty}^{\infty}v(m)I(m)z^{-m/D}=\sum_{m=-\infty}^{\infty}v(m)[\frac{1}{D}\sum_{k=0}^{D-1}e^{j\frac{2\pi km}{D}}]z^{-m/D} \quad (9.6)$$

$$Y(z)=\frac{1}{D}\underbrace{\sum_{k=0}^{D-1}\sum_{m=-\infty}^{\infty}v(m)\left(e^{j\frac{-2\pi k}{D}}z^{1/D}\right)^{-m}}_{V(z)|_{z=e^{j\frac{-2\pi k}{D}}z^{1/D}}}$$

$$Y(z)=\frac{1}{D}\sum_{k=0}^{D-1}V(e^{j\frac{-2\pi k}{D}}z^{1/D})=\frac{1}{D}\sum_{k=0}^{D-1}X(e^{j\frac{-2\pi k}{D}}z^{1/D})H_D(e^{j\frac{-2\pi k}{D}}z^{1/D}). \quad (9.7)$$

Since $V(z)=X(z)H(z)$. DTFT of the above expression is written as

$$Y(\omega_y)=\frac{1}{D}\sum_{k=0}^{D-1}X\left(\frac{\omega_y-2\pi k}{D}\right)H_D\left(\frac{\omega_y-2\pi k}{D}\right). \quad (9.8)$$

Here we have assumed that $z=e^{j\omega}y$ and $Y(\omega_y)=Y(e^{j\omega}y)$. ω_y is the decimated signal $y(m)$ frequency. Frequency relation can be understood as

$$F_y=\frac{F_x}{D} \text{ or } T_y=DT_x$$

$$\omega_y=\frac{2\pi F}{F_y}=2\pi f_y=2\pi FT_y$$

$$\omega_x=\frac{2\pi F}{F_x}=2\pi f_x=2\pi FT_x$$

$$\omega_x=\frac{2\pi F}{F_x/D}=D\omega_x$$

(9.9)

Thus output frequency is stretched by a factor of D. Frequency spectrum of signals in decimation process is shown in Fig.9.5.

9.3 INTERPOLATION

Interpolation is the process of increasing the sampling rate of a signal by inserting additional samples between existing samples. It is used to increase signal resolution or achieve smoother signal reconstruction.

In interpolation, new samples are generated between existing samples using interpolation tech- niques such as linear interpolation, cubic interpolation, or sinc interpolation. The number of inserted samples and their values depend on the interpolation factor.

Time domain input and interpolated signal relation is shown in Fig.9.6, where we can observe that $I-1$ samples are inserted between two consecutive samples.

Interpolation block diagram is shown in Fig.9.7, where LPF is used to remove the multiple (shifted) copy of the signal after interpolation. Input and output signals relation in frequency domain is shown in Fig.9.8. Interpolation output signal by a factor of *I* is expressed as

$$v(m) = \begin{cases} x\left(\frac{m}{I}\right), if\ m = 0, I, 2I, \ldots \\ 0, otherwise \end{cases}$$

The sampling rate of *v(m)* and *y(m)* are same as $F_y = IF_x$. Z-transform of *v(m)* is expressed as

$$V(z) = \sum_{-\infty}^{\infty} v(m)\, z^{-m} = \sum_{-\infty}^{\infty} x(m/I)\, z^{-m}$$

$$V(z) = \sum_{-\infty}^{\infty} x(m)\, z^{-mI} = X(z^I)$$

Or $V(\omega_y) = X(I\omega_y)$. Final output is expressed as

$Y(z) = V(z)H_I(z) = Y(\omega_y) = V(\omega_y)H_I(\omega_y)$.

Filter response is expressed as

$$H_I(\omega_y) = \begin{cases} C, if\ 0 \le |\omega_y| \le \pi/I \\ 0, \text{otherwise.} \end{cases}$$

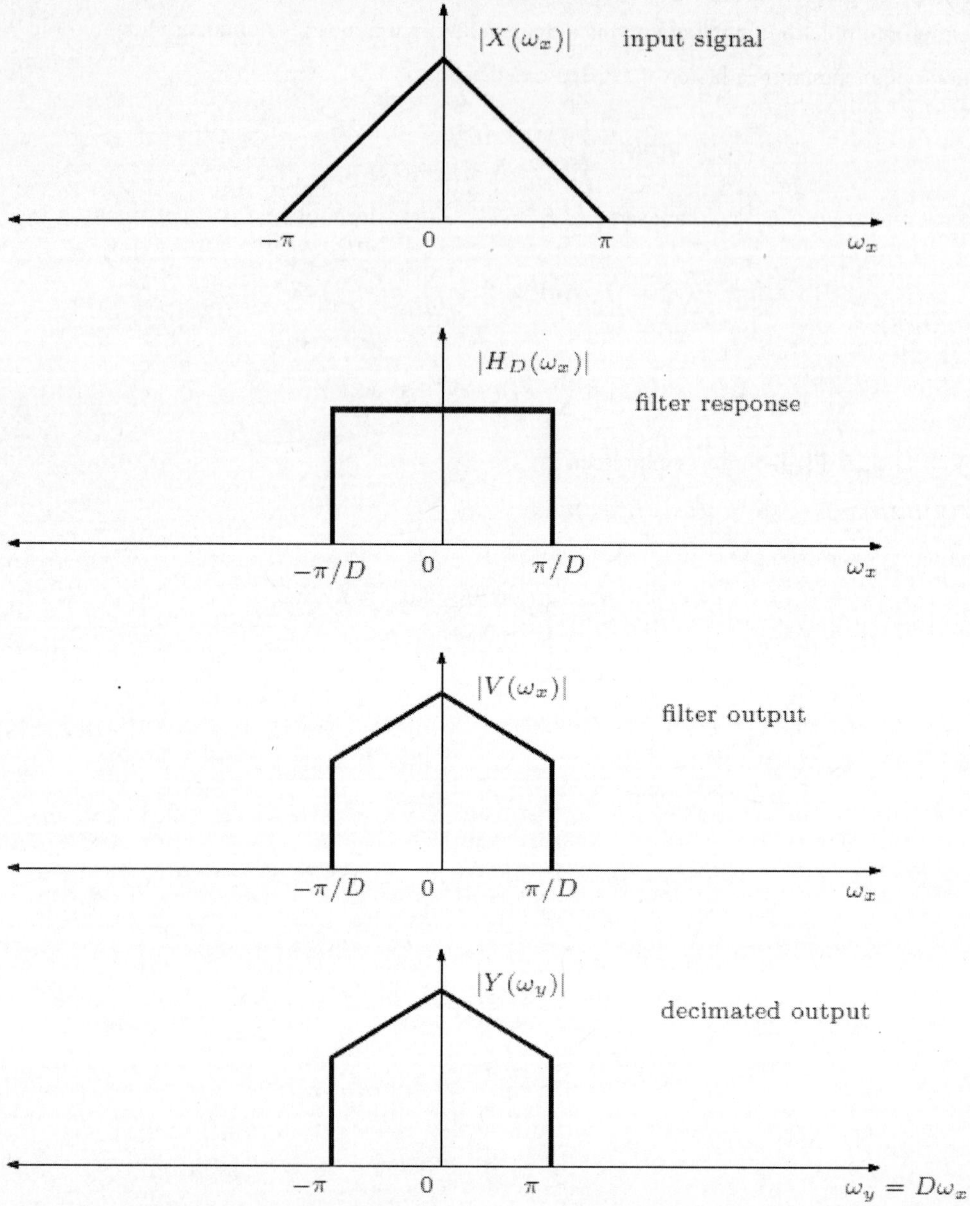

Fig.9.5: Spectra of input to output signals.

Thus output is

Relation between ω_y and ω_x is

$$\omega_y = \frac{2\pi F}{F_y} = \frac{2\pi F}{IF_x} = \frac{\omega_x}{I}.$$

$$Y(\omega_y) = \begin{cases} CX(w_y I), if\ 0 \le |\omega_y| \le \pi/I \\ 0, \text{otherwise} \end{cases}$$

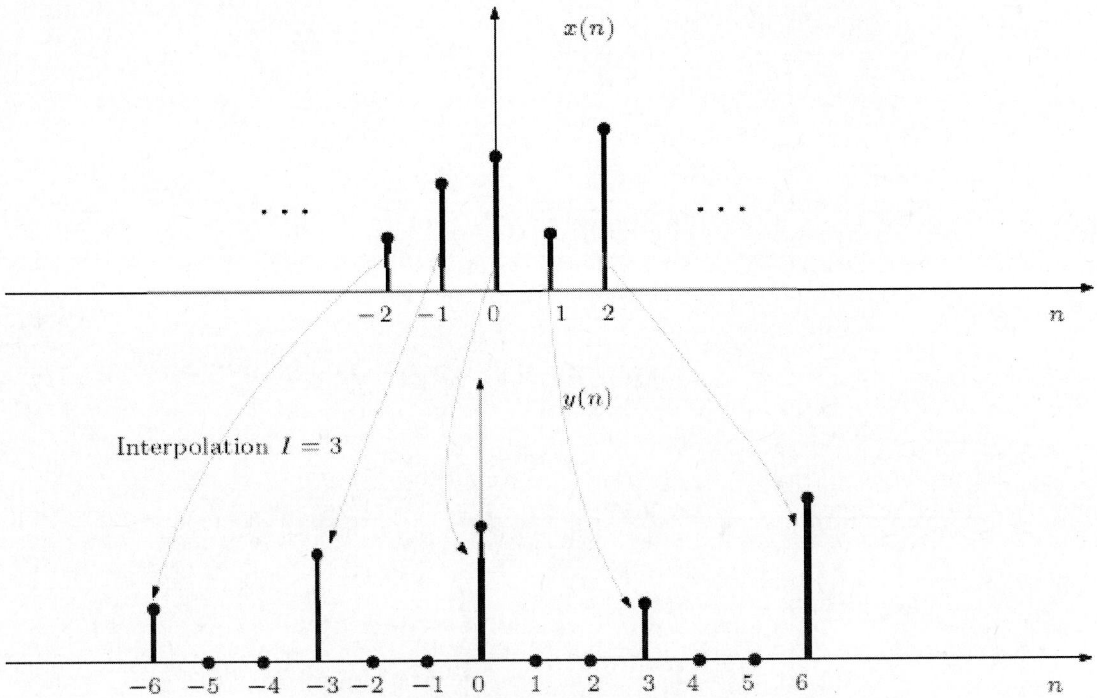

Fig. 9.6: Time domain input to output signals in interpolation

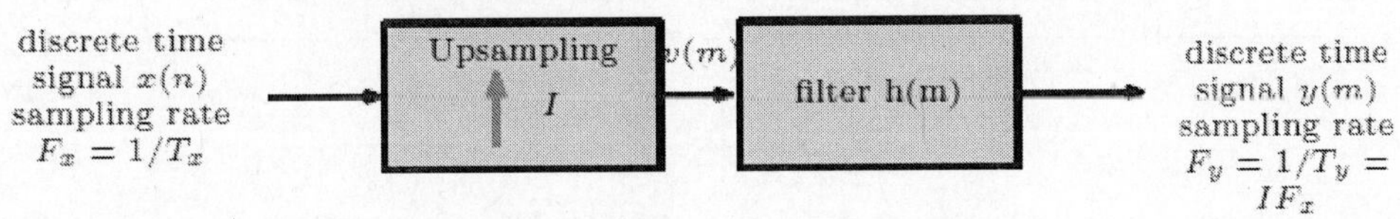

Fig. 9.7: Interpolation block diagram

9.4 SAMPLING RATE CONVERSION

Sampling rate conversion often involves a combination of decimation and interpolation. For ex- ample, to convert a signal from a higher sampling rate to a lower sampling rate, one might first interpolate the signal to increase its sampling rate and then decimate it to achieve the desired lower sampling rate. Conversely, to convert a signal from a lower sampling rate to a higher sampling rate, one might first decimate the signal to reduce its sampling rate and then interpolate it to increase its sampling rate.

Sampling rate conversion involves first interpolating the signal by a factor of *I*, followed by dec- Imation by a factor of *D*, as illustrated in Fig.9.9. Consequently, the output signal's sampling rate is IF_x/D, where F_x is the input signal sampling rate.

Interpolator output and decimator input have lowpass filters with following specifications

$$H_I(\omega_v) = \begin{cases} 1, if\ |\omega_v| \le \pi/I \\ 0, \text{otherwise} \end{cases}$$

and

$$H_D(\omega_v) = \begin{cases} 1, if\ 0 \le |\omega_v| \le \pi/D \\ 0, \text{otherwise} \end{cases}$$

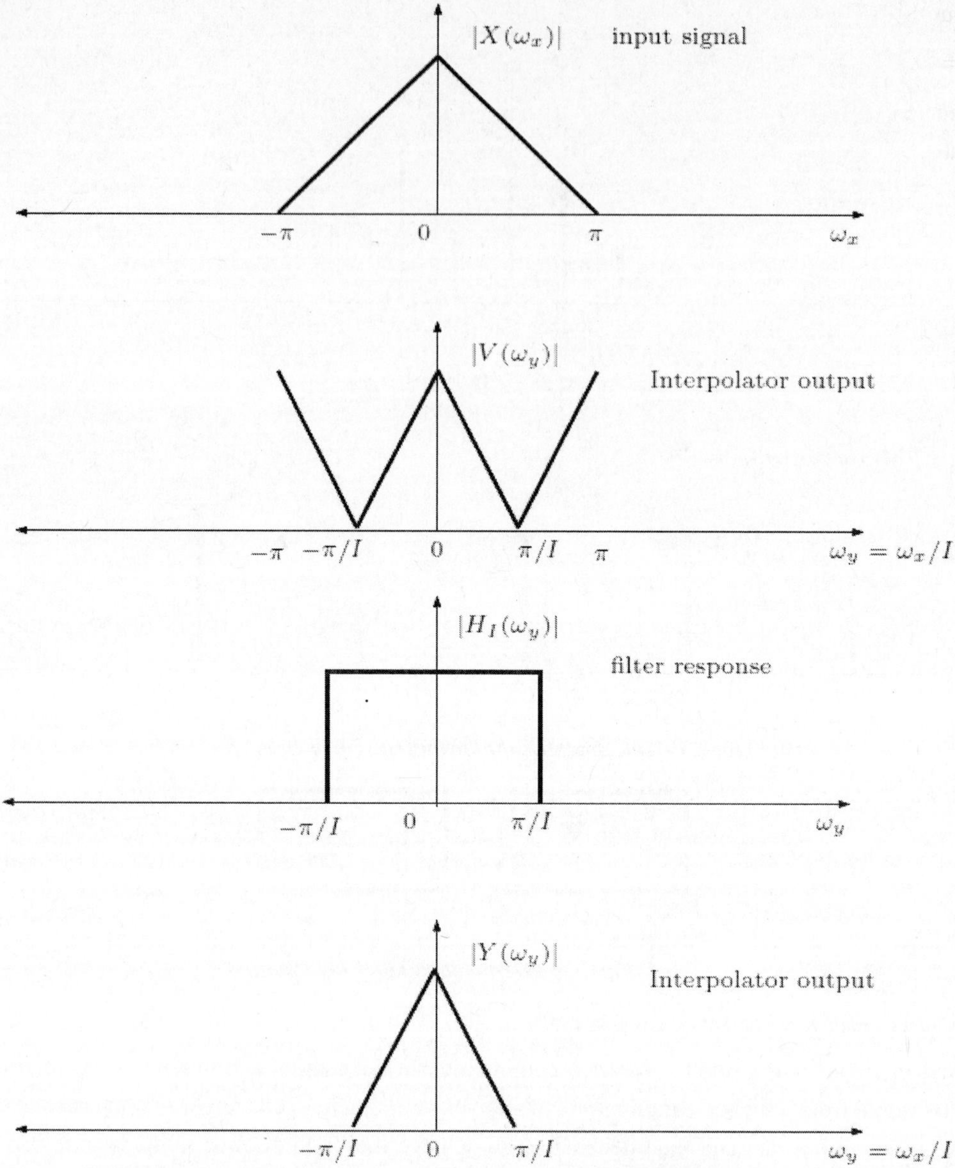

Fig.9.8: Frequency domain input and output signals in interpolation.

Thus the common lowpass filter characteristics are expressed as

$$H(\omega_v) = \begin{cases} 1, if\ 0 \le |\omega_v| \le \min\{\frac{\pi}{D}, \frac{\pi}{I}\} \\ 0, \text{otherwise} \end{cases}$$

Here $\omega_v = 2\pi F/F_v = 2\pi F/IF_x = \omega_x/I$. In the time domain, the output sequence of the upsampler is given by:

$$v(\text{k}) = \begin{cases} x\left(\frac{k}{I}\right), if\ k = 0, \pm I, \pm 2I, \ldots \\ 0, \text{otherwise} \end{cases}$$

LPF output is

$$v(k) = \sum_{l=0}^{\infty} v(l)\, h(k-l) = \sum_{l=0}^{\infty} x(l/I)\, h(k-l) = \sum_{l=0}^{\infty} x(l)\, h(k-Il) \tag{9.10}$$

Final output is expressed as

$y(m) = w(mD) = \sum_{l=0}^{\infty} x(l)\, h(mD - Il)$. (9.11)

The frequency-domain relationships can be derived by merging the outcomes of both the inter- polation and decimation operations. Hence, the spectrum at the output of the linear filter with impulse response *h*(*k*) is

$$V(\omega_v)=H(\omega_v)X(I\omega_v)$$

or

$$H(\omega_v) = \begin{cases} \mathrm{I}X(\mathrm{I}\omega_v), if\ 0 \le |\omega_v| \le \min\{\frac{\pi}{D}, \frac{\pi}{I}\} \\ 0, \text{otherwise} \end{cases}$$

Output spectrum after decimation is obtained as

$$Y(\omega_y) = \frac{1}{D}\sum_{k=0}^{D-1} \mathrm{V}\left(\frac{\omega_v - 2\pi k}{D}\right)$$

Here $\omega_y = D\omega_v$. Output is also expressed as

$$H(\omega_y) = \begin{cases} \mathrm{I/D}X(\omega_y/\mathrm{D}), if\ 0 \le |\omega_y| \le \min\{\frac{\pi}{D}, \frac{\pi}{I}\} \\ 0, \text{otherwise} \end{cases}$$

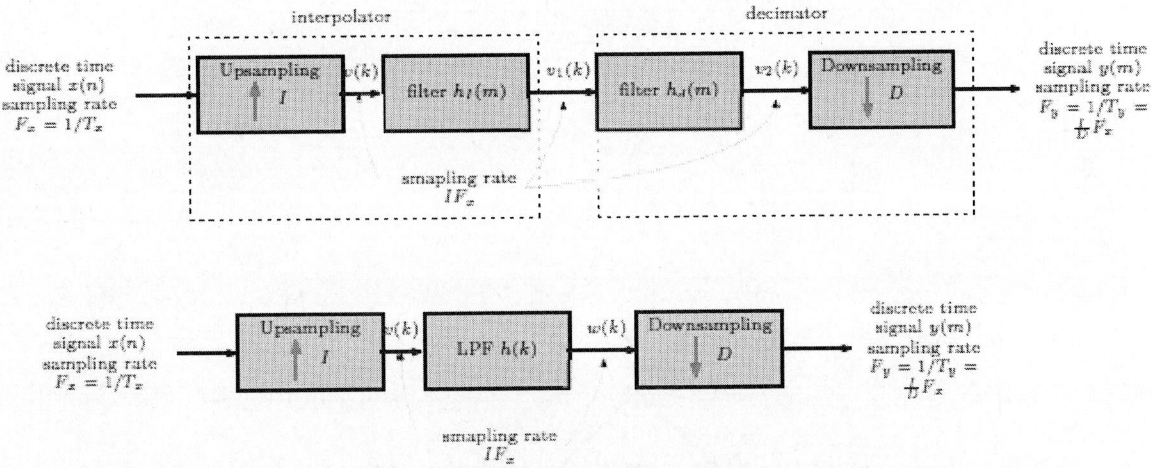

Fig.9.9: Sampling rate conversion by I/D.

9.5 POLYPHASE FILTER STRUCTURES

Polyphase filters decompose a filter into multiple "phases" or branches, each processing a fraction of the input signal. By splitting the filter into phases, redundant computations can be eliminated, leading to significant savings in computational complexity.

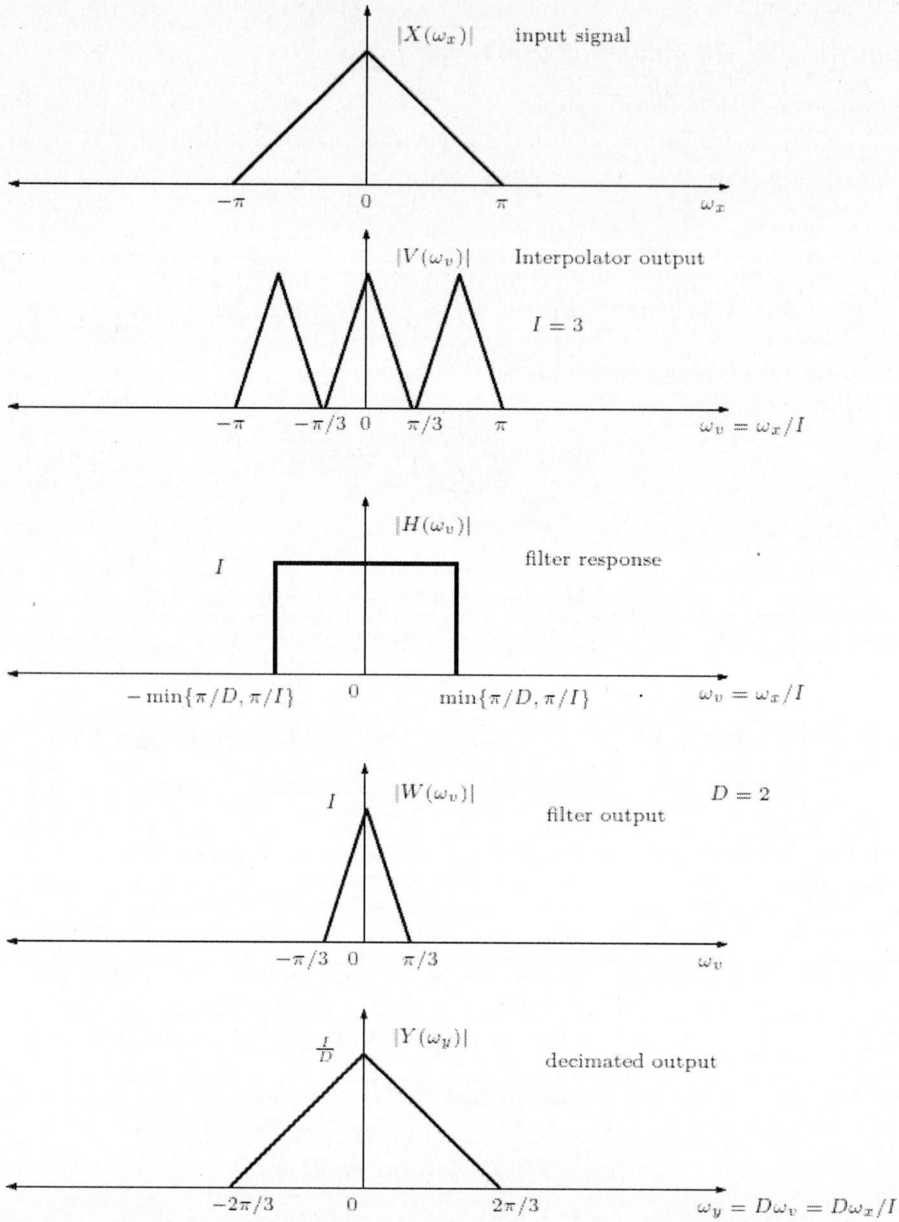

Fig.9.10: Frequency domain sampling rate conversion by I/D=3/2.

The process begins by decomposing the original filter into its constituent polyphase components. This involves partitioning the filter's impulse response into multiple subfilters, each corresponding to a specific phase. The impulse response of each subfilter is obtained by selecting every Mth Sample from the original filter's impulse response, where M is the number of phases.

Once the filter has been decomposed into polyphase components, each subfilter is implemented as a separate branch in the filter bank. The input signal is split into M parallel paths, each passing through a different polyphase component. After filtering, the outputs of all branches are combined to produce the final filtered output as shown in Fig.9.11.

FIR filter response can be written as

$$\begin{aligned} H(z) &= \sum_{k=-\infty}^{\infty} h(k)z^{-k} \\ &= \cdots + h(0) \qquad h(M)z^{-M} + \ldots \\ &\quad \cdots + h(1)z^{-1} \qquad h(M+1)z^{-(M+1)} + \ldots \\ &\quad \vdots \\ &\quad \cdots + h(M-1)z^{-(M-1)} \qquad h(2M-1)z^{-(2M-1)} + \ldots \end{aligned} \tag{9.12}$$

Above equation can be expressed as

$$\begin{aligned} H(z) = &\left[\cdots + h(0) \qquad + h(M)z^{-M} + \ldots\right] \\ &\left[\cdots + h(1)z^{-1} \qquad + h(M+1)z^{-(M+1)} + \ldots\right] \\ &\vdots \\ &\left[\cdots + h(M-1)z^{-(M-1)} \qquad + h(2M-1)z^{-(2M-1)} + \ldots\right] \end{aligned} \tag{9.13}$$

$$\begin{aligned} H(z) = &\underbrace{\left[\cdots + h(0) \qquad + h(M)z^{-M} + \ldots\right]}_{P_0(z)} \\ &z^{-1}\underbrace{\left[\cdots + h(1) \qquad + h(M+1)z^{-M} + \ldots\right]}_{P_1(z)} \\ &\vdots \\ &z^{-(M-1)}\underbrace{\left[\cdots + h(M-1) \qquad + h(2M-1)z^{-M} + \ldots\right]}_{P_{M-1}(z)}. \end{aligned} \tag{9.14}$$

$$H(z) = \sum_{i=0}^{M-1} z^{-i} P_i(z^M), \tag{9.15}$$

where

$$P_i(z) = \sum_{k=-\infty}^{\infty} h(kM+i)(z^{-k}). \tag{9.16}$$

$H(z)$ in terms of $P_i(z)$ is called M components polyphase decomposition. Time domain polyphase component $P_i(z)$ is expressed as

$$p_i(k) = h(kM+i), \quad i = 0, 1, \ldots.$$

$H(z)$ in terms of $P_i(z)$ is called M components polyphase decomposition. Time domain polyphase component $P_i(z)$ is expressed as

$p_i(k) = h(kM+i),\ i=0,1,....$

Output signal in the z domain of the M (M=3) component polyphase structure is expressed as

$$Y(z) = X(z)H(z)$$
$$=P_0(z^3)X(z)+z^{-1}P_1(z^3)X(z)+z^{-2}P_2(z^3)X(z)$$
$$=P_0(z^3)X(z)+z^{-1}P_1(z^3)X(z)+z^{-1}P_2(z^3)X(z). \quad (9.17)$$

Polyphase filter structure for $M = 3$ is expressed in Fig. 9.11(top). Similar transpose polyphase filter structure for $M = 3$ is expressed in Fig. 9.11(bottom) by considering the transpose of FIR filter realization.

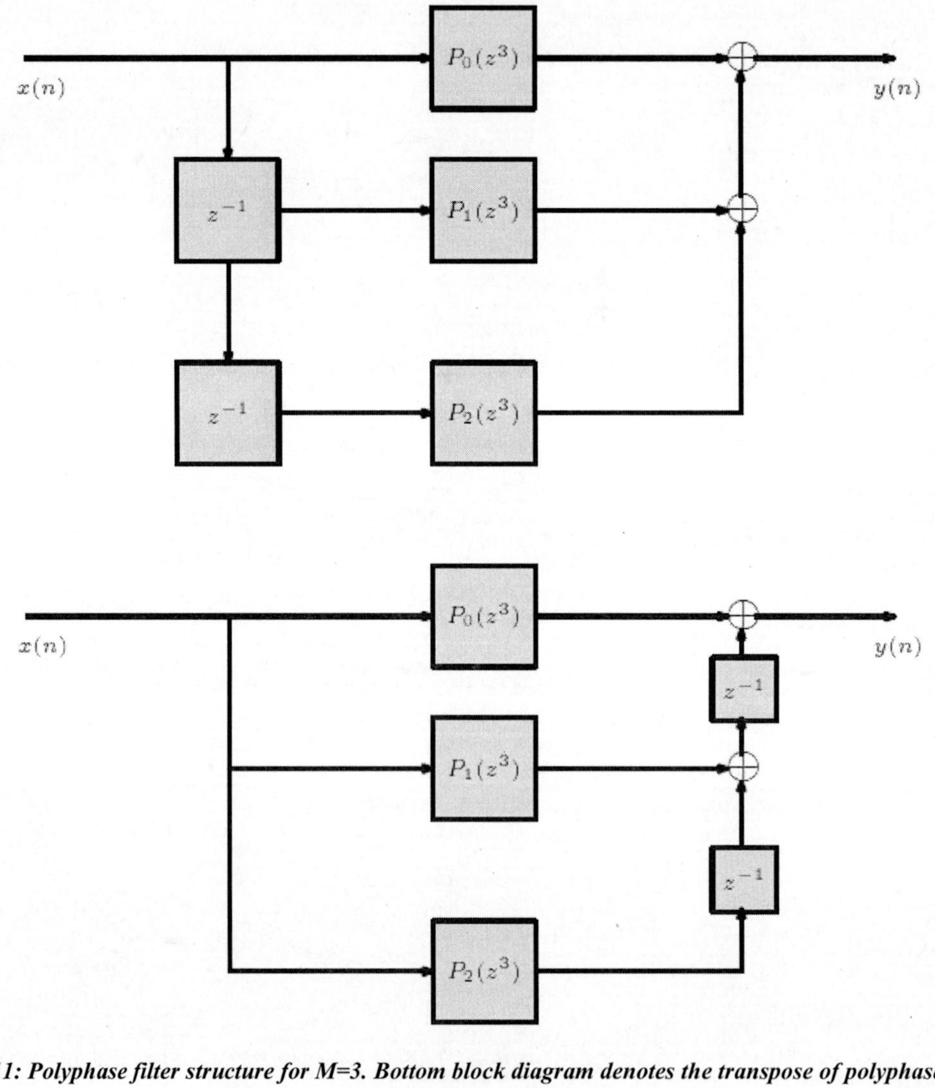

Fig. 9.11: Polyphase filter structure for M=3. Bottom block diagram denotes the transpose of polyphase filter structure for M= 3.

9.5.1 Noble identities for interpolation and decimation

In general, filters and sampling rate converters cannot be interchanged due to the time-varying nature of sampling rate converters. Below, Noble identities are derived by interchanging the positions of the filter and rate converter in the system design. For decimation input-output relation is expressed as

$$y(n) = x(nD) \quad \text{or} \quad Y(z) = \frac{1}{D}\sum_{k=0}^{D-1} X(z^{1/D}e^{-j2\pi k/D}).$$

Thus output on Fig. 9.12 is written as

$$Y(z) = V_1(z)H(z) = H(z)\frac{1}{D}\sum_{k=0}^{D-1} X(z^{1/D}e^{-j2\pi k/D}) = \frac{1}{D}\sum_{k=0}^{D-1} X(z^{1/D}e^{-j2\pi k/D})H(ze^{-j2\pi D/D}). \tag{9.18}$$

Since $e^{-j2\pi D/D} = 1$. Further, we can write

$$Y(z) = \frac{1}{D}\sum_{k=0}^{D-1} V_2(z^{1/D}e^{-j2\pi k/D}) = \frac{1}{D}\sum_{k=0}^{D-1} X(z)H(z^D)|_{z=z^{1/D}e^{-j2\pi k/D}}. \tag{9.19}$$

Therefore,

$$Y(z) = \frac{1}{D}\sum_{k=0}^{D-1} X(z^{1/D}e^{-j2\pi k/D})H((z^{1/D}e^{-j2\pi k/D})^D) = \frac{1}{D}\sum_{k=0}^{D-1} X(z^{1/D}e^{-j2\pi k/D})H(ze^{-j2\pi D/D}). \tag{9.20}$$

Thus by comparing both equations(9.18) and (9.20), we can say that both are equal, as shown in Fig.9.12.

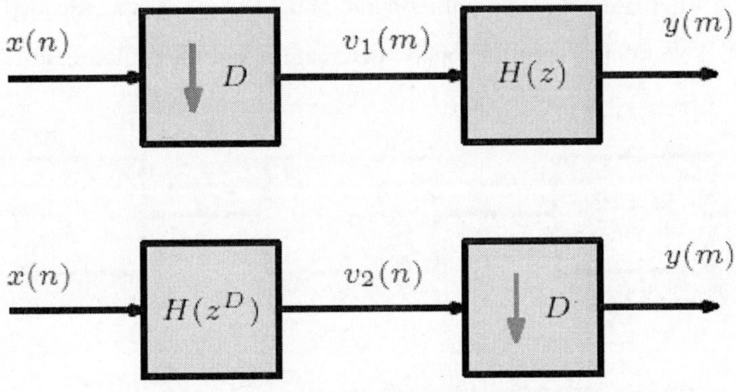

Fig.9.12: Noble identity for down-sampling.

Similarly for interpolation input-output relation is expressed as

$$y(n)=x(n/I) \text{ or } Y(z)=X(z^I).$$

Thus output on Fig.9.12 is written as

$Y(z) = V_1(z^I) = \underbrace{X(z^I)H(z^I)}_{V_1(z)=X(z)H(z)}$ (9.21)

Further, we can write $Y(z) = V_2(z)H(z^I) = \underbrace{X(z^I)}_{V_2(z)=X(z^I)} H(z^I)$ 9.22)

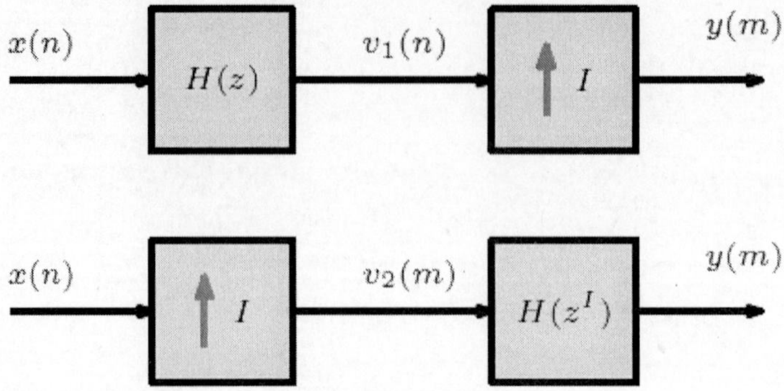

Fig.9.13: Noble identity for up-sampling.

Thus by comparing both equations (9.21) and (9.22), we can say that both are equal, as shown in Fig.9.13. The *M*th order FIR filter can be implemented as cascaded of two filters. Cascaded integrator comb (CIC) filters can also written as

$$H(z) = \sum_{k=0}^{M-1} z^{-k} = \frac{1 - z^{-M}}{1 - z^{-1}}$$

Here $1 - z^{-M}$ is comb filter and $\frac{1}{1-z^{-1}}$ is the integrator. Thus, FIR filter is a cascaded version of two filters, as shown in Fig.9.14. Two noble identities for the decimation and interpolation are shown in Fig.9.14 and Fig.9.15. respectively.

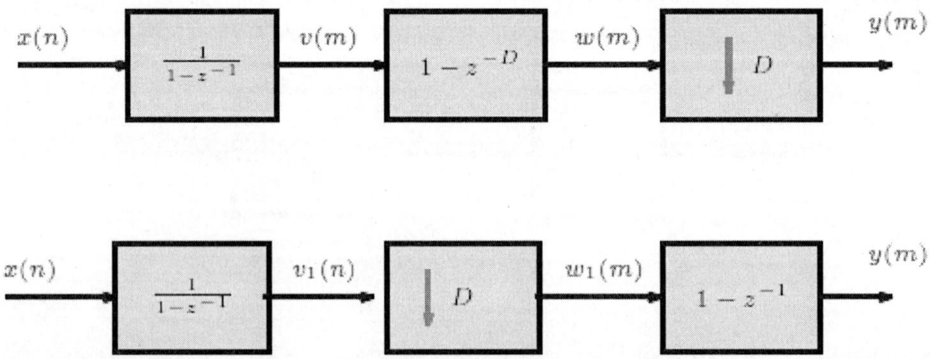

Fig. 9.14: Noble identity to implement cascaded integrator comb (CIC) filters for efficient decimator design.

9.6 POLYPHASESTRUCTURES

The decimation structure includes an anti-aliasing filter and a downsampler, as depicted in Fig. 9.16. The FIR filter is implemented using the polyphase structure, where each filter output has sampling rate F_x/D, F_x is the sampling rate of the input signal and *D* is the decimation factor. Consequently, the commutator operates from *n*=0 to *n*=*D*-1 points, and each polyphase filter is connected to the commutator switch once for every *D* samples, as illustrated in Fig. 9.17. The output is obtained continuously, as one polyphase filter out of *D* is always connected to the input.

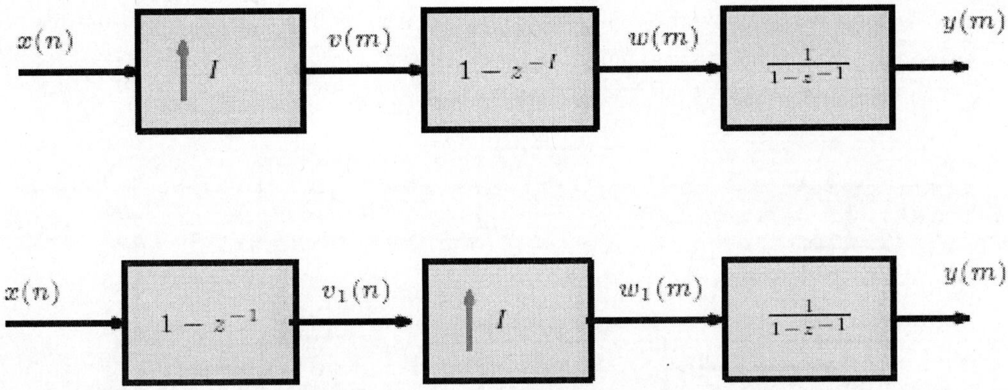

Fig.9.15: Noble identity to implement cascaded integrator comb (CIC) filters for efficient interpolator design.

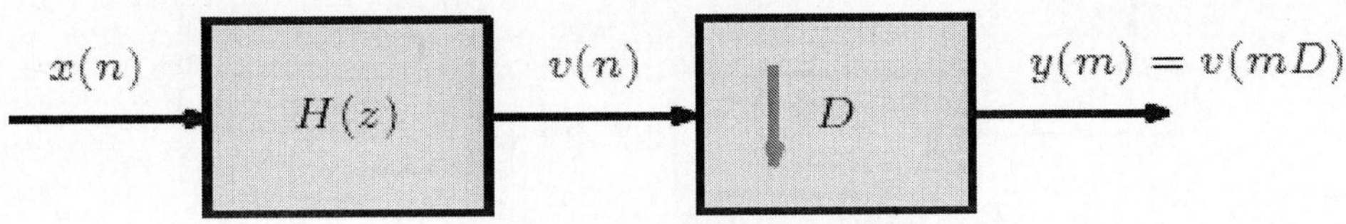

Fig.9.16: Decimation system.

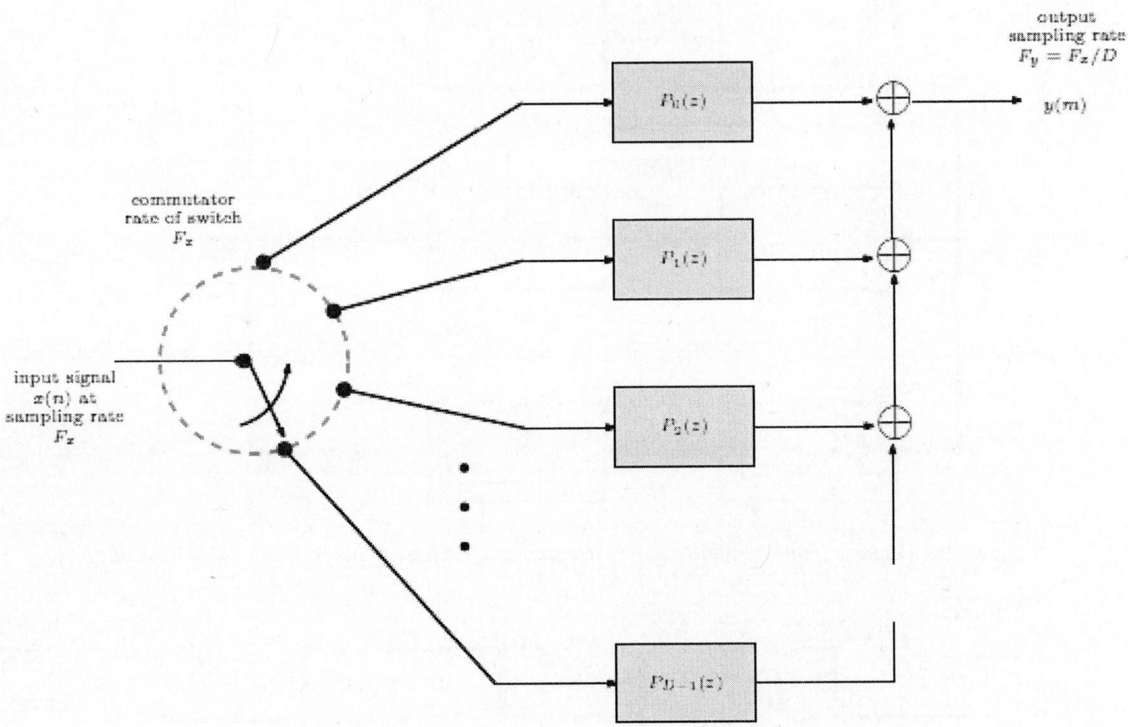

Fig.9.17: Decimation system using a polyphase filter and the commutator switch.

Polyphase structure for M= 3 using noble identity is shown in Fig.9.17.The interpolation structure includes a lowpass filter and an up-sampler, as depicted in Fig.9.19. The FIR filter is implemented using the polyphase structure, where each filter output has sampling rate IF_x, F_x is the sampling rate of the input signal and I is the interpolation factor. Consequently, the commutator operates from n=0 to n=I-1 points, and each polyphase filter is connected to the commutator switch once for every I samples, as illustrated in Fig. 9.20. Polyphase structure of an interpolator for M=3 using noble identity is shown in Fig.9.21.

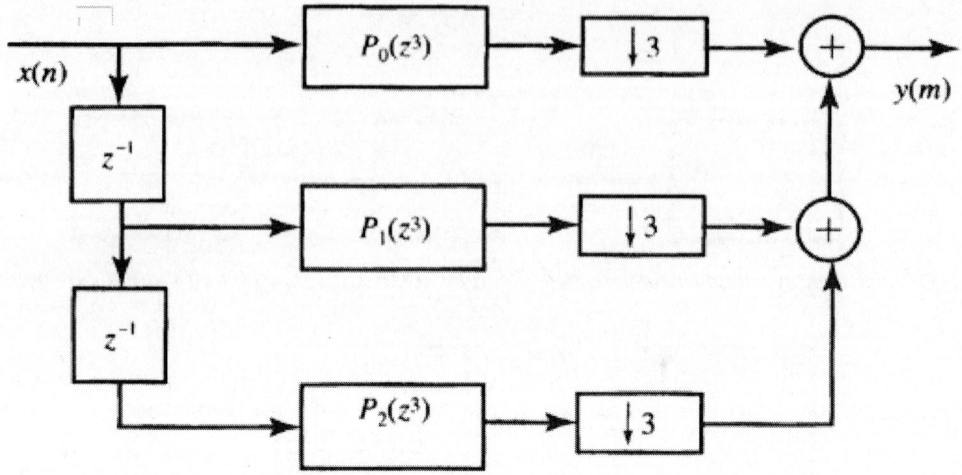

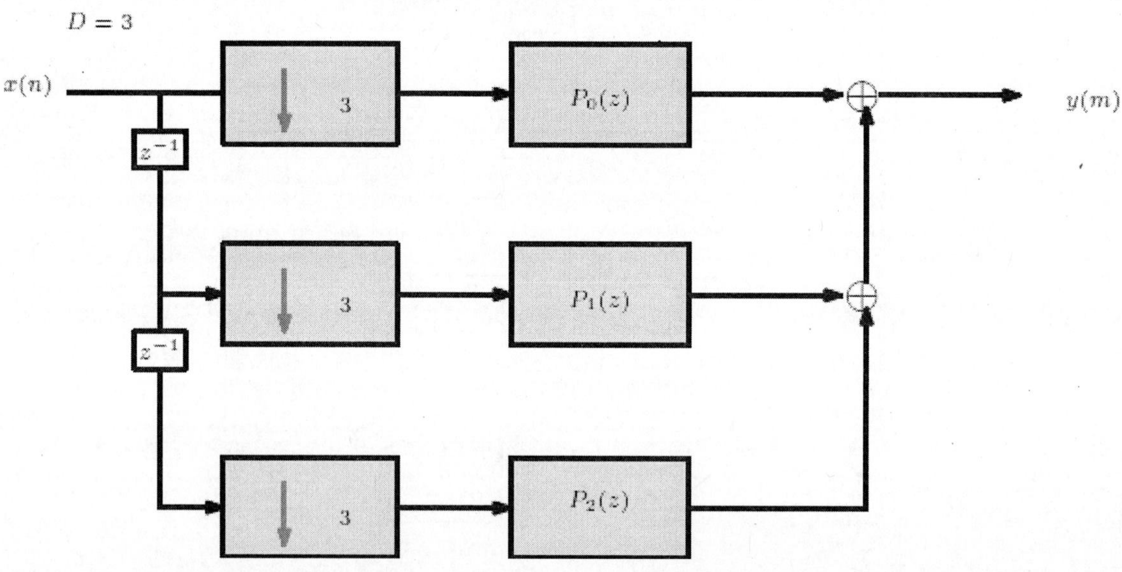

Fig.9.18: Polyphase implementation of downsampling after having invoked the noble identities.

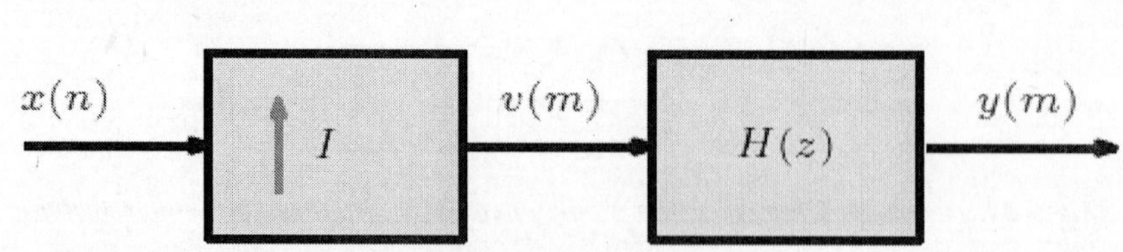

Fig. 9.19: Interpolation system.

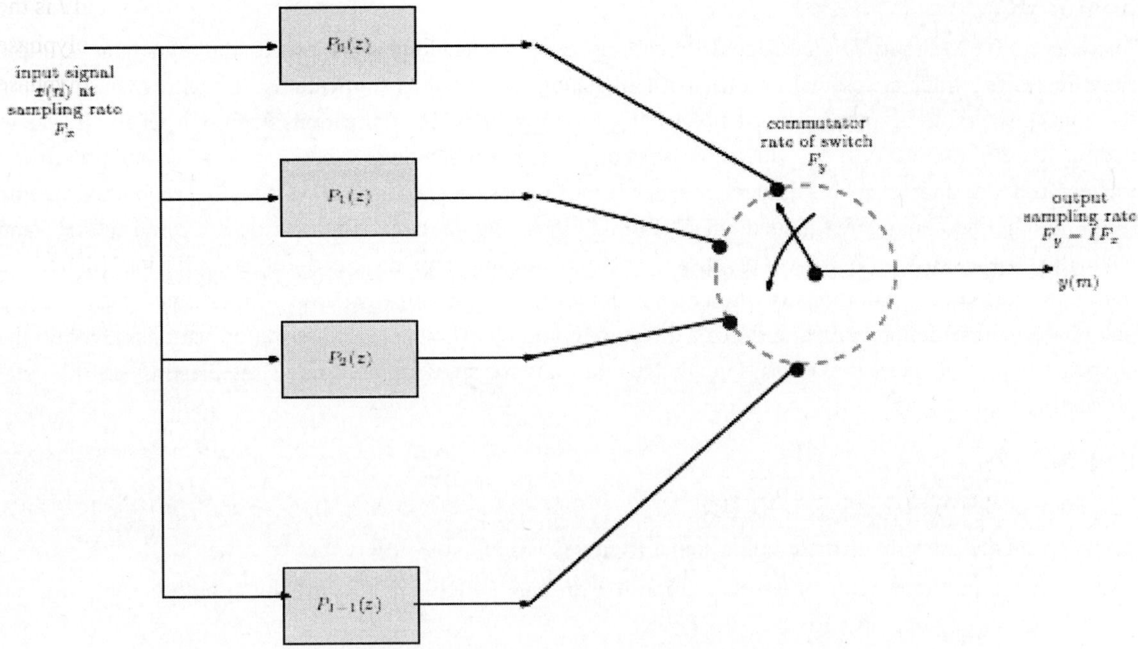

Fig.9.20: Interpolation system using a polyphase filter and the commutator switch.

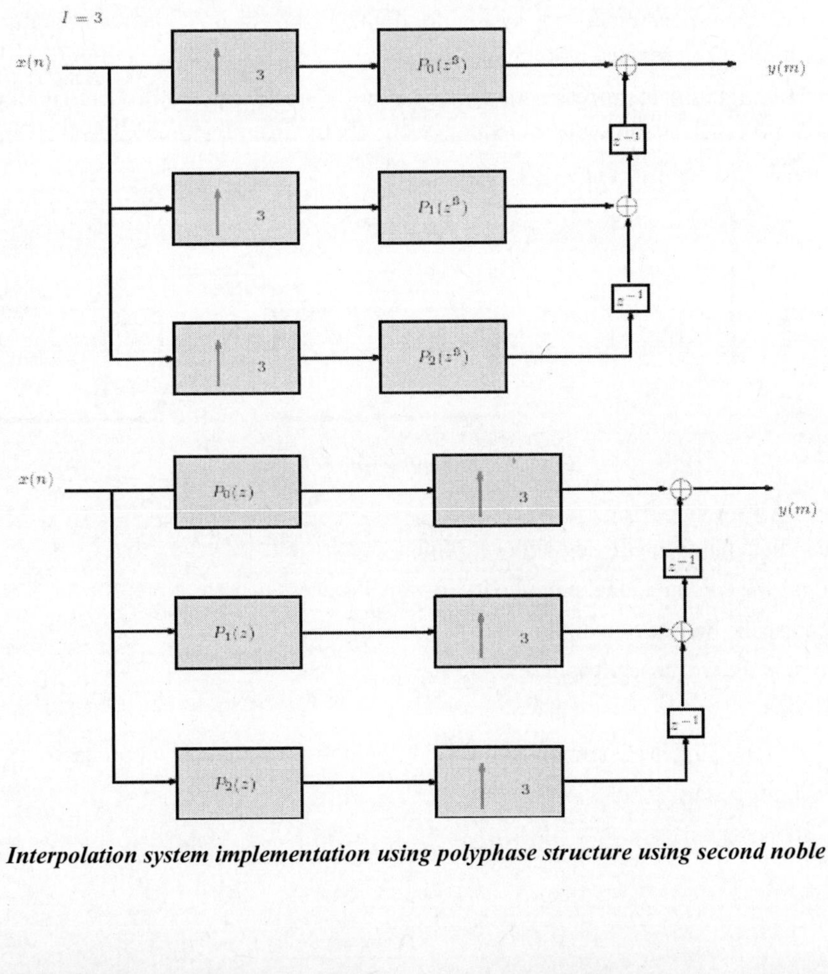

Fig.9.21: Interpolation system implementation using polyphase structure using second noble identity.

SUMMARY

The chapter on Multirate Digital Signal Processing explores techniques for processing signals at multiple sampling rates, which are crucial for efficient data handling in various applications. It begins by introducing the concept of multirate processing, emphasizing its importance in applications such as speech and audio coding, telecommunications, and video compression, where varying rates of data transmission and processing are required. The chapter covers fundamental operations such as decimation (downsampling) and interpolation (upsampling), detailing their mathematical formulations and practical implications. Key properties and challenges associated with these operations, such as aliasing and the need for anti-aliasing filters, are thoroughly discussed. Additionally, the chapter delves into the implementation of multirate systems using polyphase representation, which optimizes the computational efficiency of filtering operations. Overall, the chapter equips readers with essential knowledge and tools for applying multirate strategies in various signal processing applications.

EXERCISES

1. For signal $x(n)=\{-2,2,3,-3,4,-4,\mathbf{1},-1,2-,2,1,2,3\}$. Plot signals $y(m)=x(mD)$, $D=3$ and $y(m)=x(m/I)$, $I=2$.
2. Explain the process of converting a signal from a given rate to a different rate.
3. Design a multirate signal processing algorithm to scale a digital image, involving both upsampling and downsampling operations.
4. Analyze how multirate signal processing is used in wireless communication systems for tasks like channelization, signal filtering, and baseband processing.
5. Develop a multirate signal processing system for digital audio equalization, incorporating techniques like polyphase filtering and frequency-domain processing.
6. Study how multirate signal processing is utilized in orthogonal frequency division multiplexing (OFDM) systems for tasks such as subcarrier mapping, cyclic prefix insertion/removal, and channel equalization.
7. Plot the signal $v(m)$ and $y(k)$ in Fig.9.22 below.

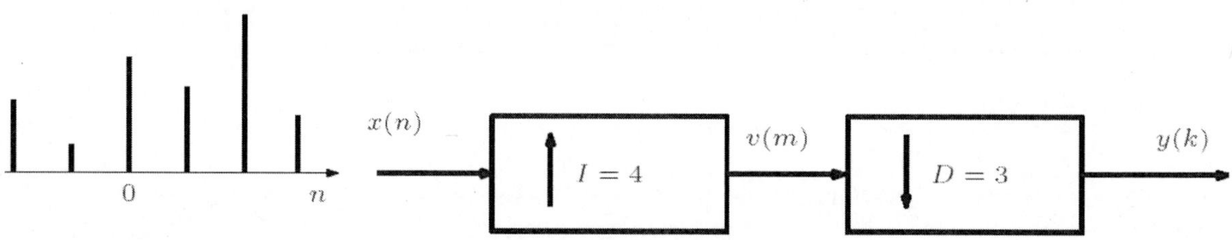

Fig.9.22: Sampling rate conversion.

Multiple Choice Questions

1. What is the main purpose of using multirate signal processing?

   A) To reduce the computational complexity of signal processing operations

   B) To increase the bit rate of a digital signal

   C) To improve the frequency response of a filter

   D) To eliminate noise from a signal

2. Which of the following is a common application of multirate digital signal processing?

   A) Audio compression

   B) Image enhancement

C) Radar signal detection

D) Video playback

3. In the context of multirate DSP, what does 'downsampling' refer to?

A) Increasing the sampling rate of a signal

B) Decreasing the sampling rate of a signal

C) Filtering a signal to reduce its bandwidth

D) Amplifying a signal

4. When downsampling a signal by a factor of M, what is the main problem that can occur if the signal is not properly filtered beforehand?

A) Aliasing

B) Quantization noise

C) Clipping

D) Phase distortion

5. What is 'upsampling' in multirate signal processing?

A) Increasing the amplitude of a signal

B) Increasing the sampling rate of a signal

C) Applying a low-pass filter to a signal

D) Reducing the bit depth of a signal

6. In upsampling by a factor of L, what type of filter is typically used after inserting zeros between samples?

A) High-pass filter

B) Low-pass filter

C) Band-pass filter

D) Notch filter

7. Which term describes a system that changes the sampling rate of a signal by a rational factor L/M?

A) Decimator

B) Interpolator

C) Resampler

D) Oversampler

8. What is the effect of decimating a signal by a factor of M?

A) It increases the bandwidth of the signal.

B) It decreases the signal's data rate.

C) It decreases the signal's frequency resolution.

D) It increases the power of the signal.

9. In a two-stage multirate system with downsampling by M_1 followed by M_2, what is the overall downsampling factor?

A) M_1

B) M_2

C) M_1+M_2

D) $M_1 \times M_2$

10. Which of the following is true for the spectrum of a signal after upsampling by a factor of L?

    A) The spectrum is expanded.

    B) The spectrum is compressed.

    C) The spectrum has periodic repetitions.

    D) The spectrum has more noise.

11. What is the primary function of a half-band filter in multirate DSP?

    A) To eliminate the need for downsampling

    B) To reduce computational complexity in decimation and interpolation

    C) To amplify high-frequency components

    D) To provide an all-pass filtering effect

12. Which of the following describes the polyphase representation in multirate DSP?

    A) A method for implementing filters in a more computationally efficient manner

    B) A technique for estimating the power spectral density

    C) A way of encoding signals for transmission over long distances

    D) A type of modulation used in digital communication

ANSWERS

1	2	3	4	5	6	7	8	9	10	11	12
A	A	B	A	B	B	C	B	D	C	B	A

KNOW MORE

For more information related to this topic scan the QR code.

OR

Type this link in your browser

https://archive.nptel.ac.in/courses/108/106/108106136/

REFERENCES AND SUGGESTED READING

1. John G. Proakis, and Dimitris G. Manolakis "*Digital signal processing: principles, algorithms, and applications, 4/E*," *Pearson Education India*, 2007.
2. Alan V. Oppenheim, Alan S. Willsky, and S. Hamid Nawab "*Signals & Systems*," *Pearson Education India*, 1997.
3. Steven W. Smith "*Digital Signal Processing: A Practical Guide for Engineers and Scientists*," *California Technical Publishing*, 1999.
4. Barrie W. Jervis, and Emmanuel C.I feachor "*Digital Signal Processing: A Practical Approach*," *Pearson Education India*,2002.
5. S. K. Mitra "*Digital Signal Processing: A Computer Based Approach*," *McGraw-Hill Higher Education New York*, 2006.

Chapeter-10: Application of Digital Signal Processing

UNIT SPECIFICS

In this chapter, we discuss digital signal processing (DSP) applications in various domains such as image processing, radar signal processing, and communication theory. We include various MATLAB-based signal processing examples for a better understanding for readers.

RATIONALE

After understanding the fundamentals of signal operations in DSP, it is essential to apply them to real-world applications across various areas.

PRE-REQUISITE

Fundamentals of LTI systems and signal processing aspects.

UNIT OUTCOMES

List of outcomes of this unit is as follows:

U10-O1: Applications of digital signal processing

U10-O2: MATLAB-based examples

U10-O3: Sampling rate conversion

Unit-10 Outcomes	EXPECTED MAPPING WITH COURSE OUTCOMES (1- Weak Correlation; 2- Medium correlation; 3- Strong Correlation)					
	CO-1	CO-2	CO-3	CO-4	CO-5	CO-6
U10-O1	1	2	1	2	2	3
U10-O2	1	2	1	2	2	3
U10-O3	1	2	1	2	2	3

Digital Signal Processing (DSP) finds extensive application in various fields, including speech and radar signal processing. Here's how DSP is applied in these domains:

10.1 SPEECH SIGNAL PROCESSING

Speech Compression: DSP techniques like discrete cosine transform (DCT) and linear predictive coding (LPC) are used for compressing speech signals to reduce bandwidth requirements in telecommunications and storage systems. Speech compression steps are shown in Fig. 10.1.

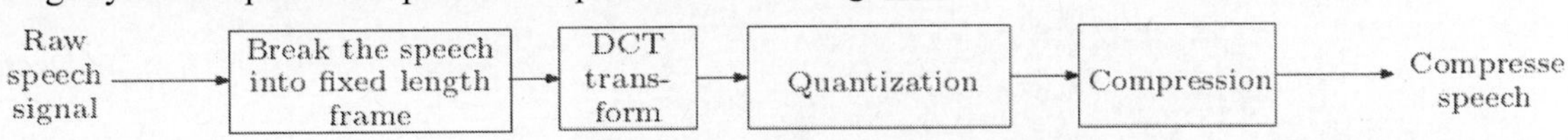

Fig. 10.1: Block diagram of speech compression.

Speech signals are inherently non-stationary, with properties that vary over time, capturing the dynamic nature of human speech. Key elements include the phonetic structure, pitch, and formants, where phonemes are the fundamental sound units, pitch corresponds to the fundamental frequency of vocal cord vibrations, and formants represent the resonant frequencies of the vocal tract. Spectral characteristics show a rich harmonic content in voiced sounds like vowels, while unvoiced sounds, such as certain consonants, are more noise-like.

Speech signals typically have energy concentrated in the lower frequencies, primarily below 4 kHz, though they can extend up to about 8 kHz. This frequency range is crucial for capturing intelligible speech. Prosody, which includes rhythm, stress, and intonation, adds depth to speech, conveying meaning and emotional context. Additionally, speech signals exhibit a wide dynamic range and significant variability due to differences in speaker characteristics like age, gender, and accent.

Speech Recognition: DSP algorithms, such as hidden Markov models (HMMs) and neural networks, are employed for automatic speech recognition (ASR) in applications like virtual assistants, dictation systems, and voice-controlled devices.

Speech Enhancement: DSP methods like spectral subtraction, Wiener filtering, and adaptive filtering are used to improve speech quality by reducing noise, echo, and reverberation in communication systems and audio recording devices.

Speaker Identification: DSP techniques are used to extract distinctive features from speech signals, enabling speaker identification and verification in security systems, forensic analysis, and biometric authentication.

10.2 RADAR SIGNAL PROCESSING

Pulse Compression: DSP algorithms such as matched filtering and fast Fourier transform (FFT) are used for pulse compression in radar systems to enhance range resolution and target detection capability.

Doppler Processing: DSP techniques are employed to analyze the Doppler shift in radar returns, enabling target velocity estimation, moving target indication (MTI), and ground clutter suppression, as shown in Fig. 10.2.

Target Tracking: DSP algorithms like Kalman filtering and particle filtering are used for target tracking and estimation in radar systems, providing accurate information about target position, velocity, and trajectory.

Synthetic Aperture Radar (SAR): DSP methods are used for SAR image formation, fo- cusing, and reconstruction, allowing high-resolution imaging of ground terrain and target detection in remote sensing applications.

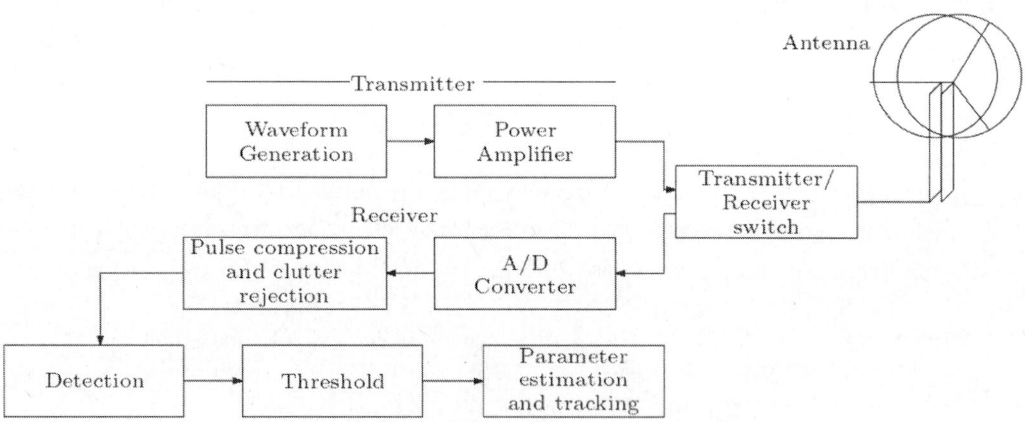

Fig. 10.2: Block diagram of Radar processing.

10.3 MATLAB based examples

Example 10.3.1 Change the signal sampling rate by a factor 4/8, where signal is

$x(t) = \cos(400\pi t) + 1/2 \sin(800\pi(t - pi/4)) + 1/4 \cos(1600\pi t)$ Sampling rate $F_x = 500$ Hz

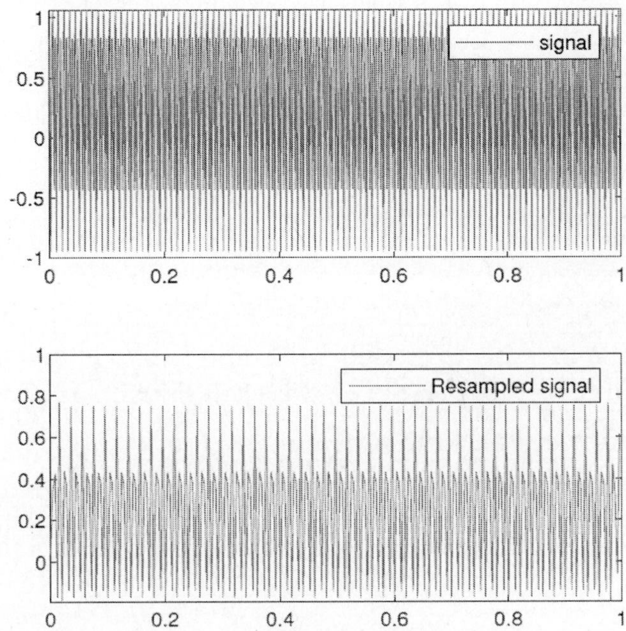

Fig. 10.3: Original signal and resampled signal at the rate F_y =4/8 F_x.

Example 10.3.2 Create a sinusoidal signal sampled at 2 kHz. Decimate it by a factor of 5.

t = 0:1/4 e3 : 1 ;

x = s i n (2∗ p i ∗30∗ t) + s i n (2∗ p i ∗60∗ t) ;

y = decimate (x , 5) ;

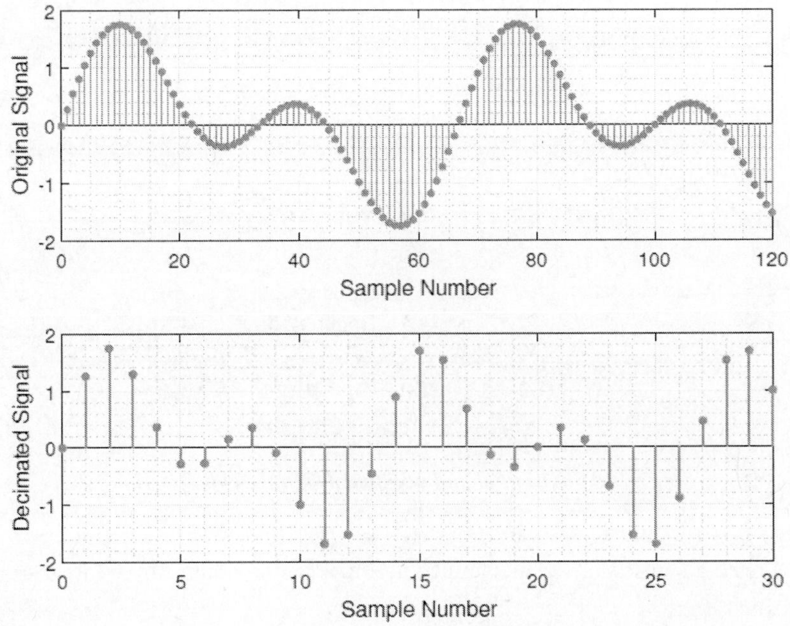

Fig. 10.4: Decimation by 5

Example 10.3.3 Create a signal with two sinusoids. Decimate it by a factor of 15 using a Cheby- shev IIR filter of order 7. Plot the original and decimated signals.

```
r = 1 5;
n = 1 6 : 3 6 5 ;
l x = l e n g t h (n) ;
x = s i n (2* p i *n/253) + cos (2* p i *n / 2 2 7 ) ;
p l o t ( 0 : l x −1,x , ' o ' )
h o l d on
y = decimate ( x , r , 7 ) ;
stem( l x −1:−r : 0 , f l i p l r ( y ) , ' ro ' , ' f i l l e d ' , ' mar k e r s i z e ' , 4 )
l e g end ( ' Or i g ina l ' , ' Decimated ' , ' Location ' , ' south ' )
x l a b e l ( ' Sample number ' )
y l a b e l ( ' Signa l ' )
```

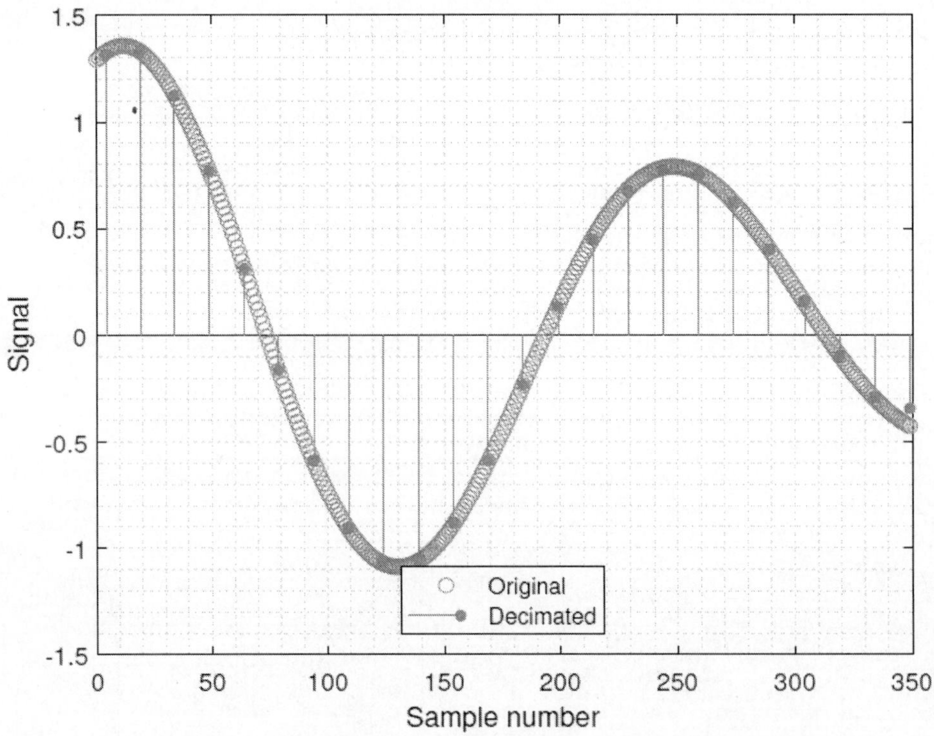

Fig. 10.5: Original and decimated signals with D = 15.

Example 10.3.4 Create a sinusoidal signal sampled at 2 kHz. Interpolate it by a factor of six. The signal is $x(t) = \sin(60\pi t) + \sin(120\pi t)$.

```
t = 0:1/2 e3 : 1 ;
```

```
x=sin(2*pi*30*t)+sin(2*pi*60*t);
y=interp(x,6);
subplot(2,1,1)
stem(0:30,x(1:31),'filled','MarkerSize',3)
grid on
xlabel('Sample Number')
ylabel('Original')
subplot(2,1,2)
stem(0:420,y(1:421),'filled','MarkerSize',3)
grid on
xlabel('Sample Number')
ylabel('Interpolated')
```

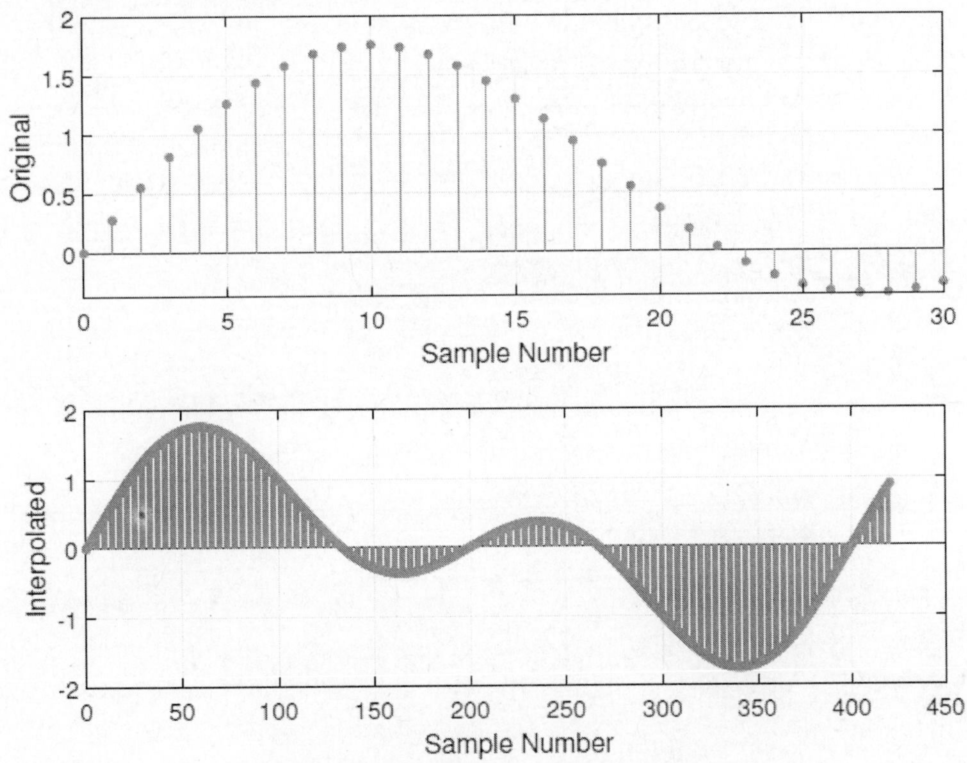

Fig. 10.6: Original and interpolated signals with I = 6.

Example 10.3.5 Plot the Fourier series (FS) of the signal $x(t) = |\sin(120\pi t)|$, as shown in Fig. 10.7.

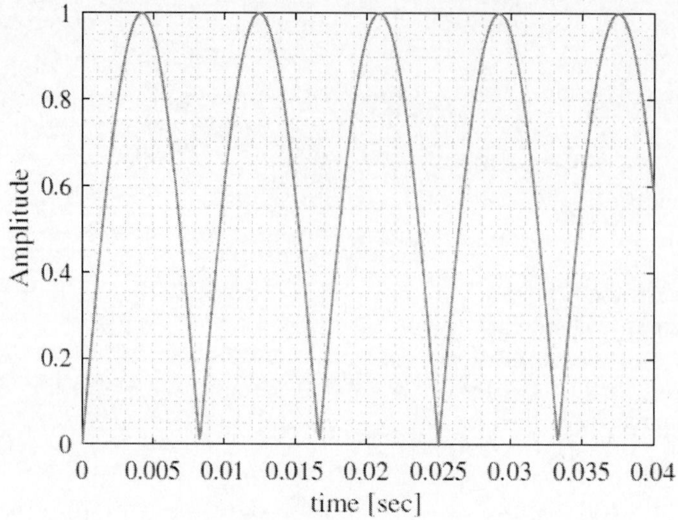

Fig. 10.7: Periodic signal x(t).

FS coefficients c_k are shown in Fig. 10.8 of the signal x(t).

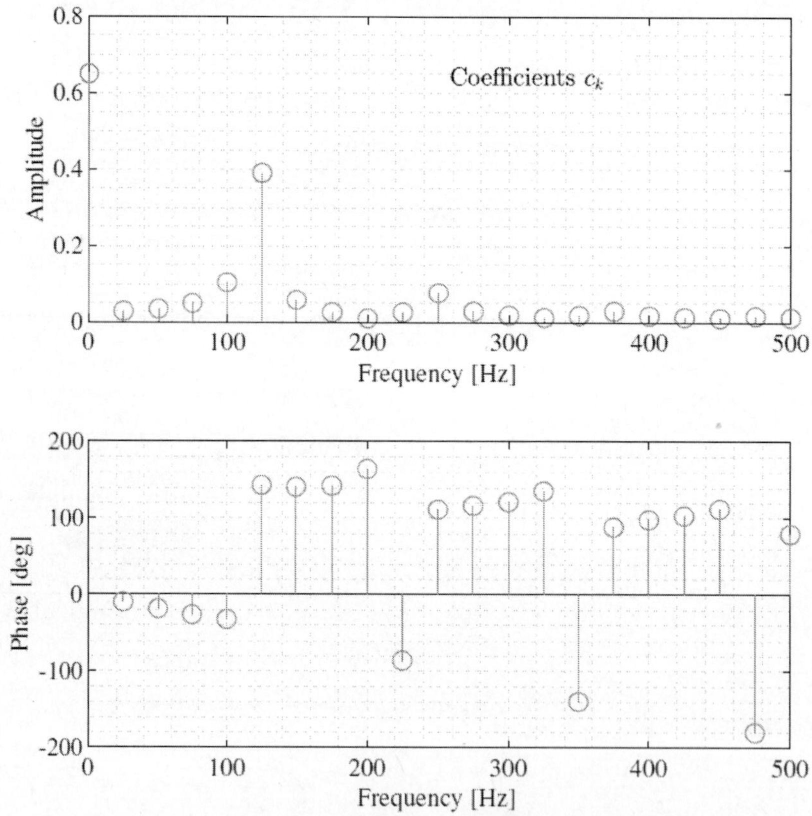

Fig. 10.8: Periodic signal x(t).

Example 10.3.6 Plot the Fourier series (FS) of the signal x(t) = 1.2| sin(120πt)|+0.6| sin(240πt)|+ 0.1| sin(360πt)|, as shown in Fig. 10.9.

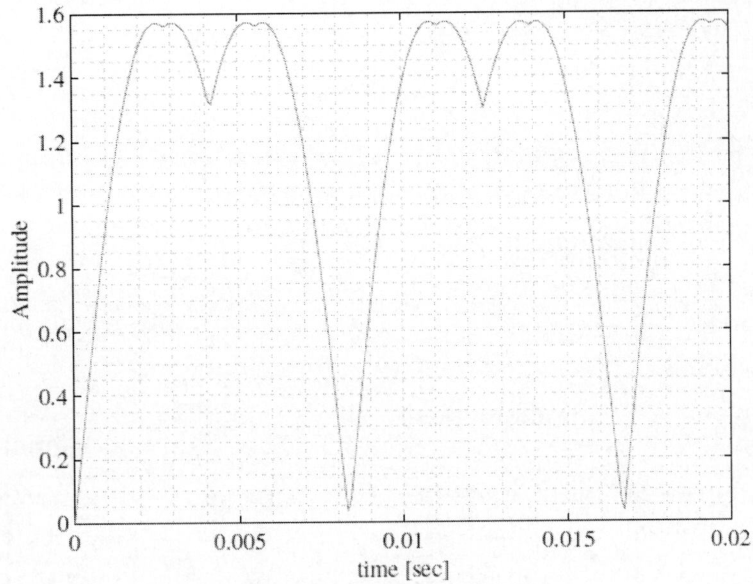

Fig. 10.9: FS coefficients of signal x(t).

FS coefficients c_k are shown in Fig. 10.10 of the signal x(t).

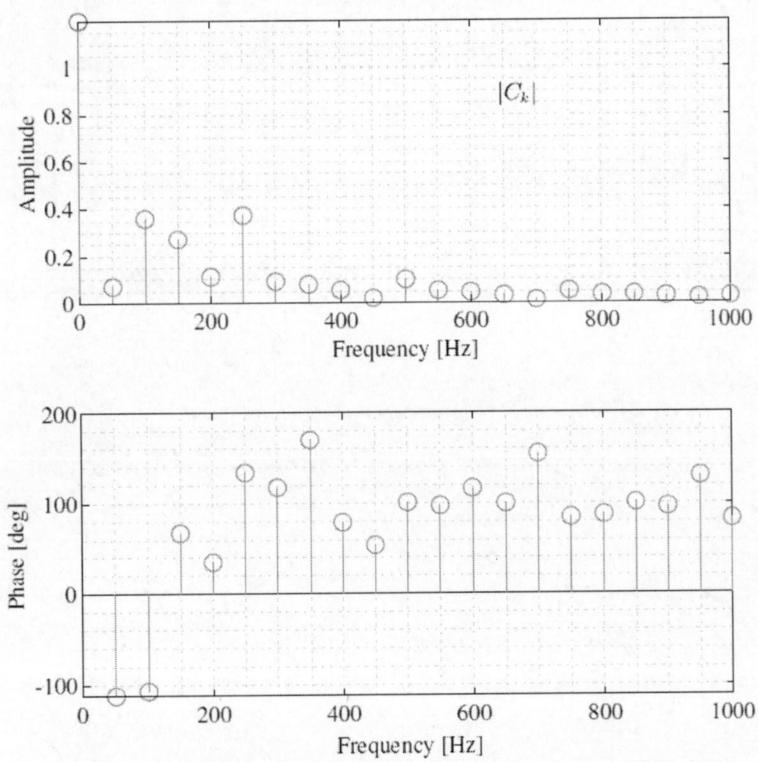

Fig. 10.10: FS coefficients of signal x(t).

Example 10.3.7 Quantization of a signal $x(t) = |4 * \sin(2\pi t)|$ is shown in Fig. 10.11. Three quantization levels B = 3 are used. Further, ten samples are considered in one complete sine cycles.

```
R = 1 0 ;
B = 3 ;
x = −5 : . 1 : 1 5 ;
x1=abs (4∗ s in (2∗ p i ∗x ) ) ;
y = adc_NU( x1 ,R,B) ;
t = 0 : l e n g t h ( x1 )−1;
```

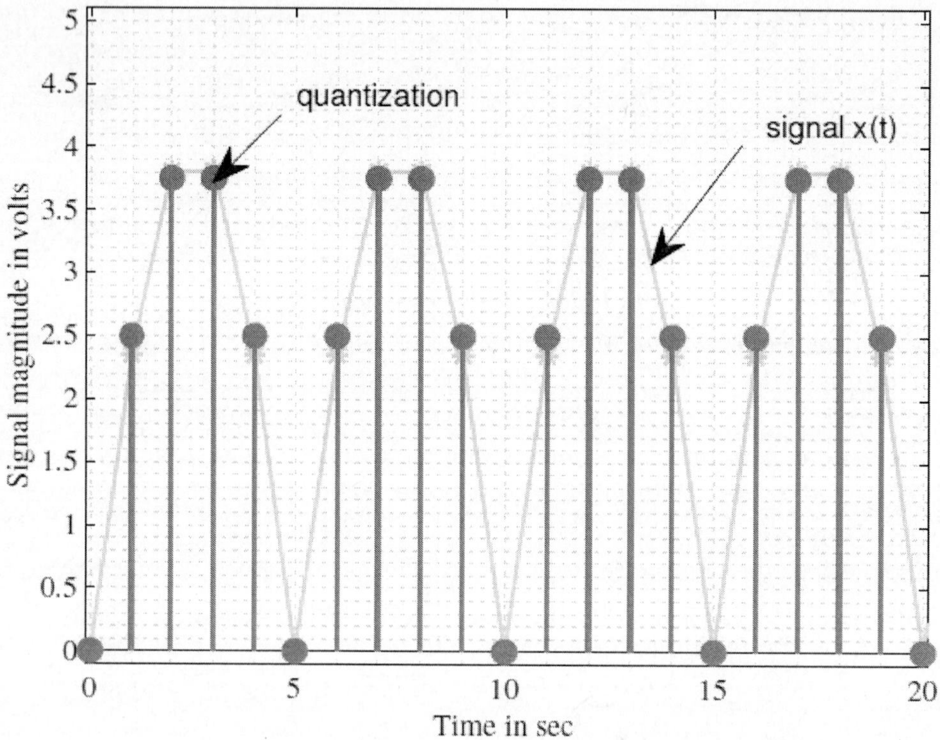

Fig. 10.11: Signal x(t) and its quantitation.

Example 10.3.8 Three signals $s_1(t)$, $s_2(t)$, $s_3(t)$ are shown in Fig. 10.12.

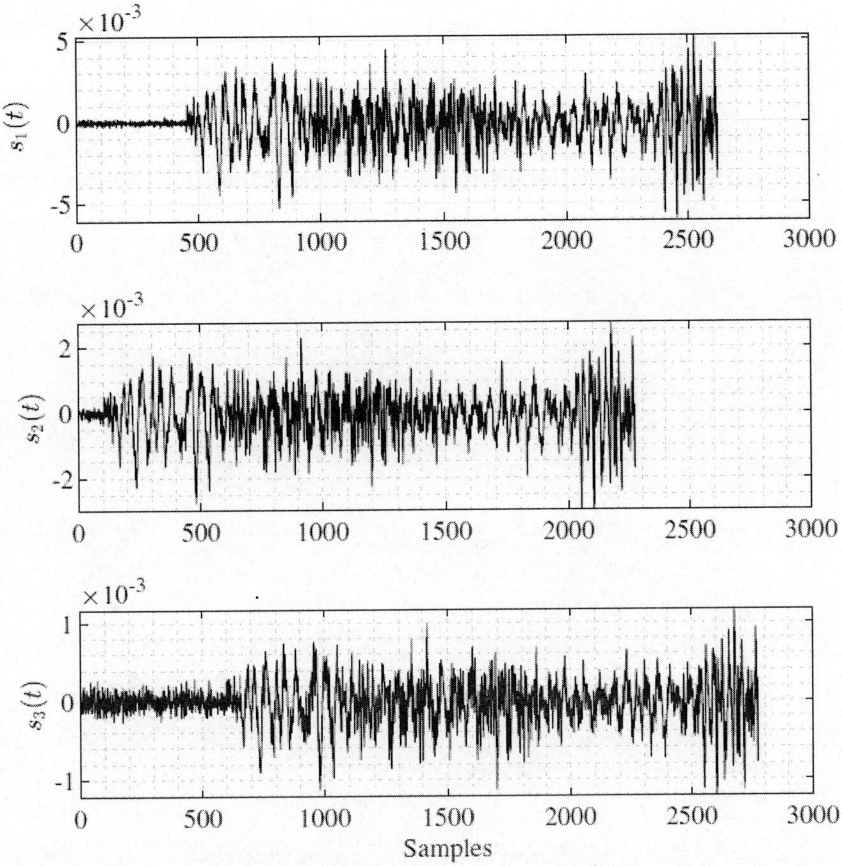

Fig. 10.12: Three different signals in the time domain.

Cross-correlations are shown in Fig. 10.13. The cross-correlations between the three pairs of signals are normalize so their maximum value is one.

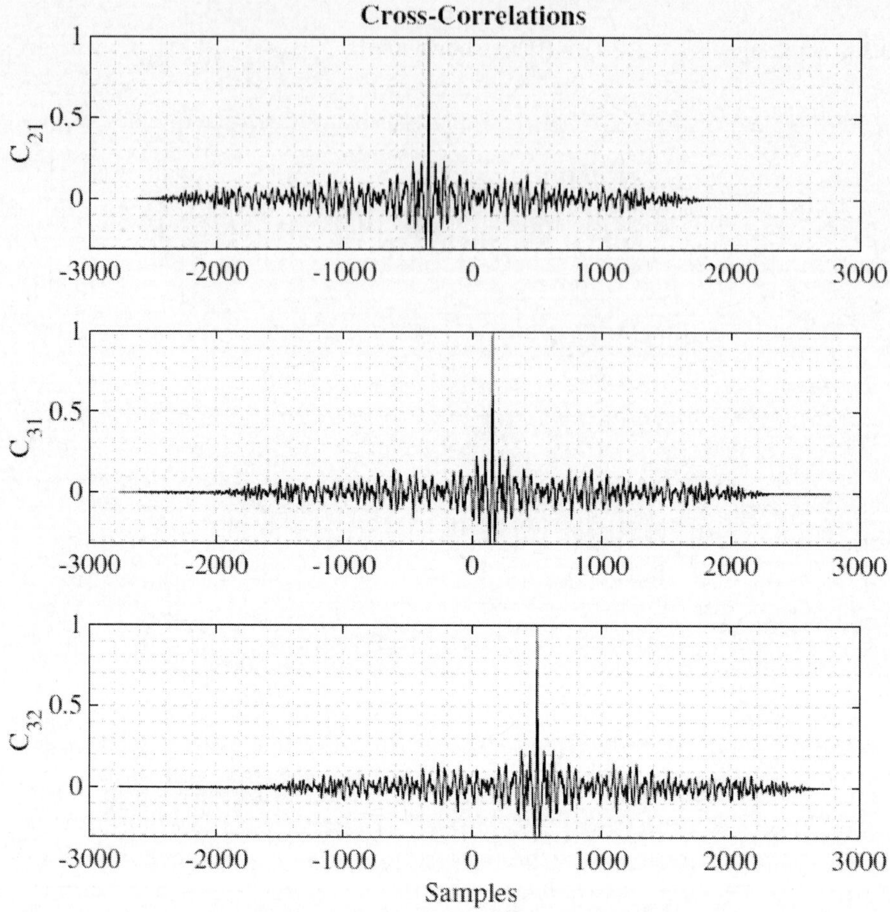

Fig. 10.13: Cross-correlation among the signals.

Example 10.3.9 A signal x(t) = 2 sin(400πt) is corrupted by a noise. Estimate the signal frequency using the DSP techniques. We have used DSP techniques and the power spectral density (PSD) of the signal is shown in Fig. 10.14.

```
c l o s e a l l ; c l e a r a l l ; c l c ;
% Assume we c a p tur e 8192 samples a t 1kHz sample r a t e
Nsamps = 8192;
fsamp = 1000;
Tsamp = 1/ fsamp ;
t = ( 0 : Nsamps−1)∗Tsamp ;
% Assume t h e no i s y s i g n a l i s e x a c t l y 123Hz
f s i g = 200;
s i g n a l = 2∗ s in (2∗ p i ∗ f s i g ∗ t ) ;
no i s e = 1∗ randn (1 ,Nsamps ) ;
x = s i g n a l + no i s e ;
```

```
% Pl o t time−domain s i g n a l
s u b p l o t ( 2 , 1 , 1 ) ;
p l o t ( t , x ) ;
y l a b e l ( ' Amplitude ' ) ; x l a b e l ( 'Time ( s e c s ) ' ) ;
a x i s t i g h t ;
t i t l e ( ' Noisy Input Si gnal ' ) ;
% Choose FFT s i z e and c a l c u l a t e spectrum
Nf f t = 1024;
[ Pxx , f ] = pwelch ( x , gausswin ( Nf f t ) , Nf f t /2 , Nf f t , fsamp ) ;
% Pl o t f r e q u enc y spectrum
s u b p l o t ( 2 , 1 , 2 ) ;
p l o t ( f , Pxx ) ;
y l a b e l ( 'PSD' ) ; x l a b e l ( ' Frequency (Hz ) ' ) ;
g r i d on ;
% Get f r e q u enc y e s t ima t e ( s p e c t r a l peak )
[~ , l o c ] = max(Pxx ) ;
FREQ_ESTIMATE = f ( l o c )
t i t l e ( [ ' Frequency e s t ima t e = ' , num2str (FREQ_ESTIMATE) , ' Hz ' ] ) ;
```

Estimated frequency 200 Hz is shown in Fig. 10.14.

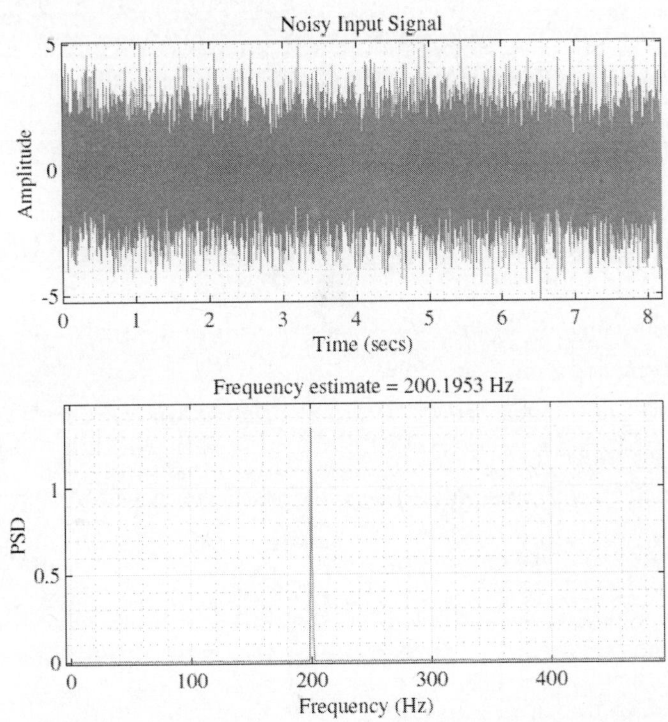

Fig. 10.14: Three different signals in the time domain.

SUMMARY

The chapter on Application of Digital Signal Processing (DSP) provides a comprehensive overview of the diverse fields and scenarios where DSP techniques are applied to enhance signal analysis and processing. It begins by exploring fundamental applications in audio and speech processing, including noise reduction, and echo cancellation, highlighting how DSP algorithms improve sound quality and intelligibility. The chapter also addresses applications in telecommunications, such as channel equalization, modulation, and demodulation, which are critical for efficient data transmission and reception. Additionally, it delves into image and video processing, discussing techniques like image enhancement, compression, and object recognition, which are essential for modern multimedia applications. Practical examples and case studies illustrate the impact of DSP in real-world scenarios, equipping readers with insights into how digital signal processing transforms and optimizes numerous applications in everyday life and advanced technology. Overall, this chapter underscores the critical role of DSP in solving complex problems and enhancing system performance across a wide array of domains.

KNOW MORE

For more information related to this topic scan the QR code.

OR

Type this link in your browser

https://www.analog.com/en/lp/001/beginners-guide-to-dsp.html

REFERENCES AND SUGGESTED READING

1. B. P. Lathi, "*Principles of Linear Systems and Signals*," *Oxford Second edition*, 2009.
2. John G. Proakis, and Dimitris G. Manolakis "*Digital signal processing: principles, algo- rithms, and applications, 4/E*,"*Pearson Education India*, 2007.
3. Alan V. Oppenheim, Alan S. Willsky, and S. Hamid Nawab "*Signals & Systems*,"*Pearson Education India*, 1997.
4. Steven W. Smith "*Digital Signal Processing: A Practical Guide for Engineers and Scien- tists*,"*California Technical Publishing*, 1999.
5. Barrie W. Jervis, and Emmanuel C. Ifeachor "*Digital Signal Processing: A Practical Ap- proach*,"*Pearson Education India*, 2002.
6. S.K. Mitra "*Digital Signal Processing: A Computer Based Approach*,"*McGraw-Hill Higher Education New York*, 2006.

Bibliography and Suggested Reading

1. John G. Proakis, and Dimitris G. Manolakis "*Digital signal processing: principles, algo- rithms, and applications, 4/E*,"*Pearson Education India*, 2007.
2. R.E. Crochiere, L.R. Rabiner "*Interpolation and decimation of digital signals— A tutorial review*,"*Proceedings of the IEEE*, vol. 69, no. 3, pp. 300-331, 1981.
3. Alan V. Oppenheim, Alan S. Willsky, and S. Hamid Nawab "*Signals & Systems*,"*Pearson Education India*, 1997.
4. S.K. Mitra "*Digital Signal Processing: A Computer Based Approach*,"*McGraw-Hill Higher Education New York*, 2006.
5. L.R. Rabiner, and B. Gold"*Theory and Application of Digital Signal Processing*,"*Englewood Cliffs: Prentice-Hall*, 1997.
6. A. V. Oppenheim, and R. W. Schafer"*Discrete-Time Signal Processing*,"*Pearson Education India*, 2014.
7. Barrie W. Jervis, and Emmanuel C. Ifeachor "*Digital Signal Processing: A Practical Ap- proach*,"*Pearson Education India*, 2002.
8. Steven W. Smith "*Digital Signal Processing: A Practical Guide for Engineers and Scien- tists*,"*California Technical Publishing*, 1999.
9. P. Singh, A. Singhal, B. Fatimah, A. Gupta; S. Dutt Joshi "*Proper Definitions of Dirich- let Conditions and Convergence of Fourier Representations [Lecture Notes]*,"*IEEE Signal Processing Magazine*, vol. 39, no. 5, pp. 77-84, 2022.
10. P. Singh, A. Gupta, and S. Dutt Joshi "*General Parameterized Fourier Transform: A Unified Framework for the Fourier, Laplace, Mellin and Z Transforms*,"*IEEE Transactions on Signal Processing*, vol. 70, pp. 1295-1309, 2022.
11. Guoan Bi and Sanjit K. Mitra "*Sampling Rate Conversion in the Frequency Domain [DSP Tips and Tricks]*,"*IEEE Signal Processing Magazine*, vol. 28, no. 3, pp. 140-144, 2011.
12. Behnam Shahrrava "*Closed-Form Impulse Responses of Linear Time-Invariant Systems: A Unifying Approach [Lecture Notes]*,"*IEEE Signal Processing Magazine*, vol. 35, no. 4, pp. 126-132, 2018.
13. Gerald Matz, Helmut Bölcskei, and Franz Hlawatsch "*Time-Frequency Foundations of Com- munications: Concepts and Tools*,"*IEEE Signal Processing Magazine*, vol. 30, no. 6, pp. 87-96, 2013.
14. A. Enis Getin, Omer N. Gerek, and Yasemin Yardimci "*Equiripple FIR filter design by the FFT algorithm*,"*IEEE Signal Processing Magazine*, vol. 14, no. 2, pp. 60-64, 1997.
15. Stephen So, and Kuldip K. Paliwal "*Reconstruction of a Signal from the Real Part of Its Discrete Fourier Transform*,"*IEEE Signal Processing Magazine*, vol. 35, no. 2, pp. 165-172, 2018.

Digital Signal Processing Laboratory

Aim: **To compute the Discrete Fourier Transform (DFT) and its inverse for a given digital signal.**

Software: MATLAB, Python

Theory:

DFT:

$$X(k) = \sum_{n=0}^{N-1} x(n) e^{-\frac{j2\pi kn}{N}}, \quad k = 0, 1, ..., N-1$$

IDFT:

$$x(n) = \frac{1}{N} \sum_{k=0}^{N-1} X(k) e^{\frac{j2\pi kn}{N}}, \quad n = 0, 1, ..., N-1$$

Algorithm:

Step-I: Get the input sequence.

Step-II: Find the DFT of the input sequence using direct equation of DFT. Step-III: Find the IDFT using the direct equation.

Step-IV: Plot DFT and IDFT of the given sequence using MATLAB command stem. Step-V: Display the above outputs.

Example: Find 8-point DFT of the sequence $x(n)$ = [1, 2, 3, 4, 3, 2, 1, 2].

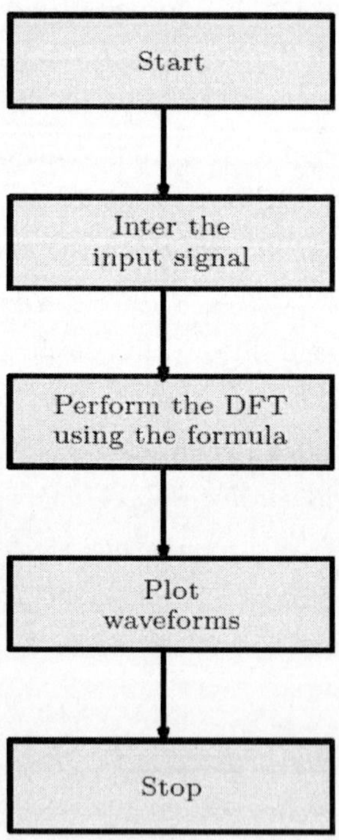

Fig. 1: Flow chart

Aim: To compute the linear convolution of two finite-length sequences. Software: MATLAB, Python

Theory:

Linear convolution is a fundamental operation in signal processing that involves combining two finite-length sequences to produce a third sequence representing their convolution. This process is essential for analyzing and processing signals in various applications, including audio and image processing, communication systems, and more. In linear convolution, each sample of the output sequence is computed by summing the products of corresponding samples from the input sequences, with appropriate shifting and scaling. The resulting sequence provides valuable insights into the relationship between the original sequences, helping to extract useful information and features for further analysis and processing.

Linear Convolution:

$$y(n) = \sum_{n=-\infty}^{\infty} h(k)x(n-k) = \sum_{n=-\infty}^{\infty} x(k)h(n-k)$$

Algorithm:

Step-I: Give input sequence $x(n)$

Step-II: Give impulse response sequence $h(n)$

Step-III: Find the convolution $y(n)$ using the MATLAB command *conv* or manual code. Step-IV: Plot all signal $x(n)$, $h(n)$ and $y(n)$

Example: Inter the signals as $x(n) = [1, 2, 3, 4, 3, 2, 1, 2]$ and $h(n) = [0.1, 1, .0.5, -2]$.

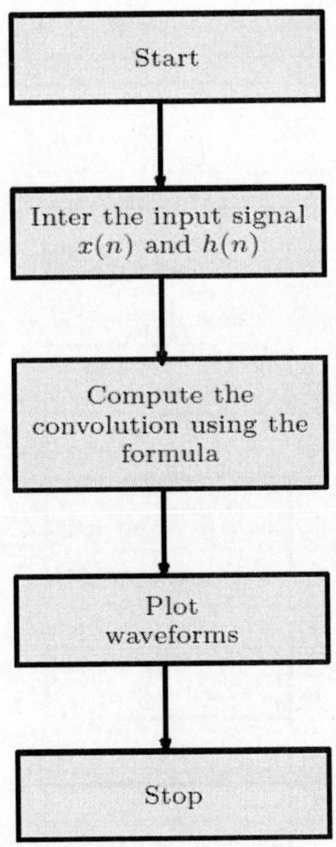

Fig. 2: Flow chart

Aim: To calculate the autocorrelation between two sequences.

Software: MATLAB, Python

Theory:

Autocorrelation, a fundamental concept in statistics and time series analysis, refers to the correlation of a signal with a delayed version of itself over successive time intervals. It measures the degree of similarity between observations in a time series at different lags. In simpler terms, autocorrelation quantifies the extent to which a series is predictable based on its own past values. Positive autocorrelation implies that values tend to follow a consistent pattern over time, while negative autocorrelation suggests an alternating pattern. Analyzing autocorrelation helps in detecting seasonality, trend behavior, and potential dependencies within time series data, providing valuable insights for decision-making in fields such as finance, economics, meteorology, and engineering.

Cross-correlation $r_{xx}(l)$:

$$r_{xy}(l) = \sum_{n=-\infty}^{\infty} x(n)y(n-l), \quad l = 0, \pm1, \pm2, ...$$

$$r_{xx}(l) = \sum_{n=-\infty}^{\infty} x(n)x(n-l), \quad l = 0, \pm1, \pm2, ... \tag{1}$$

Algorithm:

Step-I: Give input sequence $x(n)$

Step-II: Give impulse response sequence $y(n)$

Step-III: Find auto correlation $r_{xx}(l)$ (cross correlation $r_{xy}(l)$) using the MATLAB command *xcorr* or manual code.

Step-IV: Plot all signal $x(n)$, $h(n)$ and $r_{xx}(l)$

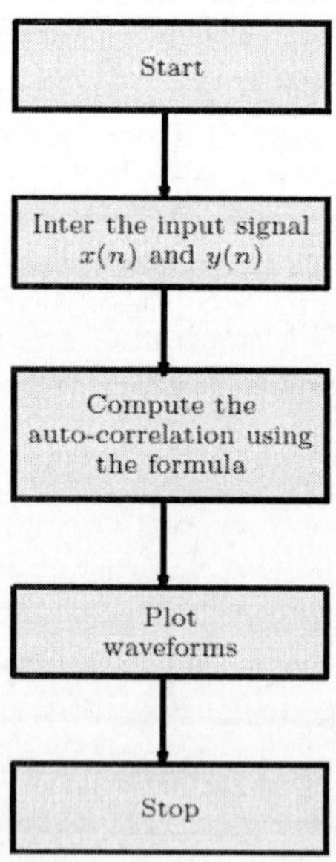

Fig. 3: Flow chart

Example: Inter the signals as $x(n) = [1, 2, 3, 4, 3, 2, 1, 2]$ and $y(n) = [0.1, 1, .0.5, -2]$.

Aim: To compute the Fast Fourier Transform (FFT) of a given sequence Software: MATLAB, Python

Theory:

The Fast Fourier Transform (FFT) is a computational algorithm that efficiently computes the Discrete Fourier Transform (DFT) of a sequence, typically a time-domain signal or data set. Developed by Cooley and Tukey in the 1960s, the FFT revolutionized signal processing by dramatically reducing the computational complexity of Fourier analysis.

FFT

$$X(k) = \sum_{n=0}^{N-1} x(n)e^{-j2\pi kn/N}, \quad k = 0, 1, ..., N-1$$

Algorithm:

Step-I: Give input sequence $x(n)$

Step-II: Find the length of the input sequence using length command or manual code. Step-III: Find FFT and IFFT using using the MATLAB command *FFT* and IFFT *or* manual code.

Step-IV: Plot all signal $x(n)$, $X(k)$

Step-V: Plot magnitude and phase response of X(k)

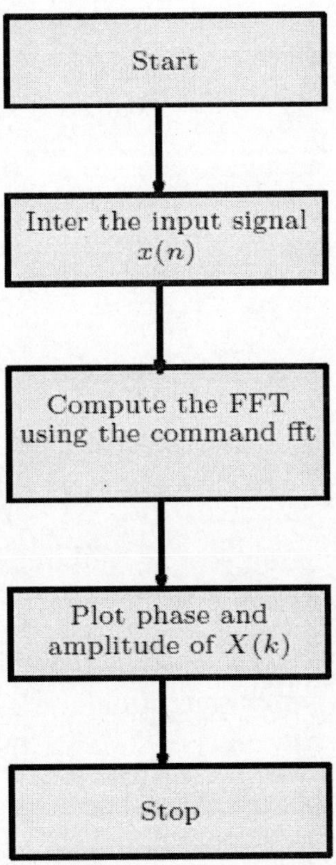

Fig. 4: Flow chart

Example: Inter the signal as $x(n) = [1, 2, 3, 4, 3, 2, 1, 2]$.

Aim: To compute Power Spectrum of a Given Signal Software: MATLAB, Python

Theory:

The power spectrum is a fundamental concept in signal processing and spectral analysis, representing the distribution of power or energy across different frequencies within a sig- nal. It provides crucial insights into the frequency components present in a signal and their respective strengths. The power spectrum is often obtained by calculating the squared mag- nitude of the Fourier transform of a signal, commonly using techniques like the Fast Fourier Transform (FFT). By decomposing a signal into its constituent frequencies and quantifying their power levels, the power spectrum enables the identification of dominant frequency components, analysis of periodic phenomena, detection of noise, and characterization of signal properties.

FFT: $|X(\omega)|^2 = X(\omega)X^*(\omega)$

Algorithm:

Step-I: Give input sequence

Step-II: Give sampling frequency, input frequency and length of the spectrum. Step-III: Find power spectrum $P(\omega)$ of input sequence using MATLAB command *spectrum*

Step-IV: Plot all signal $x(n)$, $P(\omega)$

Step-V: Plot power spectrum using *specplot*.

Example:

```
N = 12 8;
x = [ s q r t ( 2 ) 1/ s q r t ( 2 ) ] . ∗ exp (1 j ∗ pi . / [ 4 ; 3 ] ∗ ( 0 :N−1 ) ) . ' ;
[ p , f ] = pspectrum( x ) ;
pl o t ( f / pi , p)
hold on
stem( 0 : 2 /N:2−1/N, abs ( f f t ( x )/N) . ^ 2 )
hold o f f
a x i s ( [ 0 . 1 . 5 0 2 ] )
legend ( ' Spectrum ' , ' Using FFT' )
g r id minor
```

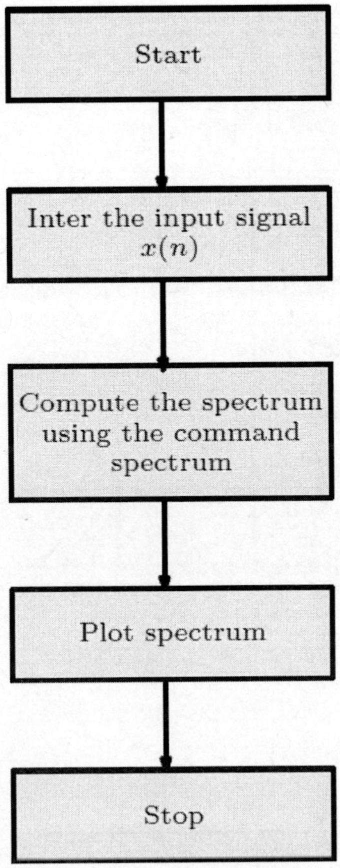

Fig. 5: Flow Chart

Aim: To deploy a Low Pass Finite Impulse Response (FIR) filter for a provided sequence

Software: MATLAB, Python

Theory:

Kindly refer the FIR filter design methods in the book.

FIR filters are digital filters characterized by a finite duration of their impulse response. They are often referred to as non-recursive digital filters since they lack feedback within their structure. FIR filters offer two significant advantages over IIR designs:

Firstly, due to the absence of a feedback loop, FIR filters inherently exhibit stability. In contrast, the stability of an IIR filter requires careful assessment due to the presence of feedback.

Secondly, FIR filters can achieve a linear-phase response, which is a notable advantage. Linear-phase response ensures that all frequencies within the signal are delayed by the same amount, preserving the signal's timing characteristics. This advantage distinguishes FIR filters from IIR designs. Additionally, despite offering similar filtering specifications, an IIR filter typically necessitates a lower order than an FIR filter.

Some common FIR filters designs are

– Window design method

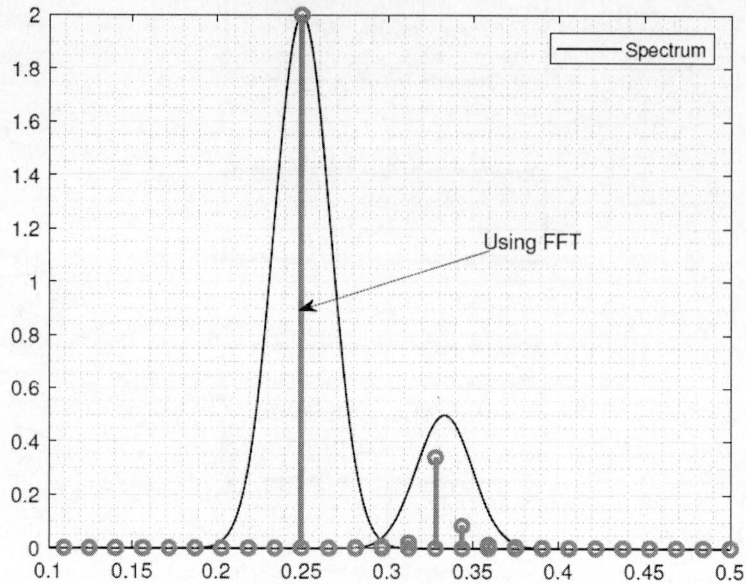

Fig. 6: Spectrum plot

- Frequency Sampling method
- Weighted least squares design

Algorithm:

Step-I : Enter the pass band frequency (f_p) and stop band frequency (f_s). Step-II : Get the sampling frequency (F_s), length of window M.

Step-III : Calculate the cut off frequency f_c

Step-IV : Use *boxcar*, *hamming*, *blackman* commands in MATLAB to design windows. Step-V : Design filter by using above parameters.

Step-VI : Find frequency response of the filter using MATLAB command *freqz*. Step-VII : Plot the magnitude response and phase response of the filter.

Example:

```
M=30;
fp=100;
f s =200;
Fs=1000;
fn=2*fp /Fs ;
window=blackman (M+1);
b=f i r 1 (M, fn , window ) ;
[H W]= f r e q z (b , 1 , 1 2 8 ) ;
subplot ( 2 , 1 , 1 ) ;
pl o t (W/ pi , abs (H) ) ;
```

```
t i t l e ( 'Magnitude r e spons e o f LPF' ) ;
y l a b e l ( 'Gain in dB---------->');
x l a b e l ( ' Normalized frequency ------->');
subplot ( 2 , 1 , 2 ) ;
pl o t (W/ pi , angl e (H) ) ;
t i t l e ( ' Phase r e spons e o f LPF' ) ;
y l a b e l ( ' Angle--------->');
x l a b e l ( ' Normalized frequency ------->');
```

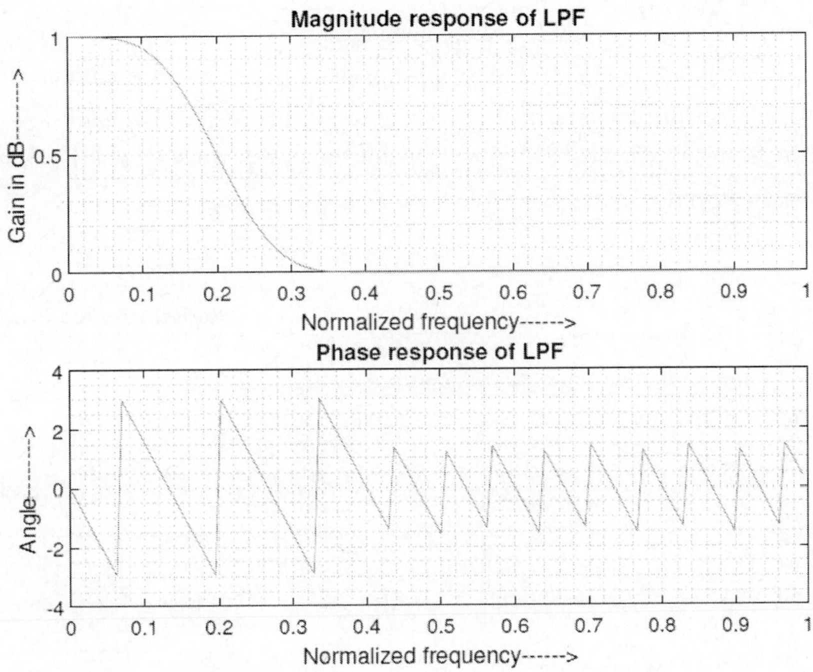

Fig. 7: Filter response

Aim: Design of FIR Filter

Generate different windows and plot their spectrum

Software: MATLAB, Python

Theory:

The design of FIR filters involves crafting a set of coefficients that manipulate the input signal to achieve desired frequency response characteristics, such as low-pass, high-pass, band-pass, or band-stop filtering. One common method for designing FIR filters is the win- dowing technique, where a desired frequency response is shaped by multiplying the desired response with a window function. Another approach is the frequency-sampling method, which directly specifies the filter's frequency response at specific frequencies. Additionally, optimization algorithms like the Parks-McClellan algorithm can be utilized to design FIR filters with optimal properties, such as minimizing the ripple in the passband or stopband. Overall, the design of digital FIR filters requires a balance between achieving the desired frequency response and minimizing implementation complexity, making them versatile tools in digital signal processing systems.

Generate and plot the following windows for different values of M. Also compare their spectrums.

- Rectangular
- Barlett
- Hanning
- Hamming
- Blackman
- Kaiser

Kindly refer the filter design chapter in the book for more details.

For example use the digital FIR low pass filter with the following specifications: passband edge frequency $\omega_p = 0.5\pi$, pass-ripple $\delta_1 = 0.25$ dB, stopband edge frequency $\omega_s = 0.65\pi$, stop-band ripple $\delta_2 = 23$ dB. Choose an appropriate window function from table. Determine the impulse response and provide a plot of the frequency response of the designed filter.

Here we use Kaiser window function.

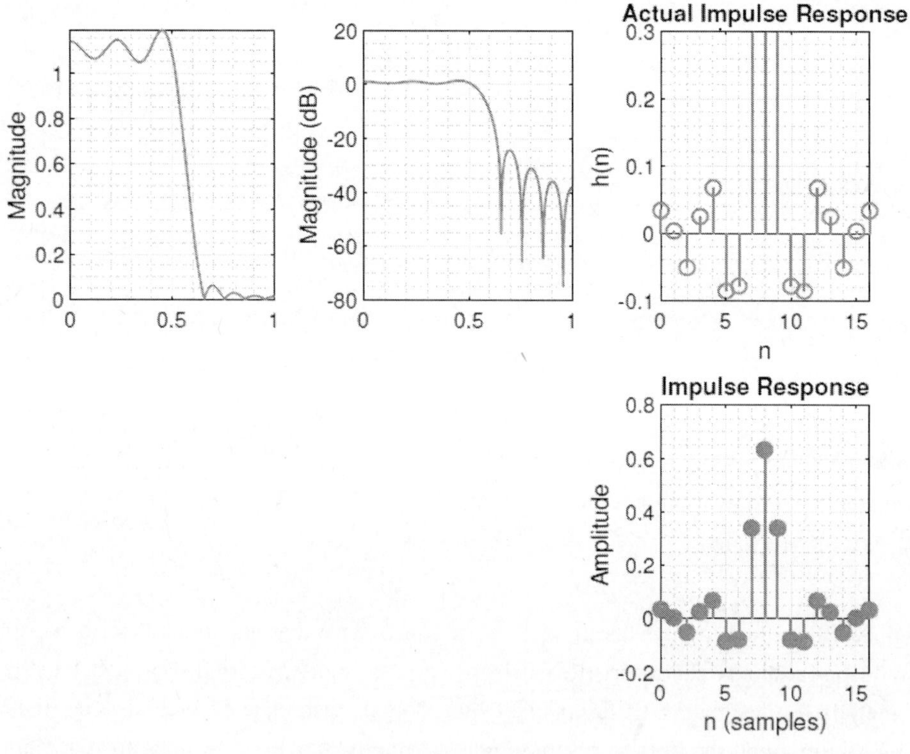

Fig. 8: Filter response

Aim: To design a Digital IIR filter, using bilinear transformation method. The two filters that are to be used are Butterworth and Chebyshev filter. The specified requirements for the filters are as follows:

1. Sampling frequency: 2KHz

2. Low pass band edge frequency = 200Hz
3. Stop edge frequency = 600Hz
4. Maximum attenuation in pass band=1.938dB
5. Maximum attenuation in stop band=13.98dB

Software: MATLAB, Python

Theory:

Kindly follow the digital filter design theory.

Bilinear:

$$\Omega = \frac{2}{T}\tan(\omega/2)$$

Invariance:

$$z = e^{sT}$$

Steps for designing any IIR filter :

- Acquiring the digital filter specifications, which define the desired characteristics of the filter.
- Deriving specifications for the prototype continuous filter, such as a Butterworth or Chebyshev filter, based on the given digital specifications.
- Once the specifications for the continuous-time filter are determined, obtaining its transfer function, denoted as *H*(*s*).
- Utilizing an appropriate transformation method, such as bilinear or impulse invari- ance, to convert the continuous-time transfer function *H*(*s*) into the desired digital filter transfer function, denoted as *H*(*z*).

Algorithm:

Step-I: Give input specification

Step-II: Compute filter order Step-III: Compute *H*(*s*) Step-IV: Convert *H*(*s*) to *H*(*z*) Step- V: Plot filter response

[NUMd,DENd] = b i l i n e a r (z , p , k , f s)

Example:

```
c l e a r a l l
c l c
c l o s e a l l
%% Di g i t a l F i l t e r S p e c i f i c a t i o n s
% wp = 0.5∗ pi ; % d i g i t a l Passband f r e q in Hz
% ws = 0.65∗ pi ; % d i g i t a l Stopband f r e q in Hz
% Rp = 1 . 1 1 0 3 ; % Passband r i p p l e in dB
% As = 2 3 . 0 9 8 ; % Stopband a t t enua t i on in dB
```

```
%% Analog s e p e c i f i c a t i o n
f s = 2 e3 ;
f 1 = 200; wp =2*atan ( pi * f 1 / f s ) ;
f 2 = 600; ws = 2* atan ( pi * f 2 / f s ) ;
Rp = 1 . 9 3 8 ; % Passband r i p p l e in dB
As = 1 3 . 9 8 ; % Stopband a t t enua t i on in dB
%% Analog Prototype S p e c i f i c a t i o n s : Inv e r s e mapping f o r f r e q u e n c i e s
T = 1 ; % Set T=1
Wp = (2/T)* tan (wp/ 2 ) ; % Prototype Passband f r e q
Ws = (2/T)* tan (ws / 2 ) ; % Prototype Stopband f r e q
%% Analog Butterworth Prototype F i l t e r Ca l cul a t i on
N = c e i l ( ( log10 ( (1 0^(Rp/10)−1)/(10^(As/10) −1)))/(2* log10 (Wp/Ws) ) ) ;
f p r i n t f ( ' \ n*** Butterworth F i l t e r Order = %2.0 f \n ' ,N)
Wc = Wp/( (10^(Rp/10)−1)^(1/(2*N) ) ) ;
[ z , p , k ] = buttap (N) ;
p = p*Wc;
k = k*Wc^N;
B = r e a l ( poly ( z ) ) ;
bs = k*B;
as = r e a l ( poly (p ) ) ;
%% Bi l i n e a r t r ans f o rma t i on
[ b , a ] = b i l i n e a r ( bs , as , 1 /T) ;
b=b . * 1 . 1 ;
[H,w] = f r e q z (b , a ) ;
grp = grpdelay (b , a ,w) ;
subplot ( 2 2 1 ) ; pl o t (w/ pi , abs (H) ) ; g r id on ; y l a b e l ( 'Magnitude ' )
subplot ( 2 2 2 ) ;
pl o t (w/ pi , 20* log10 ( abs (H) + eps ) ) ; g r id on ; y l a b e l ( 'Magnitude (dB) ' )
subplot ( 2 2 3 ) ; impz (b , a ) ; g r id on ;
subplot ( 2 2 4 ) ; pl o t (w/ pi , grp ) ; g r id on ; y l a b e l ( 'Group Delay ' )
```

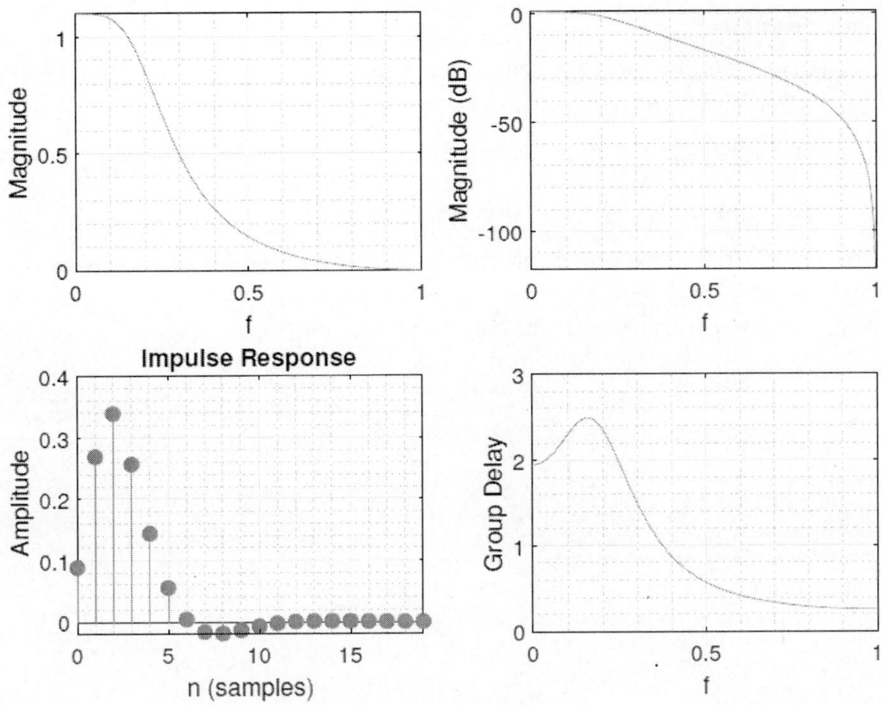

Fig. 9: FIR filter design plots

Aim: To generate the discrete time signal $x(n) = \sin(2\pi\, 0.0625\, n) + 0.3\, \sin(2\pi\, 0.2\, n)$ and plot the signal $x(n)$ and its spectrum.

Decimate the signal by a factor of $D = 2$ and plot the decimated signal and its spectrum.

Interpolate the decimated signal by the same factor $I = 2$ to obtain the signal. Observe the waveform and spectrum of the interpolated signal.

Software: MATLAB, Python

Theory:

Kindly follow the multirate rate signal processing theory.

The decimator and interpolator are essential devices in signal processing, serving to adjust the sampling rate of a signal. The decimator decreases the sampling rate by an integer factor of D, while the interpolator increases it by a factor of I, as discussed in one of the book chapter. In various applications, such as digital mobile receiver systems, altering the sampling rate is necessary for effective signal processing. For instance, in such systems, the received signal often has a high frequency that exceeds the capabilities of the analog-to-digital converter (ADC). Therefore, an RF analog down-conversion is performed to convert it to a lower frequency, termed the intermediate frequency. Subsequently, a FIR filter selects the desired bandwidth, after which the signal is either downsampled or upsampled to achieve an appropriate sampling rate. Downsampling involves reducing the sampling rate of an already sampled signal by an integer factor D, effectively resampling the signal. This reduction in sampling rate, known as subsampling, involves retaining only every D-th sample of the signal while discarding the rest.

Algorithm:

Step-I: Give input sequence

Step-II: Give sampling frequency, input frequency and length of the spectrum. Step-III: Find power spectrum of input sequence using MATLAB command *freqz*

Step-IV: Decimate the signal and plot all the signals Step-V: Interpolate the signal and plot signal

Example:

```
c l e a r a l l ;
n=0:99;
x=s i n (2* pi *0.0625*n)+0.3* s i n (2* pi *0.2* n ) ;
x1=0: l ength ( x)−1;
subplot ( 3 , 2 , 1 ) ;
stem( x1 , x ) ;
[ xz w]= f r e q z (x , 1 , 5 1 2 ) ;
subplot ( 3 , 2 , 2 ) ;
pl o t (w/ pi , abs ( xz ) ) ;
%%%%%%%%
y=downsample (x , 2 ) ;
y1=0: l ength ( y)−1;
subplot ( 3 , 2 , 3 ) ;
stem( y1 , y ) ;
[ yz w]= f r e q z (y , 1 , 5 1 2 ) ;
subplot ( 3 , 2 , 4 ) ;
pl o t (w/ pi , abs ( yz ) ) ;
%%%%%%%%%
xdown=i n t e r p (y , 2 ) ;
re_xdown1=0: l eng th (xdown)−1;
subplot ( 3 , 2 , 5 ) ;
stem( re_xdown1 , xdown ) ;
[ yz1 w1]= f r e q z (xdown , 1 , 5 1 2 ) ;
subplot ( 3 , 2 , 6 ) ;
pl o t (w1/ pi , abs ( yz1 ) ) ;
```

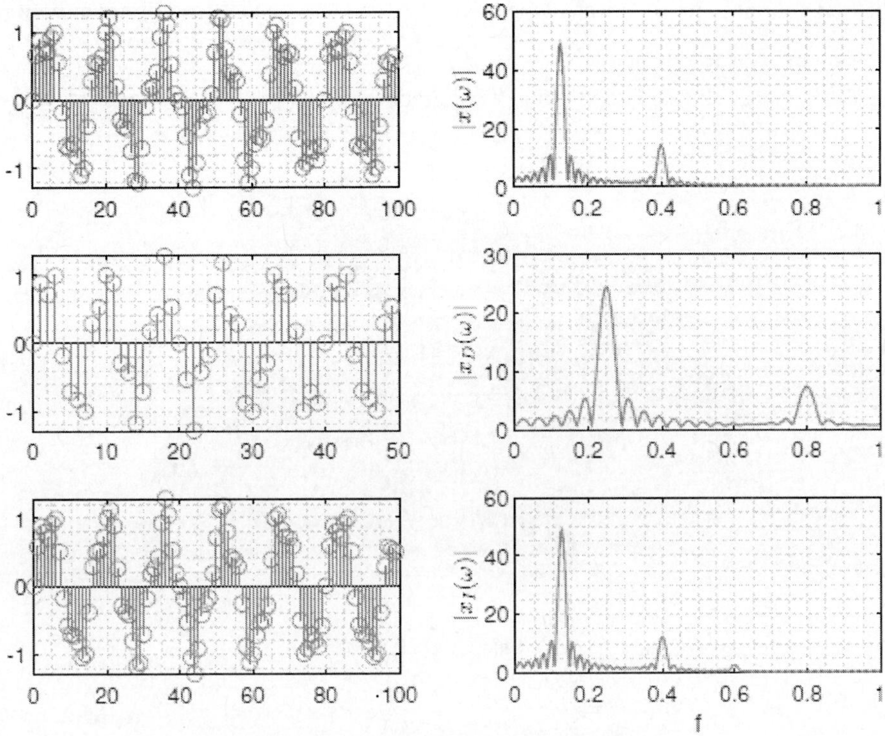

Fig. 10: Signals and their spectrum

Generate different signals and decimate and interpolate the corresponding signals using the different D and I.

Aim: To compute the N point DFT of the given sequence

Equipments: Host (PC) with windows, TMS320C5515 DSP Starter Kit (DSK).

Software: C, MATLAB, Python

Theory:

Kindly follow the DFT theory

Read the TMS320C5515 DSP System kit instructions set

Algorithm:

Step-I: Give input sequence

Step-II: Give sampling frequency, input frequency and length of the sequence Step-III: Take sampled data and apply DFT algorithm

Execution Procedure:

- Navigate to the File Menu and choose the Import option.
- In the Import Window, opt for Existing CCS/CCE Eclipse project, then proceed by clicking Next.
- Browse for the project file's root directory where it is stored.
- Select the DFT Project folder and click Finish to complete the import process.
- Connect the DSP Kit to the PC and launch it, following the manual procedure outlined in TMS320C5515 DSP Starter Kit.

- Right-click on your Dft. out file located under Binaries and choose the Load Program option.
- Now, go to Target and select Run.
- From the Tools menu, choose Graph (Dual Time), configure its properties as needed, and select OK to confirm.

Fig. 11: DSP Kit

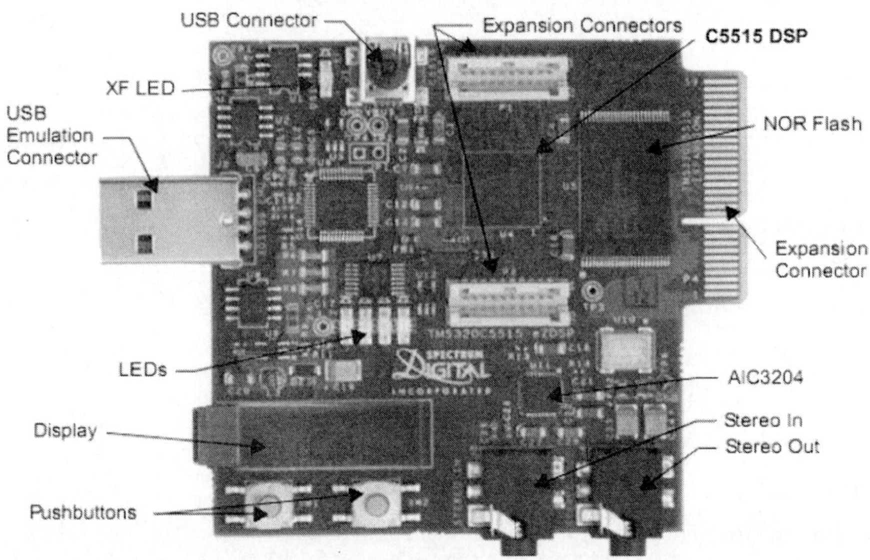

Fig. 12: Key features of DSP Kit

Example:

```
// df t . c N−point DFT computation o f a sequence read from lookup
\\t a b l e
#inc lude <s t d i o . h>
#inc lude <math . h>
#d e f i n e PI 3.14159265358979
#d e f i n e N 64
```

```
#d e f i n e TESTFREQ 10000.0
#d e f i n e SAMPLING_FREQ 64000.0
typede f s t r u c t
{
f l o a t r e a l;
f l o a t imag ;
} COMPLEX;
f l o a t x1 [N] , y1 [N] ;
COMPLEX samples [N] ;
void df t (COMPLEX *x )
{
COMPLEX r e s u l t [N] ;
i n t k , n , i ;
f o r ( k=0 ; k<N ; k++)
{
r e s u l t [ k ] . r e a l =0.0;
r e s u l t [ k ] . imag = 0 . 0 ;
f o r (n=0 ; n<N ; n++)
{
r e s u l t [ k ] . r e a l += x [ n ] . r e a l * cos (2*PI*k*n/N) +
x [ n ] . imag* s i n (2*PI*k*n/N) ;
r e s u l t [ k ] . imag += x [ n ] . imag* cos (2*PI*k*n/N) −
19
x [ n ] . r e a l * s i n (2*PI*k*n/N) ;
}
}f
o r ( k=0 ; k<N ; k++)
{
x [ k ] = r e s u l t [ k ] ;
}
p r i n t f ( " output " ) ;
f o r ( i = 0 ; i < N ; i++) // compute magnitude
{
x1 [ i ]=( i n t ) s q r t ( r e s u l t [ i ] . r e a l * r e s u l t [ i ] . r e a l +
r e s u l t [ i ] . imag* r e s u l t [ i ] . imag ) ;
p r i n t f ( " \ n%d = %f " , i , x1 [ i ] ) ;
```

```
}
}
void main ( ) //main func t i on
{
i n t n;
f o r (n=0 ; n<N ; n++)
{
yl [ n ] = samples [ n ] . r e a l = cos (2*PI*TESTFREQ*n/SAMPLING_FREQ) ;
samples [ n ] . imag = 0 . 0 ;
p r i n t f( " \ n%d = %f " , n , samples [ n ] . r e a l ) ;
}
p r i n t f( " r e a l input data s t o r ed in array samples [ ] \ n " ) ;
p r i n t f( " \ n " ) ; // pl a c e breakpoint here
df t ( samples ) ; // c a l l DFT func t i on
p r i n t f( " done ! \ n " ) ;
}
```

```
x[n].real*sin(2*PI*k*n/N);
                    }
                }
                for(k=0;k<N;k++)
                {
                    x[k] = result[k];
                }
                printf("output");
for(i=0;i< N;i++) //compute magnitude
                {
x1[i]=(int)sqrt(result[i].real*result[i].real +r
esult[i].imag*result[i].imag);
printf("\n%d = %f",i,x1[i]);
                }
            }
            void main() //main function
            {
                int n;
                for(n=0;n<N;n++)
                {
y1[n] = samples[n].real = cos(2*PI*TESTFREQ*n/SAMPLING_FREQ);
samples[n].imag = 0.0;
printf("\n%d = %f",n,samples[n].real);
                }
printf("real input data stored in array samples[]\n");p
rintf("\n"); // place breakpoint here
dft(samples); //call DFT functionpri
ntf("done!\n");
            }
```

CO AND PO ATTAINMENT TABLE

Course outcomes (COs) for this course can be mapped with the programme outcomes (POs) after the completion of the course and a correlation can be made for the attainment of POs to analyse the gap. After proper analysis of the gap in the attainment of POs necessary measures can be taken to overcome the gaps.

Table for CO and PO attainment

Course Outcomes	**Attainment of Programme Outcomes** *(1- Weak Correlation; 2- Medium correlation; 3- Strong Correlation)*											
	PO-1	**PO-2**	**PO-3**	**PO-4**	**PO-5**	**PO-6**	**PO-7**	**PO-8**	**PO-9**	**PO-10**	**PO-11**	**PO-12**
CO-1												
CO-2												
CO-3												
CO-4												
CO-5												
CO-6												

The data filled in the above table can be used for gap analysis

Index